W9-ACM-758

For our dear friends
Alice & Teo

with love

Bratislava,
June 12, 2009

Zora
& Martin
Bútora

This publication is the result of a project called *Plus for Women 45+* by the EU Community Initiative EQUAL, number 95/04-I/33-4.1, financed by the European Social Fund.

The project *Plus for Women 45+* is being implemented by a development partnership comprising the following organizations:

- The Institute for Public Affairs (www.ivo.sk)

- The EsFem civic association (www.esfem.sk)

- The FOCUS agency (www.focus-research.sk)

- The Hlava 98 civic association (www.hlava98.sk).

The *Plus for Women 45+* development partnership is part of the international partnership of the *European Gender Equality and Diversity Network* (http://frauen-europa.de/index.php?id=71).

European **Social** Fund

INSTITUTE FOR
PUBLIC AFFAIRS

Edition
**STUDIES
AND
OPINIONS**

ZORA BÚTOROVÁ et al.

SHE AND HE IN SLOVAKIA

GENDER AND AGE IN THE PERIOD OF TRANSITION

Authors

Monika Bosá
Zora Bútorová
Jarmila Filadelfiová
Oľga Gyárfášová
Milan Minarovič
Martina Sekulová
Sylvia Šumšalová
Marián Velšic

INSTITUTE FOR
PUBLIC AFFAIRS

Bratislava 2008

TABLE OF CONTENTS

Jarmila Filadelfiová

Oľga Gyárfášová – Zora Bútorová – Jarmila Filadelfiová

Monika Bosá – Milan Minarovič – Martina Sekulová

Zora Bútorová – Jarmila Filadelfiová

Zuzana Bartošová

FOREWORD

WOMEN ON THE CATWALK

An interactive installation that is hard to forget. Those were the words of a critic reviewing the cult interactive multimedia artwork created in 1998 by Ilona Németh, a Slovak artist of Hungarian origin and one of the most expressive figures of the Central European art scene, whose creations have met with a wide international response. Its central feature is the catwalk, a platform on which models display clothes during fashion shows. This time, however, it is open for the visitors to the exhibition – and once they enter it, they appear in the world of castings, flashing flights, spotlights, music and sounds of applause. They no longer belong to themselves; they lose their privacy, and for a brief moment become part of the public domain where they are exposed to media manipulation. As soon as they leave the catwalk, darkness sets in again. As if Ilona Németh were ironically commenting on the modern world, in which people's actions are often guided by pre-calculated media effects rather than by their inner beliefs and values.

This publication's cover captures the fleeting moment of this unique interactive artwork. We chose it primarily because we were impressed by the more general metaphor offered by Ilona Németh's artwork.

The illuminated catwalk sets the stage for several ephemeral silhouettes. It is not entirely clear whether they belong to a single woman or a number of them. Not that it matters much; what is truly important is the overall set.

The *catwalk* represents the public sphere in which our lives take place. The stage ablaze sets the tone: it determines what is "in", what is "correct", what is "appropriate", but also what is attractive and noteworthy. In a way, it embodies society that predetermines how individuals should live their lives. The catwalk symbolizes the pressure of society's normative expectations, which blend tradition with modernity and the fashionable influences we are exposed to in today's increasingly interconnected and global world.

The *ephemeral nature of the flitting silhouettes* symbolizes not only the plurality of our identities and the variety of the social roles we fulfill during our lives, but also the fluidity and volatility of our current situation, *here and now*. Here, we should remind the reader that the stage of our book is Slovakia, a country that rejected communism less than two decades ago, and which has since been undergoing deep and dramatic economic, political and social changes. These changes create new challenges for women and men and often surprise them with unexpected demands and requirements. Although we cannot see inside the women on the catwalk, we are nonetheless able to imagine some of their feelings, including the fear of tripping, the anxiety caused by their fierce desire to succeed, their determination to pull off this challenging task, and perhaps even joy at the unique opportunity to step from the shadows into the limelight.

Another surprising feature is the *casual outfits* worn by the women on the catwalk. They certainly do not resemble the "professional beauties" from the celebrity world. The image of a woman in trousers and a sweater on the one hand and the concept of a catwalk designed to flaunt attractive images of glittering feminine beauty on the other hand is the principal source of contrast and tension.

Unwittingly, one gets the impression that we are witnessing a rehearsal for a media presentation rather than a "hard-core" fashion show. This draws a parallel with the process of socialization, during which girls and young women prepare to become "perfect" women; they practice appropriate behavior and adopt social values and standards, adherence to which will be monitored, rewarded or punished by society.

All these images provoke contemplation.

SHE, HE AND THE GENDER PERSPECTIVE

This is the principal mission of the present publication – to encourage readers to give thought to the overall situation of women in our society, to what has changed and what has remained the same since 1989, as well as to what could and should be different. Of course, as the book's title suggests, it is not written merely for girls on the threshold of adulthood, but for a broader circle of readers – i.e. women and men from various age categories. The publication features ample factual material based on rich hard statistical data as well as on data from qualitative and quantitative sociological surveys. It will hopefully stimulate readers to reflect on the gender order of Slovak society, on the similarities and differences in the life situation of women and men, but also on how they perceive, interpret and cope with their social status and gender roles. That is why the book literally teems with numbers and facts. Its 153 tables and 117 graphs are not meant to discourage readers but to help them grasp the life situations, opportunities, opinions and behavioral patterns of Slovak women and men from multiple perspectives.

The book you are holding bears a title that is similar to one of our former publications, *She and He in Slovakia: Gender Issues in Public Opinion*, which was released in 1996. It summed up the research findings of a sociological survey carried out in the mid-1990s by the FOCUS agency, which was later dubbed "a unique gender-specific survey" (Cviková, 2003). This publication's introduction argued that it was necessary to view the developments in Slovakia after the fall of communism also from a gender perspective, and asked a series of questions, including the following.

What is the situation of women and men in a rapidly changing Slovakia? Is the social burden of transition towards a market economy distributed evenly between women and men? How is the role of women changing in a society that lends an ear to voices urging women to become anchored in the family again, something that has been taboo for decades? What are the similarities and differences between the image of "the ideal woman" and that of "the ideal man"? How have the deep political and economic changes after November 1989 affected the reproductive behavior of people in Slovakia? How do women and men arrange relationships and divide responsibilities for taking care of the family and the household? To find answers to these and many other questions, we examined the views of women as well as men.

Shortly after the book was published, I learned that asking such questions and emphasizing gender perspective was not considered obvious. I will probably never forget the bewildered reaction of one protagonist of the Velvet Revolution, for whom a single glance at the book's title was enough to reject it with unconcealed disgust: "So, you have become a feminist too?" he asked. I was so baffled that all I could do was gasp for breath.

Of course, that was back in 1996. It was a difficult period for Slovakia, a time when the democratically-oriented citizens were struggling against increasing authoritarian tendencies. The book's critic, who was deeply devoted to the ideals of freedom and democracy, was apparently one of those educated men who believed that Slovakia was facing "too many other problems to be able to deal with something like feminism", as Jana Juráňová ironically noted five years after the Velvet Revolution (Juráňová, 1995).

Perhaps he was convinced that in the ongoing fight to stop liberal democracy from relapsing into authoritarianism, it was necessary to seek a common platform instead of wasting energy on particular problems. At that point, many people held the opinion that feminism was the kind of *luxury* that a fledgling and fragile democracy struggling to stay alive could ill afford, and that its time would come once the main issues had been resolved. Under such circumstances, they argued, the drive to strengthen democracy must not be fragmented.

Or perhaps I am wrong, and he was simply one of those people who view efforts to develop a true partnership between women and men or – using modern terminology – to eliminate gender inequalities and promote gender equality as a fruitless outcome of (left-oriented) European culture, rather than part of the sound conservative traditions of Slovak society.

This question was answered after the 1998 parliamentary elections when we learned a telling lesson. Neither the defeat of authoritarianism nor the subsequent two tenures of Mikuláš Dzurinda pro-reform administrations, nor even Slovakia's successful endeavor to join the European Union (EU), has brought about an improvement in the attitude of the country's political elite and its public administration to women's issues and gender inequalities in our society.

One part of the political elite overlooked these issues as irrelevant. Most of the measures it took to protect and strengthen women's rights were reactions to pressure from the domestic non-governmental sector or from abroad, rather than based on its own initiative.

The other category of political leaders explicitly rejected influences or inspirations from the EU and warned of dangerous displays of "social engineering" that – in their view – threatened to undermine Slovakia's traditional Christian values.

As a result, attempts to eliminate gender inequalities were pushed out of the mainstream of pro-reform government policy (Filadelfiová – Bútorová, 2007a). The situation did not improve after 2006, when Dzurinda's center-right administration was replaced by the ruling coalition consisting of the party Smer – Social Democracy (Smer-SD), Slovak National Party (SNS) and People's Party Movement for a Democratic Slovakia (ĽS-HZDS). While the leading party (Smer-SD) formally subscribes to leftist values, neither its rhetoric nor its actions suggest any serious intention to address the issue of gender inequalities, which is embraced by social-democratic parties in developed democracies.

True, one can hardly deny that Slovakia's accession to the EU has catalyzed the passage of legislative changes, particularly in the field of labor law. Under pressure from the EU, Slovakia also adopted strategic documents dealing with gender equality and reflected the gender dimension in strategic documents in other areas. The EU pressure was the most intense between 2000 and 2004. Unfortunately, it subsided immediately after the country became an EU member state.

Despite the aforementioned legislative amendments, a typical feature of contemporary Slovakia is the significant gap between formally approved documents and their implementation in practice. Moreover, the government has neglected to prepare analyses of the gender impacts of its public policies.

The continuing lack of interest in promoting gender equality on the part of the political elite in Slovakia, as well as in other Central and Eastern European countries, corroborates the views of the prominent Czech philosopher Hana Havelková, who argued that while the gender issue did become a public interest issue for a certain period of time, it was merely a side product of accomplishing another public interest goal, i.e. joining the EU (Havelková, 2000). Therefore, the principal challenge is finding a way to encourage the country's political leaders, public administration and society in general to take an interest in eliminating gender inequalities and in gender issues in general, without the "carrot and stick" of the pre-accession period.

It is clear that this tough and long-term challenge is addressed primarily *pro domo*, i.e. to those who wish to trigger a positive change in this respect. That is the main reason why we have kept the "gender glasses" on since the mid-1990s until the present day, and why the issue of gender equality is also the principal focus of our most recent publication. We are convinced that this perspective is far from exhausted, and by no means should be taken for granted – either on the level of intellectual reflection or on the level of everyday life.

RECENT INITIATIVES

Although changes within the country's political sphere, public administration and public mentality take time, one must not ignore what has been accomplished in recent years, especially in the second half of the 1990s. Women's non-governmental organizations in Slovakia began to thrive as seen in a gradual increase in their self-awareness and self-confidence, the intensification of their joint activities, and the emergence of several platforms and networks. Recently, they have been focusing on agendas like cultivating gender sensitivity among the general public; promoting the introduction of gender-sensitive teaching; addressing violence against women; increasing women's participation in political decision-making; lobbying for the acknowledgement of the gender equality agenda and the creation of institutional mechanisms to support it; strengthening women's status on the labor market; and helping endangered and disadvantaged categories of women (Bútorová – Filadelfiová – Marošiová, 2004; Bútorová – Filadelfiová, 2006; Filadelfiová – Bútorová, 2007a).

In 2001, the Center for Gender Studies was established at the Faculty of Arts of Comenius University in Bratislava, which is involved in research activities, as well as educational activities. In recent years, teaching on gender issues have spread to other departments at Comenius University as well as to other Slovak universities in Prešov, Banská Bystrica and Nitra; however, no Slovak university yet has a full-fledged department of gender studies.

Along with the intense quantitative and qualitative development of women's non-governmental organizations, the shelves of bookstores, libraries and reading rooms in Slovakia have begun to feature an increasing number of publications by domestic as well as foreign experts, as well as websites specializing in gender issues. The most outstanding publisher of such titles has been the women's association Aspekt; however, research and publishing projects examining gender issues have also been pursued by other organizations, for instance the International

Center for Family Studies, which was later transformed into the Research Institute of Labor and Family; the Institute for Public Affairs; the Center of Gender Studies; several institutes at the Slovak Academy of Sciences (the Institute of Sociology, Institute of Ethnography, Institute of Philosophy and Department of Social and Biological Communication); Prešov University; Matej Bel University in Banská Bystrica; and a number of civic associations, particularly Občan a demokracia [Citizen and Democracy], Klub feministických filozofiek [Club of Feminist Philosophers] and Možnosť voľby [Freedom of Choice].

Also, the readers have been able to choose from several works of fiction by domestic and foreign authors, or inspiring theatre performances that promoted gender sensitivity. Recent book titles by Slovak authors include *Travesty šou* [Travesty Show] by Uršula Kovalyk, *Stalo sa* [It Happened] by Etela Farkašová, *Orodovnice* [Intercessors] by Jana Juráňová, *Vtedy v Bratislave* [Once Upon a Time in Bratislava] by Žofia Langerová, or the most recent publication by Irena Brežná titled *Na slepačích krídlach* [Upon Chicken Wings].

As for theatre productions, two shows combined top-notch artistic performance with effective gender education. The first was an imaginative show for children as well as adults called *Anička Ružička a Tonko Modrinka* [Annie the Rose and Tony the Bruise] by the *Na rázcestí* [On the Crossroad] puppet theatre in Banská Bystrica; the other was the staging of *Shirley Valentine*, a cult monodrama by British playwright Willy Russell featuring top Slovak actress *Zuzana Krónerová*.

The aim of the authors of the present publication is to join hands with all these civic initiatives, intellectual voices, publishing acts and cultural performances that are striving to eliminate gender-blind approach.

The book *She and He in Slovakia. Gender and Age in the Period of Transition* is the now the 11th separate publication released by the Institute for Public Affairs that deals with gender issues. It is also a continuation of no less than 15 previous studies of the women's problems; 5 were released as part of the Institute's annual *Global Reports on the State of Society*, and the remaining 10 were part of its other broadly outlined publications.[1] On top of that, some members of the team of authors have also published studies on gender issues with other institutions. In all modesty, we might say that we are not exactly navigating uncharted waters.

---

[1] Unfortunately, there is not enough space to render a complete account of all publications or studies examining gender issues released by the Institute for Public Affairs (IVO). Still, it is necessary to cite at least the two "trailblazers". First was a chapter "Gender Issues in Slovakia" in a publication *Slovakia 1998 – 1999: A Global Report on the State of Society* (Bútorová – Filadelfiová – Guráň – Gyárfášová – Farkašová, 1999) that was followed by similar studies in annual *Global Reports* published in 2002 and 2007 (Bútorová – Filadelfiová – Cviková – Gyárfášová – Farkašová, 2002; Filadelfiová – Bútorová, 2007a). Second was a book titled *Krehká sila. Dvadsať rozhovorov o životných cestách žien* [Fragile Strength: Twenty Interviews about the Life Stories of Women] (Bútorová, 2001), which featured in-depth interviews with Slovakia's prominent female personalities as well as male professionals who deal with gender issues. Several other studies examined gender issues in the broader context of politics, parliamentary elections and electoral behavior (e.g. Gyárfášová, 2002; Gyárfášová – Pafkova, 2002; Filadelfiová – Bútorová – Gyárfášová, 2002; Filadelfiová, 2003). In 2004, the IVO published the book *Keď ľahostajnosť nie je odpoveď. Príbeh občianskeho združovania na Slovensku po páde komunizmu* [When Indifference Is Not the Answer: The Story of Civic Associating in Slovakia after the Fall of Communism] that included a chapter on women's non-governmental organizations (Bútorová – Filadelfiová – Marošiová, 2004). Shortly afterwards, the IVO released a study by a broader team of authors titled *Násilie páchané na ženách ako problém verejnej politiky* [Violence against Women as a Public Policy Issue] (Bútorová – Filadelfiová, 2005). After 2005, gender research in IVO received a strong impetus in the form of two projects financed by the EQUAL Community Initiative: one was *Plus for Women 45+* that focused on women in mature age and the other was *We Perceive the World Differently and Therefore We Achieve More Together: Maternity Centers and Furthering Equal Opportunities on the Labor Market* that focused on mothers of minor children. These projects inspired a number of separate publications (e.g. Marošiová – Šumšalová, 2006; Filadelfiová – Bútorová, 2007b; Bútorová, 2007; *Women 45+...*, 2007; Marošiová, 2008; Bútorová, 2008). Most of the cited studies were published also in English or featured an English résumé.

SHE, HE AND THE AGE PERSPECTIVE

The present publication strives to overcome the prevailing gender-blind approach toward the public and private spheres in which women and men live their everyday lives, and replace it with a gender-sensitive approach. Its added value for Slovakia lies especially in the fact that besides "gender glasses", its authors also wear "age glasses". In other words, the book does not limit itself to general statements regarding the objective conditions or subjective opinions of women and men, but instead tries to add an age dimension that allows for a study of specific life situations of women and men from different generations.

In doing so, we paid attention to women over 45, who often face double discrimination on the labor market – both as women and as older persons. This focus was due to the fact that the publication was anchored in a broader project called *Plus for Women 45+*, which was financed by the EQUAL Community Initiative and implemented between 2005 and 2008.

This joint project of the Institute for Public Affairs, the FOCUS agency, the EsFem civic association and Hlava 98 civic association responded to two paradoxes in current Slovak society.

First, as we have already pointed out, while the Slovak Republic officially subscribes to the principle of equal opportunities for women and men, most of these good intentions remain largely on paper. This publication illustrates the strong prevalence of gender inequalities in real life.

Second, population ageing in Slovakia has highlighted the need to prolong working life of people. Although current legislation envisages a gradual increase in the retirement age of men and especially women, Slovak society has not yet adequately embraced the concept of active ageing. A number of circumstances on the labor market as well as within the family and in wider society reduce the chances of older women in particular, and even push them out of their workplaces. That goes against the approach that is currently being adopted by developed European countries, where decision-makers are considering how to make the best of the older generation's working potential. Needless to say, Slovakia has lots of "undiscovered silver", i.e. women and men in their mature years whose skills and experience could be better used for the benefit of the society, as well as of the older people themselves.

The problem of population ageing has been neglected in Slovakia perhaps even more than the issue of gender equality. The key postulates of the concept of active ageing were laid out in the *International Plan of Action on Ageing* from 2002, which declared that elderly people should have the opportunity to work as long as they want and as long as they are able (*Report of the Second...*, 2002). Carrying this vision into effect requires a complex and multilayered change that includes the following measures:

1. Steering macroeconomic policies toward increasing employment.
2. Increasing employers' awareness of the advantages of keeping elderly people employed.
3. Introducing measures to increase the employability of elderly employees that take into account their specific needs, for instance:
   - Flexible work arrangements;
   - Employee-friendly working conditions along with improved health and safety standards;
   - Improved medical care, prevention and rehabilitation;
   - An active approach to lifelong learning;

- Flexible retirement age;
- Reintegration of the unemployed and handicapped into the labor market.

4. Striving for age diversity and a balanced gender make-up in workplaces.

5. Implementing programs to use the experience and skills of elderly and senior employees in training their younger and junior colleagues.

6. Eliminating age barriers by promoting the recruitment of elderly employees.

7. Restricting incentives and other factors that motivate people to retire early, and removing the barriers that prevent people from working past their retirement age.

8. Pursuing family-friendly and gender-sensitive policies that allow employees to harmonize their professional and domestic duties.

9. Encouraging employees to make informed decisions on the potential financial, health and other implications of extended economic activity.

10. Promoting realistic evaluations of the qualifications and skills of elderly employees, and correcting negative stereotypes.

Similar postulates were articulated in a number of recent documents of broad international scope, for instance a working document of the European Commission from May 2007 that addressed Europe's demographic future (*Europe's Demographic…*, 2007). Another international organization to call for ending the practice of "edging out" elderly people from the labor market was the International Labor Organization (ILO), which urged important social actors – governments, employers associations and trade unions – to join this effort (Ghosheh, 2007).

Obviously, implementing these principles will require a deep cultural change, which will take time even in the most developed European countries (*Employment Initiatives…*, 2006). It will take even longer in Slovakia, as the country so far has used a narrower conceptual framework in drafting strategic documents to encourage the employment of elderly women and men (*Súhrnná správa…*, 2006).

The age-sensitive approach views age diversity as an important dimension of the diversity of the labor force. It respects the specific needs of particular age categories of employees. It is relatively rare among Slovak employers, who often fear that measures promoting work ability of ageing employees could be misinterpreted as violating the principle of equal opportunities for all employees and discriminating younger workers. Moreover, employers tend to yield to age stereotypes. On the one hand, they appreciate senior employees for their professional skills, life experience, reliability, and loyalty as well as their solid work ethic and discipline; on the other hand, they often assume that all these employees will have a lower work performance and show less flexibility, less ability to respond to new situations, an insufficient command of foreign languages, poor digital literacy and a lack of interest in lifelong education (*Anketa…*, 2007).

WHY THE *PLUS FOR WOMEN 45+* PROJECT?

Having in mind the aforementioned deficiencies in the approach of strategic government documents and employers' organizations in Slovakia to the issue of active ageing, the members of the *Plus for Women 45+* development partnership set the following goals:

1. Conducting a series of qualitative and quantitative surveys to learn more about the life and work of women over 45 and to examine gender and age stereotypes in Slovak society.

2. Disseminating research findings and making them available to target groups as well as to the general public

3. Carrying out gender and age sensitive education as well as a social campaign to increase society's gender and age sensitivity, to empower women over 45 and to strengthen their status on the labor market.

The book *She and He in Slovakia. Gender and Age in the Period of Transition* is the fourth and final publication released within the framework of this project. The first book, published in 2007 and titled *Ženy, muži a vek v štatistickách trhu práce* [Women, Men and Age in Labor Market Statistics], authored by Jarmila Filadelfiová and edited by Zora Bútorová, provided data on Slovakia's labor market, using gender and age perspectives. Against this backdrop, the publication offered a statistically documented portrait of women over 45 and their status on the labor market compared to their male counterparts as well as to younger women.

The second book, titled *Tu a teraz: sondy do života žien 45+* [Here and Now: Probes into the Lives of Women 45+], edited by Zora Bútorová and authored by Jana Andruchová, Zora Bútorová, Janka Debrecéniová, Lýdia Marošiová, Martina Sekulová and Sylvia Šumšalová, was exclusively qualitative in nature. The principal research method used in four case studies was in-depth semi-standardized interviews with female respondents that were conducted in four different regions and social environments around Slovakia. The first case study examined the working and living conditions of businesswomen over 45 from Slovakia's south-eastern Lučenec and its surroundings; the second study explored the situation of women over 45 living in the tourist region of northern Slovakia; the third case study analyzed the working conditions of seamstresses in northeast Slovakia; finally, the fourth study mapped out the living conditions of women from the Humenné area in the country's far east, who are directly or indirectly affected by labor migration abroad.

These four case studies formed an integral part of the project's broader methodological design, which was to *combine various methodological approaches*. When outlining the methodology of in-depth interviews, the authors built on a previous qualitative survey that applied the method of focus group discussions.[2] Both qualitative approaches were based on analyses of hard statistical data as well as on previous representative surveys carried out in September 2005 and August 2006. In summer 2007, we carried out a poll among employers in order to learn more about their individual attitudes as well as their corporate policies towards older employees (*Anketa...*, 2007). In November 2007, at the end of the project's research phase, we carried out a final representative sociological survey that examined public opinion regarding equal opportunities for women and men of different ages. Last, but not least, an important element of the project's research was a content analysis of select print media which scrutinized the media image of women with a special emphasis on women in their mature and older years. Its findings are discussed in the final chapter of the present publication.

We opted for such complementary methodological approaches because we supposed that they would have a synergic research effect. On the one hand, we believed that such combination

---

[2] From February through March 2006, IVO researchers conducted seven focus group discussions with employed as well as unemployed women over 45 of various professional background and educational attainment in seven different regions of Slovakia: Banská Bystrica, Rožňava, Žilina, Revúca, Martin, Nitra and Bratislava.

of different types of empirical data would allow us to overcome the limited possibilities of generalization based on qualitative research and at the same time to reach beneath the surface of hard statistical data as well as representative survey data.

The third book, titled *Ona a on na Slovensku. Zaostrené na rod a vek* [She and He in Slovakia: Focused on Gender and Age] presents a Slovak version of the present publication.

All research findings, along with a broad spectrum of other information, background material and documentation, formed a foundation on which we organized gender and age sensitive education and trainings within the framework of the *Plus for Women 45+* project. The EsFem civic association focused these education activities on three target groups: members of the Committee for Equal Opportunities of Women and Men at the Slovak Confederation of Trade Unions; students of journalism and media communication; and anchors, commentators and managers of the public service channel Slovak Radio (Mesochoritisová, 2007).

The project's research findings prepared the ground also for a social campaign called *Moja mama chce pracovať* [My Mom Wants to Work]combating gender and age stereotypes, as well as barriers to employing women in their mature years. The imaginative campaign, whose principal message was shaped in intense communication between a creative team from the Hlava 98 civic association and the sociological team of the Institute for Public Affairs, took place in February and March 2008 in several electronic media and one daily paper.[3]

ACKNOWLEDGEMENTS

This book was made possible thanks to the joint efforts of the team of eight authors: Monika Bosá, Zora Bútorová, Jarmila Filadelfiová, Oľga Gyárfášová, Milan Minarovič, Martina Sekulová, Sylvia Šumšalová and Marián Velšic. Its publication concludes a three-year research effort within the framework of the *Plus for Women 45+* project. This was a period of intense discussion, of asking questions, digging through enormous piles of accumulated empirical material, and of excitement about the answers that were surfacing. It was also a period in which the authors shared their hopes and fears, joys and sorrows emerging in their private lives. The goals set were truly ambitious, and accomplishing them required that every member of the team make some personal sacrifices. At this point, it is highly appropriate to express gratitude and acknowledgement to every one of them for their intellectual contribution and personal commitment.

Our thanks also go to our partners from the FOCUS agency, with whom we share a long history of cooperation and friendship, particularly to Ivan Dianiška and Romana Ťažká, who helped give birth to the book *She and He in Slovakia: Gender Issues in Public Opinion* in 1996, as well as to Martin Slosiarik and other members of this outstanding team.

We also would like to acknowledge the valuable contributions of our partner organizations in Finland, Germany, Lithuania and Denmark with whom we cooperated as members of the transnational partnership *European Gender Equality and Diversity Network*. In particular, we

---

[3] For further details on the campaign inspired by blogger Marína Dobošová and jointly conceived by Vladimír Talian and Juraj Johanides, please see the IVO website: http://www.ivo.sk/5300/sk/projekty/plus-pre-zeny-45-/ivo-hlava-98-a-projekt-plus-pre-zeny-45-odstartovali-kampan-%84prekonajme-bariery-pri-zamestnavani-zien-v-zrelom-veku%93; http://www.ivo.sk/buxus/docs//Plus_pre_zeny_45/Inzerat_Plus_pre_zeny.pdf

appreciate the inspiration of Kaisa Kauppinen and Juhani Ilmarinen of the Finnish Institute of Occupational Health.

Of course, this book could not have been published without the contributions of several other people. We hereby express our gratitude to research assistant Janka Fedorková for her precision and flexibility, translator Daniel Borský and copy editor Tom Nicholson for their excellent language skills, and graphic designers Gabriela Farnbauer and Peter Hajdin for their proficiency in typesetting and imaginative design of the book's cover, respectively. We should not forget the contribution by Zuzana Velková of the Institute for Public Affairs, who showed outstanding professionalism in tackling financial and accounting problems.

Our special thanks go to visual artist Ilona Németh, whose artwork on the book's cover sets the tone and perfectly captures its main topic. This was the outcome of our cooperation with art historian Zuzana Bartošová, who picked works of art by four outstanding Slovak female artists for all four publications released within the framework of the project. An essay about their artistic output written by this prominent expert put a symbolic coda on the end of the present book as well as the entire series of publications.

Last but not least, we would like to thank our colleagues as well as our nearest and dearest for showing understanding and encouraging us in our efforts. They all helped us deliver a book we firmly believe will make a contribution to exploring the gender and age dimensions of life in Slovakia in this complex and changing time.

Zora Bútorová

Head of the team of authors

and of the *Plus for Women 45+* project

1. WOMEN AND MEN IN LIGHT OF SOCIETY'S EXPECTATIONS

Zora Bútorová

1. WOMEN AND MEN IN LIGHT OF SOCIETY'S EXPECTATIONS

One of the most stable pillars supporting our culture is the conviction that the different roles that women and men play within society ensue naturally from the biological differences between them. Like in other countries, most women and men in Slovakia perceive their gender as a biological attribute rather than a socially construed identity (Marody – Giza-Poleszczuk, 2000, p. 151). Few realize that the bipolar "pink" and "blue" world which girls and boys are born into and which is presented to them as "natural" or given is historically, socially and in a broader sense culturally conditioned (Cviková, 2003, p. 10). According to Josef Alan, society strengthens the biological dissimilarity of women and men during the socialization process of "forming sexually differentiated behavior that links the biological differences with the dichotomous socio-cultural content of masculinity and femininity" (Alan, 1989, p. 145).

Since 1980s, the distinction between sex and gender became an important part of the reflection in the science, education, politics and general practice in Western societies. However, in countries of East Central Europe from behind the Iron Curtain, this process was delayed and could evolve only after the fall of communism.

Gender analysis offers a particularly interesting perspective from which to examine societal developments that Slovakia underwent for nearly two decades after the Velvet Revolution in November 1989. According to Polish sociologists Mira Marody and Anna Giza-Poleszczuk, rapid institutional changes precipitated by the transition to democracy and a free market have changed the social context in which women and men understand and carry out their social roles. On the one hand, women and men are under pressure from the changing and often contradictory expectations that come from various institutions such as the labor market, the family, the media or the church. The clash between these expectations is also reflected in the public debate on what behavior by women and men is suited to the new era. On the other hand, a fascinating struggle is taking place in which individual women and men are striving to adapt to the new social conditions and to succeed in them as best they can. The long-term effects of this process will shape the key attributes of female and male identities as well as everyday relations between women and men.

The process of gender formation, the Polish sociologists continue, draws on two main sources. The first is the world of everyday life, as circumscribed by the labor market, the level of salaries and wages, the adequacy of public services, the legal regulations of marriage, social welfare, and childcare facilities, among other. The second is the world of discourse, contained in traditional and popular culture, mass media reporting, and especially advertising. The former world defines the opportunities and constraints that shape individual actions of women and men. The latter world offers idealizations of appearance, personality, and behavior that become attached to gender and gender relations (Marody – Giza-Poleszczuk, 2000, p. 152).

In the following chapter, we will examine the gender identities that these circumstances have formed in Slovakia. More precisely, we will describe the expectations that Slovak society creates of "the ideal woman" and "the ideal man".

Before we proceed to our analysis, we should point out two facts. First, normative notions of concrete women and men about "the ideal woman" or "the ideal man" may differ substantially from their actual behavior. This contradiction will resurface repeatedly in this publication, which addresses not only what women and men wish for or what they formally declare, but also describes how they actually behave and what they actually do in the public and private spheres.

Second, although gender cannot be completely separated from biological sex, and although gender stereotypes tend to "cluster" around the latter, variability of value orientations, beliefs and behavior within the group of women or the group of men may be more pronounced than the distinction between women and men as groups (Gyárfášová – Slosiarik, 2008). That is why our identification of the image of "the ideal woman" and "the ideal man" uses an approach that avoids juxtaposing these images as incompatible, dichotomous and mutually exclusive opposites, but instead allows for an empirical examination of the degree of their differences and the extent to which concrete qualities are represented among the dominant attributes of femininity and masculinity.

1.1. THE IMAGE OF "THE IDEAL WOMAN" AND "THE IDEAL MAN"

1.1.1. CONTEMPORARY GENDER EXPECTATIONS

What ideas do Slovak women and men have about the qualities that the ideal woman and the ideal man should possess? In order to answer this question, the Institute for Public Affairs carried out a survey in which respondents were asked to choose these qualities from a list of 16 attributes. [1]

Table 1.1 illustrates the normative expectations concerning the ideal woman and the ideal man in 1995, and how they had changed by 2006. Let us first analyze the more recent findings from 2006. A glance at Table 1.1 and Graph 1.1 reveals striking differences between the concepts of "the ideal woman" and "the ideal man". The dominant attribute of the ideal woman is her ability to take care of the household, which was viewed as important by 70% of the population; 44 % of respondents believed that this feature was important for the ideal man. On the other hand, the key attribute of the ideal man, according to 79% of respondents, is his ability to provide for his family, while only 18% considered this quality to be very important for the ideal woman.

Unlike the ideal man, most people in Slovakia expect the ideal woman to be a pleasant companion (58% vs. 43%) and to be tactful and empathic concerning the problems of others (51% vs. 40%); the ideal woman is also more frequently expected to look good than the ideal man (42% vs. 15%). On the other hand, the ideal man should have physical strength according to 34% of respondents, while only 7% said the same of women.

Other important attributes of the ideal man is the ability to succeed professionally (63%), the ability to decide independently (61%), and resourcefulness, shrewdness and drive (60%). All these qualities are far less frequently expected of the ideal woman (32%, 48% and 34%, respectively).

---

[1] Respondents could rate individual qualities as "very important", "rather important", "rather unimportant" and "completely unimportant". The following analysis is based only on those qualities rated as "very important".

The ideal man is more frequently expected to be rational than the ideal woman (54% vs. 46%), to enjoy authority at home and within the family (46% vs. 35%), to be well educated (32% vs. 24%), and to show interest in public affairs (14% vs. 10%).

These differences in gender expectations allow us to identify three types of attributes:

A. *Specific feminine attributes*, i.e. qualities people expect much more frequently of women.[2] These include particularly the ability to take care of the household, to be a pleasant companion, to be tactful and empathic, and to look pretty.

B. *Specific masculine attributes*, i.e. characteristics more frequently expected of men. These include providing for the family, professional success, thinking and deciding independently, being resourceful and shrewd, having authority at home, and physical strength.

C. *Other attributes* that have a less distinct "gender identity".[3] Tolerance of others, for example, is expected more often of women, while rational thought, good education, a desire to excel at work, interest in public affairs, and the ability to make sacrifices for one's society, country or nation are somewhat more frequently expected of men. However, the differences are not significant.

Clearly, the overall normative image of the ideal man accentuates an active and assertive attitude towards professional or public activities, as well as a focus on performance and success. On the other hand, the image of the ideal woman combines three dimensions: first, she is expected to be an exemplary mother and homemaker; second, she is supposed to be a comforter and invigorator who is willing to lend an "empathic ear"; finally, she should be attractive, which is

Table 1.1
Very important qualities of the ideal woman and the ideal man as viewed by the entire population in 1995 and 2006 (%)

	Ideal woman		Ideal man	
	1995	2006	1995	2006
Ability to take care of the household	86	70	46	44
Ability to be a pleasant companion	51	58	39	43
Tactfulness, empathy for the problems of others	71	51	38	30
Ability to decide independently	50	48	72	61
Tolerance of others	50	45	45	42
Rational thinking	52*	46	57*	54
Pleasant appearance, beauty	38	42	8	15
Authority at home, within the family	40	35	53	46
Resourcefulness, shrewdness, drive	16**	34	42**	60
Ability to succeed professionally	NE	32	NE	63
Highest possible education	10	24	17	32
Ability to provide for the family	23	18	92	79
Desire to excel at work	16	17	29	25
Interest in public affairs	6	10	13	14
Ability to sacrifice for society, country or nation	8	8	13	11
Physical strength	5	7	33	34

Note: The sample comprised respondents older than 15.
NE – was not examined.
* In 1995, the survey used the term "prudence".
** In 1995, the survey used only the term "resourcefulness".
Source: FOCUS, June 2005; Institute for Public Affairs, August 2006.

---

[2] Here, we refer to at least a 10% difference in evaluating a particular quality as very important.
[3] Differences in evaluating a particular quality as very important for women and men are smaller than 10%.

a prerequisite for her success in both the public and the private spheres. These imperatives are reproduced and amplified by the media (for details, see Chapter 8 in this publication).

Graph 1.1
Specific feminine and specific masculine attributes as viewed by the entire population (%)

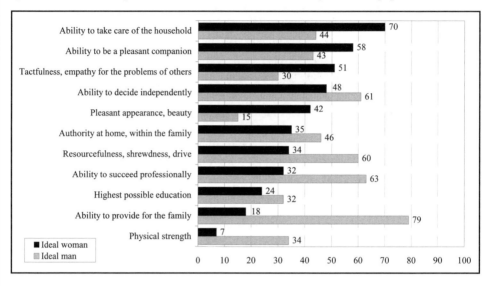

Note: The sample comprised respondents older than 15.
Source: Institute for Public Affairs, August 2006.

1.1.2. SHIFTS IN GENDER EXPECTATIONS

Let us look at the shifts in normative concepts of the ideal woman and the ideal man over the past decade. Before we comment on them, we should note that the whole socio-economic environment in which ordinary Slovak women and men live their lives has changed substantially.

Since 1995, Slovak society has gone through radical economic, social and political changes. The country implemented fundamental economic reforms that on the one hand sparked solid economic growth but on the other hand deepened social and regional disparities and brought a dramatic increase in unemployment that peaked in 2004 and has been going down since. The dividing line between winners and losers of the economic transformation has become their ability to succeed on the labor market due to their education, flexibility, communication skills, and self-confidence – in other words, on the basis of a social capital that is more common among more educated, younger and urban people. At the same time, Slovak society underwent a period of strengthening authoritarian tendencies, but after parliamentary elections in 1998 embarked on a path towards liberal democracy, which culminated in its joining the European Union and NATO in 2004. Integration into euro-Atlantic structures further opened Slovakia's economy, which brought influx of foreign direct investment, more jobs, and greater labor migration of Slovak workers.

How have these macro-social changes affected the normative notions about the ideal woman and the ideal man? As Table 1.1 shows, two traditionally dominant gender expectations changed between 1995 and 2006: the ideal woman is less frequently supposed to be the home-maker (a decline of 16 percentage points); on the other hand, the ideal man is less frequently expected to be the breadwinner for the family (a decline of 13 percentage points). Although these qualities remain the most common virtues of the ideal woman and the ideal man, re-spectively, their dominance over other gender attributes has decreased significantly.[4]

Why did this happen? The decline of expectations that men provide for their families can have several reasons. These include more intense public discourse on gender issues in Slovakia, which has emphasized the fact that most women help to support their households and many are even the principal breadwinners in their families. The discourse has also highlighted the difficulties that some men have in finding job and providing for their families. This problem is more common in regions with high unemployment, and among men with low social capi-tal – i.e. little education, poor language skills, no computer skills, etc. Moreover, the number of households has increased in which women earn more than their spouses.

The reduced expectations that women take care of the household may have been catalyzed by stronger criticism of the double burden of professional and family obligations that many women carry, as well as greater disapproval of the unjust division of labor in the private sphere, when employed women are expected to be perfect homemakers and at the same time turn in a strong performance in the workplace.

In this context, it is interesting that the share of people who expect the ideal woman and the ideal man to enjoy authority within the family declined by 5 and 7 percentage points, respec-tively. This decline is probably related to the increasing preference of the partnership family model. At the same time, deficiencies in the authoritative methods of raising children are more frequently highlighted in public discussion than they were before (see Section 1.1.6. of this chapter).

Other noteworthy shifts include the increase of the expectations that women as well as men should be resourceful and shrewd (by 18 percentage points for each). This process is linked also with a stronger emphasis on two "external" characteristics that women and men should have – pleasant appearance and ability to be good companions. As we shall demonstrate, it is mostly men who demand these qualities of the ideal woman and primarily women who expect them from the ideal man. This trend has been catalyzed not only by the media and advertisers but also by employers (*Kult tela…*, 2005).

Furthermore, these shifts combine with a substantial decline in the normative demand that women and men treat other people tactfully and empathically. In 1995, this quality was the second most desired attribute of femininity; 11 years later, demand for it had dropped by 20 percentage points, putting it behind the ability to be a pleasant companion, which is a far more external quality. In the case of the ideal man, the demand for tactfulness and empathy for the problems of others fell by 8 points.

These trends are particularly disturbing because tactfulness, sensitivity and empathy are quali-ties that make good parents, good partners, and good friends, as well as other intimate per-

---

[4] In the European context, Slovakia continues to rank among countries with a relatively conservative perception of the role of women in society. This was the conclusion of the ISSP 2002 comparative survey in which Slovakia ranked 6 among 36 countries examined. Back then, about one in two respondents agreed with the assertion that "the man's role is to earn money while the woman's role is to take care of the home and family". Between 2002 and 2006, this traditional perception of gender roles faded somewhat (cited in Bahna, 2006, p. 45).

sonal relationships. Moreover, empathy for other people is also a prerequisite for performing well in many professions and roles in public life.

Over the past decade, people in Slovakia increasingly emphasized the importance of education for the ideal woman (increase by 14 percentage points) as well as for the ideal man (by 15 percentage points). This may be a natural reaction to the fact that modern society rewards professional performance, and education is one of keys opening better opportunities on the labor market and in the broader society. The division of Slovak people into winners and losers of the transition largely hinges on their educational attainment (Bútorová – Gyárfášová, 2007).

Graph 1.2
Attributes of the ideal woman and the ideal man as viewed by the entire population in 1995 and 2006 (%)

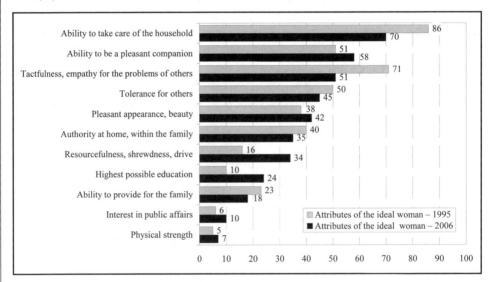

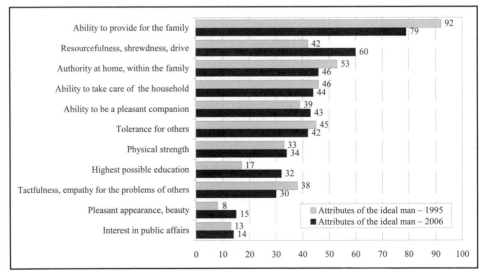

Source: FOCUS, June 1995; Institute for Public Affairs, August 2006.

Finally, active citizenship continues to play a very small role in people's expectations of the ideal woman and the ideal man. Only few people in Slovakia view an interest in public affairs or an ability to make sacrifices for one's society, country or nation as very important attributes of the ideal woman (10% and 8%, respectively) or the ideal man (14% and 11%, respectively). Despite a moderate increase in the share of people who believe that interest in public affairs is a very important quality of the ideal woman, civic participation continues to be less frequently expected of women than of men.

1.1.3. VIEWS OF WOMEN AND MEN

Let us now look at the notions that women and men have about the ideal woman. As Graph 1.3 shows, they are similar. Yet, there are some remarkable differences. Women attribute a greater importance to assertiveness and other qualities that allow them to be effective and successful at work as well as within the family, such as the ability to decide independently; resourcefulness, shrewdness and drive; highest possible education and an interest in public affairs; the ability to provide for the family, authority at home and within the family, and even physical strength.

This finding, corroborating our finding from 1995 (Bútorová, 1996), is in accordance with the conclusion made by prominent Czech sociologist Ivo Možný 25 years ago according to whom "women perceive themselves as more masculine than their partners perceive them" (Možný, 1983).

On the other hand, this self-image of women includes also stronger demands that they be tactful, empathetic and tolerant.

Men, for their part, tend to expect the ideal woman to be reliable in taking care of the household, to be a pleasant companion and to look pretty, i.e. they emphasize the elements of traditional femininity.

Graph 1.3
Attributes of the ideal woman as viewed by women and men in 2006 (%)

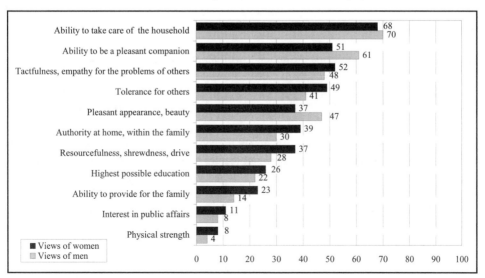

Source: Institute for Public Affairs, August 2006.

As Graph 1.4 shows that the ideal man is also perceived somewhat differently by women and men. The key difference is not that men put a greater emphasis on their ability to provide for the family, their resourcefulness, shrewdness and ability to succeed professionally – i.e. on traditionally interpreted masculinity. Nor is it that men put much more weight on their authority within the family. The most important difference is that women far more frequently emphasize the ability of men to be a pleasant companion (49% vs. 36%), to be tolerant (48% vs. 34%) and to be tactful and empathic to the problems of others (37% vs. 22%). Women also wish men to be able to take care of the household more often than men expect it of themselves (46% vs. 42%). In other words, women want the ideal man to possess qualities that used to be expected primarily of women.

Graph 1.4
Attributes of the ideal man as viewed by women and men in 2006 (%)

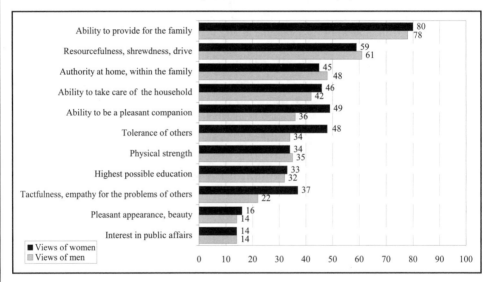

Source: Institute for Public Affairs, August 2006.

Like in 1995, women's notions of the ideal woman and the ideal man are based more on qualities needed for a balanced partnership between a woman and a man, as well as on virtues important to women's success in their professional and public life. On the other hand, men's ideas are more rooted in traditional distinction of gender roles (Bútorová, 1996).

One of the positive trends since 1995 is that both women and men increased their emphasis on highest possible education as an important feature of the ideal woman and the ideal man. This trend was more significant among women and indicates that they have become more aware of the importance of education as the key to their social advancement and professional success in a market economy.[5]

---

[5] Today, it is women who more frequently consider highest possible education as a very important asset of the ideal woman. This was not the case in 1995. It should be noted, however, that there are still more Slovak women who perceive highest possible education as a part of the image of "the ideal man" than as a part of the image of "the ideal woman".

1.1.4. VIEWS OF YOUNGER AND OLDER PEOPLE

The foregoing analysis showed that women's and men's notions of the ideal woman and the ideal man differ significantly. In the following section, we examine to what extent these gender expectations are affected by age.

Let us examine how the attributes of the ideal woman are seen by women and men younger than 45 and older than 45. As Table 1.2 shows, younger people have higher expectations than the older ones. They put a greater emphasis on the qualities that are important to women's success in the public sphere and particularly on the labor market, such as the ability to decide independently and advance professionally, resourcefulness, shrewdness and highest possible education. The ideal woman is also expected to be able to provide for the family. At the same time, however, she should cultivate her appearance and manners and be tactful, empathetic and tolerant of others. In other words, the ideal woman according to younger people must be assertive in an acceptable way, not at the expense of her femininity. Only two attributes of the ideal woman are less frequently mentioned by younger women and men than by their older counterparts: the ability to take care of the household and authority within the family.

It is interesting that in 8 out of 13 listed qualities, the differences in the views of older and younger women were greater that those in the views of older and younger men. While women's views show a rather significant generational gap, younger men seem to be more conservative and tend to stick with their fathers' ideals.

Table 1.2
Attributes of the ideal woman as viewed by younger and older women and men in 2006 (%)

	People under 45		People over 45	
	Women's views	Men's views	Women's views	Men's views
Ability to take care of the household	69	69	68	72
Ability to be a pleasant companion	56	63	49	57
Tactfulness, empathy for problems of others	54	49	50	47
Ability to decide independently	55	44	49	42
Tolerance of others	51	42	47	38
Authority at home, within family	43	28	35	32
Resourcefulness, shrewdness, drive	41	29	33	27
Pleasant appearance, beauty	42	51	31	40
Ability to succeed professionally	39	31	32	22
Highest possible education	29	25	22	19
Ability to provide for family	26	17	18	11
Interest in public affairs	12	9	9	7
Physical strength	8	6	9	4

Source: Institute for Public Affairs, August 2006.

And how do younger and older people view the ideal man? As Table 1.3 shows, younger people are slightly more demanding. As with the ideal woman, they expect the ideal man to have qualities that allow him to succeed in the public life and particularly on the labor market, i.e. the ability to decide independently and succeed professionally, resourcefulness, shrewdness and a good education. At the same time, the ideal man should be tactful, empathetic and tolerant of others, and should not neglect his appearance. It is particularly noteworthy that younger women and men put a stronger emphasis on the ability of the ideal man to take care of the household. There are only three qualities of the ideal man that are less important for the younger women and men than for their older counterparts: they care less about his ability to provide for the family, authority within the family, and physical strength. Needless to say, all these features are typical of the traditional concept of masculinity.

Table 1.3
Attributes of the ideal man as viewed by younger and older women and men in 2006 (%)

	People under 45		People over 45	
	Women's views	Men's views	Women's views	Men's views
Ability to provide for the family	79	76	79	79
Ability to succeed professionally	65	63	58	58
Resourcefulness, shrewdness, drive	60	63	54	56
Ability to decide independently	59	68	55	56
Ability to be a pleasant companion	52	38	42	35
Ability to take care of the household	49	43	43	40
Tolerance of others	48	36	47	32
Authority at home, within family	46	46	44	48
Tactfulness, empathy for problems of others	40	23	34	22
Highest possible education	35	35	31	27
Physical strength	34	33	34	38
Pleasant appearance, beauty	21	15	10	11
Interest in public affairs	15	14	12	15

Source: Institute for Public Affairs, August 2006.

Let us now change perspective and examine the differences in the views of women and men belonging to the same generation. Are younger women's ideas of the ideal woman and the ideal man closer to younger men's views than is the case with the older generation? Or is it the other way round, and the gap between the ideas of younger women and younger men is greater than between the views of their older counterparts?

As for the concept of the ideal woman, the views of younger women and men are more dissimilar than those of older women and men. Compared to their older counterparts, but also to men of the same age, younger women more frequently expect the ideal woman to be resourceful and shrewd, to decide independently, to be able to provide for the family, and to enjoy authority at home.

Also when it comes to the concept of the ideal man, the differences between the perceptions of younger women and men are greater than in older generation. Younger women, more frequently than their older counterparts or men of the same age, demand that the ideal man be a pleasant companion, take care of the household, be gentle and sensitive, and have attractive appearance. Younger women also more often expect the ideal man to provide for his family.

Another interesting finding is that younger women and younger men attach equal importance to the authority that the ideal man should wield within his family. However, while younger women expect the ideal woman's authority to match that of the ideal man, younger men see authority within the family primarily in the hands of men, and expect women to follow the lead of "the head of the family".

These findings indicate that the differences between the gender expectations of women and men have widened within the younger generation. Younger women are abandoning the traditional patriarchal model and drifting towards a family model based on an equal partnership between a more sovereign, active, assertive and educated woman and a less patriarchal but more pleasant, tolerant and sensitive man who does not neglect his appearance. Still, they expect the ideal man to be resourceful and shrewd and able to provide for the family.

This increased gap in the expectations that young women and men have of themselves and their partners is a source of tension. Young women, especially those with university degrees, often have problems finding a partner who meets their expectations. Many educated young men were raised in traditional families and tend to prefer less demanding female partners and more hierarchical family relations in which they hold the upper hand.

1.1.5. THE IMAGE OF THE IDEAL WOMAN AS VIEWED BY MATURE WOMEN

So far, our findings indicate that women over 45 have slightly less demanding expectations of the ideal woman than younger women. But when we divide the large category of women over 45 into 10-year sub-groups, we see that age 55 is an important turning point (Graph 1.5). Soon after women reach this age, their emphasis on almost all of the attributes of the ideal woman weakens. This applies particularly to those qualities that are essential for women's performance on the labor market, such as the ability to decide independently and to succeed professionally, resourcefulness and shrewdness, a good education and an interest in public affairs. As women age, they seem to become less demanding and their concept of the ideal woman becomes more passive.

Why is the age of 55 such a watershed? One reason is the relatively low retirement age for women, which has been in force in Slovakia for several decades. The previous pension system has set women's "mental clock" in such a way that after they reach 55 many of them begin to withdraw from the labor market. This explanation is supported by the fact that men over 55 do not show a similar weakening of their self-image; over the decades, they have apparently become accustomed to staying longer active in the public sphere than women.

Currently, the retirement age for women is being gradually increased to 62 years (for details, see Chapter 3 in this publication). Therefore, the contemporary generation of women in mature years is facing the challenge of adopting the concept of active ageing. This entails extricating themselves from the stereotypical conviction that the best choice for women over 55 is to abandon their careers and to become non-working pensioners whose activity is limited to their families. The coming changes will demand that mature women cease to withdraw from active participation in public life prematurely.

Needless to say, the necessity to embrace the concept of active ageing reflects also inexorable demographic trends: similarly to other European countries, Slovakia's population undergoes a process of ageing.[6] Moreover, such a redefinition of ageing is interconnected with the fact that the "baby boomers" from the 1960s are approaching retirement age. This generation differs from its predecessors by substantially greater educational attainment and significantly better health. Slovak women and men may draw inspiration from the United States and other Western democracies where the concept of active ageing is not only a topic of public discussion, but is also increasingly reflected in changing lifestyles of older peoples (Aburdene – Naisbitt, 1992; Friedan, 1993; Rowe – Kahn, 1999; Braun Levine, 2005; Steinhorn, 2006; Ilmarinen, 2006).

---

[6] One of the arguments in favor of redefining the concept of ageing is the Slovakia's strong economic growth, which is creating new jobs and increasingly depleting the available domestic workforce.

Graph 1.5
Attributes of the ideal woman as viewed by women over 45 in 2006 (%)

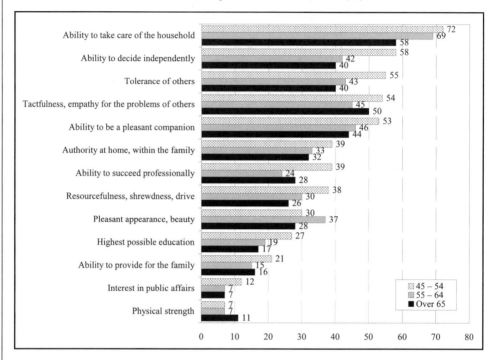

Source: Institute for Public Affairs, August 2006.

1.1.6. NOTIONS OF IDEAL RELATIONS WITHIN THE FAMILY

As we saw in the previous analysis, 70 % of people in Slovakia perceive the ability to take care of the household as a very important attribute of the ideal woman, while only 44 % see it as a very important attribute of the ideal man. On the other hand, the authority within family is less frequently attributed to women than to men (35 % and 46 %, respectively). Let us explore, in how far are these normative expectations in accordance with a more general concept of ideal relations within the family.

As for the division of labor within family, few people in Slovakia nowadays openly subscribe to the view that taking care of children and the household is primarily a woman's responsibility (Table 1.4). This opinion was presented by only one in five women (21%) and two in seven men (29%). On the other hand, 62% of women and 52% of men said that both partners should participate equally in performing these duties. While the ideal woman should be able to take care of the household, it does not mean that all responsibilities should be left on her shoulders. Preference for the partnership model is stronger among women, as well as among people with higher education.

Obviously, Table 1.4 presents the publicly expressed views of respondents. One cannot rule out that some of them were being "politically correct", and that their declarations may not correspond to their actual behavior. An analysis of the real division of labor in Slovak households suggests that they often do not (for details, see Section 6.2.). In Slovakia, the burden of

Table 1.4
"Which of the following statements do you support?" (support of A : undecided : support B – in %)

	Educational Attainment	Women's views	Men's views
Division of labor within family (2007)			
In the ideal family, the woman is primarily responsible for taking care of the children and the household.	Elementary	26 : 23 : 51	38 : 21 : 41
	Secondary without A levels	21 : 13 : 66	29 : 20 : 51
In the ideal family, both parents should jointly take care of the children and the household.	Complete secondary	22 : 15 : 63	21 : 18 : 61
	University	7 : 20 : 73	21 : 18 : 61
	Total	21 : 17 : 62	29 : 20 : 52
Decision-making within family (2002)			
The man is the head of the family, which is why he should decide on important matters.	Elementary	15 : 15 : 70	31 : 18 : 51
	Secondary without A levels	7 : 12 : 81	23 : 19 : 59
Man and woman are partners and therefore they should decide on important matters together.	Complete secondary	3 : 12 : 85	16 : 14 : 70
	University	3 : 10 : 87	8 : 10 : 82
	Total	8 : 13 : 79	23 : 16 : 61
Education of children (2002)			
When raising children, parents should teach them complete obedience. Children should not be involved in discussing or deciding on family matters.	Elementary	19 : 31 : 50	26 : 32 : 42
	Secondary without A levels	13 : 26 : 61	21 : 28 : 51
	Complete secondary	8 : 20 : 72	12 : 24 : 64
When raising children, parents should consult them and get them involved in deciding on family matters.	University	5 : 24 : 71	9 : 25 : 66
	Total	13 : 25 : 62	20 : 28 : 52

Source: Institute for Public Affairs, June 2002 and November 2007.

household chores is still primarily borne by women, and a just division of labor remains an ideal rather than an everyday reality.

But let us remain focused on the ideal notions comprised in Table 1.4. A comparison with the findings of a similar previous survey indicates that even proclaimed support for the partnership model of the division of labor within the family has declined in recent years. Between 2002 and 2007, the percentage of people who prefer equal division of care of the children and the household dropped from 68% to 62% among women and from 55% to 52% among men (Bútorová – Filadelfiová – Cviková – Gyárfášová – Farkašová, 2002; *Empirical Data…*, 2005b; *Empirical Data…*, 2007c).

This trend suggests that the positive shift in professed values has frozen and people's support of gender equality in everyday family life has not become stronger. One reason may be the insufficient public discourse about the participation of men in carrying out household and family responsibilities (for details, see Chapter 8 in this publication). Another factor might be the failure of the school system to implement gender-sensitive education into curricula (Filadelfiová, 2008). So far, attempts to introduce such an education were mostly initiated by women's non-governmental organizations and have had a limited impact.[7]

Let us now look at the opinions of Slovak women and men about another aspect of the family model, i.e. the role of women and men in decision-making on important family matters. In a survey from 2002, four in five women (79%) and three in five men (61%) agreed with the assertion that men and women are partners and therefore should decide on important matters together. The opposite view, based on the patriarchal concept of the man as the head of the family,

---

[7] For further details on women's non-governmental organizations specializing in promoting gender sensitivity, see Bútorová – Filadelfiová – Cviková – Gyárfášová – Farkašová, 2002; Bútorová – Filadelfiová – Marošiová, 2004; Bútorová – Filadelfiová, 2005. One of the best outcomes of the endeavour to identify gender stereotypes and examine their implications is the book *Ružový a modrý svet* [Pink and Blue World] (Cviková – Juráňová, 2003) and a related project of the same name (www.ruzovyamodrysvet.sk).

holding all decision-making power in his hands, was only endorsed by 8% of women and 22% of men. The concept of joint decision-making within the family found a stronger support among women. An important factor affecting men's views was their educational attainment.

Again, we have to bear in mind that the views presented in Table 1.4 are declaratory. So what does decision-making in Slovak families actually look like? An answer to this question was provided by one of our previous surveys, carried out in 2000 (*Empirical Data...*, 2000), which found that the share of women and men who endorsed the partnership model of decision-making within the family was higher than the share of those who actually practiced this model (see Graph 1.6). The statement that important family matters should ideally be decided jointly by both partners was supported by 95% of women and 82% of men.[8] However, only 77% of women and 76% of men said they actually used this model when deciding on family matters. The survey also documented a generation gap, as only 60% of female respondents and 57% of male respondents reported that their parents had decided important matters together.[9] Contemporary families practice joint decision-making more frequently than one generation earlier, but still not as frequently as they would like to see.

Graph 1.6
Deciding on important family matters – views and experiences (% of affirmative answers)

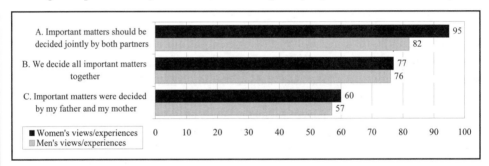

Note: The sample comprised respondents who live in a partnership and grew up in a complete family.
Source: Institute for Public Affairs, March 2000.

Finally, let us look at people's views of yet another dimension of the family model, i.e. the preferred model of raising children. According to Table 1.4, over three in five women (62%) and over one in two men (52%) believe that parents should consult their children and get them involved in deciding on family matters. The opposite opinion, that children should be taught obedience without any role in discussions of family matters, was approved by 13% of women and 20% of men. Both women and men clearly preferred the participative model of raising children over the directive one, and horizontal communication with children over the vertical one. This preference was more pronounced among women than among men.

If we look at all three examined aspects of family life, we see that women are stronger advocates of the partnership model than men. However, significant differences are also found within

---

8   The higher percentage of respondents endorsing the partnership model of decision-making in the survey from 2000 compared to the survey from 2002 was probably the result of a differently formulated question. In 2002, the survey used a pair of opposite statements and gave respondents a chance to take also an ambivalent position. In 2000, respondents were only asked to express their approval or disapproval of statement A in Graph 1.7.

9   Almost one in four female respondents (24%) and almost one in three male respondents (31%) said important matters in their families were decided by the father, while only 14% of female respondents and 9% of male respondents said they were decided by the mother.

categories of women and men. The patriarchal model is typically preferred by less educated women and men; older people; unskilled blue collar workers; people who see themselves as members of the lowest social class. On the other hand, better educated and younger women and men who identify with the middle class tend to favor the partnership family model.

However, the strongest factor determining people's support of particular family model is the educational attainment. The higher it is, the less likely women and men are to endorse the patriarchal family model, which puts decision-making in the hands of the father, exempts the father from taking care of the children and the household, and favors an authoritative style in raising children.

Table 1.4 also shows differences in the positions of women and men in all education categories, as well as a "phase shift" between the views of women and men. The distribution of views among men with university education is not similar to that among women with university degrees, but rather to that among women with elementary or incomplete secondary education. Analogous "phase shift" can also be seen within particular age categories. The youngest women prefer the partnership family model more frequently than their male counterparts who are more inclining toward the traditional patriarchal model.[10]

1.2. MATURE WOMEN AND MEN AS LIFE MODELS
1.2.1. DO PEOPLE HAVE LIFE MODELS?

In the previous section, we discussed normative notions of the ideal woman and the ideal man in Slovakia. Now, we take another angle and explore whether people in Slovakia know women or men in their immediate or wider surroundings who meet their expectations sufficiently to be viewed as life models. We assume that the status of women and men in society does not depend merely on their formal position in the public sphere, but also on the way they affect other people's values and behavior. We focus primarily on life models who are women and men in their mature years. The following analysis is based on a survey carried out by the Institute for Public Affairs, which yielded unique findings on this phenomenon that were previously unavailable in Slovakia.[11]

In the survey, the respondents spontaneously identified a broad spectrum of mature women and men whom they viewed as life models. Table 1.5 provides a comprehensive "map" of such models without specifying the frequency of their occurrence. It distinguishes between models according to gender (i.e. female and male models) and according to the sphere of origin (i.e. life models from the private sphere that people have personal knowledge of and direct interaction with, and life models from the public sphere that can further be divided into domestic and foreign ones).

Let us now fill this chart of life models with concrete research findings. Graph 1.7 shows the distribution of life models within the Slovak population. Surprisingly, less than two in five

---

[10] For details on the perpetuation of gender stereotypical socialization in various institutions in Slovakia, i.e. within the families, schools and informal education, see Cviková, 2003; Bosá, 2005; Bosá – Minarovičová, 2005. Empirical findings on gender stereotypes in the attitudes of schools teachers were published in Minarovičová, 2003 and Filadelfiová, 2008b. For more information on gender stereotypes in the media, see also Mesochoritisová, 2005.

[11] It would be interesting to study also the life models in younger years, as it could well be that such models are strongly preferred by young people. Unfortunately, such an analysis would exceed the scope and space of the present publication.

Table 1.5
Categorization of life models in mature years

		Female models	Male models
Private sphere		Mother	Father
		Grandmother	Grandfather
		Other older female relative	Other older male relative
		Wife	Husband
		Other female relative (coeval or younger)	Other male relative (coeval or younger)
		Female friend, acquaintance, neighbor, colleague	Male friend, acquaintance, neighbor, colleague
		Female superior	Male superior
		Female teacher	Male teacher
		Female doctor (personal)	Male doctor (personal)
Public sphere	Domestic	Local female politician	Local male politician
		National female politician	National male politician
		Female cultural, scientific, economic or civic figure	Male cultural, scientific, economic or civic figure
		Female spiritual authority	Male spiritual authority
		Female show business star	Male show business star
		Sportswoman	Sportsman
	Foreign	Foreign female politician	Foreign male politician
		Female cultural, scientific, economic or civic figure	Male cultural, scientific, economic or civic figure
		Female spiritual authority	Male spiritual authority
		Female show business star	Male show business star
		Foreign sportswoman	Foreign sportsman

Note: Categorization of respondents' answers to an open-ended question.
Source: Institute for Public Affairs, August 2006.

women (38%) and less than one in three men (30%) know a person in mature years that they see as their life model.

Graph 1.7
"Would you be able to identify a person in mature years (i.e. over 45) that you regard as your life model?" (%)

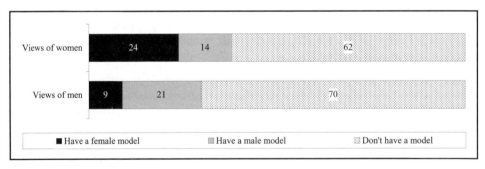

Source: Institute for Public Affairs, August 2006.

Graph 1.7 also answers the question whether women or men have a greater chance of becoming life models. It largely depends on who makes the choice. Female models in their mature years inspire women more frequently than men, as 24 % of women but only 9% of men reported a female life model. On the other hand, male models in their mature years are more appealing to men, as they were cited by 21% of male and 14% of female respondents.

The graph also shows that women choose male models more frequently than men choose female ones. We believe that this asymmetry reflects the weaker position of women within

Slovak society. This is probably why men are more reluctant to follow female examples while women are more inspired by male examples.

What walk of life do most life models come from? As Graph 1.8 shows, those from the private sphere strongly prevail over those from the public sphere. Life models from the private sphere were mentioned by 30% of women and 23% of men, while life models from the public sphere were cited by only 8% of women and 7% of men.

Graph 1.8
"Would you be able to identify a person in mature years that you regard as your life model?" (%)

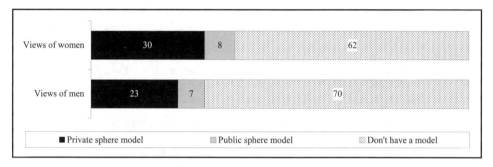

Source: Institute for Public Affairs, August 2006.

Let us now distinguish between female and male life models from the private sphere and from the public sphere. Female life models more often come from the private sphere than male models (see Table 1.6).

While 21% of women said they had a female life model from the private sphere, only 3% had a female model from the public sphere. That means that 88 % of women's female life models hail from the private sphere while 12% come from the public sphere. Men tend even more to prefer female life models from the private sphere; 8% of male respondents were inspired by female life models from the private sphere and none of them mentioned a female model from the public sphere.

Male life models are distributed somewhat more evenly, but the private sphere is still dominant. While 15% of men have a male life model from the private sphere, only 7% have a male model from the public sphere. Among women, 9% cited a male model from the private sphere and 5% from the public sphere.

Table 1.6
Personalities in their mature years who are life models for women and men (%)

Life models of women				Life models of men			
38				30			
Private sphere		Public sphere		Private sphere		Public sphere	
30		8		23		7	
Female model	Male model	Female model	Male model	Female model	Male model	Female model	Male model
21	9	3	5	8	15	0	7

Note: The remainder of the 100% figure comprises the 62% of female and the 70% of male respondents who said they did not have any life model.
Source: Institute for Public Affairs, August 2006.

1.2.2. WHO TYPICALLY HAS LIFE MODELS?

So far, we have been interested in the kind of life models professed by women and men. Let us now examine the role of age in recognizing life models. As Graph 1.9 shows, the general image of young people as rebels who reject older authorities is not adequate: it is primarily younger women and men who respect some figure in mature years as their life model.[12] Older women and men are less likely to have some kind of life model, particularly one from the private sphere. On the other hand, this decline does not apply to life models from the public sphere.

What does this trend indicate? One explanation may be that as people grow older they become more skeptical and/or realistic. In other words, mature women and men rarely "reach for the stars"; instead, they tend to look at "what lies at their feet" for help in tackling everyday obstacles. Also, they may feel they don't need life models because they have greater life

Graph 1.9
"Would you be able to identify a person in mature years that you regard as your life model?"
(Percentage of affirmative answers of women and men – by age)

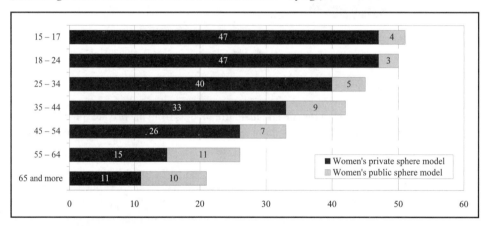

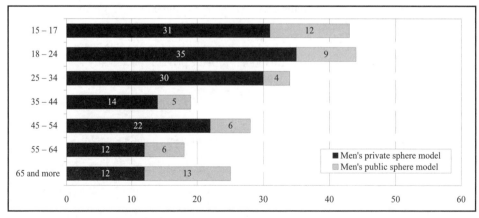

Source: Institute for Public Affairs, August 2006.

---

[12] Among younger women, educational attainment plays an important role: the higher it is the greater is the share of women who have a life model. No such correlation was found among younger men.

experience. When dreams and desires collide with the realities of life, people may also think that it is better to remain "down-to earth" instead of trying to follow a life model whose example may be unattainable or "unusable" in a concrete situation. Moreover, life models may also lose some of their previous glamor. As years go by, people tend to be more critical of their life models and see some of their problematic features they did not realize before.

1.2.3. MOST COMMON LIFE MODELS

Let us now focus on the concrete life models of Slovak women and men. Graph 1.10 indicates that parents have an unrivalled position. Women tend to prefer their mothers (cited by 13% of female respondents) followed by their fathers (4%). On the other hand, men favor their fathers (cited by 8% of male respondents) followed by their mothers (5%).

Graph 1.10
Most common life models of women and men (%)

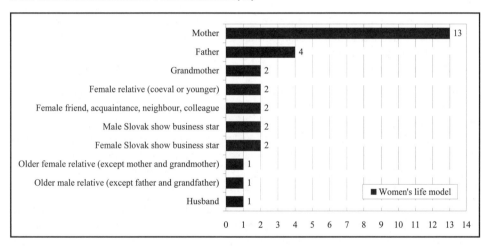

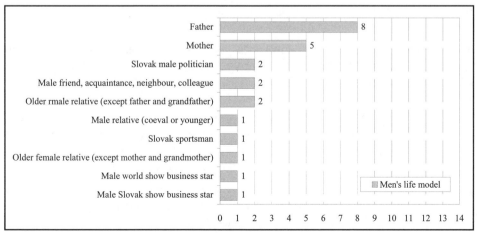

Note: This was an open-ended question. The graph shows the percentage of respondents.
Source: Institute for Public Affairs, August 2006.

It is noteworthy that the father's position in the eyes of men is weaker than the mother's position in the eyes of women (8% vs. 13%). Also, the father is a slightly less inspiring model to women than the mother is to men. One of the reasons of this difference may be that men participate to a lesser extent in the everyday life of the family – a situation that weakens the bond between father and child and that cannot be fully compensated by the effort of many fathers to fulfill their role as breadwinners.

Let us now examine ten life models most frequently cited by women. Eight of them originate from the private sphere while only two hail from the public sphere, more specifically from Slovak show business: one represents female celebrities, the other male stars.

Other life models from the public sphere that are not included in Graph 1.10 were mentioned by less than one percent of women: it was a Slovak male politician and a male spiritual authority.

Domestic and foreign sportswomen, female political leaders, businesswomen and outstanding women from the domain of culture, science or civil society appeared only marginally in women's answers.

The virtual absence of female political leaders and businesswomen among women's life models may be due to the fact that top politics and business are primarily male domains in Slovakia. This state of affairs is exacerbated by the media image of women, which often follows traditional gender stereotypes (for details, see Chapter 8 in this publication).

It is more surprising, however, that those public sectors where women are relatively visible and undoubtedly successful (e.g. sports, science, research, teaching, medicine, etc.) only rarely supply life models for Slovak women. Even more paradoxical is the fact that women see almost no models in the ranks of female activists and leaders of non-governmental organizations. It indicates that they are insufficiently aware of the important role these women have played for almost two decades in developing civil society and improving the quality of life in Slovakia (Fialová, 1997; Bútorová – Filadelfiová – Marošiová, 2004).

We may conclude that the life models of Slovak women largely reflect their prevailing orientation towards the private sphere. As we have pointed out, the only public figures listed among the top 10 life models by Slovak women were show business celebrities, who can hardly present true and "useful" life models that would inspire women, accompany them throughout their life, and give them strength to overcome obstacles.

And what about the life models of Slovak men? According to Graph 1.10, six from the most frequently cited models originated in the private sphere while four came from the public sphere. Compared to women's top 10 list, life models of men from the private sphere were not as dominant.

Models from the public sphere that were the most frequently mentioned by male respondents included domestic political leaders, followed by domestic sportsmen and male stars of domestic and world show business. Other models from the public sphere that did not make it to the top 10 list included male cultural, scientific, business and civic figures.

To sum up, the spectrum of life models from the public sphere identified by male respondents is more diverse than that of women. As we shall see later, it is also a bit more colorful and rich in terms of the virtues that men appreciate (see Table 1.7).

The top 10 life models respected by men included eight male models but only two female models; on the other hand, the women's top 10 list comprised six female and four male models.

Perhaps even more important is the fact that there was not a single female model among the five models from the public sphere most frequently identified by male respondents. However, female respondents were not much better off in this respect, as four out of their five models from the public sphere were male models and only one was female. These findings corroborate the above mentioned gender asymmetry.

1.2.4. VIRTUES FOR WHICH PEOPLE ADMIRE LIFE MODELS

Based on the spontaneous answers of respondents to an open-ended question, the virtues for which Slovak people respect or admire their life models may be grouped into seven categories. Women and men value the most self-sacrifice for the family (see Table 1.7), followed by vitality, vigor and creativity. Third on the list is education, wisdom and life experience, followed by humanity, tolerance of others. According to male respondents, civic virtues such as bravery, honor, standing up for the rights of others and working for the community ranked fifth. These were followed by outstanding professional achievement, and finally by personality, authority and charisma. According to female respondents, the latter three virtues were equally important.

The overall perspective of women differs slightly from that of men. The virtue of making personal sacrifices for the family was more frequently emphasized by women (35%) than by men (27%); the same was true of humanity, tolerance of others (13% vs. 11%, respectively).

> "I had a grandmother ... She was perfect, she never complained. She was always self-reliant; she never needed anything from anybody. She was 82 years old when she died ... She worked at an agricultural cooperative. One day she came home from work, washed herself, changed her clothes, tidied up the room, and all of a sudden she got sick and died. She was one unique woman ... She was simple but at the same time very wise and just." (Anna, 52, a clerk from Martin)

> "I had my first child when I was 20. What life models does one have at that age? I only wondered whether I could be as self-sacrificing a mother as my mother was." (Terézia, 59, a laboratory technician from Nitra)

Table 1.7
"What do you value or admire the most about this person?" (%)

	Valued virtues		Origin of life models with valued virtues (private sphere : public sphere)	
	Women's views	Men's views	Women's views	Men's views
Self-sacrifice for family	35	27	35 : 0	26 : 1
Vitality, vigor, creativity	20	19	17 : 3	15 : 4
Education, wisdom, life experience	15	16	9 : 6	10 : 6
Humanity, tolerance, respect for others	13	11	10 : 3	8 : 3
Life's work, outstanding professional achievement	6	10	5 : 1	6 : 4
Bravery, honor, promoting rights of others, working for the community	6	9	3 : 3	5 : 4
Personality, authority, charisma	6	7	4 : 2	4 : 3

Note: This was an open-ended question; respondents could give three answers. Percentages in columns were calculated from the answers of those respondents who had a life model.
Source: Institute for Public Affairs, August 2006.

"I admired my mother because although she was not an educated woman, she was very wise and clever ... I very much wanted to be like her so I too could manage everything just like she did. That's why I can paint a room, bake a cake and do whatever needs to be done ... But at the same time I thought to myself, no way, I'm not going to live like my mother did, I'm not going to fuss over a man. My father wouldn't even slice bread because he had been raised in a family where work was strictly divided between men and women; so, when he was hungry he waited for someone to feed him – even though the meal was cooked and ready." (Magdaléna, 53, an unemployed teacher from Žilina)

"When I was 20, I had a model – the director of the clothing factory in Trenčín. She was the first woman to ever get that post. An incredible achiever and hard worker. I yearned very much to be like her. I even wanted to enroll into a textile machinery faculty, but I couldn't due to family reasons." (Ester, 53, a technician from Žilina)

"I became interested in Maria Curie-Skłodowska, especially for working her way up from such a background. When I was at a college, I read a book about her ... She studied at the Sorbonne and had to work in order to put herself through her studies. She was my model. But besides her, I had no models." (Viera, 55, a state sector manager from Bratislava)

"I have admired my grandmother. She had children, her husband died in the war; she suffered a lot; she kept a homestead with fields and did all the mowing and everything by herself. But I never took [her life] as a model because I never wanted to have such a hard life." (Ľubomíra, 47, a tradeswoman from Martin)

"I had a model – my father's sister. She was a nurse. Back then, nurses wore those bonnets. As a child, I fell in love with that and played doctor. Nothing topped a hospital for me. I always found her so clean and noble. That was my model. I hoped to be like her one day." (Oľga, 60, a nurse from Rožňava)

Men, for their part, more frequently praised their life models for their life's work and outstanding professional achievement (10% of men and 6% of women) as well as for civic virtues (9% and 6%, respectively). Generally speaking, though, gender differences in views of the qualities of life models are not very significant.

The two far right columns of Table 1.7 provide information on the "origin" of life models that are appreciated for various virtues. They show that Slovak women and men attribute the most valued qualities to models from the private sphere. Most respondents admired the sacrifice that their life models from private sphere have made for their families. Somewhat surprisingly, they attributed them also vitality, vigor and creativity that ranked second on the list.

Other virtues were distributed more evenly between life models from the private and the public spheres. For men, these included three attributes in particular: life's work and outstanding professional achievement; civic virtues such as bravery, honor and willingness to defend the rights of others and to work for the community; and finally, personality, authority and charisma. Women, for their part, appreciated only the latter two virtues.

The key virtue for which many women and men perceive their mothers or fathers as their life models is their ability to make sacrifices for the family. This largely corresponds to the fact that according to a majority of population, the dominant attribute of the ideal woman is her ability to take care of the family and household, while the most important quality of the ideal man is his ability to be the principal breadwinner.

After a significant gap, the second most appreciated virtue of mothers and fathers is their vitality, vigor and creativity, followed by their education, wisdom and life experience.

Interesting differences could be found in respondents' views of their parents: while mothers are more frequently than fathers valued for their self-sacrifice, fathers inspire their children more frequently than mothers through their charisma and authority, as well as through their life's work and outstanding professional achievement.

Particularly noteworthy is the way how women interpret the most appreciated attribute of a female life model, i.e. self-sacrifice for the family. For some women, this virtue is not only commendable but also indisputable. This attitude can be illustrated by the authentic

"I guess our parents mean the most to us. But I also admire Madeleine Albright. I read her biography and learned about everything she had to go through. Her life wasn't easy and yet she achieved what she did." (Margaréta, 51, a manager from Bratislava)

"I admire Mother Theresa, who did so much for this world... If the Earth carried a couple more people like her, I guess it would look quite different." (Anna, 58, a PR manager from Bratislava)

"I admire women in high executive posts, for instance that woman with Slovenská sporiteľňa bank, the Austrian [Regina Ovesný-Straka]... for succeeding in working their way up to these posts. Young girls should certainly be inspired by their ambitions ... They should not remain stuck as a clerk for thirty years." (Marta, 56, a food chemist from Nitra).

statements of Anna and Terézia – two participants in a focus group discussion carried out in 2006 by the Institute for Public Affairs (see page 39).

On the other hand, women's admiration for such self-sacrifice may not be unconditional. It is often accompanied by ambivalent feelings and doubts whether such a life model, corresponding to the traditional concept of "the ideal woman" who bravely puts up with everything, is actually worth following as a "life manual" for the modern era. This ambiguity can be found in the spontaneous statements of Magdaléna and Ľubomíra (see page 40).

Last but not least, let us present the statements of other female respondents – Ester, Viera, Oľga, Margaréta, Anna, and Marta – who respect their life models not for their family virtues but because of their inspiring work ethics, their ability to win professional recognition or to succeed in the public sphere, and their contribution to the broader community or the progress of mankind.

2. WOMEN, MEN AND THE INCREASING DIVERSITY OF LIFE

Zora Bútorová – Jarmila Filadelfiová

Zora Bútorová is the author of Section 2.2. and the co-author of Section 2.1. Jarmila Filadelfiová is the co-author of Section 2.1.

2. WOMEN, MEN AND THE INCREASING DIVERSITY OF LIFE

2.1. CHANGES IN REPRODUCTIVE AND PARTNERSHIP BEHAVIOR[1]

2.1.1. PERIOD OF INCREASING DIVERSITY

Before 1989, the patterns of family and partnership behavior of Slovak population showed considerable uniformity. Besides a long-term decline in the birth rate, hallmarks of the reproductive behavior included a low mean age of women at first childbirth (approximately 22 years) and a high share of pregnant brides entering marriage (approximately 50%).

In terms of the marriage and divorce rates, Slovakia was rather traditional; compared to some Western European countries, it had a high marriage rate and a relatively low divorce rate. The mean age at first marriage was also very low; among women only about 21 years. These characteristics were shaped by traditional attitudes regarding the institution of matrimony as well as by the communist regime's social policy. In the 1970s, many family policy measures were made conditional on people's being married. By pegging social policy measures to reproductive behavior, the government hoped to reverse the negative trends in the birth rate. The effects were short-lived: the birth rate increased for several years but then returned to its previous downward trend.

In the 1980s, due to the overall decline in the birth rate, the two-child family model became dominant. The relatively high marriage rate, and the fact that the mean age at first marriage was almost identical to the mean age at first childbirth, meant that beginning a marriage was virtually the same as starting a family. Over 90% of all children were born in matrimony. Most women became mothers shortly after completing their education; after their maternity leave, they joined the labor market on a more or less permanent basis. In other words, the period of entering marriage and of bearing children overlapped for most women, and preceded their entry to the labor market.

After the November 1989 Velvet Revolution that marked the fall of Communism, the partnership and reproductive behavior of the Slovak population began to change dramatically. While some trends were rooted in the past, others surfaced over the next two decades. The weakening of the previously strong welfare state, the deepening social disparities in the new free market economy, the increased financial challenges of starting a family, as well as the broadening variety of new life options and career opportunities for young people, the new demands of the labor market, more diverse lifestyles, weaker social control, especially in cities, the diversity of the new value systems (e.g. the cultivation of respect for human rights, the dissemination of religious values, the penetration of consumerism), the "opening" of various issues previously seen as private or taboo (sexuality, family planning, domestic violence, etc.), greater freedom of speech, the increased openness of society to outside influences, growing contact with foreign cultures – all these and other factors produced a drift towards greater

---

[1]   This chapter is a continuation of several previous studies (e.g. Guráň – Filadelfiová, 1995; Filadelfiová – Guráň, 1997, 1998; Bútorová, 1996; Filadelfiová, 2005a, 2005c, 2006a, Filadelfiová – Bútorová, 2007b).

diversity in family and partnership patterns, and as a result triggered significant demographic changes. The cultural preference for the dominant family model began to fade. "Various solutions are being sought, and people are taking different decisions according to their own preferences" (Možný, 2006, p. 191). Changing partnership and reproductive behavior is also part of society's overall trend towards permissiveness, which apart from the fundamental change in people's attitudes to their lives and activities also encompasses changed views on work, lifestyles, culture, and leisure time (Petrusek, 2006, p. 236).

2.1.2. TRENDS IN BIRTH RATE AND FERTILITY

In Slovakia, the number of live-births per 1,000 population fell throughout the 20th century. This decline came in three major waves. The first wave swept the country between 1925 and 1940, when the crude birth rate dropped from 35.3 to 22.8 live-births per 1,000 population. The second drop took place between 1952 and 1968, when the crude birth rate fell to 17 live-births per 1,000 population. After a brief recovery came a third wave, which was the longest and most dramatic and saw the crude birth rate fall from 20.8 in 1976 to 9.5 in 2002. Since 2003, the annual number of live-births has risen slightly.

The decline in the total number of live-births and in the birth rate was also reflected in the overall fertility of women in Slovakia. While in the 1950s the fertility rate was 3.5 children per woman, that number fell to less than 2.1 in 1990 and below 1.2 in 2002. Along with other post-Communist countries, Slovakia copied the trend in traditional South European countries that had experienced a similar fertility decline – unlike, for instance, the Nordic countries or France. Between 2004 and 2006, overall fertility rate rose moderately to 1.24. This had a lot to do with the fact that the generation of "Husák baby boomers" from the early 1970s (named after former Czechoslovak President Gustáv Husák) began to have babies of their own – belatedly but nevertheless.[2] As we mentioned above, the main reasons for the declining birth and fertility rates in the 1990s (despite strong age-groups entering

Graph 2.1
Births and abortions in Slovakia (1921 – 2006, in total numbers)

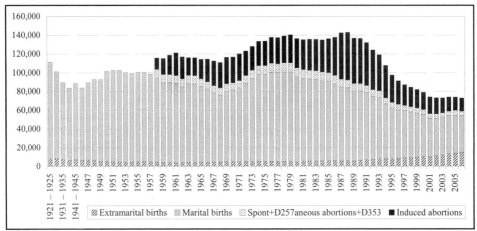

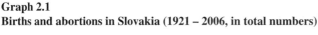

Source: *Stav a pohyb...*, 1921 – 2004; *Štatistické ročenky...*, 1985 – 2007; *Informácia o demografickom...*, 2007.

Table 2.1
Mean age of women at childbirth (1995 – 2006)

	1995	1996	1997	1999	2000	2001	2002	2003	2004	2005	2006
First child	23.00	22.86	23.10	23.56	23.93	24.14	24.53	24.88	25.26	25.66	25.97
All children	25.59	25.49	25.87	25.99	26.21	26.46	26.67	26.95	27.19	27.51	27.78

Source: Vaňo, 2003, 2005, 2007.

their reproductive years) include decisions to postpone parenthood until a later age, deteriorating conditions for starting a family, and the opening of new opportunities for young people to study or travel, which produced a greater variety of life strategies and orientations (Bodnárová – Filadelfiová – Guráň, 2001; Filadelfiová, 2005b, 2006b; Vaňo, 2003, 2005).

After 1990, several characteristics of Slovak birth and fertility rates began to change dramatically. The mean age of mothers at childbirth began to increase particularly rapidly. In 2006, the mean age of mothers at first childbirth reached 26.0 years, while the mean age of women at birth of all children increased to 27.8 years (see Table 2.1).

The structure of newborn children also changed in the first two decades after the Velvet Revolution. The share of children born out of wedlock in the total number of newborn children grew significantly, from 7.6% in 1990 to 27.6% in 2006.

Table 2.2
Children born out of wedlock in Slovakia (1950 – 2006, in total numbers and %)

Year	Number of extramarital births	% of all live-births
1950	5,538	5.4
1955	4,738	4.7
1960	4,189	4.7
1965	4,506	5.3
1970	5,048	6.2
1975	5,177	5.3
1980	5,490	5.7
1985	5,967	6.6
1990	6,134	7.6
1995	7,788	12.6
2000	10,067	18.3
2005	14,136	26.0
2006	14,820	27.6

Source: *Stav a pohyb... 1951 – 2004*; Vaňo, 2007.

2.1.3. DEVELOPMENT OF ABORTION RATE

In the course of the 1990s, there was a significant reversal of the long-term trend in the abortion rate; induced abortions, as opposed to spontaneous abortions, began to decline particularly rapidly after 1990. In 2005, the total number of women undergoing abortion dropped below 20,000, which corresponded to the level in 1958 when abortions were first legalized (see Graph 2.2). The total number of abortions continues to decline in all age categories of women. While in 1989 there were 1.29 abortions for every woman of fertile age, by 2006 that number had dropped to 0.34.

The change in the abortion rate is the most favorable trend in the reproductive behavior of the Slovak population since 1989. Most importantly, the turnaround was achieved without a

---

2   A similar turnaround took place also in the Czech Republic, where the birth rate began to increase moderately in 2002 due to the belated births of previously postponed children. But according to Czech sociologist Ivo Možný, it is difficult to predict at this point how many people who once wanted to found a family but never invested the time to do so will ever found one. The thing is that *zero reproduction strategies*, i.e. planned or voluntary childlessness, are also growing increasingly popular (Možný, 2006, p. 197). The recent popularity of non-family life is brought about by a number of factors, including the proliferation of the single lifestyle.

Graph 2.2
Birth and abortion rates in Slovakia per 1,000 population (1921 – 2006)

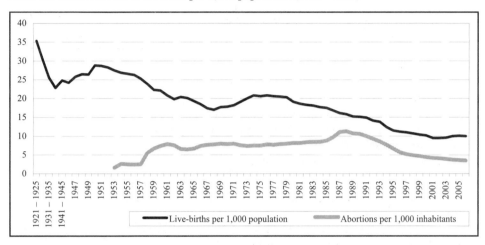

Source: *Stav a pohyb...*, 1950 – 2004; *Informácia o demografickom ...*, 2007.

legislative ban on abortions (Guráň – Filadelfiová, 1995; Filadelfiová – Guráň, 1997; Vaňo, 2003, 2007; Filadelfiová, 2005a; Filadelfiová – Bútorová, 2007b).

2.1.4. TRENDS IN MARRIAGE AND DIVORCE RATES

The long-term trend in the marriage rate saw several changes after the early 1990s (see Graph 2.3). The marriage rate began to decline rapidly after 1992 and hit an all-time low of 4.4 marriages per 1,000 population in 2001. It then grew moderately for three consecutive years to reach 5.2 in 2004, at which point it began to decline again to 4.9 marriages per 1,000 popu-

Graph 2.3
Marriage and divorce rates in Slovakia per 1,000 population (1921 – 2006)

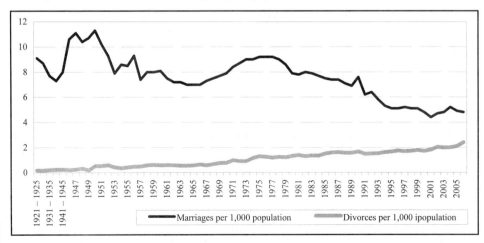

Source: *Stav a pohyb...*, 1921 – 2004; *Informácia o demografickom ...*, 2007.

lation in 2006. Alongside the declining marriage rate there has been an increase in the total number of cohabiting couples that are not formally married.

Perhaps the most significant change in the makeup of the marriages has been the increase in the mean age at marriage. Between 1995 and 2006, it rose by about four years among women as well as men (see Table 2.3). In 2006, the mean age of men at first marriage was 28.5, while the mean age of men at all marriages was 31. The mean age of women increased to 25.8 for the first marriage and to 27.9 for all marriages. More than 80% of marriages undertaken in any given year are the first ones for both partners. Repeated marriages are considerably more common among divorced men and widowers than among divorced women and widows.

Table 2.3
Mean age of women and men at marriage (1995 – 2006)

Mean age	1995	1996	1997	1999	2000	2001	2002	2003	2004	2005	2006
Men											
– first marriage	24.7	25.0	25.3	25.9	26.1	26.3	26.8	27.2	27.6	28.2	28.5
– all marriages	26.3	26.8	27.2	27.7	28.2	28.6	29.1	29.5	29.6	30.5	31.0
Women											
– first marriage	22.3	22.6	22.9	23.4	23.6	23.8	24.2	24.6	25.0	25.6	25.8
– all marriages	23.5	23.9	24.3	24.8	25.2	25.6	26.1	26.5	26.7	27.4	27.9

Source: Vaňo, 2003, 2005, 2007.

The divorce rate continued to grow slowly, and in recent years has stabilized near the level of two divorces per 1,000 population. The structure of the divorces changed as well. Both divorcees and divorced marriages grew older. In 2006, the mean age at divorce was 40 among men and 37.2 among women; the average lifespan of marriages that ended in divorce reached 14.7 years. At the same time, the share of divorced marriages involving dependent children in the total number of divorced marriages declined. While in 1995 they made up 75% of all divorces, by 2006 the share was 66.5%. Due to the overall decline in the number of children per family, the average number of children per divorce declined as well; over the long term the figure was 1.5 children, while in 2006 it was only one child. What has not changed is the dominance of women among those filing for divorce, as women continue to file two thirds of motions. Most children continue to be entrusted to the mother's care after a divorce.

2.1.5. GENDER DIFFERENCES IN MORTALITY AND LIFE EXPECTANCY

Mortality is one of the most stable demographic indicators in Slovakia (see Graph 2.4). For many years before 1990, it hovered just above 10 deaths per 1,000 population, but in 1993 it dropped below this mark. In 2006, the crude death rate in Slovakia was 9.9 deaths per 1,000 population. This mortality rate is higher than in most Western European countries; in some EU member states, it recently dropped below 8 deaths per 1,000 population (*Recent...*, 2000, 2003; Lanzieri, 2007; *Demographic...*, 2007; *Europe's...*, 2007).[3]

---

[3] In 2006, Ireland had the lowest crude mortality in the European Union (6.3 deaths per 1,000 population), followed by Cyprus (6.8), Malta (7.5) and Luxembourg (7.7). Low death rates were also recorded in France, the Netherlands and Spain (Lanzieri, 2007).

Graph 2.4
Birth and death rates in Slovakia per 1,000 population (1921 – 2006)

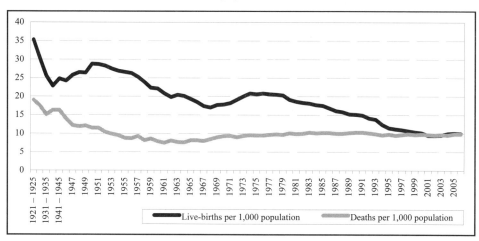

Source: *Stav a pohyb...*, 1921 – 2004; *Informácia o demografickom ...*, 2007.

The most frequent causes of death in Slovakia are cardiovascular diseases and cancer. Other frequent causes include accidents (three times more frequent among men than among women), respiratory system diseases and digestive system diseases.

As in other countries, mortality in Slovakia shows marked gender differences over the long term. There are fewer than 9 deaths per 1,000 women but almost 11 deaths per 1,000 men. In all age categories, men show higher mortality than women. The death rate among men starts to increase dramatically in the 45 – 49 age group, while the turning point for women comes between 60 and 64. Men in Slovakia die earlier and in greater numbers, which testifies to their poorer health and higher illness rate. This difference is also related to the fact that men tend to neglect prevention and prefer riskier lifestyles than women.

Table 2.4
Select characteristics of the mortality of women and men (2006)

	Men	Women
Total number of deaths	28,091	25,210
Mean age at death	67.1	75.5
Share of deaths in pre-productive and productive age (%)	29.7	8.9

Source: *Ženy a muži SR…*, 2007.

Due to their higher mortality, men in Slovakia have shorter life expectancy at birth than women. In 2006 it reached was 70.4 years for men and 78.2 years for women (see Graph 2.5). Since 1960, life expectancy has increased by 5.7 years for women but only by 2.7 years for men. In recent years, the difference between life expectancy for men and women has grown to eight years, whereas in Western Europe the gap is between four and five years (*Recent...*, 2003; *Europe's...*, 2007; *Demographic...*, 2007; *The Life...*, 2008).

Graph 2.5
Life expectancy of Slovak women and men at birth (1960 – 2006)

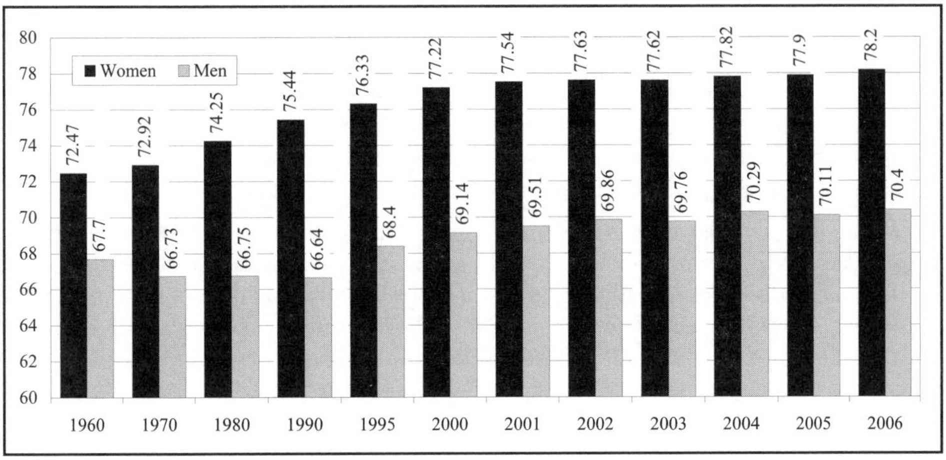

Source: *Stav a pohyb...*, 1960 – 2004; *Informácia o demografickom ...*, 2007.

2.1.6. REGIONAL DIFFERENCES IN DEMOGRAPHIC DEVELOPMENT

As of the end of 2006, Slovakia had 5,393,637 inhabitants, of whom 44.6% lived in rural areas with populations under 5,000 while 55.4% resided in towns. The country is divided into 8 regions and 79 districts; there are 2,891 municipalities, 138 of which are towns. Individual regions differ by the number of districts as well as by the number and type of municipalities.

Slovakia shows remarkable regional heterogeneity in its social, life and cultural conditions, which are subsequently reflected in demographic indicators. Most demographic disparities are long-term in nature, and many have deepened in recent years (Filadelfiová, 2005c; Jurčová, 2006).

The greatest variations can be found in the share of extramarital births in the total number of live-births. In various districts, this share may fluctuate between 4% (Námestovo) and 44% (Rimavská Sobota). The public debate on children born out of wedlock often neglects this regional diversity, which leads to erroneous interpretations. The increasing share of extramarital births is usually interpreted as evidence of "a departure from the nuclear family" and the adoption of "the Western model" of reproductive behavior. However, the highest share of extramarital births in Slovakia is to be found in the country's most backward regions, as opposed to its most "modern" ones.[4]

---

[4] Extramarital fertility in Slovakia is typical of less educated women. While 60% of all children born to women with only elementary education were born out of wedlock, that share was only 10% among women with university education (Vaňo, 2007). A similar trend may be observed in the Czech Republic. Women with higher education tend to postpone marriage and the birth of their first child; however, when they decide to have a child, they do it mostly in marriage. On the other hand, women with low education do not tend to postpone motherhood as much; they give birth at a younger age than women with higher education; and mostly as single mothers (quoted by Hašková, 2008).

Significant differences between districts can also be found in the infant mortality rate. In some districts, the annual rate is 20 deaths during the first year per 1,000 live-births (e.g. Trebišov, Gelnica, Košice-surroundings or Veľký Krtiš) while the overall average for Slovakia is seven. Slovakia's districts also differ in total mortality, life expectancy, marriage rate, divorce rate and abortion rate. Marked regional disparities are also seen in the mean age of women at first marriage and at first childbirth. Both indicators are the highest in Bratislava, where the mean age of women is over 26 at first marriage and over 27 at first childbirth. On the other hand, the lowest values were recorded in eastern Slovakia (particularly in Medzilaborce and Sobrance), where the mean age of women at first marriage as well as at first childbirth is just over 22.

The most problematic values of these demographic indicators are in marginalized regions with large Romany populations (Falťan, 2004). Employment opportunities in some districts of Slovakia are limited, leading to high long-term unemployment and mass labor migration (*National...*, 2000; Džambazovič, 2001; Vaňo, 2001; Bodnárová – Džambazovič – Filadelfiová – Gerbery – Kvapilová – Porubänová, 2004). In some districts, demographic surveys revealed an accumulation of multiple disadvantages that strongly affect the lives of local families as well as their reproductive behavior.

2.1.7. CHANGES IN THE STRUCTURE OF FAMILIES AND HOUSEHOLDS

The above outlined trends in the birth rate, marriage rate and divorce rate have shaped changes in the size and structure of Slovak families (see Graph 2.6). The share of single-parent families is gradually increasing at the expense of families with two parents. According to the most recent population census from 2001, two-parent families made up 56.4% of all households (in 1970, the share was 78.4%) while two-parent families with children under 15 made up 31.1% (10 percentage points less than in 1991). The share of one-parent families was 11.9% in 2001. Almost 90% of these families were headed by mothers and only 10% of them by fathers. But the greatest increase among all types of households was those of single individuals, who in 2001 made up 30% of all households, compared to 22% in 1991 and only 12% in 1970.

Graph 2.6
Structure of Slovak households (1961 and 2001 – in %)

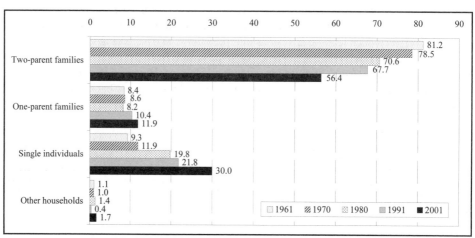

Source: *Sčítanie...*, 1992 a 2002; *Štatistická ročenka...*, 2004; *Obyvateľstvo...*, 2005.

Certain changes can also be detected in the average size of families (see Table 2.5). In all types of households examined by population censuses, the number of members declined from 3.4 members in 1970 to 2.6 members in 2001. The average two-parent family in 2001 had 3.44 members, while ten years before it was 3.52 members. On the other hand, the average number of members in one-parent families increased from 2.58 in 1991 to 2.64 in 2001.

Table 2.5
Structure and size of Slovak households (1961 – 2001, select indicators)

	1961	1970	1980	1991	2001
Household types (%)					
– Two-parent families	81.2	78.5	70.6	67.7	56.4
– One-parent families	8.4	8.6	8.2	10.4	11.9
– Single individuals	9.3	11.9	19.8	21.8	30.0
– Other households	1.1	1.0	1.4	0.4	1.7
Two-parent families					
– With children under 15 (%)	47.6	44.2	38.3	41.6	31.1
– Without children under 15 (%)	33.6	34.3	32.3	25.8	25.3
– Gainfully employed women (%)	32.8	42.6	50.1	48.9	40.0
– Housewives (%)	48.4	35.9	20.5	18.5	16.4
Average number of household members	**3.5**	**3.4**	**3.0**	**2.9**	**2.6**

Source: *Sčítanie…*, 1992 a 2002; *Štatistická ročenka…*, 2004; *Obyvateľstvo…*, 2005.

The most significant decline in the structure of households was seen among families with three or more children, whose share of all families dropped from 18.5% to 12.8%. This reflects the decline in the average number of children per family. In 1991, the average family with dependent children was raising 1.9 children, which indicated the dominance of two-child families; by 2001 that number had dropped to 1.5 (Pilinská, 2005).

According to census data, the share of cohabitations increased slightly. While in 1991 these "*de facto* marriages" made up 1.7% of all two-parent family households, by 2001 their share had grown to 2.6%. However, the actual share of this type of household is probably higher because population censuses are unable to detect a large number of such cohabitations.

2.1.8. INCREASED VISIBILITY OF SEXUAL MINORITIES

With respect to changes in partnership behavior patterns in Slovakia, a taboo has been broken on another issue of human sexuality, i.e. sexual minorities.

After the fall of Communism, Slovakia saw the emergence of several organizations representing sexual minorities, cultivating their own subculture and lifestyle or defending their civil rights.[5] Thanks to their activities, people with minority sexual orientation are more visible in Slovakia than ever before. At the same time, most public figures with minority sexual orientation tend to keep it to themselves.

---

[5] For more details on the situation of sexual minorities and their civic associations, see Šípošová – Jójárt – Daučíková, 2002; http://www.diskriminacia.sk/?q=s_sexorient; Pirošík – Janišová – Šuterová, 2001; Daučíková – Bútorová – Wallace-Lorencová, 2002; Bútorová – Filadelfiová – Marošiová, 2004; and especially the websites of non-governmental organizations such as Prvé lesbické združenie Museion [Museion First Lesbian Association] (www.lesba.sk), Iniciatíva Inakosť [Otherness Initiative] (www.inakost.sk), Ganymedes (www.ganymedes.info) or Združenie homosexuálnych kresťanov Medzipriestor [Interspace Association of Homosexual Christians] (www.medzipriestor.sk). Several associations (e.g. Altera, Prometheus, Podisea, HaB or Q-Archív) have ceased to operate due to a lack of funds or other reasons.

The issue of the rights of the members of the LGBT community (i.e. community of lesbians, gays, bisexuals and transsexuals) is highlighted also by the fact that people in Slovakia, as part of the European Union, are now more interested in developments in other member states. Many of them are not indifferent to reports that in some countries, such as the Czech Republic, Spain or Norway, efforts to strengthen the civil rights of gays and lesbians culminated in the passage of legislative amendments, or that in other countries peaceful marches by gays and lesbians are broken up by the police. A particularly important political step abroad was the enactment of registered partnerships in the neighboring Czech Republic. Slovakia still has a long way to go in terms of enacting similar legislation; however, the incorporation of the principle of equal treatment of people with the minority sexual orientation into the Antidiscrimination Act passed in 2004 and amended in 2008 was an indisputable success in this respect.

The visibility and relevance of the rights of sexual minorities is strengthened by non-governmental human rights organizations, gay and lesbian activists and even some politicians – paradoxically, even those who stubbornly turn a blind eye to this agenda. The coalition of center-right parties that ruled the country between 1998 and 2006 adopted a rather lukewarm stand on this agenda; worse, the Christian Democrats in the second half of this government's tenure made campaigning against this agenda one of their priorities. After the Smer-SD – SNS – ĽS-HZDS ruling coalition was formed following the 2006 elections, the agenda of rights for sexual minorities did not gain a stronger political foothold. Despite official hesitation, the Slovak Republic joined the 2007 European Year of Equal Opportunities for All.[6]

Public attitudes toward sexual minorities in Slovakia will be the main focus of the Section 2.3.4.

2.1.9. CULTURAL DISPUTES ON THE THRESHOLD OF THE 21ST CENTURY

The demographic trends and changes in reproductive and partnership behavior of Slovak women and men described above are subsequently reflected not only in changes in the structure of families and households, but also in the country's population structure. In many respects, these developments are similar to those in Western Europe, but in Slovakia they arrived later and under different economic and political circumstances. While in Western Europe these changes took place during a period of economic prosperity and social stability, in Slovakia they happened during the transformation period. The most notable result of the declining birth and fertility rates in combination with the moderate increase in life expectancy (particularly among women) is the ageing of the population. Due to the higher death rate among men, the overall share of women among the population is increasing, as is the feminization of old age. The declining marriage rate and the trend towards postponing marriage, along with the growing divorce rate and the increasing share of extramarital births, is reducing the average number of family members and weakening the role of families with children. These changes in the structure of households and of the population in general are putting significant pressure on the health care system, the education system, the social security system and the labor market.

---

[6] Within this program, the Otherness Initiative, which promotes coexistence without discrimination against sexual minorities, implemented a project called Days of Otherness (www.inakost.sk). Activities aimed at increasing public acceptance of sexual minorities are also pursued by the Queer Leaders Forum (QLF), an informal group of young activists that was established as part of the Museion First Lesbian Association.

The changes in reproductive and partnership behavior represent a new challenge for public policy, and are provoking intense cultural debate. Recent public disputes in Slovakia can be broken down into two principal approaches.

The first approach is based on the concept of "the decline of the family" or "the departure from family". Its advocates lament the collapse of the old system of values that included a traditional gender structure in families (with women primarily as mothers and homemakers and men as breadwinners); as well as strict sexual morals and strong social control that put taboos on various problems that arise between marital partners.

The second approach sees the recent changes in family and partnership behavior patterns in a broader social context. Its exponents argue that family life is not falling apart but is heading toward new forms of family and greater diversity. They emphasize that family values remain strong in Slovakia, as people continue to attribute great importance to family and to hold positive attitudes toward matrimony and parenthood.

The latter approach is seen in many developed European countries, where the public discourse seeks answers to two principal questions: first, what is the effect of global changes in the economic and political foundations of society on the family; and second, what is the effect of changes in families on the future of the economy and social welfare. This approach is based on the assumption that family models must change in order to adapt to the new reality; on the other hand, cultural standards, public policy and the legal system along with other institutions must also change in order to accommodate new family models. Forcing families to accept old and outdated formulas is obviously not the way to go. It is far better to accept diversity than to resist it.

Let us now characterize the two sides of the ongoing cultural discourse in Slovakia and their key issues.[7] One group of its protagonists is represented by the political, church and civic leaders of Christian conservatism, who are alarmed by what they see as threats to traditional values and the destruction of Christian morals. They condemn informal cohabitation and the raising of children in non-matrimonial families. They urge the government to promote the traditional model of the matrimonial family by passing legislative measures, adopting economic incentives and educating young people. Some criticize the very concept of family planning and birth control, in which they see the roots of what they call "abortion mentality".[8] They fervently defend the right to life of unborn fetus, even when it has genetic defects or is unwanted by the parents for social reasons.

A centerpiece of the conservative campaign is criticism of the feminist advocacy of women's rights as well as rejection of the concept of gender equality as a relic of Communist ideology. As an alternative, the conservatives advocate an even stronger anchoring of women within the family and greater appreciation for their role as mothers and wives while preserving the traditional patriarchal division of roles between partners.[9]

While defending the traditional family in their media appearances, Christian conservatives often ignore key issues related to the quality of partnership or family coexistence. These issues are the discussed primarily by liberal groups orientated at human rights protection and implementation. A crucial role among them belongs to women's non-governmental organiza-

---

[7] This discourse has been analyzed by the following studies: Bútorová, 2005; Marošiová, 2005; Mesežnikov, 2005.
[8] From an interview with Terézia Lenczová, Chairwoman of the Slovak Society for Family and Responsible Parenthood (quoted in Bútorová – Filadelfiová – Marošiová, 2004).
[9] For more details of this argument, visit the website of the Slovak Society for Family and Responsible Parenthood (www.family.sk) or see Bútorová – Filadelfiová – Marošiová, 2004.

tions that are involved in defending the right of women to live in safety and have succeeded in de-tabooing the issue of domestic violence against women in Slovakia.

Another issue missing from the conservative agenda is a more just arrangement in gender relations within the families and a more balanced division of labor between women and men. Under the concept of the traditional family, most Christian conservatives imagine a patriarchal family with a dominant man as the principal breadwinner and head of the family and a woman whose primary role is tending the family fireplace.[10]

Perhaps the fiercest criticism from Christian conservatives is aimed at the lifestyle and rights of gays and lesbians. Any attempt of the members of the LGBT community to openly present their weaker, more vulnerable position within Slovak society arouses indignation in conservative circles, who view it as a violation of some unwritten social contract which assumes that gays and lesbians should keep their sexual orientation and related problems to themselves. They believe that homosexuality should be restricted to the private sphere and gays and lesbians should not "bother" the rest of society with their problems.

These views clash with those of liberals, especially those who come from a civil society environment, who unlike conservatives lack clear political backing and a precisely defined party base (Mesežnikov, 2005; Filadelfiová, 2005a, 2005b; Bodnárová – Filadelfiová – Gerbery – Džambazovič – Kvapilová, 2006). Apart from some cultural figures and members of country's expert and academic communities (e.g. demographers, sociologists or political scientists), these liberals comprise mostly leaders of feminist organizations, human rights and environmental non-governmental organizations, and associations representing sexual minorities.[11] The position of Smer-SD, the dominant party in the incumbent ruling coalition, on the rights of sexual minorities remains very reserved, despite the fact that Smer-SD is part of the Socialist International, and that the issue is part of the traditional social-democratic agenda in Western European countries.

A detailed description of these two concepts is beyond the scope of this publication. In the following analysis we focus primarily on how these new trends in partnership and family behavior are perceived by the public in Slovakia. We will discuss the data of several representative surveys conducted mostly by the Institute for Public Affairs, and complement them with findings and quotations from a qualitative survey of the views of young people with secondary and university education carried out in two Slovak cities in 2003.[12]

2.2. NOTIONS OF IDEAL REPRODUCTIVE AND PARTNERSHIP BEHAVIOR[13]

2.2.1. IDEAL AGE FOR FIRST MARRIAGE AND FIRST CHILDBIRTH

Until the mid-1990s, a low age at first marriage was typical in Slovakia. Women entered their first marriage around the age of 22 and men around the age of 25. More than 60% of first

---

[10] It is worth noting that Christian non-governmental organizations specializing in domestic violence against women recommend separation instead of divorce even in the worst cases of domestic violence. From an interview with Terézia Lenczová, Chairwoman of the Slovak Society for Family and Responsible Parenthood (quoted in Bútorová – Filadelfiová – Marošiová, 2004).

[11] For further details on their activities, see Bútorová – Filadelfiová – Cviková – Gyárfášová – Farkašová, 2002; Daučíková – Bútorová – Wallace-Lorencová, 2002; Bútorová – Filadelfiová – Marošiová, 2004; Bútorová – Filadelfiová, 2006; www.aspekt.sk; www.moznostvolby.sk; www.oad.sk; www.diskriminacia.sk

[12] For further details see Bútorová, 2005.

[13] This section is a continuation of previous publications, particularly Bútorová, 1996 and Bútorová, 2005.

children were born within 12 months of the wedding. The mean age of mothers at first child-birth was 23 in 1995. According to the findings of a sociological survey from 1995, people's ideas of desirable reproductive behavior largely corresponded to the actual state of affairs (Bútorová, 1996).

More than two fifths of respondents (44%) at the time believed that a woman should marry before reaching the age of 21; as many as 71% put the maximum wedding age at 23 or less and 96% at 25 or below. According to public opinion, the first child should be born immediately afterwards. Over one in four respondents (27%) believed that a woman should give birth to her first child before reaching the age of 21, while 57% put that age limit before 23 and 86% at 25 or less (see Table 2.6).

The early age of marriage, which set Slovak women apart from women in more developed Western European countries, was quite normal according to public opinion. The low mean age of mothers at their first childbirth was also widely accepted.

In the mid-1990s, public opinion was more benevolent with respect to men's maximum appropriate wedding age. Only 8 % of respondents at the time believed that a man should marry before the age of 21 and 22% of them put that age limit at 23 or less. As many as 62% of respondents believed that a man should marry at 25 or less; 86% at 29 or less and 99% at 34 or less. The same was true of the ideal age of men to father the first child, which was again higher than for women.

Table 2.6
Ideal age of women and men to enter into the first marriage and have the first child (1995 and 2006 – views of the entire population, in %)

	Ideal age of women				Ideal age of men			
	to enter into marriage		to have the first child		to enter into marriage		to have the first child	
	1995	2006	1995	2006	1995	2006	1995	2006
Under 19	10	1	3	0	2	0	0	0
20–21	34	13	24	7	6	2	3	1
22–23	27	21	30	17	14	4	9	3
24–25	25	39	29	36	40	28	28	15
26–29	3	18	12	29	24	29	38	34
30–34	1	8	2	11	13	31	19	41
35 and more	0	0	0	0	1	6	2	7
Ideal mean age	22.2	24.5	23.2	25.4	25.7	27.7	26.7	28.6

Note: Views of respondents older than 15. The figures do not include the answers "I don't know" and "other answer".
Source: FOCUS, June 1995; Institute for Public Affairs, August 2006.

Already at that time, however, it was clear that the social pressure to found a family at an early age would subside in future, especially among well educated partners with professional ambitions (Bútorová, 1996). Eleven years later, we can state that this is exactly what happened, as people's views have changed significantly. The ideal age of women and men for both landmarks has increased by approximately two years. This increase took place not only in people's minds but in reality as well. Between 1995 and 2006, the mean age of women at their first marriage increased from 22.3 to 25.8, while the mean age of men increased from 24.7 to 28.5. The mean age of women at first childbirth grew from 23.0 to 26.0 (*Informácia...*, 2007).

Graphs 2.7 and 2.8 illustrate how public opinion changed between 1995 and 2006 with respect to the ideal age at which Slovak women and men should enter parenthood.

Graph 2.7
"What is the ideal age for a woman to give birth to the first child?" (views of the entire population – in %)

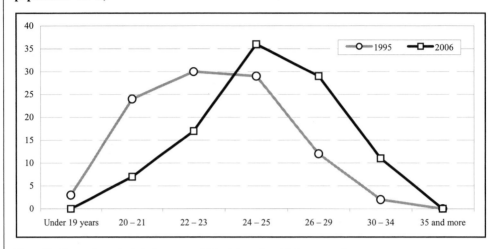

Note: The figures do not include the answers "I don't know" and "other answer".
Source: FOCUS, June 1995; Institute for Public Affairs, August 2006.

Graph 2.8
"What is the ideal age for a man to father the first child?" (views of the entire population – in %)

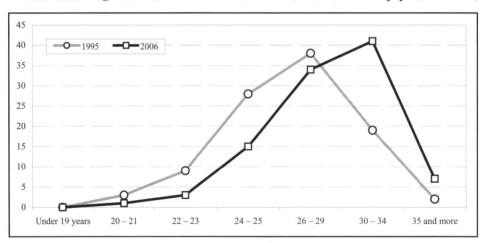

Note: The figures do not include the answers "I don't know" and "other answer".
Source: FOCUS, June 1995; Institute for Public Affairs, August 2006.

The tendency to postpone marriage and parenthood as well as the declining birth rate have been brought about by many factors, in particular more careful family planning under the pressure of the economic challenges, the increased material expectations of young families, as well as new career opportunities open to young people. The increased availability of contraception, improved sexual education and more intense public debate on moral values have also played a role. Other important factors include the absence of a state family policy that would accommodate the needs of working mothers and fathers, and the persisting dominance of traditional patriarchal family relations, which leave women with few options to reconcile their maternal and professional roles (Potančoková, 2004; Filadelfiová, 2005a; Bodnárová – Filadelfiová – Gerbery – Džambazovič – Kvapilová, 2006; Vaňo, 2007).

Let us now return to Table 2.6 and analyze people's views from 2006 in greater detail. At that time, only 35% of respondents believed that women should marry before reaching the age of 23, while eleven years earlier, this figure was twice as high (71%)! Three in four respondents (74%) put the first wedding age limit at 25 or less, and 91% at 29 or lower. The ideal age of women at first marriage according to public opinion increased from 22.2 in 1995 to 24.5 in 2006.

People's views of the ideal timing of motherhood saw changes as well. In 2006, only 24% of respondents believed that a woman should give birth to her first child before she turned 23, while in 1995, this opinion was presented by 57% of respondents. Sixty percent of respondents put the age limit for the first birth at 25 or less, and 89% at 29 or lower. The ideal age of women at first increased from 23.2 in 1995 to 25.4 in 2006.

Like eleven years ago, people in 2006 still believed that men could wait a little longer than women to found a family. Only 6% of respondents said that a man should marry before turning 23 (compared to 22% in 1995); 34% put the wedding age limit at 25 or lower, 63% at 29 or under and 94% at 34 or less. The ideal age of men at first marriage increased from 25.7 in 1995 to 27.7 in 2006.

As in the case of women, people's views of the ideal age of men for fatherhood changed (see Graph 2.8). Only 4% of respondents said a man should become a father before he turned 23; 19% put his age limit at 25, while 53% regarded 29 or less as optimum and 94% at 34 or under. The ideal age for men to father their first child increased from 26.7 in 1995 to 28.6 in 2006.

Clearly, marrying young had ceased to be the generally accepted social standard by 2006; the same may be said of having a first child at a relatively young age.

Graph 2.9
"What is the ideal age for women and men to get married?" (views of the entire population – in %)

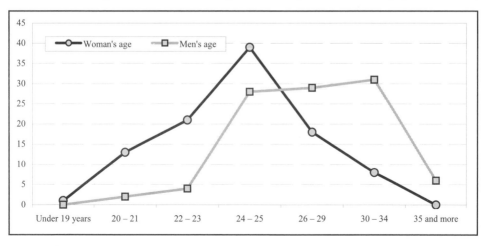

Note: The figures do not include the answers "I don't know" and "other answer".
Source: Institute for Public Affairs, August 2006.

Graph 2.10
"What is the ideal age for women and men to have their first child?" (views of the entire population – in %)

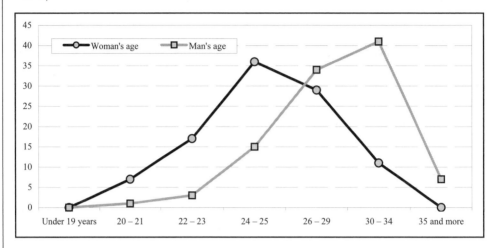

Note: The figures do not include the answers "I don't know" and "other answer".
Source: Institute for Public Affairs, August 2006.

Graphs 2.9 and 2.10 also allow us to compare people's views of the ideal period that should elapse between getting married and having the first child. The curves expressing the ideal age at which a woman should marry and give birth to her first child were very similar in 2006. As Table 2.6 documents, the period between the two is less than one year: according to public opinion, the ideal mean age of women is 24.5 at marriage and 25.4 at first childbirth.

So far, we have only examined the views of the population as a whole. Let us now take a look at social groups that favor postponing matrimony and parenthood. Women tend to peg the

Graph 2.11
"What is the ideal age for a woman to have the first child?" (views of women and men – in %)

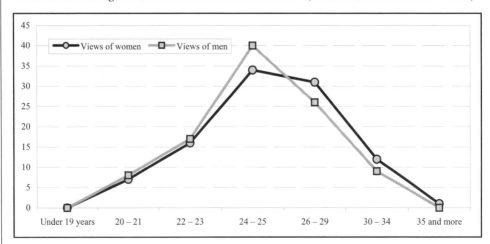

Note: The figures do not include the answers "I don't know" and "other answer".
Source: Institute for Public Affairs, August 2006.

Graph 2.12
"What is the ideal age for a woman to have the first child?" (views of women by education – in %)

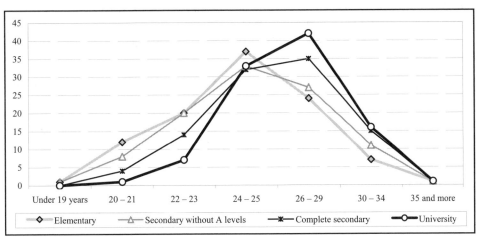

Note: The figures do not include the answers "I don't know" and "other answer".
Source: Institute for Public Affairs, August 2006.

ideal age of marriage and first childbirth a little later than men (see Graph 2.11). Better educated people; younger women and men; the residents of larger towns, and people who are not deeply religious – these are the groups that favor postponing matrimony and parenthood (see Graph 2.12). On the other hand, less educated women and men, people over 55, residents of small villages and deeply religious people tend to adhere to the traditional concepts that prevailed until the mid-1990s.

The increasing diversity in the reproductive behavior of Slovak women and men was also reflected in regional differences in the mean age of women at first childbirth. We can expect that the trend towards postponing parenthood will continue; however, it will be weaker in more traditional settings that in more modern environments.

It should be noted that the trend towards postponing parenthood has biological and social limits (Možný, 2006, p. 197; Hašková, 2008), such as the increased risk of infertility. Therefore, we may assume that when the mean age of women at first childbirth approaches certain number of years, the current trend of postponing childbirth will slow down or completely stop.

2.2.2. ATTITUDES TOWARD ABORTIONS

One of the most significant demographic trends of the past two decades has been the fall in the total number of abortions by over 70%, a reversal that occurred without the introduction of stricter abortion legislation. This positive change was due to a range of favorable circumstances, most notably the increased availability and use of contraception, improved awareness of reproductive health, and more intense public debate on values and human rights.

How have the attitudes to abortions changed in the past decade or so? A comparison of survey findings from 1995 and 2007 indicates that they have remained virtually untouched, as a substantial majority of Slovak women and men consider abortions to be legitimate under certain circumstances (see Table 2.7). This indicates that the decline in the number of abor-

"It's up to the woman or, potentially, up to both partners. It depends on the situation. For instance, if the child will suffer from some hereditary disease or anomaly such as Down Syndrome… the decision is up to the woman. Of course, she has to live with the worry about who will take care of the child if something happens to her or her partner. Would she be happy leaving the child to the care of the state, which is notoriously poor? She has to try to put herself in the shoes of the child… We don't have children yet, but I would also agree with an abortion if I knew that the child would be severely handicapped." (Eva, 29, a veterinarian from Rimavská Sobota)

tions is primarily the result of the increased ability of women (and men) to avoid unwanted pregnancies and, therefore, of a more responsible approach to women's reproductive health.

In a survey carried out by the Institute for Public Affairs in November 2007, as many as 85 % of respondents viewed abortions as justifiable if the pregnancy threatens the mother's health (86% of women and 83% of men); 79% endorsed them if the child is likely to be handicapped (81% of women and 78% of men) or if the woman was raped (80% of women and 79% of men). However, only 48 % of respondents approved of the abortions if the parents cannot provide for the child.

Table 2.7
"Do you agree that abortions should be legal under the following circumstances?" (% of answers "certainly and rather yes" : "definitely and rather no" : "I don't know")

	1995	2003	2007
If the pregnancy threatens mother's health	85 : 9 : 6	87 : 7 : 6	85 : 9 : 6
If the child is likely to be handicapped	72 : 17 : 11	79 : 13 : 8	79 : 14 : 7
If the woman was raped	81 : 9 : 10	77 : 13 : 10	79 : 13 : 8
If the parents cannot provide for the child	47 : 38 : 15	56 : 34 : 10	48 : 43 : 9

Source: FOCUS, June 1995; Institute for Public Affairs, September 2003 and November 2007.

Since 1995, the ratio of people who endorse abortions if there is high probability that the child will be severely handicapped has increased. Evidence that women take this decision seriously is to be found in the spontaneous answers of Eva and Jela, who took part in focus group discussions conducted in 2003 by the Institute for Public Affairs.

Most people in Slovakia do not see the need for stricter abortion legislation. As Table 2.8 shows, only 16 % of respondents (20% of women and 11% of men) viewed the current abortion law as too lenient in November 2007. On the other hand, 64% of women and 57 % of men advocated either preserving the *status quo* (43% of women and 41% of men) or further liberalization to increase the availability of abortions (21% of women and 16% of men). Women's views are generally more polarized and articulate than those of men.

"I don't agree with abortions at all… But I don't know how I would react if I learned that my child would not be healthy. I don't condemn people who can't handle it and opt for abortion if their child is going to be ill. But I can't agree with parents who get rid of their child just because, for instance, they already have two." (Jela, 28, a high school teacher from Rimavská Sobota)

Views on the current abortion law vary among women as well as among men. Younger and more educated residents of large towns tend to favor preserving or liberalizing the abortion law. On the other hand, deeply religious women demonstrate above-average preference of tougher restrictions on abortions. However, even in this group of strong believers, support for stricter legislation is below 40%.

Table 2.8
"What is your opinion of Slovakia's abortion law?" (% of answers "too strict" : "just fine" : "too lenient" : "I don't know")

	2003	2007
Views of women	25 : 50 : 14 : 11	21 : 43 : 20 : 16
Views of men	21 : 47 : 8 : 24	16 : 41 : 11 : 32
Views of the entire population	23 : 49 : 11 : 17	18 : 42 : 16 : 24

Source: Institute for Public Affairs, September 2003 and November 2007.

Graph 2.13
Opinions of women and men about the abortion law in 2007 (% of answers "too strict" : "just fine" : "too lenient" : "I don't know")

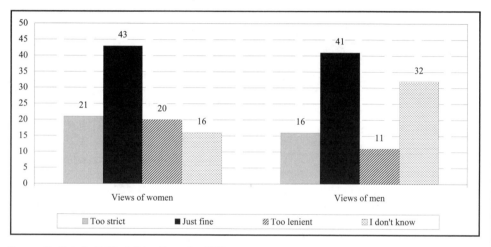

Source: Institute for Public Affairs, November 2007.

Table 2.9
Opinions of women and men about the abortion law in 2007 (% of answers "too strict" : "just fine" : "too lenient" : "I don't know" – by education and attitude toward religion)

		Views of women	Views of men
Education	Elementary	11 : 36 : 31 : 22	12 : 28 : 16 : 44
	Secondary without A levels	22 : 42 : 16 : 20	16 : 41 : 12 : 31
	Complete secondary	24 : 46 : 17 : 13	13 : 54 : 7 : 26
	University	26 : 54 : 15 : 5	29 : 41 : 4 : 26
Attitude toward religion	Strong believers	6 : 34 : 38 : 22	15 : 39 : 22 : 24
	Believers	21 : 42 : 21 : 16	15 : 36 : 13 : 35
	Undecided	27 : 46 : 11 : 16	12 : 42 : 6 : 40
	Non-believers	29 : 55 : 7 : 9	17 : 49 : 6 : 28

Source: Institute for Public Affairs, November 2007.

These differences do not alter the general conclusion that most people in Slovakia are satisfied with the abortion law currently in force that and gives women the freedom of choice. In 2003, an overwhelming majority of women and men (86 % and 84 %, respectively) believed that "instead of introducing stricter abortion legislation, society should focus on sex education and prevention of unwanted pregnancies" (Bútorová – Gyárfášová – Velšic, 2003).

2.2.3. NONTRADITIONAL PATTERNS OF FAMILY BEHAVIOR

Let us now take a closer look at three patterns of family behavior that do not correspond to the traditional concept of the matrimonial family: first, informal cohabitation by partners without marriage; second, the decision of an unmarried woman to a have child out of wedlock; third, the divorce of marriages with dependent children. Table 2.10 illustrates the distribution of people's positions on these patterns of behavior, from rejection to acceptance.

Table 2.10
"To what degree do you think the following behavior can be justified?" (% of answers "never and almost never" : "sometimes yes, sometimes no" : "always and almost always")

	Views of women	Views of men	Views of the entire population
Cohabitation between a man and a woman	16 : 24 : 59	14 : 25 : 60	15 : 25 : 59
Woman having a child out of wedlock	21 : 30 : 47	23 : 28 : 46	22 : 29 : 47
Divorce of a marriage with dependent children	27 : 42 : 31	30 : 44 : 25	28 : 43 : 28

Note: Respondents evaluated the acceptability of such behavior on a 10-degree scale. The category "never and almost never" corresponds to degrees 1 – 3, the category "sometimes yes, sometimes no" to degrees 4 – 7, and the category "always and almost always" to degrees 8 – 10. The remainder of the 100% comprises the answer "I don't know".
Source: Institute for Public Affairs, August 2006.

> "*I am absolutely comfortable with people living together as unmarried partners. I currently live in a couple like that myself. I plan to marry my partner in the near future, but not before we get everything settled... First, we looked for a place to live together, and at this point we are still studying... This has been a good experience for me.*" (Mária, 24, a civil servant from Bratislava)

> "*I live with my partner in just such an arrangement myself, but when we decide to start a family, then... I would like to bring children only into a proper family... While young people are still getting to know each other, it's okay. But as soon as they start to plan a child, it's better to have an official family and a marriage.*" (Želmíra, 25, a nurse from Martin)

The views of Slovak women and men clearly show an acceptance of informal cohabitation between partners. In 2006, this behavior was condemned as unacceptable by only 15% of respondents while 59% endorsed it. The remaining quarter of respondents took an ambivalent stance. The differences in the views of women and men were negligible. Social acceptance of cohabitation between partners prevailed also in 1995 (Bútorová, 1996).

Young people often see cohabitation as helping them to make a responsible life choice and to vet their partner. For many, it is also a way out of an unsatisfactory material situation and is often combined with a decision to postpone marriage and children. I should be stressed, however, that despite favoring this form of coexistence, young people still hold pro-family attitudes and continue to view a family as the best environment in which to raise children.

Decision by an unmarried woman to have a child out of wedlock is also accepted, but to a lesser degree. In a survey from August 2006, almost half of the respondents (47%) endorsed such behavior; 29% were ambivalent and 22% saw it as unacceptable. Compared to the mid-1990s, public views on the decision on an unmarried woman to have a child out of wedlock have remained virtually unchanged (Bútorová, 1996). Despite the continuous growth in the number of children born outside marriage, social acceptance of this type of behavior has not increased.

> *"When a woman is financially independent, has reached a certain age and is unable to establish a viable partnership, it's completely natural that she desires a baby. Under certain circumstances, I can accept it."* (Mária, 24, a civil servant from Bratislava)

Table 2.10 also shows that Slovak women and men in 2006 were slightly more reserved with respect to divorcing marriages with dependent children. Advocates and opponents of such behavior were even at 28% each, while the remaining 43% of respondents were ambivalent. It is interesting that women endorsed divorcing marriages with dependent children slightly more frequently than men.

Surveys examining value orientations indicate that the social acceptability of divorce as a way out of a failed marriage generally increased in Slovakia in the 1990s (Gyárfášová – Krivý – Velšic, 2001, p. 272). Already by the mid-1990s, almost two in three people (64%) believed that "it is better for the children to see their parents divorced than to be raised in a dysfunctional marriage". On the other hand, only one in three respondents (32%) felt that

> *"When two partners reach a point where they can do nothing but hurt each other, and especially when there is a child involved, then it is better for everybody if they get divorced and part ways. It's much worse for the children if they have to go through it... Children must not suffer for their parents' mistakes. They should be left out of it."* (Pavol, 28, a shopkeeper with a secondary school diploma from Rimavská Sobota)

Graph 2.14
"To what degree do you think the cohabitation between a man and a woman can be justified?"
(**% of answers "always and almost always" – by age**)

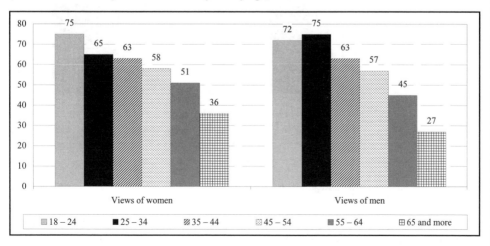

Note: Respondents evaluated the acceptability of such behavior on a 10-degree scale. The category "always and almost always" corresponds to degrees 8 – 10.
Source: Institute for Public Affairs, August 2006.

Graph 2.15
"To what degree do you think the decision of a woman to have a child out of wedlock can be justified?" (% of answers "always and almost always" – by attitude toward religion)

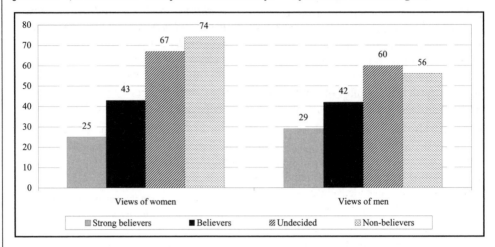

Note: Respondents evaluated the acceptability of such behavior on a 10-degree scale. The category "always and almost always" corresponds to degrees 8 – 10.
Source: Institute for Public Affairs, August 2006.

Graph 2.16
"To what degree do you think the divorce of a marriage with dependent children can be justified?" (% of answers "always and almost always" – by education)

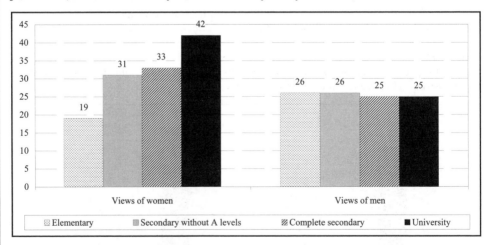

Note: Respondents evaluated the acceptability of such behavior on a 10-degree scale. The category "always and almost always" corresponds to degrees 8 – 10.
Source: Institute for Public Affairs, August 2006.

"even failed marriages should be preserved at all cost" (Bútorová, 1996). The prevailing opinion is illustrated by the statement of Pavol.

Which categories of women and men show a greater propensity for accepting nontraditional patterns of partnership and family behavior? According to the research findings, the most important factors include age, education, attitude toward religion and the size of the municipality in which the respondents live. All three behavior patterns, i.e. informal cohabitation, raising children out of wedlock and divorcing with dependent children, were more frequently accepted by younger women and men, residents of larger towns, and people who were not strong believers. The role of education showed an interesting twist: while tolerance for these "alternative" behavior patterns increased in line with greater education among women, the views of men were not affected by their educational attainment.

Despite the prevailing tolerance to nontraditional patterns of partnership and family behavior, the matrimonial family remains an almost universal choice for people in Slovakia, as more than 90% get married at least once in their lifetime (*Sčítanie...*, 2001; Pilinská, 2005). According to the findings of the European Values Survey, almost 90% of Slovaks do not consider matrimony an obsolete institution (*European Values...*, 1999/2000). The highly favorable views of this institution were also corroborated by a survey carried out in 2004 by the Research Institute of Labor and Family: only 2% of the parents of dependent children and 14% of parents of students at secondary school and university had negative views of matrimony (Bodnárová – Džambazovič – Filadelfiová – Gerbery – Pafková – Porubänová, 2004).

2.2.4. HOMOSEXUALITY AND THE RIGHTS OF SEXUAL MINORITIES

In recent years, the opinions of Slovak women and men on of sexual minorities have exhibited two remarkable and seemingly conflicting trends. On the one hand, the visibility of gays and lesbians in society has increased. While in a survey carried out in 1995 only 30% of respondents said they personally knew a gay or lesbian, that share increased to 35% by 2002 and to 42% by 2007.

On the other hand, the growing visibility of gays and lesbians does not automatically mean that people feel increasingly tolerant and empathetic towards them or that they are more ready to meet their demands. Such a trend took place in the 1990s, when Slovak society saw a general "increase in liberal tolerance and positive sensitivity for minorities" (Gyárfášová – Krivý – Velšic, 2001), which included a decline in negative views on homosexuality (Daučíková – Bútorová – Wallace-Lorencová, 2003). But this trend came to a close and was even reversed following 2003 when tolerance for sexual minorities began to decline.

Table 2.11
"Do you personally know somebody who is gay or lesbian?" (views of the entire population – in %)

	1995	2002	2007
Yes, I do	16	18	23
I think I do but I am not sure	14	17	19
No, I don't	54	62	55
I don't know	13	3	3

Source: FOCUS, June 1995; Institute for Public Affairs, June2002 and November 2007.

How do people in Slovakia perceive the status and opportunities of sexual minorities in Slovakia? As Table 2.12 shows, public is largely ambivalent and relatively confused on the issue. At the end of 2007, almost half of respondents (46%) believed that the status and opportunities of gays and lesbians were equal to those of heterosexuals, and 5% even saw them as better. On the other hand, 35% of respondents thought that their status and opportunities were worse. As many as 14% of them respondents had no opinion. Compared to 2003, the ratio of those who viewed members of sexual minorities as underprivileged decreased, while

Table 2.12
"How would you evaluate the status and opportunities of gays and lesbians compared to the rest of the population?" (views of the entire population – in %)

	2003	2005	2006	2007
Worse	39	33	38	35
Equal	33	46	41	46
Better	4	3	4	5
I don't know	24	17	17	14

Source: Institute for Public Affairs, September 2003, November 2005, August 2006 and November 2007.

the share of those who did not see any difference in the status and opportunities of gays and lesbians and of heterosexuals increased.

Women were more critical of the status and opportunities of gays and lesbians than men: 38 % of female respondents, but only 32% of male respondents viewed them as worse off compared to heterosexuals, while 44% of women and 49% of men viewed them as equal.

In recent years, the cohabitation between same-sex partners has been heatedly debated. While a majority of Slovaks did not condemn it on moral grounds at the end of 2006, nor did a majority approve of it (see Table 2.13). The share of those who viewed it as unacceptable was 37%, while the share of those who tolerated it was even lower at 25%. The remaining 38% of respondents were either ambivalent (30%) or had no opinion (8%). Women approved of cohabitation between same-sex partners slightly more frequently (28%) than men (22%).

Table 2.13
"To what degree do you think the cohabitation between same-sex partners can be justified?"
(% of answers "never and almost never" : "sometimes yes, sometimes no" : "always and almost always" : "I don't know")

	2003	2006
Views of women	30 : 31 : 28 : 11	36 : 29 : 28 : 7
Views of men	29 : 34 : 26 : 11	38 : 32 : 22 : 8
Views of the entire population	29 : 33 : 27 : 11	37 : 30 : 25 : 8

Note: Respondents evaluated the acceptability of such behavior on a 10-degree scale. The category "never and almost never" corresponds to degrees 1 – 3, the category "sometimes yes, sometimes no" to degrees 4 – 7, and the category "always and almost always" to degrees 8 – 10.
Source: Institute for Public Affairs, September 2003 and November 2006.

A comparison to the findings from 1995 indicates that the tolerance of Slovak population for cohabitation by same-sex partners did not increase in 11 years (Bútorová, 1996).

Now let us examine the degree to which Slovaks are willing to see some of the key human rights extended to members of sexual minorities. As Graph 2.17 shows, 76% of respondents that gays and lesbians should enjoy equal access to all professions, while 19% oppose it. Less than two thirds of respondents (64%) acknowledged the right of gays and lesbians to run for political posts, while almost one in three (29%) disapproved of it. In comparison with situation four years ago, slightly less people were willing to extend these rights to the members of LGBT community (Bútorová – Gyárfášová, 2008).

As for two other demands, people in Slovakia continue to be much more disapproving. When asked whether gays and lesbians should enjoy the right to form registered partnerships, respondents are divided between 41% of advocates and 51% of opponents.

As for the right to adopt and raise children, the ratio of advocates and opponents is clearly in favor of the latter, at 16% to 76%. A comparison to the survey carried out in 1995 shows that there has been no shift toward greater acceptance of this right. In 1995, only 19% of women

Graph 2.17
"In your opinion, should gays and lesbians be granted the following rights?" (views of the entire population – in %)

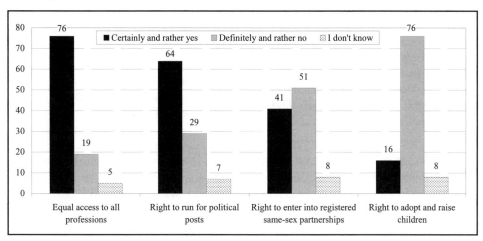

Source: Institute for Public Affairs, November 2007.

and 17% of men were prepared to grant this right to gays and lesbians, while 72% of women and 73% of men rejected it (Bútorová, 1996).

Table 2.14
"Do you believe that gays and lesbians should be granted the following rights?" (% of answers "certainly and rather yes" : "definitely and rather no" : "I don't know")

	Views of women	Views of men
Equal access to all professions	79 : 17 : 4	73 : 21 : 5
Right to run for political posts	66 : 26 : 8	61 : 32 : 7
Right to enter into registered same-sex partnerships	45 : 48 : 7	37 : 53 : 10
Right to adopt and raise children	17 : 76 : 7	15 : 76 : 9

Source: Institute for Public Affairs, November 2007.

Compared to men, women are slightly more prepared to grant all four mentioned rights to members of sexual minorities (see Table 2.14). The gender difference is most clear on the right of gays and lesbians to live as registered partners.

Should gays and lesbians publicly assert their rights? In 2007, public opinion was divided between 27 % of respondents who believed that "gays and lesbians should openly declare their sexual orientation and fight for their rights" and 33 % of those who said that "gays and lesbians should keep quiet and not demand any rights". The remaining 40% of respondents were ambivalent (31%) or had no opinion (9%). Again, women were slightly more accommodating than men.

> *"They are discriminated against because people don't know about them; they just point their fingers and say that he or she is this or that, etc. If they want this to change, they should talk about it... They must overcome that barrier and... society will accept them. But they must show their true colors and fight for themselves, for what they are and will always be. This is the only way to eliminate current discrimination."* (Želmíra, 25, a nurse from Martin)

> "*I wouldn't mind some gay or lesbian living in my vicinity... [But] if they wanted to speak out and show themselves in some way, they should take it easy because Slovakia is still rather traditional at this point. Of course, it's up to every individual to assess their private and professional environment... and to anticipate other people's reactions.*" (Rudolf, 26, an archaeologist from Bratislava)

Still, many people in Slovakia understand the complexity of coming out of the closet in given social environments. This was corroborated by a qualitative analysis carried out in 2003 by the Institute for Public Affairs, from which we present the views of Želmíra and Rudolf.

What attitudes to sexual minorities exist in various social environments? Women in Slovakia – as well as in other countries – are slightly more accommodating than men with respect to sexual minorities (Ondrisová, 2002, p. 39; *Empirical Data...*, 2008). As sociological surveys have repeatedly corroborated since the early 1990s, wary or negative attitudes are more frequent among women and men with lower education, elderly people, residents of rural areas, and strong believers (*Current Problems...*, 1993; Bútorová, 1996).

Table 2.15
"Do you believe that gays and lesbians should be granted the right to enter into registered same-sex partnerships?" (% of answers "certainly and rather yes" : "definitely and rather no" : "I don't know")

		Views of women	Views of men
Age	Under 45	55 : 38 : 7	46 : 45 : 9
	45 and more	34 : 60 : 7	25 : 65 : 10
Size of municipality (select categories)	Under 2,000 population	28 : 64 : 8	30 : 64 : 7
	Bratislava & Košice	65 : 31 : 4	56 : 42 : 2

Source: Institute for Public Affairs, November 2007.

Graph 2.18
"Do you believe that gays and lesbians should be granted the right to enter into registered same-sex partnerships?" (% of answers "certainly and rather yes" – by education)

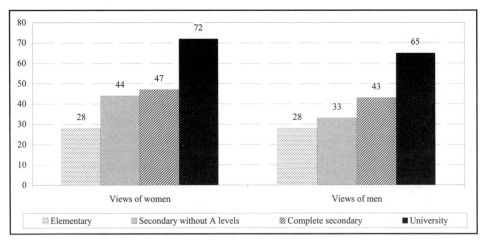

Note: The remainder of the 100% figure comprises the answers "definitely and rather no" and "I don't know".
Source: Institute for Public Affairs, November 2007.

Graph 2.19
"Do you believe that gays and lesbians should be granted the right to enter into registered same-sex partnerships?" (% of answers "certainly and rather yes" – by attitude toward religion)

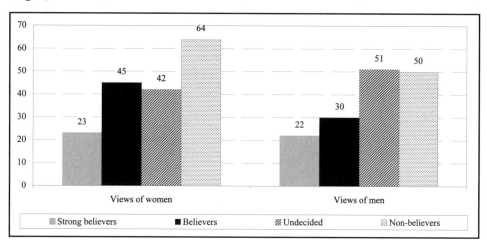

Note: The remainder of the 100% figure comprises the answers "definitely and rather no" and "I don't know".
Source: Institute for Public Affairs, November 2007.

On the other hand, educated, younger, urban and secular environments tend to be more accepting of sexual "otherness", more sensitive to the complicated situation of gays and lesbians, and are more likely to acknowledge their rights to equal access to all professions, to run for political posts, to enter into registered partnerships or to adopt and raise children. In these environments, gays and lesbians face fewer risks from disclosing their sexual orientation (Bútorová, 1996; Daučíková – Bútorová – Wallace-Lorencová, 2003; Bútorová, 2005).

A qualitative survey conducted among young, educated residents of urban areas suggested that people from this environment often view homosexuality as a minority variant of sexual orientation that is normal rather than deviant or contemptible. They also have greater understanding for members of sexual minorities who actively assert their rights instead of withdrawing into their private world. Several respondents advocated the need for more education of general public in this area. The statements of young respondents such as Fridrich and Mária showed respect for the "live and let live" principle.

Obviously, any overall increase in the tolerance of the society for members of sexual minorities will

"It's a question of age. Older people mind and younger ones don't. For instance, I don't mind." (Fridrich, 28, a manager with a multinational company from Bratislava)

"I think it's more we who should learn to view them as normal people who are no different from us. Perhaps we should be given some more positive examples because we tend to be rather reserved and apprehensive, based on some negative examples that are presented particularly by the media. I believe that these are merely exceptions, just like with us heterosexuals. That's why we should be taught that they are people just like ourselves." (Mária, 24, a civil servant from Bratislava).

require the LGBT community to continue its effort to eliminate prejudices against homo-sexuality and sexual minorities, to help the majority understand their situation, to communicate their interests clearly and convincingly, to wage an effective campaign for their rights; and last but not least, to acquire new allies in the wider civil society as well as among politicians.

3. ACTIVE AGEING AS A CHALLENGE

Zora Bútorová – Jarmila Filadelfiová

Zora Bútorová is the author of Sections 3.2. and 3.3.
Jarmila Filadelfiová is the author of Section 3.1.

3. ACTIVE AGEING AS A CHALLENGE

3. 1. POPULATION IN MOTION
3.1.1. AGE STRUCTURE OF THE POPULATION

Due to its declining birth rate, Slovakia faces two problems: lower fertility and ageing of the population. The increasing life expectancy further intensifies the process, while the higher death rate among men puts the principal weight of the ageing process on the shoulders of women.

Population in Slovakia and in the European Union

In 2006, the crude birth rate in the European Union's 27 member states fluctuated between 15.1 (Ireland) and 8.2 (Greece) newborns per 1,000 inhabitants. In Slovakia, the crude birth rate was 10.0. Overall, 15 EU member states recorded higher birth rates than Slovakia, while only countries from Eastern and Southern Europe recorded lower birth rates.

The crude death rate in the EU-27 fluctuated between 14.7 (Bulgaria) and 6.3 (Ireland) deaths per 1,000 inhabitants. In Slovakia, the crude death rate was 9.9. Again, 15 EU member states – mostly from Western Europe – recorded lower death rates than Slovakia.

Slovakia ranked even lower on the list of EU-27 countries according to the mean life expectancy of women and men at birth. The mean life expectancy of women at birth exceeded 80 years in 18 EU member states, while another two member states recorded values very close to that limit. Slovakia, with its values of 78.2 years for women and 70.4 for men, ranked seventh worst in the EU.

Source: *Europe's...,* 2007.

Graph 3.1
Basic age groups of women and men (1945 – 2006, in total numbers)

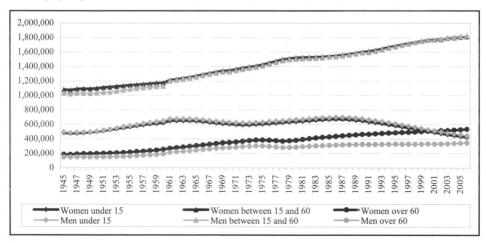

Source: *Slovstat,* 2008.

As Graph 3.1 shows, the decline in the total number of newborns that began in the late 1980s continues to the present day. Together with that trend, the size of the middle generation increased while the overall share of the oldest category grew more moderately. In other words, population ageing took place primarily within the middle generation. This presented Slovakia with a window of opportunity – to use the time and resources to prepare for a rapid increase in the number of people in their post-productive years. Recent trends indicate that the country has reached the threshold of this period, which according to population projection will peak between 2020 and 2025 (*Vývoj...*, 2004; Bleha – Vaňo, 2007).

Since the mid-1970s, the total number of women over 60 has increased much faster than the number of men of the same age. As a result, besides population ageing, the gradual feminization of old age is becoming a major trend in Slovakia's demographic development.

Both of these trends along with other indicators are illustrated by Table 3.1. The mean age of women is about three years greater than that of men, while the mean age of both women and men rose by roughly four years between 1990 and 2006. Another rapidly increasing indicator is the ageing index, which expresses the ratio of the oldest to the youngest female and

Table 3.1
Mean age of women and men and ageing index (1990 – 2006)

	1990	1995	2000	2001	2002	2003	2004	2005	2006
Mean age									
Women	34.9	36.0	37.5	37.7	38.0	38.4	38.4	39.0	39.3
Men	32.1	33.0	34.4	34.6	34.9	35.2	35.5	35.8	36.1
Ageing index									
Women	51.0	61.5	75.8	77.5	80.8	84.2	87.5	90.8	94.5
Men	32.3	37.3	44.5	44.9	46.5	48.1	49.7	51.6	53.5

Note: Ageing index = number of persons older than 65 per 100 children under 15.
Source: Vaňo, 2003, 2007.

Graph 3.2
Age structure of women and men (2006 – in total numbers)

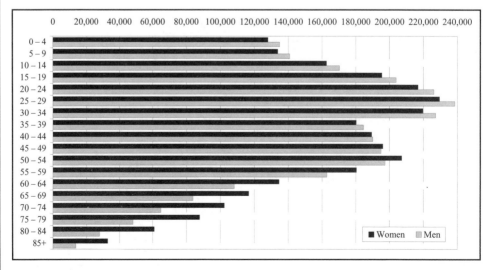

Source: *Slovstat,* 2008.

male generations. Again, this index shows much higher values and growth pace for women than for men (94.5 vs. 53.5 in 2006).

Let us take a closer look at the age structure of women and men (see Graph 3.2). In 2006, women made up 51.5% of Slovakia's population. Men slightly outnumber women in the younger age groups, but their numerical edge declines with increasing age. The ratio of women to men is equal around the age of 45; from this point on, women's prevalence increases. In 2006, the overall share of women in the 45 – 49 age group was 50.1%, whereas in the 65 – 69 age group it was 58.2% and in the 85+ group it was 70.9%.

3.1.2. SIZE AND STRUCTURE OF THE 45+ AGE GROUP

Let us now examine the total number of the age group over 45. As Graph 3.3 shows, the size of this age group increased from less than 900,000 to over 2,000,000 in less than six decades. The gap between the total number of women and men over 45 began to increase in the 1970s, and has been growing ever since.

Graph 3.3
Women and men over 45 (1950 – 2006, in total numbers)

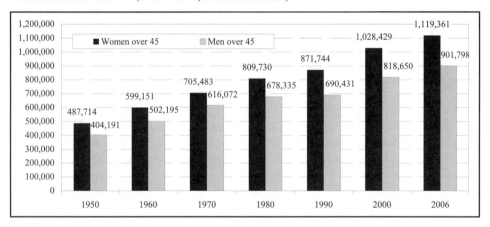

Source: *Slovstat,* 2008.

Graph 3.4
Share of women and men over 45 in the total population (2006 – in %)

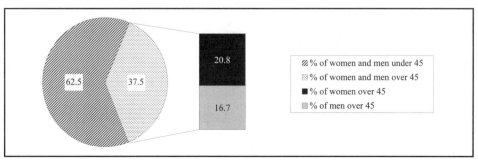

Source: *Slovstat,* 2008.

At the end of 2006, the 45+ age group made up 37.5% of total population; the share of women over 45 was 20.8%, while the share of men over 45 was 16.7% (see Graph 3.4).

Let us take a closer look at the age structure of the 45+ age category among women and men. Graph 3.5 shows that people between 45 and 64, i.e. economically active people are the most numerous in both groups.

Graph 3.5
Changes in the age structure of women and men over 45 (1945 – 2006, in total numbers)

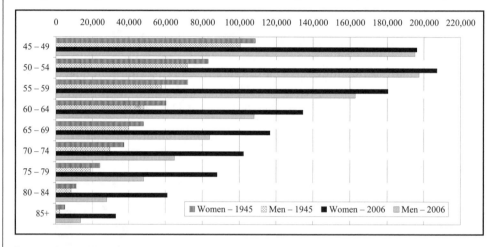

Source: *Slovstat,* 2008.

When we compare the changes that occurred in the age structure of women and men between 1945 and 2006, we see two basic trends. First, women's numerical superiority over men grew stronger in recent decades, particularly in the older age groups. Second, the total number of economically active people over 45 increased enormously, particularly in two youngest age groups, 45 – 49 years and 50 – 54 years.

How did the age structure of women over 45 change over the same period? Data from Table 3.2 show a numerical increase in all age groups. While in 1950 only the two youngest age

Table 3.2
Age structure of women over 45 (1950 – 2006, in total numbers)

Age group	1950	1960	1970	1980	1990	2000	2006
45 – 49	112,527	118,507	152,761	139,674	144,004	209,533	196,078
50 – 54	102,052	120,809	86,982	143,133	131,821	174,569	207,162
55 – 59	75,564	104,349	115,238	144,893	132,406	137,764	180,437
60 – 64	63,857	91,170	112,363	81,025	131,732	122,736	134,606
65 – 69	51,297	62,636	92,782	99,869	126,257	117,342	116,678
70 – 74	36,397	46,694	71,851	89,374	65,097	107,822	102,301
75 – 79	25,920	29,789	42,286	61,465	67,785	88,400	88,011
80 – 84	13,557	14,151	20,965	34,525	45,682	35,869	61,096
85+	6,543	11,046	10,255	15,772	26,960	34,394	32,992
All women over 45	**487,714**	**599,151**	**705,483**	**809,730**	**871,744**	**1,028,429**	**1,119,361**
Women between 45 and 64	**354,000**	**434,835**	**467,344**	**508,725**	**539,963**	**644,602**	**718,283**

Source: *Slovstat,* 2008.

groups exceeded 100,000, by 2000 six of them did so. At the same time, the most numerous female group grew older: In 2006, the youngest age group of women over 45 ceased to be the largest one, giving way to the 50 – 54 years age group. In the future, the 55 – 59 age group will become the largest one.

Graph 3.6 illustrates the cyclical developments from previous decades as well as the regroupings that may be expected in the near future. It shows that the two youngest age groups have already peaked and have begun to decline in numbers, while the next two age groups (i.e. women between 55 and 64) are currently expanding. The female labor force is growing older and this process will likely continue in the next two decades.

Graph 3.6
Age groups of women 45 – 64 (1945 – 2006, in total numbers)

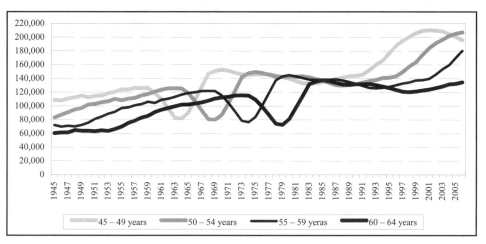

Source: *Slovstat,* 2008.

3.2. LIFE STAGES AND AGE IN THE EYES OF WOMEN AND MEN

3.2.1. POINT AT WHICH MIDDLE AGE BECOMES OLDER AGE

According to prevailing public opinion in Slovakia, older people have less chance on the labor market than middle-aged people (see Section 5.1. of this book). So at what age do people perceive that middle age becomes older age?

Graph 3.7 reveals two telling facts. First, people's views of the point at which middle age becomes older age range widely. Some believe it comes before the age of 40, while according to others it comes after 60; however, most people – approximately one third of the population – place it at between 45 and 50 years.

Second, most people believe that women enter their older years slightly earlier than men. According to the public opinion, the point that separates middle age from older age is 48.9 years on average for women and 51.3 years on average for men.

Graph 3.7
"At what age do you think middle-aged women and men enter older age?" (views of the entire population – in %)

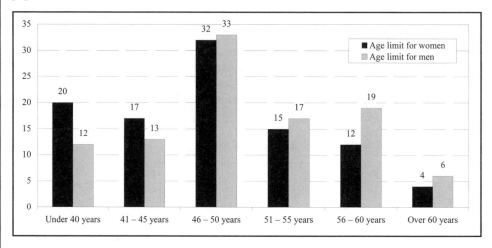

Note: This was an open-ended question for respondents older than 15. The answers "I don't know", "didn't answer" and "other answer" were disregarded.
Source: Institute for Public Affairs, August 2006.

Since the public as a whole believes that women age more rapidly than men, it is legitimate to ask whether women share this view as well. The data presented in Table 3.3 testify to the affirmative, as women largely agree with men that women age faster.

Table 3.3
"At what age do you think middle-aged women and men enter old age?" (views of women and men – in %)

	Age limit for women			Age limit for men		
	Under 45	Between 45 and 55	Over 55	Under 45	Between 45 and 55	Over 55
Views of women	35	47	18	25	48	27
Views of men	38	47	15	25	52	23

Note: This was an open-ended question. The answers "I don't know", "didn't answer" and "other answer" were disregarded.
Source: Institute for Public Affairs, August 2006.

How is the point separating middle age from older age perceived by women between 45 and 64? According to Graph 3.8, almost four in five women (79%) placed it over the age of 45 and one in three women (33%) located it between 46 and 50, while 21% put it between 50 and 55, 20% between 56 and 60, and 5% put the mark even higher. According to women between 45 and 64, the mean age at which middle-aged women enter their older years is 51.7; compared to the views of the population as a whole (48.9), these women locate this point at an older age.

Graph 3.8 also reveals where women between 45 and 64 see the point separating middle age and older age for men. According to them, the average age at which middle-aged men enter their older years is 53.8, i.e. it comes two years later than in case of women.

Graph 3.8
"At what age do you think middle-aged women and men enter older age?" (views of women between 45 and 64 – in %)

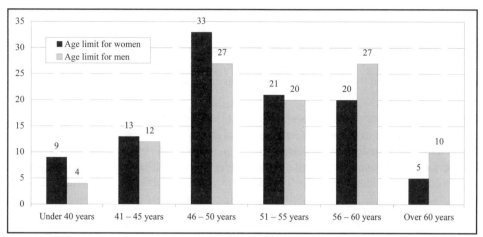

Note: This was an open-ended question. The answers "I don't know", "didn't answer" and "other answer" were disregarded.
Source: Institute for Public Affairs, August 2006.

These findings indicate that people in Slovakia – both men and women alike – believe that women age faster than men. This differing perception has grave implications because it creates a breeding ground for discrimination against women. Older people are often seen as those who have a lower work performance, less adaptability and flexibility, less ability to learn new things and, consequently, less attractiveness for employers. As we have shown, women accept the interpretation that they age faster than men. This is one of the reasons why they passively accept discrimination from their superiors or employers.

Let us try to outline the factors behind the different perceptions of ageing for women and men. The first and most obvious explanation is the simultaneous influence of the youth cult and the beauty myth, whose negative synergic effect hurts women far worse than men. For instance, David Brinkerhoff and Lynn White state the existence of a *double standard of ageing* as "the signs of age – wrinkles, loose skin or grey hair – are considered more damaging for women than for men" (Brinkerhoff – White, 1988, p. 326). The problem is that female beauty is usually defined as having to do with youth.

Donald Light, Suzanne Keller and Craig Calhoun note that "both men and women confront negative age stereotypes, but since society values youth and beauty more highly in women than in men, women suffer a greater loss as they age" (Light – Keller – Calhoun, 1989, p. 161).

In other words: since old age is usually associated with negative stereotypes, greater sensitivity to ageing symptoms in the case of women gives rise to prejudices and discrimination against women. At the root of this attitude is the *lookism*: discrimination against or prejudice towards others based on their appearance (Kauppinen, 2007). As the content analysis of select Slovak dailies and weeklies in Chapter 8 of his publication shows, the media in Slovakia significantly contribute to the reproduction of a *double standard of ageing* and of ageist beauty norms.

Betty Friedan, a feminist philosopher, also speaks of negative stereotypes with respect to old age and elderly people, particularly elderly women, which give rise not only to a *feminist mystique* but also to an *age mystique*. The author also elaborates on the negative effects of the youth and beauty myth, claiming that old age degrades women to the status of "socially rejected and useless sexual objects" (quoted by Sýkorová, 2007, p. 33).

According to Czech sociologist Dana Sýkorová, men are also the victims of ageist attitudes and behavior; however, women face a double threat of sexism and ageism. Reduced physical attractiveness and the end of fertility is socially degrading for women; furthermore, they are broadly viewed as weak and in need of help (Sýkorová, 2007, p. 51).

Obviously, it would be wrong to reduce the double standard of ageing with respect to women and men to the issue of women's declining sexual attractiveness, given that it has to do with the broader understanding of the role of women in society. This broader concept was examined by Leonard Steinhorn, who analyzed attitudes towards older women within American society and noted "hidden contempt for older women and the subtle discrimination that arises from it". According to Steinhorn, "this is a contempt driven partly by outmoded images of beauty and partly by the lingering notion that women don't have much of value to offer once they've raised children" (Steinhorn, 2007, p. 246).

It could be objected that Steinhorn's interpretation overestimates the role of women as mothers and underestimates the other important family roles that women play as grandmothers or nurses of other relatives. Nonetheless, his concept is inspiring because it shifts the debate about the reasons for the different interpretations of the ageing of women and men from the notion of women as "sexual objects" toward a broader understanding of their role in society.

We believe that one of the roots of the widespread notion that women age faster than men is that women retire earlier in Slovakia, a fact that has affected the social perception of the ageing of women and men for many decades. Although this difference is gradually being removed as the result of the pension reform introduced in 2004, people still believe in a simple "equation": women retire earlier, *ergo* they age faster. Here we are dealing with the gender-specific effects of one of the myths of old age as identified by Helena Haškovcová: the myth of *simplifying demography*, which defines the beginning of old age by way of the retirement age (quoted by Sýkorová, 2007, p. 49).

Last but not least, the belief that women age faster is supported by women themselves, who tend to give up on their ambitions in public life soon after they reach the age of 50, as we discussed in the opening Section 1.1. In doing so, women of mature years complete the vicious circle on the labor market: the glass ceiling of their ambitions ceases to be a phenomenon that affects them merely from the outside; instead, it becomes part of their personality and mentality.

One of the consequences of the widespread perception that women age faster is greater tolerance among people from different age groups to discrimination against women of mature years.

3.2.2. AGE IDENTIFICATION OF WOMEN AND MEN

In the previous section, we examined where people draw the line between middle age and older age. Now let us examine their self-classification in terms of age. We will base our conclusions on the assumption, corroborated by numerous research findings, that "age identity is a subjective measure of age that encompasses social and psychological meanings rather than chronological age *per se*" (Sýkorová, 2007, p. 66). We were interested in which age categories women and men of different ages see themselves as belonging to.

According to the Finnish expert on ageing Juhani Ilmarinen, subjective or psychological age or age identification has practical implications as well. It not only affects the individual age attitude of people, but also "has a predictive value because it may indicate a general well-being and belief in the future, both of which affect health" (Ilmarinen, 2006, p. 131). Gerontologists agree that subjective age is a more important factor of physical and mental well-being than chronological age. Seniors who perceive themselves as younger enjoy better morale, greater satisfaction, better health, fewer somatic disorders, better mobility and greater optimism than those who feel older than they are.

Comparative surveys examining the linkage between chronological age and psychological or subjective age among people from various countries have produced two principal findings: first, people usually feel younger than they actually are; second, the difference between people's chronological and subjective age tends to increase as they grow older (Ilmarinen, 2006, pp. 128 – 131).

Table 3.4 illustrates what age identity is claimed by Slovak women and men of different ages. It shows that people's age identification changes as they get older. At first glance, the shifts among women and men seem very similar; however, a careful look reveals certain dissimilarities. In three age groups, women feel slightly older than men. The first is the 35 – 44 age group, where 64% of female respondents defined themselves as middle-aged, while among men from the same age group only 54% felt this way, and more male respondents felt that they were in their younger years (i.e. in younger middle age) or even young. A similar phenomenon was seen in the 55 – 64 and especially 65+ age groups, where more women tended to put themselves in the old age category, while men preferred to call themselves older (i.e. of older middle age) rather than old.

Table 3.4
"Do you consider yourself to be young, in your younger age, middle-aged, in your older age or old?" (age identification of women and men – in %)

	Age identification of women					Age identification of men				
	Young age	Younger age	Middle age	Older age	Old age	Young age	Younger age	Middle age	Older age	Old age
18 – 24 years	88	10	2	0	0	89	10	1	0	0
25 – 34 years	35	50	15	0	0	33	53	13	1	0
35 – 44 years	3	30	64	2	1	7	34	54	2	2
45 – 54 years	0	3	71	25	1	0	2	67	27	4
55 – 64 years	0	0	23	62	15	0	1	24	68	7
Over 65 years	0	0	1	30	69	0	0	0	44	56

Note: The answers "I don't know" and "didn't answer" were disregarded. The percentages in rows for women and men add up to 100%.
Source: Institute for Public Affairs, August 2006.

3.2.3. HOW WOMEN OVER 45 PERCEIVE THEIR AGE

In the following section, we will examine age identification of women between 45 and 64. In this age group, 48% of women describe themselves as being middle-aged and 43% as be-

"There is a great difference be-
tween a woman who lives in a
town and one who lives in the
country... The one from the vil-
lage has to take care of the prop-
erty and work around the house...
When these women come into our
surgery, one can tell right away
that they come from the country...
They look older, much older, at
least ten years older." (Oľga, 60,
a nurse from Rožňava)

ing older. Eight percent believe they are old, while only 1% think they are still in younger age (i.e. younger middle age). None of them feels young.

Of course, when we divide this large age group of women into five-year intervals, we find that their self-perception dramatically changes according to their actual age. A huge majority of women between 45 and 49 feel middle-aged (90%), but in the 50 – 54 age group their share drops to 54%, while the share of those who feel older increases to 40%. In the 55 – 59 age group, the share of women who describe them-selves as being middle-aged declines to 30%, while the share of those who feel older increases to 61%. Finally, two in three women between 60 and 64 feel

older (67%) but one in four already feels old (26%). The share of women who feel middle-aged tends to decline dramatically with age; however, such women can be found in every age group, including the oldest one.

Graph 3.9
Age identification of women over 45 (%)

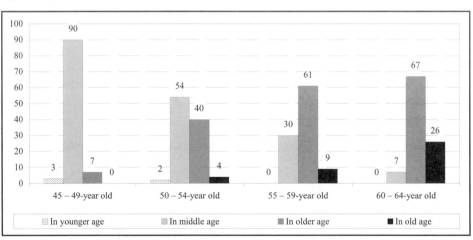

Note: The answers "I don't know" and "didn't answer" were disregarded.
Source: Institute for Public Affairs, August 2006.

The age identification of women be-tween 45 and 64 is affected not only by their age but also by social factors such as their educational attainment and eco-nomic activity. Less educated women tend to perceive themselves as older, while women with more education feel younger. A detailed analysis revealed that education has this effect in all age

"It also depends on who does what. Those who
work hard physically feel tired, exhausted and
weary soon after they break 50. But those who
are in some office, if they are not managers
and are free of stress, those women can feel
young for a long time." (Magdaléna, 53, an
unemployed teacher from Žilina)

groups. This ensues largely from the fact that women with lower education usually work in blue-collar professions that entail greater physical strain and negative health consequences. Consequently, they feel wearier and often less able to perform well in their current jobs. Unfortunately, the scope of potential job opportunities these women have is limited by their low educational attainment. Due to all these circumstances, they often feel older than they actually are. According to the statements of participants in a qualitative survey by the Institute for Public Affairs in 2006, Slovak women are clearly aware of this linkage.

> *"As long as people feel well and are fit, they are still in their middle age. I don't think I'm old yet, although my grandchildren tell me that I am."* (Oľga, 58, a school manager from Banská Bystrica)

The economic status of women has a similar effect on their age identification. Employed women, including employed pensioners, feel somewhat younger than unemployed women or non-working pensioners who are of the same age. But again, we should not forget the crucial link between women's educational attainment and their willingness to retain

> *"I don't think it can be limited by age. It depends more on how people feel or think – and how they radiate on the outside... I feel that I am in my prime ... I have the feeling that I am finally maturing. But when I will truly begin to feel mature – that I have no idea."* (Eliška, 46, a culture manager from Bratislava)

their job or their ability to stay on the labor market and avoid unemployment. In any case, we may conclude that higher educational attainment and active participation in the labor process slow down the feeling of ageing among women.[1]

3.3. EMPLOYMENT AND RETIREMENT

3.3.1. WORK OF THE ELDERLY IN THE CONTEXT OF THE LABOR FORCE SHORTAGE

Like many other European countries, Slovakia has an ageing population. At the same time, it also suffers from a shortage of labor force. What does the public think of the various strategies for tackling this situation? As Table 3.5 shows, most people support opening up more jobs for older women and men, although by this they do not mean increasing the retirement age of either women or men. The fact that nine in ten respondents opposed increasing the retirement age indicates that people see opening jobs for older people as a matter of eliminating barriers to employment for women and men in their pre-retirement years.

Seven in eight respondents (87%) also supported the strategy of opening more jobs for handicapped citizens. A slightly lesser but still comfortable majority (70%) saw the solution in including more Roma into the labor market; this strategy had slightly higher support among more educated people.

On the other hand, there is strong opposition to opening the country's labor market to foreigners; this solution was endorsed by one in four respondents (25%) and rejected by almost

---

[1] A similar linkage was established by a survey carried out in Finland in 2002. It revealed that employed women over 50 were healthier and more optimistic about their age and ageing compared to women of the same age that were not working (quoted according to Kauppinen, 2007).

three in four (70%). Younger and more educated people were somewhat more supportive, but even they expressed caution.

The public emphatically rejects the idea of introducing longer working weeks or cutting vacations, which was opposed by 91% of respondents. The idea of working longer and harder is simply unattractive for most ordinary people.[2]

Finally, almost all respondents (97%) would welcome a rather wishful solution: increasing wages in Slovakia to a level that would prevent people from seeking jobs abroad or make those who have already left return.

Table 3.5
"Slovakia is suffering from a labor force shortage and this situation must be solved. To what degree do you agree with the following suggestions?" (% of answers "certainly and rather yes" : "definitely and rather no" : "I don't know")

	2005	2007
Increase wages in order to prevent our people from seeking jobs abroad or to make them return home	NA	97 : 2 : 1
Open up more jobs for older women	92 : 5 : 2	89 : 10 : 1
Open up more jobs for the handicapped	87 : 10 : 3	88 : 10 : 2
Open up more jobs for older men	NA	87 : 11 : 2
Open up more jobs for the Roma	61 : 34 : 5	70 : 26 : 4
Open our labor market to people from other countries	22 : 69 : 9	25 : 70 : 5
Gradually raise the retirement age of men	8 : 88 : 4	10 : 87 : 3
Gradually raise the retirement age of women	4 : 92 : 4	6 : 92 : 2
Introduce longer working weeks or cut vacations	6 : 91 : 3	NA

Note: NA – the question was not examined.
Source: Institute for Public Affairs, September 2005 and November 2007.

The views of people on how to tackle the labor force shortage resemble those of people in other EU member states. According to the *Eurobarometer 2006* survey, the least popular strategies include increasing the number of legal weekly working hours, increasing the legal retirement age and encouraging immigration of workers from outside the EU. Citizens in most EU member states were more in favor of discouraging early retirement, supporting a greater number of children, encouraging non-working women to participate in the labor market, and encouraging part-time workers to change to full-time work (*Europe's...*, p. 52).

3.3.2. VIEWS OF THE IDEAL RETIREMENT AGE

Effective January 1, 2004, Slovakia launched a pension reform envisaging a gradual increase in the retirement age for women and men to 62 years. While men have been required to work only two years longer, the change has been particularly dramatic for women; for instance, women with two children will see their retirement age increase by seven years.

---

[2] People in Slovakia are no exception in this respect; also people in other European countries attribute great importance to their leisure time. This is what sets Europeans apart from Americans (Kohout – Stokes, 2006, p. 230). On the other hand, one should note that working hours of the Slovaks are much longer compared to people in developed European countries. Slovakia along with Hungary ranked third among all EU member states in terms of average working hours per week for men (45 hours; the EU-27 average is 42 hours) and along with Poland it ranked first in terms of average working hours per week for women (41 hours; the EU-27 average is 35 hours) (*Working Conditions...*, 2007).

According to the previous legislation, the retirement age for women was three years earlier than that of men and also depended on the number of children they had. Childless women became eligible for retirement at 57, women with one child at 56, women with two children at 55 and so on. According to the new legislation, eligibility for retirement will no longer depend on the number of children. The new retirement age for women will be phased in by 2013.

What does the public think about the ideal retirement age? A survey carried out by the Institute for Public Affairs in 2006 showed that people's views differed from the newly introduced official retirement age; in the case of women, the difference was substantial (see Graph 3.10).

As for the ideal retirement age for men, almost two in three respondents (62%) agreed it should be set at 60, while one in four (26%) wanted it even lower. Only one in eight respondents (13%) placed this limit beyond 60 years, where the new legislation put it. On average, respondents saw the optimum retirement age for men at 59.3, which is almost three years below the new limit of 62 years.

As for the ideal retirement age for women, almost all respondents (98%) imagined lower values than the 62 years stipulated by law. On average, they placed the ideal retirement age for women at 55.4, which is almost seven years below the new limit.

Graph 3.10
"What in your opinion is the ideal retirement age for women and men?" (views of the entire population – in %)

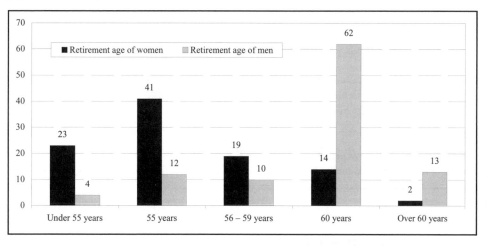

Note: This was an open-ended question. The answers "I don't know", "didn't answer" and "other answer" were disregarded.
Source: Institute for Public Affairs, August 2006.

These findings illustrate not only the strong inertia of public opinion, but especially people's lack of understanding of the concept of *active ageing*. After the pension reform was launched, people did not accept the increased limit of the ideal retirement age; on the contrary, most of them saw the optimum retirement age as even younger than the previous one. The increase in the retirement age for women sparked indignation rather than enthusiasm. This is not surprising when we realize that the previous retirement ages for women and men had been in place for several decades. People had become used to them and embraced them both as natural landmarks in their life course and as important factors in planning their lives after retirement, often on a three-generation or even four-generation basis (i.e. in the context of relations with parents, partners, children and grandchildren).

As described by French sociologist Anne-Marie Guillemard, there are two types of age culture, namely *the culture of the right to early exit from the labor market* and *the culture of the right to employment for all age groups* (Guillemard, 2007, p. 21). Our findings indicate that the former culture prevails in Slovak society, particularly with respect to women, whose early retirement was until very recently institutionally supported and internalized by the public as appropriate and just. The pension reform of 2004, which sought to cope with the impact of population ageing, was the first step toward creating an institutional framework for gradually strengthening the latter type of age culture. Of course, in order for this culture to earn public acceptance, an entire complex of other conditions should be met, including enough jobs, an age-sensitive attitude on the part of employers toward their employees, medical care for ageing workers, opportunities for lifelong learning, and the existence of a network of institutions providing social services and care for children or adult relatives in need of help.

Let us now examine what are the views on the ideal retirement age of women between 45 and 64 years of age. Two in three (67%) believed that this point should not exceed 55 years. Only one in three advocated a higher age, and only 1% believed it should be higher than 60.

While women with lower education more frequently advocated an earlier exit from the labor market, women with university education preferred the retirement age to be set between 56 and 59 years. As we see, women with higher education not only feel younger but are also more prepared to accept a higher retirement age, although not higher than 60.

3.3.3. OPINIONS ON RAISING THE RETIREMENT AGE FOR WOMEN

In 2006, almost four in five women (78%) and three in four men (67%) condemned the decision to increase the retirement age for women to 62 as unjust to women (see Graph 3.11). Criticism of women was more resolute and pronounced.

Graph 3.11
"Previously, the retirement age of women was lower than that of men, but now they are scheduled to converge gradually. In your opinion, is this just?" (views of women and men – in %)

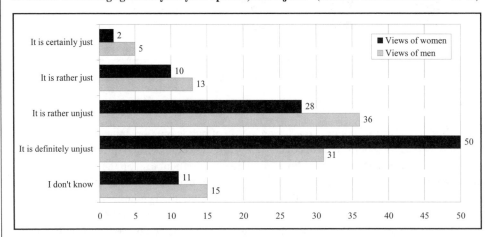

Source: Institute for Public Affairs, August 2006.

Why do some people consider increasing the retirement age for women to be just while others condemn it? We examined the arguments of both opinion groups through people's spontaneous answers to an open-ended question. First, let us take a closer look at the group of the supporters of this legislative change that was much smaller than that of the opponents. It comprised just 12% of all female and 18% of all male respondents.

Table 3.6
"Why do you find it just that the retirement age for women will gradually converge with that of men?" (most frequent arguments of women and men – in %)

	Arguments of women	Arguments of men
Because equality demands it: women should not be privileged and men discriminated against. Women and men work equally hard and age equally fast, which is why they should retire at the same age.	72	57
Women live longer than men; they are less exhausted than men; they are efficient until an old age.	33	37
The lower retirement age was discriminatory for women.	9	13
It gives women a chance to earn a better pension and be more self-reliant.	5	8
Work keeps women fresh and gives them self-fulfillment; staying home and looking after the household gets them down.	4	8

Note: This was an open-ended question. Respondents who endorsed the convergence in the retirement ages of women and men could give three answers, which is why the total sum exceeds 100%.
Source: Institute for Public Affairs, August 2006.

As Table 3.6 shows, there are two basic arguments in favor of increasing the retirement age of women: first, it will put an end to the discrimination against men; second, women live longer and are less exhausted than men and therefore can and should work longer. The former argument was much more frequently cited by women (72% of women and 57% of men), while the latter had slightly more advocates among men (33% of women and 37% of men). Also, the former argument was cited by better educated women and men, while the latter was more typical of less educated respondents.

Other arguments were cited more rarely. One in eleven women (9%) and one in eight men (13%) pointed out the need to eliminate discrimination against women, which ensued from their early retirement; 5% of women and 8% of men saw it as a chance for women to earn better pensions; finally, 4% of women

"I take it as an inevitability... who would otherwise work to support pensioners? But there are certain things that should function properly so we're not as worn out. I wish there were services available; I wish we could afford domestic help. Of course, I would like to work longer... But there are an awful lot of things that do not work properly and exhaust us... So, I would say the problem lies somewhere else, not with the retirement age." (Viera, 47, a financial manager from Bratislava)

"I don't find it unjust that I will not be allowed to retire earlier because of my two children. Of course, I invested some energy into them, but I hope that they will soon stand on their own feet... If I raised them well, perhaps I will get something back from them. And I think that I will have more time for myself, which includes time to work... Of course, I hope they will not expect me to be a kindergarten. Instead, the government should create the conditions for them to have kids and take care of them. I would expect this to work." (Eliška, 46, a culture manager from Bratislava)

> *"That's too long. For instance, we carry those canisters; I can't even imagine myself dragging these canisters around as a 62-year old."* (Anna, 46, a cook from Rožňava)

and 8% of men believed that work is an important source of self-fulfillment for women.

So much for the arguments used by respondents in the 2006 representative survey. However, focus group discussions with women between 45 and 64 from seven Slovak towns carried out by the Institute for Public Affairs in spring 2006 uncovered another argument that conditioned approval for any increase in the retirement age for women on certain requirements. Respondents emphasized the need to create the financial and institutional conditions that would alleviate the double burden on women – both women in pre-retirement age and younger women who often depend on help from their mothers while raising their children.

Let us now examine the arguments of the much more numerous opposing group, composed of critics of the legislative change (78% of women and 67% of men). As Table 3.7 shows, their main argument was that women are more exhausted and age faster due to the double burden of work and family duties; this was cited by 100% of female and male respondents.

Table 3.7
"Why do you find it unjust that the retirement age for women will gradually converge with that for men?" (most frequent arguments of women and men – in %)

	Arguments of women	Arguments of men
Women are more exhausted and age more rapidly due to the double burden of work and family duties.	100	100
Women are physically not as fit as men, they cannot take as much.	21	23
Women should retire earlier because they take care of the family; men are the breadwinners and should work longer.	10	10
Older women have fewer chances to succeed on the labor market due to high unemployment; they should make way for younger workers.	5	6
The retirement of women should be individual and flexible; it should depend on the type of their work, the state of their health, the number of children they have, and other factors.	3	3

Note: This was an open-ended question. Respondents who opposed the convergence in the retirement ages of women and men could give three answers, which is why the total sum exceeds 100%.
Source: Institute for Public Affairs, August 2006.

Approximately one in five women and men (21% and 23%, respectively) said that women are not as physically fit as men and therefore should not work as long. One in ten respondents argued that the traditional gender division of labor should be respected and women should be allowed to take care of the family and the household while men should continue to fulfill their role as principal breadwinners. Finally, 5% of women and 6% of men pointed out that raising the retirement age for women was unjust because older women had fewer chances to succeed on the labor market due to high unemployment.

> *"I think that a woman wears out earlier than a man. I mean, a woman must take care of her family; she must go to work; she must take care of everything. And those births, for instance... today it makes no difference whether a woman has four children or two children as it used to before. Or a woman with no kids retires at the same age... no, I don't think it's just."* (Katarína, 45, a waitress from Martin)

As Table 3.7 shows, all these arguments were almost evenly cited by women and men. A detailed analysis has also revealed that they were evenly distributed among women of different age, education and professional background. The remarkable consensus on this issue was also corroborated by statements from participants in the above-mentioned qualitative survey of the Institute for Public Affairs.

> "*It is different working after retirement and working before retirement. [A pensioner] that is too tired to work can simply quit and has a guaranteed income. But like this, you are under constant stress as to whether you will manage or not, but you have to anyway. Even if you crawl to work, you must get there or else you may lose your apartment and everything else.*" (Eva, 52, a seamstress from Rožňava)

A comparison of the arguments presented by the advocates and opponents of raising the retirement age of women indicates there are three different notions of gender discrimination in Slovak society. First, *advocates of earlier retirement for women* perceive it as a just solution that corresponds to the different roles of women and men; consequently, they view the decision to converge the retirement ages of women and men as discriminatory with respect to women. Second, *advocates of increasing the retirement age for women* perceive the previous model as discriminatory with respect to men, who were forced to work longer. Finally, a small share of people sees the previous model as discrimination against women because they were forced out of the labor market earlier than men.

How deeply rooted in public opinion is the logic of *gender justice* based on the previous retirement age for women? The answer can be found in a survey carried out by the Institute for Public Affairs in November 2007. According to its findings, almost four in five women (78%) and two in three men (67%) believe that "it is appropriate if a woman retires earlier than a man"; the opposite opinion, that "it is appropriate for a woman to work as long as a man instead of retiring earlier" was endorsed by only 8% of women and 9% of men (*Empirical Data...*, 2007c). These opinions indicate that the earlier retirement age for women is firmly woven into the fabric of normative expectations in Slovak society.

3.3.4. PROLONGING WORKLIFE IN THE CONTEXT OF FAMILY EXPECTATIONS

Where should we look for the roots of the reluctance to prolonging the participation of women in the labor market? One reason is family expectations regarding women in their mature years.

According to prevailing opinion, Slovak women generally find it difficult to harmonize their professional careers and family lives. In a survey carried out by the Institute for Public Affairs in 2005, this opinion was presented by three in four respondents (76%). Women face a challenge in reconciling their roles at work and in the family not only while raising their own children, but also during the so-called "the sandwich" years, i.e. when they begin to take care of other family

> "*By retiring earlier, women help their daughters to jumpstart their professional careers earlier. They should take care of their grandchildren while they still can. So I think women should retire earlier than men... A grandmother is more capable of helping the grandchildren.*" (Anna, 52, a social worker from Martin)

> *"I work as a pensioner myself, but I don't think it is right to have the same retirement age for women and men… children often need a grandmother to help with their children. Because they are workaholics, these young people nowadays. Their wages are different, too. We retired on a poor wage. Our children will need their mothers to help them… but they will still be employed."* (Mária, 58, an agricultural expert from Bratislava)

Graph 3.12
"To what degree is it acceptable for a grandmother to postpone her retirement even though her grandchildren need her?" (views of women and men – in %)

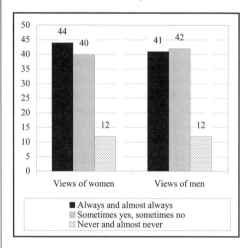

Note: Respondents evaluated the acceptability of such decisions on a 10-degree scale. The category "never and almost never" corresponded to degrees 1 – 3, the category "sometimes yes, sometimes no" to degrees 4 – 7, and the category "always and almost always" to degrees 8 – 10. The remainder of the 100% comprises the answer "I don't know".
Source: Institute for Public Affairs, August 2006.

members such as older relatives or grandchildren (Brinkerhoff – White, 1988, p. 321). For some women, their obligations related to other family members may reduce their motivation and limit their possibilities to continue their professional career.

Expectations that mature women will be active in their roles as grandmothers are relatively strong in Slovakia. This was indirectly corroborated by people's views on the best ways of taking care of infants under three. In 2005, almost three in four respondents (70%) considered the participation of grandmothers in taking care of little children as second best only to active care by the mothers (90%); this solution was considered even better than having the mother and father alternate (52%) in raising the children (see Marošiová – Šumšalová, 2006). The opinion that the right place for mature women is with their grandchildren can also be illustrated by the statements of Anna and Mária – the participants in a qualitative survey of the Institute for Public Affairs from 2006.

Of course, that is not to say that a majority of people in Slovakia would condemn an older woman's decision to postpone her retirement. As Graph 3.12 shows, only 12% of women and men consider such a decision unacceptable. On the other hand, more than two in five women (44%) and men (41%) think that it should be accepted always or almost always. About the same share of respondents (40% of women and 42% of men) is ambivalent. Tolerance for decisions by older women to postpone their retirement is significantly higher in more educated and urban environments.

As Eliška, one of the participants of the focus group discussions put it, older women should be free to choose if they help in taking care of their grandchildren. It should never be the only solution to the unavailability of adequate schooling facilities.

Let us now examine people's views about taking care of elder relatives (see Graph 3.13). Almost three in four women (71%) and almost three in five men (58%) agreed with the statement that "if there is an elderly person requiring help in the family, then it should be jointly provided by a woman (e.g. daughter or daughter-in-law) and a man (e.g. son or son-in-law)".

The opposite opinion that such help should be provided solely by a woman was advocated by one in eight women (12%) and one in four men (23%). This distribution of opinions as similar in all age groups of women and men.

> "I am also looking forward to my grandchildren. But the system should be here to help... The education system is a catastrophe. That's where the problem is. Why should we dump everything on the grandmother? If she volunteers, okay. But little children depending on their grandmother, that's a nightmare." (Eliška, 46, a culture manager from Bratislava)

But everyday family reality may differ vastly from this ideal model of a division of labor between partners. The need to take care of a dependent partner or parent may compel a woman to cut down on her work hours or abandon her job altogether because it is usually women who take care of dependent relatives. According to a survey carried out in 2005 by the Research Institute of Labor and Family (Bodnárová – Filadelfiová – Gerbery, 2005), women made up 71% of all people in Slovakia who provided care to dependent relatives. The remaining 29% were men – usually husbands taking care of their wives and sons taking care of their mothers. The same survey showed that the most frequently required and provided kind of help in Slovakia is domestic care. The largest group of people receiving such help were senior citizens over 70, of whom 56% were women.

Graph 3.13
"Which of the following statements do you support:
A. If there is an elderly person requiring help in the family, then it should be provided solely by a woman;
B. If there is an elderly person requiring help in the family, then it should be jointly provided by a woman and a man."
(support of statement A : undecided : support of statement B – in %)

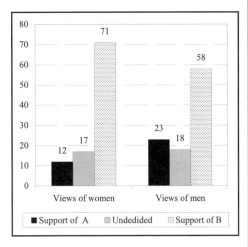

Source: Institute for Public Affairs, November 2007.

3.3.5. OPINIONS ON THE LOWER PENSIONS OF WOMEN

The gradual convergence of the retirement ages of women and men has one more important dimension that should be seen in the context of gender equality or inequality. Under the previous model, the earlier retirement of women negatively affected their old-age pensions and contributed to the feminization of poverty in old age. Of course, this was not the only factor, as women's generally lower pensions were also the result of their discontinuous professional careers, during which most of them took care of children in the earlier stages and some of them took care of other family members in the later stages. The formula for calculating old-age pensions subsequently reproduced the already lower income of women.

As Graph 3.14 illustrates, three in four women (75%) and one in two men (51%) do not consider this model of calculating old-age pensions to be fair. The opposite statement, that "men

Graph 3.14
"Which of the following statements do you support:
A. Men are entitled to higher pensions because they earned higher wages during their professional careers.
B. Women should not be punished by lower pensions for taking care of children and the family during their professional careers."
(support of statement A : undecided : support of statement B – in %)

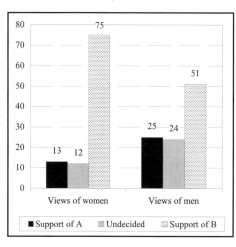

Source: Institute for Public Affairs, November 2007.

are entitled to higher pensions because they earned higher wages during their professional careers", was endorsed by one in eight women (13%) and one in four men (25%).

According to a substantial majority of people in Slovakia the current formula for calculating old-age pensions is unjust to women. It may be assumed that this awareness significantly affects people's widespread conviction about a weaker position of women in society. In this context, it is paradoxical how little critical attention in the ongoing public debate on pension reform is being paid to the fact that the period of caring for children is not included into the formula for calculating old-age pensions, which therefore ignores a great deal of the unpaid work that most women perform during their lives.

As long as this model is preserved and the work women invest into raising their children is considered "unproductive", those mothers who choose to stay home with their children for a longer period of time will continue to pay twice for their decision: first, by receiving a lower income throughout their professional careers; and second, by receiving lower old-age pensions throughout their retirement. Besides, many of these women are likely to spend the final years of their lives without partners, either as widows or as divorcées. It remains to be seen to what degree their adult children will be able and willing to repay their "debt" and take care of them when they need it most. As the total number of newborns continues to decline, the urgency of this issue is increasing because the burden of caring for old parents, who will continue to live longer on average, will fall on fewer adult children.

3.3.6. INDIVIDUAL RETIREMENT STRATEGIES

The retirement strategies of employed women and men in Slovakia are very similar. As Graph 3.15 shows, more than two in three (70%) women and men under 50 would like to work either until they become eligible for retirement (49% of women and 46% of men) or as long as they can past their retirement age (20% of women and 25% of men).

Men are slightly more interested in prolonging their professional careers. On the other hand, women seem to prefer early retirement more frequently (12%) than men (7%). But we should note that this option does not have the same meaning for female as for male respondents: when the survey was carried out, women were just trying to come to grips with the substantial increase in their retirement age.

In any case, it is clear that a significant proportion of women and men take different approaches to their retirement than respecting the legal retirement age. The broad spectrum of people's notions about the timing of their retirement corroborates the observation of French sociologist Anne-Marie Guillemard about "the erosion of the standardized age limit for retirement" (quoted by Havlíková, 2007, p. 195 – 196).

Graph 3.15
"What is your idea of retirement? Until what age do you plan to work?" (views of employed women and men under 50 – in %)

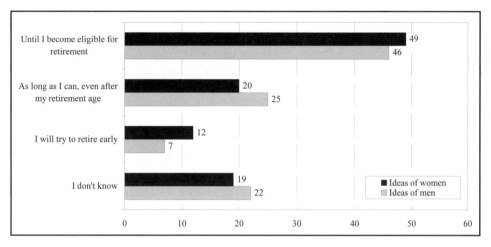

Source: Institute for Public Affairs, August 2006.

The figures in Graph 3.15 also indicate that many women and men under 50 have rather vague ideas about their retirement. This is particularly true of younger respondents who consider this landmark too far in the future. For instance, two in five (41%) employed women between 18 and 24 answered "I don't know", but only 14% of employed women between 45 and 49 gave the same response. Among male respondents, the share of vague answers was very similar.

Table 3.8
"What is your idea of retirement? Until what age do you plan to work?" (% of answers "until I become eligible for retirement" : "as long as I can, even after my retirement age" : "I will try to retire early" – by degree of handling physical and mental demands of work and by job satisfaction)

		Views of women	Views of men
I handle physical demands of my work:	Very well	47 : 25 : 6	36 : 32 : 9
	Rather well	50 : 18 : 14	54 : 20 : 5
	Neither well, nor poorly + rather poorly + very poorly	54 : 11 : 21	61 : 6 : 11
I handle mental demands of my work:	Very well	47 : 22 : 5	39 : 28 : 6
	Rather well	50 : 20 : 14	49 : 25 : 7
	Neither well, nor poorly + rather poorly + very poorly	50 : 13 : 16	57 : 11 : 11
I am satisfied with my job:	Yes	49 : 22 : 9	44 : 25 : 7
	No	51 : 8 : 27	57 : 20 : 0

Note: Views of employed women and men younger than 50. Percentages in rows add up to 100%. The remainder of the 100% comprises the answer "I don't know".
Source: Institute for Public Affairs, August 2006.

Retirement strategies of women – and even more so of men – are strongly affected by their ability to cope with the demands of their work. People who have difficulties coping with the physical load and mental demands of their work, rarely consider prolonging their worklife and prefer remaining employed only until they become eligible for retirement. Those who find their work too challenging also tend to contemplate early retirement more often. This option is more frequently considered by women than by men.

Another important factor affecting people's retirement strategies is their overall job satisfaction. Women who are happy in their jobs more frequently consider extending their work past the retirement age and rarely contemplate early retirement. Satisfied men, for their part, are less interested in exiting from the about market immediately upon becoming eligible for retirement.

The individual retirement strategies of women are also affected by other factors, most importantly their cultural capital. As Table 3.9 shows, the more educated women are, the more they would like to continue working past their retirement age, and the less they are interested in early retirement. Fluency in foreign, particularly Western languages, and computer literacy have similar effects.

Another important factor is the type of job. Women in blue-collar professions are less interested in extending their employment past the retirement age, unlike clerks, executive professionals and especially creative professionals.

Marked differences can also be seen between the retirement strategies of women with various status self-identification. Those who identify with the upper class or upper middle class are more inclining toward the option of working as long as possible.

Table 3.9
Women's ideas of retirement (% of answers "until I become eligible for retirement" : "as long as I can, even after my retirement age" : "I will try to retire early" – by education, profession, fluency in Western languages and status self-identification)

		Ideas of women
	Elementary	53 : 0 : 27
Education	Secondary without A levels	43 : 18 : 13
	Complete secondary	54 : 18 : 10
	University	43 : 34 : 10
	Unskilled blue-collar workers	48 : 9 : 14
	Skilled blue-collar workers	44 : 13 : 26
Profession (select types)	Clerical workers	45 : 20 : 15
	Executive professionals	51 : 25 : 9
	Creative professionals	43 : 36 : 7
	No language	50 : 14 : 15
Fluency in Western languages	One language	52 : 23 : 8
	More languages	35 : 41 : 7
	Lower class and lower middle class	50 : 16 : 11
Status self-identification	Middle class	51 : 19 : 12
	Upper class and upper middle class	37 : 41 : 11

Note: Views of employed women younger than 50. Percentages in rows add up to 100%. The remainder of the 100% comprises the answer "I don't know".
Source: Institute for Public Affairs, August 2006.

What are the motives behind the retirement strategies that employed women choose? Table 3.10 shows that women place the greatest emphasis on the circumstances related to the nature of their work.

Women who want to work past their retirement age view their jobs primarily as a way of satisfying their non-material needs and not merely as a source of income. More than half of these women (53%) described work as the "substance of life" that allows them to remain vital and energetic and to capitalize on their knowledge and skills. They stress that work satisfies their need of social contacts, and that they fear feeling useless, passive and lonely after retirement. Only one in seven (14%) said financial reasons played a role in their desire to extend their careers. On the other hand, these women perceive retirement as their right to a well-earned rest (27%), and said any extension of their careers was conditional on their good health (18%). On the other hand, very few (5%) describe their work as too physically or mentally challenging.

Respondents who prefer early retirement differ from the rest especially in their emphasis on the financial reasons for their decision (47%) and, almost equally frequently, on their right to a well-earned rest after tiring years of work (45%). Almost one in three of these women (29%) cited the physical and mental challenges of their professions.[3]

The third and the largest group comprises women who intend to remain employed until they become eligible for retirement; their views place them between the first and second groups.

Table 3.10
Arguments of women in favor of individual retirement strategies (%)

	Until I become eligible for retirement	As long as I can, even after my retirement age	I will try to retire early
Work is a way to satisfy non-material needs	29	53	31
Financial reasons in favor of late or early retirement	26	14	47
Right to a well-earned rest, weariness of work	21	27	45
Physically or mentally challenging profession	17	5	29
Valid legislation, social conventions	18	17	0
Decision will depend on state of health	12	18	10
Desire to spend time with family (e.g. partner, husband, grandchildren)	7	4	0
Shortage of jobs	5	0	9
Desire to pursue hobbies and travel	4	0	6

Note: Views of employed women younger than 50. Respondents were free to choose three answers, which is why the total sum exceeds 100%.
Source: Institute for Public Affairs, August 2006.

3.3.7. NOTIONS OF THE IDEAL LIFE AFTER RETIREMENT

How do employed women imagine their ideal retired life? Are their notions different from those of men? The answers can be found in Table 3.11, which summarizes the reactions of female and male respondents to an open-ended question.

Most women (57%) and men (59%) believe that an ideal retirement should allow them to spend time with their closest relatives – especially their partner, children and grandchildren. An interesting paradox can be observed here. On the one hand, female respondents did not identify the desire to spend time with their families as an important factor affecting the timing of their retirement (see Table 3.10). On the other hand, they cited devotion to family life

---

[3] In real life, women opt for early retirement also due to the lack of available job opportunities (*Empirical Data...*, 2006b).

Table 3.11
"What kind of retired life would you imagine for yourself? What would you like to spend most of your time doing?" (ideas of employed women and men – in %)

	Notions of women	Notions of men	Notions of women between 45 and 54
Enjoying family life (with partner, children, grandchildren, etc.)	57	59	46
Traveling	42	42	46
Doing housework and gardening (e.g. cooking, baking, craftwork, gardening, taking care of pets, repairing car, etc.)	32	36	33
Pursuing hobbies, spending time "on myself"	30	23	39
Relaxing, enjoying leisure time	28	26	34
Spending time actively outdoors (e.g. pursuing sports, hiking, visiting spas, fishing, hunting, staying in a summer house)	15	26	11
Pursuing cultural activities (e.g. reading, theatre, artwork, etc.)	12	9	8
Having enough money	8	7	7
Cultivating social contacts with friends and acquaintances	7	4	3
Having a paid job	6	4	5
Enjoying good health	3	6	0
Pursuing pro bono and charity activities	1	0	0
Pursuing educational activities	1	3	0

Note: This was an open-ended question to which respondents were free to choose three answers, which is why the total sum exceeds 100%.
Source: Institute for Public Affairs, August 2006.

as a key attribute of an ideal retirement (see Table 3.11). It is also interesting that men presented this opinion even more frequently than women; this may reflect their desire to compensate their relatives for the long years of work during which their participation in family life was rather limited.

The next on the list of favorite retirement activities envisioned by employed women is traveling (42%), doing housework and gardening (32%), pursuing unspecified hobbies (30%), relaxing (28%), spending time actively outdoors (15%) and pursuing cultural activities (12%). As for employed men's notions of the ideal retirement, they more often include working in and around the house (36%) and spending time actively outdoors (26%). Women, for their part, dream more frequently of simply spending time on themselves and their hobbies (30%) and pursuing cultural activities (12%).

It is interesting that relatively few women (6%) viewed paid work as an attractive part of an ideal retirement, despite the fact that – as we demonstrated earlier – finances are an important factor affecting women's retirement strategies. On the other hand, some female respondents said having enough money was an important prerequisite for an ideal retirement (8%).

Special attention should be paid to the fact that very few employed people (1% of women and 3% of men) mentioned studying as part of an ideal retirement. The concept of lifelong learning has clearly not yet taken root in Slovakia. For Slovak women and men, an ideal retirement simply does not include the ambition to learn new things and "hone one's skills".[4]

An even tinier share of employed people (1% of women and 0% of men) realizes that retirement could be used to pursue *pro bono* or charity activities or other forms of participating in

---

[4] This is not to say that there are no older people in Slovakia who feel the need for further learning and education. The government created institutional framework for this type of education after 1990. Gradually, a network of 13 universities of the "third age" was established. In the 2007/2008 academic year, they were attended by 5,069 women and men over 55 (Hrapková, 2007, pp. 12 – 40; Čornaničová, 2007, pp. 6 – 11).

the life of the local community. From this perspective, Slovakia lags behind the US and other developed countries where senior citizens constitute important actors in public and political life.

All these findings support the conclusion that, in the eyes of employed women and men in Slovakia, retirement means voluntarily withdrawing into the family or into private circles rather than using the spare time to help tackle problems in the local community or on the national level. This conclusion comes as little surprise when one realizes that active civic involvement – regardless of age – forms a relatively small part of normative expectations of the ideal woman and the ideal man (see Section 1.1. of this book). The syndrome of civic passivity seems particularly strong among retired people. In other words, when thinking of retirement, most people in Slovakia do not imagine helping to tackle problems that concern most of citizens, nor do they intend to get involved in defending and furthering the interests of senior citizens, i.e. a social group they will at some point become a part of. The ideals of the "silver revolution", aimed at increasing the civic participation of elderly people, have not yet gained a foothold in Slovakia. Civic activism among senior citizens is rather uncommon.[5]

Let us now take a look at the last column of Table 3.11, which shows the notions of the ideal retirement shared by women in their pre-retirement years, i.e. between 45 and 54. When we compare their ideas to the expectations of all employed women, we see that during the decade immediately before retirement, women's expectations shift toward a desire to enjoy life in the form of traveling, pursuing hobbies and relaxing. As if they grew tired of their usual chores and wished to spend more time enjoying themselves. Compared to the entire sample, women from this age group less frequently emphasize the intense cultivation of family life as an indispensable part of an ideal retirement.

Finally, let us compare how employed women shortly before retirement (i.e. women between 45 and 54) and pensioners shortly after retirement (i.e. women between 55 and 64) see their ideal retirement. As Graph 3.16 shows, the views of the latter are already affected by reality, which often modifies their original notions and "clips their wings". While enjoying family life remains central (47%), the most favored activity of retired women is not traveling but working in the household and around the house (55%). The significantly lower emphasis on travel (only 29% compared to 46% of women in their pre-retirement years) may be explained by worries about finances (14% of retired respondents said that the prerequisite for an ideal retired life is enough money, while 8% cited having a paid job as an important part of retirement) and more frequent health problems (5% of retired respondents mentioned the importance of good health, compared to 0% of employed respondents). Only one in ten retired respondents (10%) compared to one in three employed respondents (34%) said that an ideal retirement requires enough time for resting and relaxing, which indicates that time for them apparently ceased to be as scarce a commodity as it used to be in the hectic pre-retirement period. On the other hand, women's emphasis on social contacts with friends and acquaintances increased to 11% compared to 3% before retirement. The importance of educational, *pro bono* and charity activities did not increase, even though they might well form a natural part of pensioners' social contacts and help them integrate into the life of a broader community.

---

[5] The public remains rather unaware of activities pursued by civil organizations associating elderly people. This can be illustrated by the fact that respondents in their spontaneous answers did not mention a possibility to participate in activities of the Slovak Union of Pensioners or civic associations such as Strieborné hlavy [Silver Heads], Fórum pre pomoc starším [Forum for Helping the Elderly] or Regióny.sk that launched a web portal for senior citizens in spring 2007 (www.senior.sk). The respondents either did not know of their activities or did not find them relevant enough to associate them with their post-retirement lives.

Graph 3.16
Women's notions of the ideal retired life before and after retirement (%)

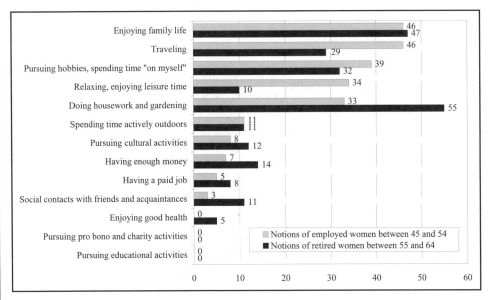

Note: This was an open-ended question to which respondents were free to choose three answers, which is why the total sum exceeds 100%.
Source: Institute for Public Affairs, August 2006.

These findings also help outline the desirable future scenario for senior citizens in Slovakia. We believe that the main emphasis should be on promoting an active lifestyle for elderly people and strengthening their participation in the public sphere including labor market, civil society and politics. Furthering this scenario should be the main aim of the new paradigm of old age policy in Slovakia, which should aim to activate older people in two basic dimensions: first, prolonging their work life by postponing their retirement; second, helping them to attain an active retirement by encouraging them to participate in the life of the local community, as well as broader society.

Slovakia should avoid drifting toward the model of the old age as a "role-less role",[6] when almost nothing is expected of the elderly person, or toward an old age model as an exclusively private stage in the life of individuals who are isolated from the community and broader society. We believe that the optimum scenario for individuals and for society is to adopt the model of "continuing engagement with life that takes two main forms: maintaining relations with other people and performing activities that are, in the broadest sense, productive" (Rowe – Kahn, 1999, p. 51).[7]

---

[6] The notion of role-less role was developed by Ernest W. Burgess in his publication *Aging in Western Societies* (1960) (quoted according to Sýkorová, 2007, p. 35).

[7] This perception is in direct contradiction with a so-called disengagement theory developed by American gerontologists Elaine Cumming and William Henry in their famous book *Growing Old* (1961). According to their theory, people's gradual disengagement from society and decline in social activities is considered a "normal", healthy adjustment to age, functional for both the individual and society (quoted according to Friedan, 1993, pp. 79 – 80; Brinkerhoff – White, 1988, p. 323; Schaefer, 1989, pp. 299 – 300).

4. WORK IN THE LIFE OF WOMEN AND MEN

Jarmila Filadelfiová – Zora Bútorová – Marián Velšic – Sylvia Šumšalová

Jarmila Filadelfiová is the co-author of Sections 4.1.1, 4.1.3., 4.1.4., 4.1.5., 4.1.6., 4.1.8. and 4.1.9.
Zora Bútorová is the author of Sections 4.1.7. and 4.2.6. and co-author of Sections 4.2.1., 4.2.2., 4.2.3., 4.2.4., 4.2.5., 4.2.7., 4.2.8. and 4.2.9.
Marián Velšic is the author of Section 4.1.2. and co-author of Sections 4.2.1., 4.2.2., 4.2.3., 4.2.7., 4.2.8. and 4.2.9.
Sylvia Šumšalová is the co-author of Sections 4.2.4. and 4.2.5.

4. WORK IN THE LIFE OF WOMEN AND MEN

4.1. WOMEN AND MEN IN LABOR MARKET STATISTICS

This section outlines the recent trends in the economic activity and employment of women and men in Slovakia. It describes the basic differences in their academic and professional orientations as well as in their employment. It also characterizes the differences between men and women employed in various segments of the national economy, points out the similarities and differences in their professional careers and remuneration, and outlines the specific parameters of the jobs of women and men. In analyzing these issues, we combined the gender dimension with the age dimension.

4.1.1. EDUCATION AND PROFESSIONAL ORIENTATION OF WOMEN AND MEN

Educational Attainment

The most important factor affecting people's success on the labor market is their educational attainment, as well as the orientation of their education. Over the past three decades, the overall level of education of the entire Slovak population has increased significantly (see Graph 4.1). According to the last two population censuses, the share of people with elementary and incomplete education dropped from 60.7% in 1970 to 27.4% in 2001. The greatest increase was in the category of people with complete secondary education. Over the same period, the share of people with complete university education increased from 3.0% to 9.7%. While this

Graph 4.1
Structure of Slovak population over 15 by education (1970 and 2001 – in %)

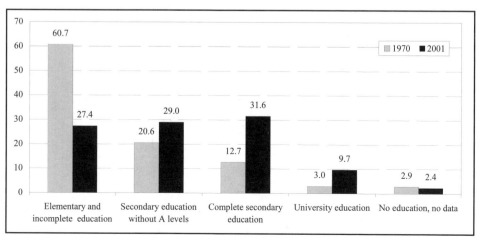

Source: *Obyvateľstvo…*, 2005.

Graph 4.2
Percentage of elementary and university education among Slovak women and men over 15 (2001)

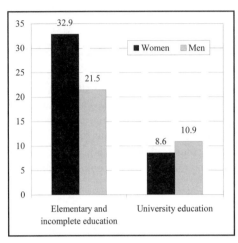

Source: *Obyvateľstvo...*, 2005.

represents a remarkable improvement, Slovakia continues to lag behind western EU member states, where the share of people with university education is about 20% of the entire population older than 15 (*Key...*, 2007).

According to the most recent population census, the overall educational attainment of women has increased substantially thanks to a dramatic increase in the share of women with complete secondary education, which is already higher than among men. However, women continue to lag behind men due to their above-average representation among people with elementary and incomplete education and their below-average representation among people with university education (see Graph 4.2).

Let us now take a closer look at the education structure of employed women and men. As Table 4.1 shows, women's educational attainment is slightly higher. In 2007, most employed women had complete secondary education (45.9% of women compared to 34.0% of men). Among employed men, the largest group was made up of those with vocational education without A levels (38.2% of men compared to 24.3% of women). At both poles of the education continuum, the share of women was higher than that of men: 16.9% of employed women, but only 14.6% of men had university education; similarly, 5.6% of employed women but only 3.6% of employed men had elementary education.

Table 4.1
Structure of employed women and men by education (1995 – 2007, in %)

		1995	1996	1997	1998	1999	2000	2001	2002	2003	2004	2005	2006	2007
Elementary	Women	13.7	13.4	13.5	12.2	10.3	9.1	8.3	7.3	6.5	6.5	6.0	6.1	5.6
	Men	8.7	8.2	8.6	7.6	6.0	5.1	4.5	4.2	3.9	3.9	3.5	3.5	3.6
Vocational without A levels	Women	24.8	23.8	22.8	24.3	26.1	26.5	27.7	30.0	25.1	25.1	24.0	24.4	24.3
	Men	40.3	39.3	38.2	40.3	43.0	42.4	43.1	43.6	40.5	40.5	37.7	38.1	38.2
Secondary without A levels	Women	5.9	5.5	5.9	5.1	3.8	3.2	2.4	2.0	1.7	1.7	2.2	2.2	2.3
	Men	8.6	8.3	9.3	8.5	5.8	4.9	3.1	2.6	2.7	2.7	2.8	2.7	2.8
Complete vocational	Women	2.3	2.5	3.6	4.0	4.0	3.3	3.7	3.8	4.0	4.0	3.7	3.8	3.8
	Men	3.9	4.3	5.4	5.6	5.5	5.8	5.8	5.9	6.1	6.1	6.4	6.4	6.3
Complete secondary (general)	Women	5.8	6.4	7.1	8.3	7.8	7.4	7.0	6.2	6.4	6.4	6.5	6.4	6.1
	Men	2.7	3.4	3.1	3.7	3.8	3.6	3.2	2.8	2.8	2.8	2.7	2.8	2.9
Complete secondary (vocational)	Women	36.4	37.3	35.3	34.5	36.3	37.8	37.2	38.3	40.1	40.1	40.5	39.7	39.8
	Men	22.4	24.9	23.3	22.2	23.9	26.2	27.5	28.4	29.7	29.7	30.8	30.0	31.1
University	Women	12.8	12.5	11.8	11.6	11.7	12.6	13.7	14.4	15.1	15.1	15.5	16.0	16.9
	Men	14.7	12.9	12.1	12.0	11.9	12.1	12.7	12.4	13.8	13.8	15.5	15.9	14.6

Source: *Štatistické...*, 1996 – 2004; *Slovstat*, 2008.

Over the past decade, the ratio of people with only elementary education to the total number of employed women and men has declined substantially. On the other hand, the ratio of people with complete secondary and university education has increased. These trends testify not only to the overall growth in the level of education of employed women and men, but also to the gradual elimination of women and men with few or no qualifications from the labor market.

Academic Orientation of Women and Men

Over the long term, women in Slovakia focus on different fields of study than Slovak men. According to long-term statistics, boys traditionally choose secondary vocational schools while girls prefer secondary schools completed with a final examination. In 2006, the overall share of girls studying at secondary vocational schools was 28.2%, but at secondary trade schools the figure was 56.6% and at secondary academic schools 58.3%. Compared to 2000, the overall share of girls attending secondary academic schools increased while their share at secondary vocational and trade schools declined (see Graph 4.3).

Graph 4.3
Percentage of girls among students at particular types of secondary schools (2000 and 2006)

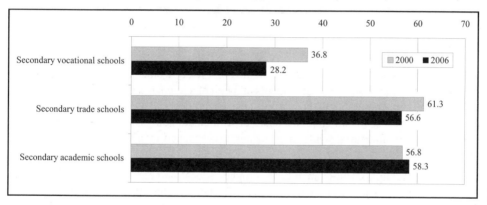

Source: *Štatistické...*, 2001 and 2007.

Even within specific categories of secondary school, girls have different academic interests than boys. Girls attending vocational schools are attracted to light industry or services, and study to become seamstresses, dressmakers, saleswomen, shoemakers, waitresses or cooks. Boys, for their part, tend to focus on engineering as they are attracted to technical, mechanical or construction studies. The same difference is typical of girls and boys attending secondary trade schools. Boys are interested in technical colleges or forestry schools, where they form 75% and 85% of the student body, respectively. Girls specialize in fields related to the health service and education; in the long term, the share of girls attending secondary medical schools is at 90% and at secondary pedagogical schools it approaches 100%. Girls also dominate at librarian and economic secondary schools. The ratio of boys and girls is balanced only at secondary agricultural schools and conservatories; all other types of secondary schools are clearly dominated by one or the other sex. The structure of students at secondary schools over the past decade indicates that the academic orientation of girls and boys is relatively stable (see Graph 4.4).

Similar differences can also be seen at universities. The total share of women attending public and private universities is higher than that of men. In 2006, women made up 59.6% of all university students in Slovakia. Again, the shares of women and men at various faculties differ significantly. The greatest gender gap is in among students attending technical faculties, where

Graph 4.4
Percentage of girls among full-time students at secondary trade schools (1995 and 2006)

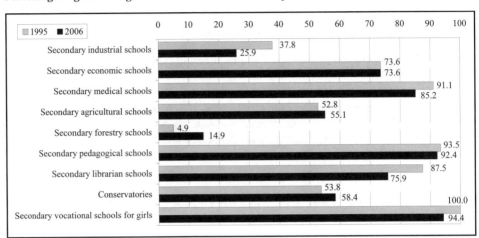

Source: *Štatistické...*, 1996 and 2007.

the share of women was 23.7% in 2006. On the other hand, women clearly dominate in universities as they make up 80.4% of students at medical and pharmaceutical faculties, 67.5% at social science faculties, 60.3% at cultural science faculties, and over 57% at natural science faculties. Between 2000 and 2006, the share of women attending social science, artistic and medical faculties increased while men further strengthened their dominance at technical faculties.

Generally speaking, Slovak women have a higher education potential, but their interest in particular fields of study has a significantly different structure than that of men. Gender segregation on the labor market originates in the process of choosing a secondary school and a study field at university.

4.1.2. DIGITAL LITERACY OF WOMEN AND MEN

The penetration of modern information and communication technologies (ICT) into various areas of society brings the urgent question whether the population is prepared to use them to the full. In this respect, academic experts and political leaders speak of the need to increase the population's "digital literacy".

What is digital literacy?

Digital literacy encompasses the ability to understand and use information in multiple formats from a wide range of sources when it is presented via computers.

Paul A. Gilster

The digital literacy of the Slovak population was examined in detail by two surveys carried out by the Institute for Public Affairs in 2005 and 2007 (*Empirical Data...*, 2005a; *Empirical Data...*, 2007b). A comparison of their findings indicates that the overall level of digital literacy among Slovak adults increased. While in 2005 the overall *digital literacy index*[1] was 0.31, two years later it had increased to 0.34. During this period, Slovaks improved especially their abilities to use modern ICT as a means of communication. They also strengthened their skills in operating computer hardware and software. It is particularly positive that they improved mostly those computer skills that are viewed as more challenging and sophisticated.

The ongoing informatization of society is catalyzing a new line of social division between those who have access to modern ICT and those who do not. This phenomenon is usually referred to as the digital divide or the digital gap.

According to the surveys from 2005 and 2007, the digital gap in Slovakia is increasing. The younger, urban, more educated and wealthier segments of the population are continuing to improve their computer skills rapidly; on the other hand, the older, rural, less educated and poorer segments are increasingly lagging behind, although they also made progress during the specified period. People with low or no digital literacy are not only less motivated to improve their computer skills, but they have significantly worse access to modern ICT. From the socio-demographic viewpoint, digital literacy is strongly influenced by education status. Higher educational attainment in combination with well-paid jobs and wealthier households are associated with higher digital literacy.

What are the basic differences between Slovak women and men in terms of digital literacy? Gender does not play a very strong role. As Graph 4.5 shows, the digital literacy of women and men increased between 2005 and 2007. On the other hand, the progress of women was slightly less rapid than that of men. While the digital literacy index among women increased from 0.30 to 0.33, among men it grew from 0.32 to 0.37.

Graph 4.5
Index of digital literacy of women and men (average evaluation)

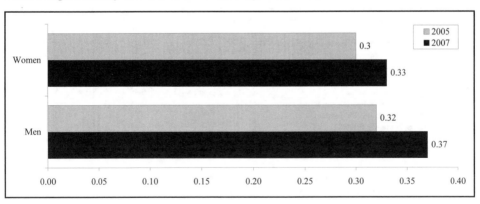

Note: Average grades on a scale from 0 (digital illiteracy) to 1 (full digital literacy).
Source: Institute for Public Affairs, July 2005 and August 2007.

These findings undermine the stereotypical notion that men are technically oriented and skilled, unlike women who are traditionally viewed as detesting anything technical. Table 4.2

---

[1]   Digital literacy is a relatively complex phenomenon that may be effectively measured by a synthesizing indicator called a digital literacy index. The index comprises 27 partial indicators that measure the population's ability to use modern information and communication technologies, applications and services. In two surveys carried out by the Institute for Public Affairs in 2005 and 2007, respondents were asked to rate their computer knowledge and skills on a scale of 1 ("I have an excellent command") to 5 ("I have no command"). The indicators are divided into four basic segments: operating hardware; operating software; working with information in a virtual space; communicating with information and communication technologies. They represent partial indexes that are combined to calculate a total index expressing an overall level of digital literacy. The figures are presented on a scale ranging from 0 (digital illiteracy) to 1 (full digital literacy). For more details see Velšic, 2005 and 2007.

illustrates that women can compete with men in most computer skills, for instance working with a personal computer, printing documents, working with a word processor, a table processor or a database software, using an Internet browser, sending and receiving e-mails, using various on-line services, chatting via the Internet and mobile communication. What sets men apart from women are more sophisticated skills such as working with a portable computer, installing various hardware and software applications, working with computer graphics and multimedia or using databases, archives and so on.

Table 4.2
Skills of women and men in working with various information technologies (average evaluation)

	Women	Men
Working with a personal computer (PC)	0.45	0.44
Working with a portable/pocket PC	0.25	0.33
Printing documents on a PC printer	0.43	0.43
Working with a scanner	0.28	0.33
Recording of data on a medium (CD-R, USB memory stick, diskette, etc.)	0.32	0.39
Installing of peripheral devices (printers, scanners, mouse, etc.)	0.23	0.35
Transferring/copying data or files in LAN (Local Area Network)	0.24	0.29
Working with a word processor	0.44	0.42
Working with a table processor	0.35	0.35
Working with a database software	0.23	0.24
Working with a graphics software	0.24	0.30
Working with a multimedia software	0.24	0.32
Working with an Internet browser	0.32	0.37
Installing software to a PC and setting their basic functions	0.21	0.32
Searching for various information and services on the Internet	0.42	0.43
Registering to access information and services on the Internet	0.36	0.39
Using internet banking – banking services via the Internet	0.23	0.25
Shopping for goods or services via the Internet (e-Shopping)	0.23	0.26
Searching for various information in LAN	0.21	0.25
Searching for various information stored in databases and archives	0.26	0.32
Downloading various files and data to a PC from the Internet	0.25	0.34
Sending and receiving e-mails	0.45	0.44
Participating in discussion forums on the Internet	0.25	0.30
Making phone calls from a cellular phone	0.79	0.78
Making phone calls via the Internet	0.27	0.31
Sending messages (SMS, MMS or e-mails) from a cellular phone	0.73	0.69
Chatting via the Internet	0.31	0.34

Note: Average grades on a scale from 0 (digital illiteracy) to 1 (full digital literacy).
Source: Institute for Public Affairs, August 2007.

Let us now examine the differences within both gender groups as determined by age, education and type of economic activity. As Table 4.3 indicates, digital literacy declines rapidly with increasing age among women as well as among men. For instance, the digital literacy index of women between 18 and 24 was 0.49, among women between 55 and 64 it was 0.14, and among women over 65 it was only 0.02, which means virtual digital illiteracy. An important gender difference is that the digital literacy index of men under 45 is substantially higher (0.52) than that of the same category of women (0.45). After the age of 45, the digital literacy of women levels out with that of men (0.20 and 0.23, respectively).

Digital literacy also increases hand in hand with education. For instance, the digital literacy index of people with only elementary education was 0.20 while among people with university education it reached 0.65. Women lag behind men at the level of elementary education, as well as secondary education without A levels, but they catch up with men at the level of complete secondary and university education. At the level of elementary education, the digital literacy index was 0.24 for men and 0.13 for women; at the level of university education, women had almost closed the gap with men as the digital literacy index was 0.67 for men and 0.63 for women.

Similar differences can be observed between women and men with the same type of profession. For instance, among blue-collar workers, the digital literacy index was 0.26 for men and 0.19 for women; among people in intellectual professions it was 0.69 for men and 0.61 for women; among entrepreneurs and tradespersons it was 0.54 vs. 0.51; among students it was 0.73 vs. 0.60; among the unemployed it was 0.27 vs. 0.24; and among pensioners it was 0.07 vs. 0.06.

Digital literacy is strongly affected by the frequency of using computers and the Internet. Here, the surveys established relatively significant differences between women and men of different ages. As many as 60% of men, but only 41% of women between 18 and 24 use PCs on an everyday basis. The ratio is reversed in the next age group, 25 – 34, where everyday use of PCs was common among 53% of women but only 48% of men. Though shrinking, the ratio remains in favor of women until the 45 – 54 age group; after that, it flips back and increases in favor of men.

It is interesting that women with secondary and university education use PCs more than their male counterparts. In the category of people with secondary education, PCs are used on an everyday basis by 48% of men and 51% of women; among people with university education the ratio is 74% to 78%, respectively.

Men are slightly more often using the Internet. This is true particularly of the 18 – 24 age group, where everyday use of the Internet was declared by 49% of men, but only 39% of women. As in the case of PC use, women catch up with men in the next age group (25 – 34), but immediately after that fall behind men again.

A survey from 2005 revealed that women between 24 and 55 years of age attach greater importance to the role of modern ICT in everyday life than their male counterparts. For instance, 69% of women but only 62% of men between 25 and 34 acknowledged the importance of modern ICT in their life. Among women and men, the share of those who consider ICT important in their everyday life declines rapidly after they reach the age of 55.

Table 4.3

Index of digital literacy of women and men by age and education (average evaluation)

		Women	Men
Age	18 – 24	0.49	0.68
	25 – 34	0.49	0.49
	35 – 44	0.34	0.40
	45 – 54	0.25	0.30
	55 – 64	0.14	0.16
	Over 65	0.02	0.03
Education	Elementary	0.13	0.24
	Secondary without A levels	0.14	0.24
	Complete secondary	0.46	0.52
	University	0.63	0.67

Note: Average grades on a scale from 0 (digital illiteracy) to 1 (full digital literacy).
Source: Institute for Public Affairs, August 2007.

Table 4.4

Daily computer use among women and men by age and education (%)

		Women	Men
Age	18 – 24	41	60
	25 – 34	53	48
	35 – 44	39	36
	45 – 54	32	31
	55 – 64	13	15
	Over 65	0	4
Education	Elementary	11	21
	Secondary without A levels	10	22
	Complete secondary	51	48
	University	78	74

Source: Institute for Public Affairs, August 2007.

The more educated people are, the greater their appreciation of modern ICT. At the same time, the importance of ICT was acknowledged by 88% of women with university education but only 83% of their male counterparts. Female entrepreneurs and tradespersons were also more likely to acknowledge the importance of ICT (83% of women and 66% of men) than female blue-collar workers (35% vs. 31%) and unemployed women (27% vs. 20%).

The greater importance women tend to attach to information technologies stems from the fact that they are more closely tied to women's qualifications and professional careers. In comparison to men, women tend to put greater emphasis on the importance of ICT in areas such as career and employment as well as study and education (see Graph 4.6). They also more often appreciate ICT when searching for information and services and communicating with institutions and authorities. Men, for their part, more frequently emphasize the role of ICT in entertainment and relaxation and in the everyday life of the household.

Graph 4.6
Importance of information technologies in various fields of life (% of affirmative answers)

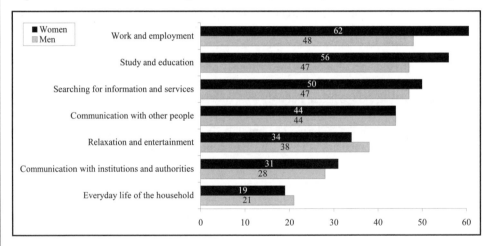

Source: Institute for Public Affairs, July 2005.

ICT is important particularly to women between 25 and 54. Sixty eight percent of women but only 51% of men between 25 and 34 emphasized the importance of ICT for their work and careers. Among respondents between 35 and 44, this opinion was shared by 75% of women and 55% of men; finally, in the 44 – 54 age group the share was 58% among women and 52% among men. After women and men reach the age of 55, the share of those who appreciate the importance of ICT falls below 30%.

The survey also showed that the attitude of women and men to ICT is closely related to their overall ability to adapt to modern technologies. According to Table 4.5 there were no significant differences between groups of women and men. However, the adaptability of women and men tends to decrease with the increasing age. Generally speaking, the pattern of the previous findings applies here as well, as women between 25 and 54 are better than men from the same age groups at adapting and learning to operate modern ICT. Table 4.5 also indicates that women as well as men experience serious problems with adaptability after they reach the age of 55.

Table 4.5
"How do you adapt to and learn to work with information technologies?" (% of answers "easily" : "with difficulty" : "I don't adapt" – by age)

	Views of women	Views of men
18 – 24	75 : 16 : 9	82 : 12 : 7
25 – 34	59 : 20 : 19	55 : 20 : 24
35 – 44	50 : 25 : 24	45 : 31 : 23
45 – 54	39 : 29 : 32	32 : 32 : 35
55 – 64	12 : 20 : 67	14 : 19 : 67
Over 65	2 : 8 : 90	3 : 8 : 88
Total	**43 : 21 : 36**	**40 : 22 : 38**

Note: The remainder of the 100% figure comprises the answer "I don't know".
Source: Institute for Public Affairs, July 2005.

As Graph 4.7 shows, women feel greater social pressure to learn how to use modern ICT and broaden their knowledge and skills (45% of women and 34% of men, respectively). The main reason is higher expectations that face women on the labor market.

Graph 4.7
"Have you ever experienced a situation in which you were forced to learn how to use information technologies or broaden your knowledge and skills?" (%)

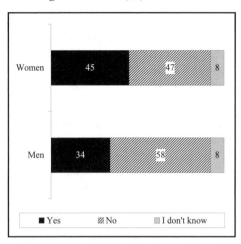

Source: Institute for Public Affairs, July 2005.

In recent years, Slovakia's labor market has witnessed expansion of new information and communication technologies. The ubiquitous presence of foreign or international companies combined with informatization of labor processes are strengthening demand for qualified workers with a command of foreign languages and computer skills.

Women feel this pressure more than men (18% vs. 11%), particularly when applying for jobs and commencing new employment. But women and men are also expected to improve their digital literacy within their existing jobs, whether due to modernization (e.g. introducing new software, hardware or technologies) or promotion. Forty-five percent of female respondents claimed they have been forced to adapt to a new job description. It is also important to note that stricter requirements in terms of digital literacy concern especially employed women and men over 45. This applies to both women and men: 61% of them claimed they have been forced to learn how to use new information technologies at work.

Our analysis also showed that digital literacy is a competitive advantage particularly for younger female job applicants. Thirty-two

Graph 4.8
"Have you personally experienced a situation in which skills with a PC and the Internet helped you get a job?" (% of affirmative answers)

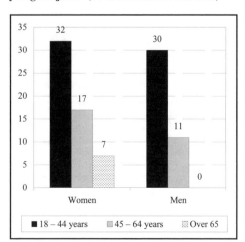

Note: The remainder of the 100% figure comprises the answers "no" and "I don't know".
Source: Institute for Public Affairs, July 2005.

percent of women between 18 and 44 but only 17% of women between 45 and 64 managed to get a job based on their command of ICT. As Graph 4.8 indicates, women stand a slightly better chance of success than their male counterparts of the same age.

Even more interesting is the situation in which people fail to get a job due to their digital illiteracy; 11% of female respondents and 9% of male respondents reported this kind of experience. Digital illiteracy was the main reason for not getting a job for 13% of women and 9% of men in intellectual professions, for 8% of female and 11% of male entrepreneurs and tradespersons and even for 12% of women and 10% of men in blue-collar professions. This shows that requirements regarding digital literacy now affect all job applicants across the labor market spectrum.

One of the main reasons why women feel greater pressure to improve their digital literacy than men is the different make-up of their professions and job positions, which require from them greater flexibility and adaptability in using information technologies. While men dominate in the field of manual labor, as they make up 86.1% of all craftsmen and qualified producers, women prevail in the administrative professions (67.9% of women compared to 32.1% of men) as well as among technical, medical and pedagogical professionals (58.3% vs. 41.7%) and scientists and intellectual workers (58.3% vs. 41.7%).

How do women and men perceive their digital literacy in the near future? In general, women feel a slightly stronger motivation (54%) to learn and acquire new skills in the field of ICT compared to men (48%). As many as 73% of women under 45 but 38% of women over 45 were interested in improving their skills in the field of ICT; still, women from both age categories showed greater determination than their male counterparts (70% of men under 45 : 31% of men over 45).

People's willingness to improve their digital literacy increases with their educational attainment. For instance, 85% of women and 82% of men with university degrees said they were planning to improve their command of

Graph 4.9
"Regardless of your skills in the field of modern information technologies, are you planning to improve your skills or learn new things in the near future?" (% of affirmative answers)

Table 4.6
"Regardless of your skills in the field of modern information technologies, are you planning to improve your skills or learn new things in the near future?" (% of answers "yes" : "no")

		Women	Men
Age	18 – 24	83 : 14	83 : 14
	25 – 34	79 : 15	65 : 32
	35 – 44	59 : 34	63 : 31
	45 – 54	53 : 41	43 : 51
	55 – 64	18 : 78	17 : 84
Education	Elementary	29 : 64	23 : 72
	Secondary without A levels	39 : 57	39 : 58
	Complete secondary	71 : 24	69 : 27
	University	85 : 11	82 : 17
Total		54 : 41	48 : 48

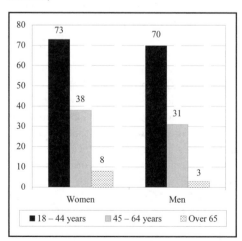

Note: The remainder of the 100% figure comprises the answer "I don't know".
Source: Institute for Public Affairs, July 2005.

Note: The remainder of the 100% figure comprises the answers "no" and "I don't know".
Source: Institute for Public Affairs, July 2005.

ICT. Women showed greater determination than men also in the category with complete secondary education (71% vs. 69%), among people with elementary education (29% vs. 23%) and even among the unemployed (44% vs. 38%).

Let us summarize. According to survey data, the gender stereotypes that claim that men have stronger ties to modern information technologies than women are unfounded. It is true that the youngest men between 18 and 24 are slightly more advanced than their female counterparts in terms of overall digital literacy or the frequency with which they use computers and the Internet. However, the balance tips in favor of women in the higher age categories, particularly at the age when women begin to enter the labor market and launch their professional careers. The surveys confirmed that work and employment as well as study and education constitute a powerful engine that propels women towards greater adaptability and improved skills in the field of modern information technologies. For most women, a solid command of computers, the Internet and mobile communication is becoming an important prerequisite to success on the labor market, as well as in everyday life.

4.1.3. ECONOMIC ACTIVITY OF WOMEN AND MEN

Development of the Economically Active Population

Since the beginning of the 1990s, the ratio of people in their productive years to the total population of Slovakia (and, consequently, the total number of economically active people) has increased. In 2007, economically active population in Slovakia reached 2,649,200 people (1,465,100 men and 1,184,100 women). The number of economically inactive persons outside the labor market was 1,859,800 (699,800 men and 1,160,000 women). This latter figure was made up mostly of pensioners (1,038,800), students and apprentices (522,300) and household members (125,500), as well as persons on maternity or parental leave (64,500), people unfit for work (64,300), people who had abandoned the labor market (15,300) and other economically inactive persons (29,100).

Since the mid-1990s, the rate of economic activity in Slovakia has stabilized at around 60%, and in recent years has shown signs of a moderate decline (see Table 4.7). There is a significant difference between the rate of economic activity of women and men; in 2007, it was 50.5% for women and 67.7% for men. In other words, there were almost 51 economically active women per 100 women older than 15, and 68 economically active men per 100 men older than 15.

Compared to 1993, the overall rate of economic activity of the Slovak population has decreased. The decline recorded among women was slightly more substantial (by 3.9%) than among men (by 2.8%).

Table 4.7
Rate of economic activity of women and men (1993 and 2007 – in %)

	1993	1995	1997	1999	2001	2002	2003	2004	2005	2006	2007
Women	54.4	51.5	51.8	52.0	53.0	52.6	52.9	52.5	51.3	50.7	50.5
Men	70.5	68.9	68.6	68.7	69.2	68.5	68.4	68.5	68.4	68.2	67.7
Total	62.1	59.8	59.9	60.0	60.7	60.2	60.3	60.2	59.5	59.1	58.8

Note: Rate of economic activity = percentage of economically active persons (i.e. employed and unemployed) in the total number of inhabitants in their productive and post-productive years (i.e. older than 15).
Source: *Štatistické...*, 1994 – 2005; *Slovstat*, 2008.

Structure of Economically Inactive Women and Men

Let us now examine what categories of women and men drain the most from Slovakia's total labor force. Table 4.8 shows that the total number of economically inactive men increased from 617,600 in 1995 to 699,900 in 2007 (or by 82,300), while the total number of economically inactive women increased from 1,042,200 to 1,160,000 (or by 117,800) over the same period. The number of economically inactive women thus grew faster than that of economically inactive men. In 2007, the difference between the two groups was almost 500,000.

Table 4.8
Structure of economically inactive women and men (1995 and 2007 – in thousands)

	Women		Men	
	1995	2007	1995	2007
Pensioners	619.4	659.7	364.8	379.2
Students	200.2	263.1	210.0	259.2
Household members (e.g. housewives)	102.8	117.1	2.4	8.4
People on maternity (parental) leave	70.2	64.4	0.9	0.2
People unfit for work	37.8	33.7	25.4	30.6
People who refuse to work or are discouraged	3.4	6.7	4.4	8.4
Participants in retraining programs	0.4	0.0	0.4	0.1
Other kinds of inactive people	8.0	15.2	9.5	13.9
Total	1,042.2	1,160.0	617.6	699.9

Source: *Slovstat*, 2008.

Table 4.8 shows that the largest group of economically inactive population was pensioners, followed by students of secondary schools and universities. In 2007, the total number of women in both of these categories was higher than that of men. There were 659,700 retired women compared to 379,200 retired men; the number of women studying at secondary schools and universities was 263,100 compared to 259,200 men.

The next two categories of economically inactive people are substantially smaller and are strongly dominated by women: people who stay at home and those who are on maternity or parental leave. In 2007, the number of housewives was 117,100 while the number of househusbands was only 8,400. In the latter category, the gender difference was even greater as there were 64,400 women but only 200 men on parental leave. This huge difference illustrates that taking care of children and household continues to be the principal domain of women.

In the remaining four categories of economically inactive people, gender differences were not so significant. The number of persons unfit for work is traditionally higher among women; in 2007 there were 33,700 such women and 30,600 such men. On the other hand, the category of people who were 'discouraged' or who had dropped out of the labor market is dominated by men (8,400 men as compared to 6,700 women). The number of people undertaking retraining programs has dropped in recent years. In 2007 there were more women than men among the group of "other inactive people"; however, in the previous period, that ratio was reversed.

These figures illustrate that women in Slovakia stay more often outside the labor market than men. Women retire earlier than men; they take more time to prepare for their professional careers; and last, bur not least, it is primarily women who take care of children and household.

Economic Activity of Women and Men of Different Age

What is the age structure of the female and male components of the Slovak labor force and how is it developing? Table 4.9 divides both women and men into two age categories – under 45 and over 45. It shows that the Slovak labor force gradually grew older between 1994 and 2007, and that this process was faster among women. While in 1994 the share of persons over 45 was higher among men, by 2007 it was higher among women. During this period, the share of the older age category increased from 23.6% to 35.2% among economically active women and from 25.4% to 34.5% among economically active men.

Let us take a closer look at the largest age groups within the female and male labor force (see Graph 4.10). In 2007, the male labor force was dominated by men at the outset of their professional careers as there were 224,400 economically active men in the 25 – 29 age group and 212,800 in the 30 – 34 age group. The number of economically active women in both of these age groups was much smaller, although the total numbers of women and men between 25 and 34 are almost equal. The highest number of economically active women was in the 40 – 44 age group (172,100), the 45 – 49 age group (171,300) and the 50 – 54 age group (169,500). In these groups, the number of economically active women and men is almost equal. The next two age groups are again dominated by men.

Table 4.9
Age structure of economically active women and men (1994 – 2007, in % of persons under 45 : over 45)

	Women	Men
1994	76.4 : 23.6	74.6 : 25.4
1995	76.0 : 24.0	74.2 : 25.8
1996	75.1 : 24.9	73.5 : 26.5
1997	74.5 : 25.5	73.4 : 26.6
1998	73.3 : 26.7	72.5 : 27.5
1999	72.7 : 27.3	72.0 : 28.0
2000	71.9 : 28.1	71.0 : 29.0
2001	70.8 : 29.2	70.0 : 30.0
2002	70.1 : 29.9	69.5 : 30.5
2003	69.5 : 30.5	69.1 : 30.9
2004	67.7 : 32.3	67.3 : 32.7
2005	65.9 : 34.1	66.2 : 33.8
2006	65.3 : 34.7	65.7 : 34.3
2007	64.8 : 35.2	65.5 : 34.5

Source: *Slovstat*, 2008.

Graph 4.10
Number of economically active women and men by age (2007 – in thousands)

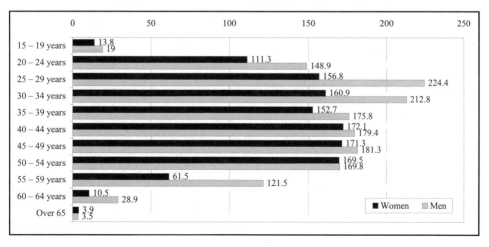

Source: *Slovstat*, 2008.

What causes these differences in the number of economically active women and men? One reason is the different course of their professional careers that may be illustrated by comparing the total number of women and men to the number of employed women and men at five-year age intervals (see Graph 4.11). Most of men enter the labor market at the age of 25 – 29. It is also the age interval in which the difference between the economic activity of women and men is the greatest. While the total number of women and men in this age group is virtually the same (approximately 230,000), there were 203,000 employed men but only 135,000 employed women in this age group in 2007. After the age of 29, the number of employed men declines slightly, and between the ages of 35 and 49 it settles at just above 160,000. After the age of 50, the number of employed men falls again, first moderately and then rapidly after the age of 55. Nevertheless, the number of employed men more or less copies the total number of men in the various age groups.

Graph 4.11
Number of women and men, employed women and men by age (2007 – in thousands)

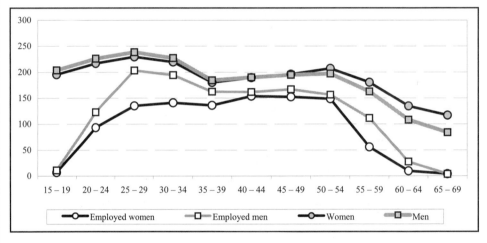

Source: *Slovstat*, 2008.

In the female population, the number of employed women in various age groups is not so closely tied to the total number of women. The correlation between the number of employed women and the total number of women is weak especially in the 25 – 39 age group and then again between 50 and 64.

Thus the gap between employed women and men widens twice: at the beginning of their professional careers and at their end. The difference in the number of employed women and men toward the end of their professional careers is mostly the result of the different retirement ages for women and men. The gradual equalization of the retirement ages should reduce the differences in the number of employed women and men, unless other factors appear to prevent women older than 50 from actively participating on the labor market. The difference in the number of employed women and men at the beginning of their professional careers is caused by the greater role that women play in taking care of children, as many women at this age interrupt their professional careers due to their maternal obligations. The numbers of employed women and men do not level off until the age of 40 – 44.

There are thus two principal ways in which people participate on the labor market: the male model, which is characterized by a continuous professional career, and the female model of an interrupted career. The interrupted professional careers of women take on various forms depending on the length of the interruptions, their frequency, the women's age, etc. Moreover, not all women choose to interrupt their careers.[2] Analyses of the participation of women on the labor market indicate that interrupting a career – particularly if the break is repeated or long-term in nature – brings multiple disadvantages to women. Their chances of investing time and energy into their careers are limited, which is subsequently reflected in a lower "payback of investments", whether in the form of a lower wage, a slower promotion, the loss of work skills or stagnation in qualifications. On the other hand, people with uninterrupted professional careers do not have to cope with these problems.

The representation of employed women and men in labor force becomes equal only in the age category 40 – 44, when a large group of middle aged women come back to the labor market upon completing their maternity leave. If the interruption is long, this return can be complicated and the women can be forced into marginal or otherwise disadvantaged segments of the labor market, such as worse paid jobs that require lower education.

Due to the gradual increase in the retirement age of women, the time that women spend at work upon their return to the labor market will increase. It can be expected that the shortage of quality job opportunities for women in their mature years will become an even more pressing problem than today.

Graph 4.12 enables a closer look at the differences in the number of economically active women and men, as it divides both groups into five-year age intervals and allows comparing the make-up of women and men according to basic categories of the labor market. It shows that there are no fundamental differences in the total number of women and men in particular age groups. The only exceptions are the two oldest age groups, which are dominated by women. However, from the viewpoint of economic activity – i.e. the ratio of employed, un-

Graph 4.12
Economically active (i.e. employed and unemployed) and inactive women and men by age (2007 – in thousands)

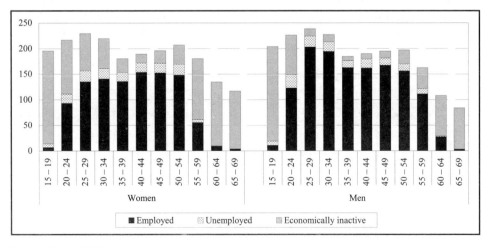

Source: *Slovstat*, 2008.

---

2 For more details on women's participation on the labor market, see also Sirovátka, 2003.

employed and economically inactive persons – the make-up of most age groups of women and men is fundamentally different. The only exception is the 15 – 19 age group, in which the structure of women and men is very similar. It is characterized by a very large share of students and a very low share of employed, as well as unemployed.

A major gender difference shows up in the age group of 20 – 24 year olds, in which the portion of economically active persons is substantially higher among men than among women. About one third of men (mostly students) remain outside the labor market, compared to one half of women (students as well as women on maternity leave and housewives).

The gender gap remains wide in the 25 – 29 and 30 – 34 age groups as well. The share of economically inactive persons in the former age group is only 6% among men but 32% among women; in the latter age group, the share of economically inactive men remains 6% while the share of inactive women falls to 27%. Most of these women are on maternity leave or are housewives whose professional career has been interrupted or postponed.

A similar gender gap, albeit a little smaller, persists also in the age group of 35 – 39: the share of economically inactive persons is still significantly higher among women than among men (15% and 5%, respectively). In the next three age groups between the ages of 40 and 54, the structure of women and men is almost identical, as both groups consist mainly of economically active persons. Still, the share of economically inactive women remains slightly higher than that of men, and includes mostly women on maternity leave, housewives as well as some pensioners.

Between the ages of 55 and 59, the gender gap grows wider again; only 25% of men but 66% of women are now economically inactive, mostly because women retire earlier. In the oldest age group, the gender gap closes once again as pensioners prevail among both women and men.

A closer picture of the make-up of economically inactive women and men by age can only be provided by representative surveys because regular statistical publications and public databases do not feature more detailed breakdowns of data. Table 4.10 summarizes the findings of such a representative survey carried out in 2006 by the Institute for Public Affairs. It illustrates an equal representation of economically inactive women and men in the youngest and the oldest age groups, as well as higher representation of economically inactive women

Table 4.10
Age structure of economically inactive women and men (2006 – in %)

Age group	Women				Men			
	Students	At home	Parental leave	Pensioners	Students	At home	Parental leave	Pensioners
15 – 19	92	1	2	0	95	0	0	1
20 – 24	26	0	15	0	32	0	0	2
25 – 29	3	0	22	0	3	0	2	0
30 – 34	0	2	25	0	0	0	0	4
35 – 39	0	4	10	1	0	0	0	2
40 – 44	0	1	7	4	0	0	0	6
45 – 49	0	0	0	3	0	0	0	5
50 – 54	0	0	0	16	0	0	0	13
55 – 59	0	1	0	67	0	2	0	29
60 – 64	0	0	0	100	0	0	0	97
Over 65	0	0	0	100	0	0	0	100

Note: The remainder of the 100% figure comprises employed and unemployed persons.
Source: Institute for Public Affairs, August 2006.

in the middle age groups. It also shows that women more frequently take parental leave or stay home as housewives.

The data in Table 4.10 also document a correlation between particular types of economic inactivity and the life cycle. While studying at secondary school and universities is limited almost exclusively to the two youngest age groups, other types of economic inactivity occur across broader age intervals. For instance, the status of pensioner is associated mostly with older age groups (starting between 55 and 59 for women and between 60 and 64 for men) but it also shows up in the middle and even younger age brackets (e.g. those on disability pensions). Although parental leave is typical of women between 25 and 34, it is not limited to this interval, and occurs in as many as six age groups, i.e. between 15 and 44, a span of almost three decades.

The distribution of reasons for economic inactivity across the broader age spectrum indicates a departure from a strictly linear sequence of life events and a shift toward more individual life courses. This trend has been noted by a number of foreign as well as domestic experts.[3] They observe that whereas the life of most individuals used to take place as a more or less linear succession of stages (i.e. birth, education, work, matrimony, family, pension, and death), in recent decades life has taken on a more cyclic nature. Various stages and activities in the field of education, work or family are repeated over the course of a person's life. For instance, people return to education after they enter the labor market or even at a greater age; they start families much later than they used to; others re-enter marriage in their retirement or do not found a family at all; people live longer in general, etc. Life has become more complex, and the prevailingly linear sequence of life events has been replaced by alternative life cycles. People's preferred employment patterns are undergoing major changes as well. For instance, a growing number of people work and study at the same time; others combine work and care for a family; still others work for employers and for themselves at the same time, and so on (Bodnárová – Filadelfiová – Gerbery – Džambazovič – Kvapilová – Porubänová, 2004; Bodnárová – Filadelfiová – Gerbery – Džambazovič – Kvapilová, 2006).

Recently, this shift in life course has come to Slovakia as well. Young families with children are gradually ceasing to be the dominant type of household; increasing life expectancy along with a trend towards postponing childbirth has changed the concept of parenthood (Vaňo, 2003 and 2007; Filadelfiová, 2005a). This shift affects family careers, as well as professional careers. Single-career family models (i.e. the man as breadwinner and the woman as housewife) which dominated in the past have gradually become minority models. In recent years, the model of the successful professional career is undergoing changes, too (from one type of profession or work for one employer towards a pattern of switching employers or even fields of work).

This new cyclical life course provides women and men with constant opportunities to change or revive their professional or family careers: to interrupt a professional career and return to it later; to start a career in one's middle age or even one's mature years; to choose a flexible working time; to migrate, etc. Some women and men choose such change voluntarily, while others are forced to do so by various events at the individual, communal or national level, such as the death or illness of a family member, the birth of a child, the loss of a job, or trans-

---

[3] These include among others experts from the International Labor Organization (ILO) Alejandro Bonilla Garcia and Jean Victor Gruat, German authors Walter R. Heinz, Helga Krüger and Ulrich Beck, Dutch authors Marc van der Meer and Frans Leijnse, Polish sociologist Zygmunt Bauman or his Czech colleague Jan Keller, etc. In Slovakia, these trends were highlighted in a publication by Daniel Gerbery, Ivan Lesay and Daniel Škobla from 2007.

formation within society. Every new life cycle brings new opportunities as well as new risks to individuals and members of their families (Filadelfiová, 2007).

4.1.4. EMPLOYMENT OF WOMEN AND MEN

In Slovakia, the total number of employed women has been lower than that of employed men. Also, the employment rate of women is substantially lower and follows a different course. As Graph 4.13 shows, the employment of men reached bottom in 2000 and 2001 and has increased by 7% since then. The employment of women was the lowest in 2004 and 2005, and only in the last two years has it increased moderately by 2%. In 2007, the employment rate was 68.4% for men and 53.1% for women. So an increase in overall employment has been accompanied by a widening of the gender gap in employment, which in 2007 reached 15% – the same as in the mid-1990s.

Graph 4.13
Employment rate of women and men (1994 – 2007, in %)

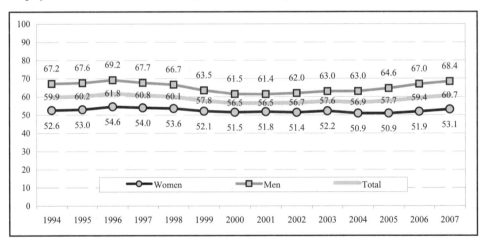

Note: Employment rate according to methodology used by labor force surveys.
Source: *Slovstat*, 2008.

Graph 4.13 shows that overall employment in Slovakia exceeded 60% in 2007 for the first time in nine years, matching the level from 1997. Despite this improvement, Slovakia continues to fall short of the goals set by the *Lisbon Strategy* for EU member states: to increase overall employment to 70% and the employment of women to 60% by 2010 (*The Lisbon...*, 2000).

Gender Differences in Employment by Education

There is a strong correlation between the employment rate and education status. By far the lowest employment rate is traditionally recorded among women and men with elementary education. According to Graph 4.14, only 8.6% of women and 11.2% of men with elementary education were employed in 2007. There are several reasons of it: first, many young people over 15 continue to study; second, some of those young people who are not studying

any more start their professional career as unemployed; third, people with elementary education mostly belong to the older age groups and are already retired.

Graph 4.14
Employment rate of women and men by education (2007 – in %)

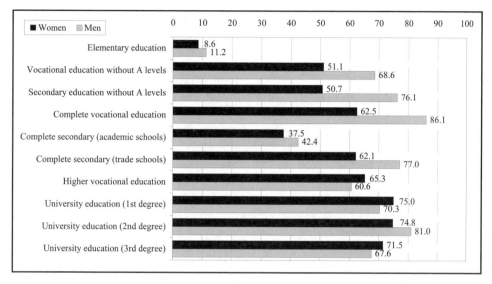

Note: Employment rate according to methodology used by labor force surveys.
Source: *Slovstat*, 2008.

The greatest difference was in the employment rates of women and men with vocational education and secondary education without A levels. Generally speaking, the employment rate
for men is substantially higher in all categories of secondary education. The only exception
is general secondary education where the difference between women and men is relatively
small and the employment rate in both groups is relatively low. The main reason is that most
graduates of secondary academic schools continue to study at universities. In the categories
of higher vocational and university education, the employment rates of women either match
or even exceed those of men.

Gender Differences in Employment by Age

In all age groups, there are differences in the employment rate of women and men. As Table
4.11 shows, the greatest differences in 2007 were recorded in the 25 – 29 (by 26.2%) and 30
– 34 (by 22.0%) age groups, as well as in the 55 – 59 (by 38.8%) and 60 – 64 (by 18.7%) age
groups.

Table 4.11 also illustrates the different course that the employment rate follows among women
and men of different ages. While the employment rate of men remains at very high levels from
the age of 25 to the age of 59, the interval of high employment of women is significantly
shorter, spanning the ages of 40 and 54. Among men, the highest employment rate in 2007
was in the 30 – 34 and 35 – 39 age groups (87.4% and 88.5%, respectively); among women,
it was in the 40 – 44 age group (80.8%) as well as in both adjacent age groups (75.6% and
76.8%, respectively). The greatest gender differences were in the 25 – 34 and 55 – 64 age

Table 4.11
Employment rate of women and men by age (1995 and 2007 – in %)

Age group	Women		Men	
	1995	2007	1995	2007
15 – 19	14.7	3.5	13.0	5.3
20 – 24	49.6	42.8	67.3	54.1
25 – 29	55.3	58.7	82.7	84.9
30 – 34	71.2	65.4	87.1	87.4
35 – 39	76.8	75.6	86.9	88.5
40 – 44	82.7	80.8	85.9	84.6
45 – 49	81.1	76.8	87.6	84.9
50 – 54	61.6	71.9	80.4	79.6
55 – 59	12.7	31.9	63.0	70.7
60 – 64	3.8	7.1	12.2	25.8
Over 65	0.9	1.0	2.8	1.5
Total	53.0	53.1	67.6	68.4

Note: Employment rate according to methodology used by labor force surveys.
Source: *Slovstat,* 2008.

groups. This indicates that the greatest obstacles to the employment of women are their maternal obligations and the parameters of the previous pension system, which allowed women to retire earlier than men.[4]

Data in Table 4.11 also reveal another important trend: the employment of women and men from the two youngest age groups has declined in recent years. This is not only the result of people's longer preparation for their careers, but probably also the result of voluntary and involuntary unemployment of young people.[5] In the middle age groups, no important trends were seen.

The employment rate grew the fastest in the older age groups. Between 1995 and 2007, the employment of women increased by 10.3% in the 50 – 54 age group, by 19.2% in the 55 – 59 age group and by 3.3% in the 60 – 64 age group. Among men, the employment rate increased by 7.7% in the 55 – 59 age group and by 13.6% in the 60 – 64 age group. The overall growth in the employment rate in recent years was thus caused primarily by higher employment among older people, particularly women.

A similar trend is visible also in the employment rate of broader age groups of women and men. Table 4.12 shows that the employment rate of women between 15 and 24 declined from 32.1% in 1998 to 22.5% in 2006, while the employment rate of women between 55 and 64 increased from 9.4% to 18.9%. The employment rate of the middle generation of women fluctuated around 70% throughout that period. The employment rate of the middle generation of men in 2006 (84.1%) was similar to that in 1998 (84.9%).

Table 4.12
Employment rate of women and men by broader age groups (1998 – 2007, in %)

Age group		1998	1999	2000	2001	2002	2003	2004	2005	2006
15 – 24	Women	32.1	29.0	28.2	26.5	25.3	25.4	24.6	23.1	22.5
	Men	38.0	32.9	29.8	28.9	28.7	29.3	28.0	28.1	29.2
25 – 54	Women	72.1	70.6	69.8	70.7	70.6	71.5	69.3	69.2	70.2
	Men	84.9	81.7	79.6	79.0	79.5	80.5	80.0	81.4	84.1
55 – 64	Women	9.4	10.3	9.8	9.8	9.5	11.2	12.6	15.6	18.9
	Men	39.1	36.8	35.4	37.7	39.1	41.0	43.8	47.8	49.8

Note: Employment rate according to methodology used by labor force surveys.
Source: *Employment in…,* 2007.

As we see, the overall growth in employment that Slovakia recorded in recent years is primarily the result of higher employment among women in higher age brackets, which is probably related to the gradual increase in the retirement age of women. Despite the improvement,

---

[4] Currently, the retirement age for women and men is being gradually equalized. By 2013, the country should reach a single retirement age of 62 years for women and men.
[5] Many young people who work abroad or study part time at universities have the status of voluntarily unemployed people in Slovakia.

though, the enormous gender gap has remained virtually unchanged at around 30%. In 2007, the employment rate of women between 55 and 64 was 18.9% while among their male counterparts it was 49.8%.

Besides the general factors influencing the labor market (e.g. unemployment, wages), the decision of women to retire or remain at work is also affected by the specific institutions of pension system (McNay, 2003; Bertola – Blau – Kahn, 2002), i.e. by formal retirement age of women, as well as by basic parameters of social protection for elderly people (i.e. rules affecting the amount of disbursed pensions, the legal conditions for early retirement, the number and structure of the pensions system's pillars, etc.). Finally, the retirement strategies of women between 55 and 64 may also be affected by the past decisions they made between the ages of 25 and 54 (e.g. how long they stayed home with their children, when did they return to work, whether they preferred a job in the neighborhood, etc.).

Let us now put the employment of Slovak women between 55 and 64 into the international context. Despite the recent growth in their economic activity, they trail their counterparts from most EU member states, as their employment rate of 18.9% is the third lowest in the EU. In 2006, the highest participation of women between 55 and 64 on the labor market was in Sweden (66.9%), Denmark (54.3%), Finland (54.3%) and Great Britain (49.1%). The EU-27 average was 34.9%. Even in the neighboring Czech Republic, the employment rate of women between 55 and 64 was substantially higher than in Slovakia, at 32.1%. As of 2006, Slovak women fell 31 percentage points short of meeting the goal set by the *Lisbon Strategy* to increase the employment of persons between 55 and 64 in EU member states to 50% by 2010 (*The Lisbon...*, 2000).

Graph 4.15
Employment rate of persons 55 – 64 in Slovakia and in EU member states (2006 – in %)

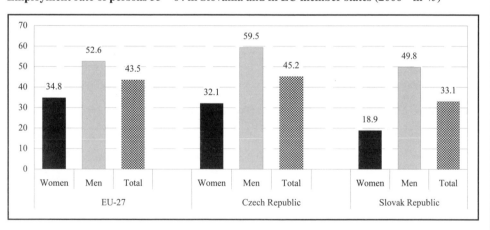

Source: *Employment in...*, 2007.

4.1.5. GENDER SEGREGATION ON THE LABOR MARKET

Comparative surveys examining the status of women and men on the labor market have noted the advanced feminization of many professions, and suggest a link between jobs dominated by women and between low pay and worse opportunities, whether in terms of promotion possibilities or further education.[6] In Slovakia, statistics from the end of the 20th and the beginning of the 21st centuries document lingering and even deepening gender segregation on both the horizontal and vertical axes.

Women and Men Employed in Public and Private Sectors

The gender make-up of employed in the private sector differs from that of employed in the public sector (see Table 4.13). From the outset, the private sector, which re-emerged in Slovakia at the beginning of the 1990s, offered better job opportunities to men. In 1995, the share of women employed within the private sector was only 34.1%, while in the public sector it reached 52.3%.

Table 4.13
Women and men employed in public and private sectors (1995 – 2006, in thousands and %)

	1995	1996	1997	1998	1999	2000	2001	2002	2003	2004	2005	2006
Employed in the public sector												
Women	454.0	414.4	576.5	541.8	524.6	518.6	513.1	468.8	448.6	429.6	413.9	390.1
Men	413.8	366.4	591.8	554.9	527.7	507.9	466.5	424.9	401.6	367.9	340.5	308.2
Total	867.8	780.8	1,168.3	1,096.7	1,052.3	1,026.5	979.6	893.7	850.2	797.5	754.4	698.3
Women (%)	52.3	53.1	49.3	49.4	49.9	50.5	52.4	52.5	52.8	53.9	54.9	55.9
Employed in the private sector												
Women	436.4	457.3	412.4	446.4	443.8	445.8	464.7	501.2	538.9	547.1	569.2	620.2
Men	842.6	878.5	625.2	655.5	636.0	629.4	679.3	731.9	775.7	825.8	892.6	982.9
Total	1,279.0	1,335.8	1,037.6	1,101.9	1,079.8	1,075.2	1,144.0	1,233.1	1,314.4	1,372.9	1,461.8	1,603.1
Women (%)	34.1	34.2	39.7	40.5	41.1	41.5	40.6	40.6	41.0	39.8	38.9	38.7

Source: *Štatistické...*, 1995 – 2007.

Although the overall number of women employed within the private sector gradually increased, by 2006 they still made up only 38.7% of all employees. On the other hand, women strengthened their long-term dominance in the public sector. In 2006, they made up 55.9% of all employees.

Graph 4.16
Self-employed women and men in Slovakia (2006 – in thousands)

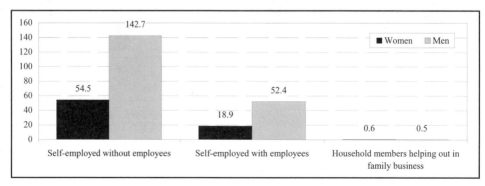

Source: *Štatistická...*, 2007.

---

6 For instance, *The Social...*, 2004; *The Story...*, 2006; or *Working Conditions and Gender...*, 2005; etc.

The gender gap is even greater in the category of self-employed, i.e. the owners of small businesses and household members helping out in family businesses (see Graph 4.16). In 2006, women made up 25.6% of all self-employed. The share of women was 25.1% among business persons without employees and 26.5% among business persons employing other people. On the other hand, women prevailed in the category of household members helping out in family businesses (54%).

Table 4.14 shows that the share of self-employed men in the total number of employed men increased from 9.5% in 1998 to 17.2% in 2006. The growth of the share self-employed women in the total number of employed women was less significant (from 4.1% to 7.5%).

A comparison between Slovakia and other EU member states shows that Slovakia is below the EU average (see Table 4.14). In 2006, the share of self-employed women in Slovakia was 5.2 percentage points lower than the EU-27 average (7.5% in Slovakia compared to 12.7% in the EU-27) , while the share of self-employed men in Slovakia was only 2.5 percentage points lower (17.2% vs. 19.7%).

Table 4.14
Share of self-employed in the total number of employed in Slovakia and in EU member states (1998 – 2006, in %)

		1998	1999	2000	2001	2002	2003	2004	2005	2006
EU-27	Women	14.5	14.3	14.0	13.8	13.4	13.2	13.0	12.8	12.7
	Men	20.2	20.0	19.9	19.8	19.9	20.1	20.1	19.7	19.7
	Total	17.8	17.6	17.3	17.2	17.0	17.1	16.9	16.7	16.6
Czech Republic	Women	10.7	11.3	11.7	11.7	12.0	12.7	12.2	11.8	12.1
	Men	20.3	21.6	21.8	21.9	22.9	24.1	24.0	23.1	22.5
	Total	16.1	17.1	17.4	17.4	18.1	19.1	18.8	18.2	18.0
Slovakia	Women	4.1	4.6	4.8	5.1	5.0	6.1	7.2	7.1	7.5
	Men	9.5	10.8	11.3	11.9	12.6	13.5	16.4	17.6	17.2
	Total	7.1	8.0	8.3	8.8	9.1	10.1	12.3	13.0	13.0

Source: *Employment in…*, 2007.

Women and Men Employed in Primary, Secondary and Tertiary Sectors

The structure of the economy is changing in all developed countries. The share of employed in the primary (agriculture) and secondary (industry) sectors is declining, while the share of those employed in the tertiary sector (services) is increasing. At the same time, there are usually substantial differences in the structure of women and men employed in each of these sectors. As Table 4.15 documents, Slovakia is no exception.

Table 4.15
Women and men employed in agriculture, industry and services (1998 – 2006, in % of total employment)

		1998	1999	2000	2001	2002	2003	2004	2005	2006
Agriculture	Women	4.6	3.8	3.3	3.2	3.2	2.6	2.4	2.0	1.9
	Men	9.0	8.2	7.6	7.2	6.6	6.1	6.1	5.1	5.0
Industry	Women	25.5	24.7	24.1	23.5	23.3	23.3	23.3	22.1	21.7
	Men	46.6	45.8	44.7	44.3	44.0	44.3	44.5	43.5	43.8
Services	Women	69.9	71.4	72.7	73.3	73.5	74.1	74.3	75.9	76.5
	Men	44.4	46.1	47.7	48.4	49.4	49.6	49.4	51.3	51.3

Source: *Employment in…*, 2007.

As Table 4.15 and Graph 4.17 show, the participation of women and men in the three main economic sectors varies significantly. The tertiary sector is predominantly feminine; it contains 76.5% of all employed women and 51.3 of all employed men. The secondary sector gives jobs to 21.7% of all employed women and to 43.8% of employed men. Finally, the primary sector employs only 1.9% of all employed women and 5.0% of all employed men. The trend of leaving the primary sector and drifting toward the tertiary sector affects both women and men; however, it is much stronger among women.

Nonetheless, Slovakia still lags behind the EU-27 average. According to Graph 4.17 illustrating the situation in 2006, the share of women and men employed in the tertiary sector in EU member states was 81.5% and 58.1%, respectively, while in Slovakia it was 75.5% and 51.3%.

Graph 4.17
Employment in Slovakia and EU member states in agriculture, industry and services (2006 – in %)

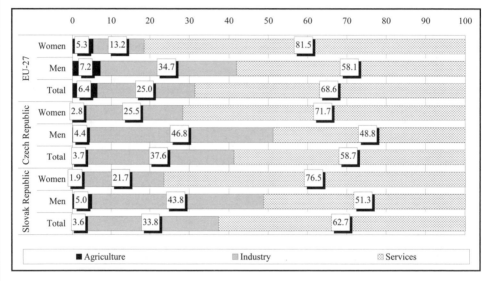

Source: *Employment in…*, 2007.

Employed Women and Men by Sector of Economic Activity

For a long time, the female and the male labor force has been unevenly distributed through individual sectors of economic activity (Filadelfiová, 2007 and 2008). In recent years, women have preserved or even strengthened their presence in sectors traditionally dominated by women. On the other hand, their representation in sectors traditionally dominated by men has declined even further (Barošová, 2006).

Table 4.16 shows that women have the strongest presence in such sectors as health and social work, (82.2% of all employed in 2007), as well as education (78.9%). Women represent a majority of employed in financial intermediation (64.1%), hotels and restaurants (63.2%) and wholesale and retail trade (56.9%). In recent years, they have also gained a majority in other public services (54.9%) and in the field of public administration and defense (50.6%). On the other hand, sectors traditionally dominated by men include construction (only 5.4% of women), mining and quarrying (5.5%), agriculture and forestry (23.5%) and transportation, storage, post and telecommunications (25.4%). In the long term, the average wage in most sectors in which women have a stronger presence is lower than the average wage in the national economy (for more details see Section 4.1.8. of this publication).

Table 4.16
Share of women in the total number of employed by sectors economic activity (1997 and 2007 – in %)

	1997	2007
Mining and quarrying	14.0	5.5
Construction	8.7	5.4
Electricity, gas and water supply	14.5	17.1
Transport, storage, post and telecommunications	30.0	25.4
Agriculture and forestry	30.6	23.5
Industry	41.3	36.4
Real estate, renting and business activities	41.7	42.8
Other community, social and personal service activities	49.0	54.9
Public administration and defense	47.9	50.6
Wholesale and retail trade	57.8	56.9
Hotels and restaurants	66.2	63.2
Financial intermediation	73.9	64.1
Health and social work	79.6	82.2
Education	80.6	78.9
Total	**44.9**	**43.9**

Source: *Slovstat*, 2008.

Employed Women and Men by Profession

Another characteristic feature of Slovakia's labor market is its vertical segregation, which means the different representation of women and men in particular types of profession.

Table 4.17
Share of women in particular types of profession (2000 and 2007 – in %)

	2000	2007
Legislators, senior officials and managers	30.8	30.9
Scientists and intellectual workers	62.1	58.3
Technical, medical and pedagogical professionals	61.2	58.3
Administrative workers (officials)	77.3	67.9
Workers in trade and services	66.5	70.1
Qualified workers in agriculture and forestry	48.7	26.4
Craftsmen and qualified producers, repairmen	19.4	13.9
Plant and machine operators	20.1	22.1
Supporting and non-qualified staff	49.7	49.4
Total	**45.9**	**43.9**

Source: *Slovstat*, 2008.

In 2007, women held less than one third (30.8%) of the best paid posts in the country, i.e. those of legislators, senior officials and managers. The low representation of women in these posts has persisted despite the significant improvement in the educational attainment of women in recent decades (see also Section 4.1.1.). This indicates that the insufficient participation of women in governing society is caused by other than educational barriers.

The representation of women is low in other professions as well, such as qualified workers in agriculture and forestry (26.4% of women), plant and machine operators (22.1%) or craftsmen, qualified producers and repairmen (13.9%).

On the other hand, women outnumber men among administrative workers, where their share exceeds two thirds (67.9%). Other highly feminized professions are workers in trade and services (70.1%), scientists and intellectual workers, as well as technical, medical and pedagogical professionals (58.3% each). The representation of women and men is most balanced among supporting and non-qualified staff (49.4%).

The overall structure of professions performed by women and men is different, too. Women are most frequently employed as technical, medical and pedagogical professionals (24.9%), as workers in trade and services (22.5%) and as scientists and intellectual workers (13.9%). Only 10.9% of women perform supporting and non-qualified jobs and 9.8% are employed as administrative workers. Female legislators, senior officials and managers make up only 3.8% of all employed women (see Graph 4.18).

The structure of employed men is dominated by craftsmen and qualified producers (28.3%), followed by plat and machinery operators (21.2%) and technical, medical and pedagogical professionals (14.0%). Other professions were performed by less than one in ten employed men; however, the share of employed men among legislators, senior officials and managers is significantly higher than that of employed women (6.7%).

Graph 4.18
Structure of employed women and men by profession (2007 – in %)

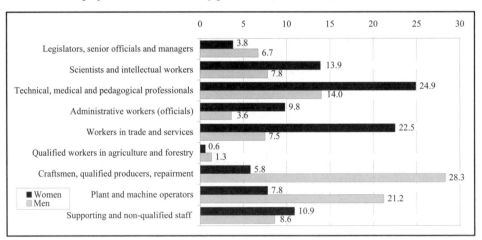

Source: *Slovstat*, 2008.

To summarize: the overall structure of employed women and men varies according to the sectors of economy and types of profession.[7] It largely corresponds to the different academic orientation of women and men during their preparation for professional careers. Nevertheless, certain discrepancies cannot be explained by differences in education. One of them is the low representation of women in the highest category of professions, which endures despite the fact that

---

[7] Several recent studies pointed out the high concentration of women in a small number of sectors or occupations. Sixty percent of them work in one of the following six economic sectors: health and social work, trade, the education, public administration, hotels and restaurants and the clothing and textile industry. According to A. Franco, more than 40% of women in Slovakia work in the five most common professions – as saleswomen; helpers and cleaning ladies; restaurant employees; clerks; and nurses (Franco, 2007b). At the same time, the concentration of women in the "female" occupations is higher than the concentration of men in the "male" occupations, as only 30 % of men work in the six most common professions (Filadelfiová, 2008a).

educational attainment of women is constantly improving. The removal of this vertical gender segregation requires not only changes in the academic preferences of girls and boys preparing for their career, but also the identification and elimination of structural barriers.

4.1.6. EMPLOYMENT PATTERNS AND WORKING TIME

Stability of Employment and Types of Contract

Slovakia is a country with largely traditional employment patterns. In other words, the employment of women and men takes mostly the form of stable work performed full time and for an indefinite term. Alternative forms of employment contracts are rather unusual.

As Table 4.18 shows, the overall share of "unstable" work – i.e. temporary, casual or seasonal – among women and men has fluctuated around 5% since 2000.

Table 4.18
Working women and men by the stability of employment (2000 – 2006, in %)

		2000	2003	2004	2005	2006
Stable jobs	Women	95.4	95.4	95.1	95.1	94.8
	Men	95.3	95.1	94.7	94.9	95.0
Temporary, casual and seasonal jobs	Women	4.6	4.6	4.9	4.9	5.2
	Men	4.7	4.9	5.3	5.1	5.0

Source: *Štatistické...*, 2002, 2005 and 2007.

The share of women and men employed for a fixed term, i.e. whose employment contract explicitly specifies the term of employment, have remained low at approximately 5% (see Table 4.19). This type of contract is generally considered less stable and offering less protection to employees than indefinite-term contract, and is much less common in Slovakia than in other European countries. According to data from 2006, the share of employed for a fixed term was 5.1% of the total number of employed in Slovakia while the EU-27 average was almost three times as high (14.4%). The share of men employed for a fixed term was 5.0% and that of women was 5.2%. In most EU member states including the Czech Republic, fixed-term employment is more common among women, but in Slovakia there is no major gender difference in this regard.

Table 4.19 also shows that the share of women employed for a fixed term in the EU-27 increased from 12.2% in 1998 to 14.9% in 2006, while the share of their male counterparts grew

Table 4.19
Share of employed for a fixed term in the total number of employed in Slovakia and EU member states (1998 and 2006 – in %)

		1998	1999	2000	2001	2002	2003	2004	2005	2006
EU-27	Women	12,2	12,5	13,0	13,3	13,2	13,3	13,8	14,4	14,9
	Men	11,1	11,3	11,7	11,7	11,6	12,0	12,7	13,5	13,9
	Total	11,5	11,8	12,3	12,4	12,4	12,6	13,2	13,9	14,4
Czech Republic	Women	7,7	9,1	9,4	8,9	9,3	10,7	10,7	9,8	10,1
	Men	5,7	6,2	7,1	7,2	7,0	7,9	7,8	7,6	7,5
	Total	6,7	7,6	8,1	8,0	8,1	9,2	9,1	8,6	8,7
Slovak Republic	Women	4,4	3,6	4,5	4,7	4,5	4,6	5,1	4,9	5,2
	Men	4,0	4,1	5,1	5,1	5,2	5,3	6,0	5,1	5,0
	Total	4,2	3,9	4,8	4,9	4,9	4,9	5,5	5,0	5,1

Source: *Employment in...*, 2007.

from 11.1% to 13.9% over the same period. In Slovakia, both shares increased less significantly, from 4.4% to 5.2% for women and from 4.0% to 5.0% for men.

Part-time employment contracts, i.e. contracts for shorter working hours, are not very common in Slovakia either (see Table 4.20). In 2007, only 4.5% of women and 1.2% of men were employed part time. Between 1998 and 2007, the number of women working shorter hours increased more rapidly than that of men.

Major gender differences can be seen in the number of "underemployed" women and men who involuntarily work shorter hours. In 2007, 1.6% of all employed women and 0.4% of all employed men were underemployed. Among women as well as men, involuntarily underemployed make up about one third of all part-timers.

Table 4.20
Women and men employed part time and underemployed (1998 – 2007, in thousands and %)

	Women				Men			
	Part-timers		Of that, underemployed		Part-timers		Of that, underemployed	
	in thousands	%	in thousands	%	in thousands	%	in thousands	%
1998	36.1	3.8	12.3	1.3	11.7	1.1	2.2	0.2
1999	29.3	3.2	10.5	1.1	12.3	1.2	2.2	0.2
2000	28.8	3.1	11.7	1.3	11.1	1.1	1.7	0.2
2001	33.2	3.5	14.8	1.6	12.6	1.2	2.3	0.2
2002	25.9	2.7	11.7	1.3	11.9	1.1	1.6	0.2
2003	35.0	3.8	13.5	1.5	13.7	1.3	2.3	0.2
2004	38.1	4.2	14.5	1.6	15.4	1.4	3.4	0.3
2005	37.1	4.1	17.8	2.0	14.7	1.4	4.7	0.5
2006	43.6	4.7	17.5	1.9	14.5	1.3	5.3	0.5
2007	42.5	4.5	15.6	1.6	13.0	1.2	4.2	0.4

Note: The term underemployed denotes those persons older than 15 who are forced to work part time because they are unable to find a suitable full-time job or because employers want them to.
Source: *Slovstat,* 2008.

Graph 4.19
Share of part-time workers in the total number of employed in Slovakia and EU member states (2006 – in %)

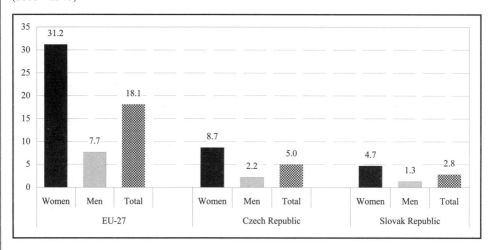

Source: *Employment in...,* 2007.

Graph 4.19 shows that the share of people working shorter hours in Slovakia is significantly lower than the EU-27 average, which in 2006 was 18.1%. In Slovakia, only 2.8% of all employed worked part time. While this type of employment is not very common in the Czech Republic either, it is almost twice as frequent as in Slovakia. Generally speaking, working part time is much less frequent in Central and Eastern European countries. On the other hand, it is rather widespread in southern Europe as well as in Finland, particularly among women. The vast differences between EU member states ensue from differences in legislation as well as from specific economic conditions and market requirements. Another important factor is the availability of pre-school educational establishments and the existence of other measures to balance work and family obligations.

Graph 4.19 also shows that women work on part-time contracts more frequently than men. In EU member states, the average share of female part-timers was 31.2% of all employed women, while the share of male part-timers was only 7.7%. The overall share of part-timers was much lower in Slovakia (4.7% of employed women and 1.3% of employed men).

Generally speaking, working part time in Slovakia is not a popular way of participating in the labor market. This finding has repeatedly been confirmed by surveys that examined people's preferences for various models of working time (*Názory...*, 2006; Filadelfiová – Bútorová, 2007b). The lack of interest of Slovak women and men in part-time jobs may be attributed to insufficient opportunities created by employers but especially to the low incomes in the country and the need of two wage earners in the families.

According to a survey carried out by the Institute for Public Affairs in 2006, part-time employment contracts are more frequent among older women and men (see Table 4.21). Among women and men between 55 and 64, the share of part-timers was 16% and 17%, respectively. Part-time employment contracts are frequent among employed pensioners, too.

Part-time employment contracts are more common among women with elementary education (18%) or secondary education without A levels (10%), who work in manual professions (18%) – unlike women with complete secondary and university education (3% and 1%, respectively).

Table 4.21
Type of employment contract of women and men (% of answers "full-time contract" : "part-time contract" : "other type of contract" – by age, education, economic status and profession)

		Women	Men
Age	Under 45	93 : 5 : 2	94 : 2 : 4
	Over 45	87 : 7 : 6	88 : 6 : 6
	Of that: 45 – 49	93 : 4 : 3	88 : 4 : 8
	50 – 54	85 : 8 : 7	97 : 0 : 3
	55 – 64	72 : 16 : 12	77 : 17 : 6
Education	Elementary	71 : 18 : 11	83 : 6 : 11
	Secondary education without A levels	88 : 10 : 2	95 : 3 : 2
	Complete secondary	94 : 3 : 3	88 : 3 : 9
	University	95 : 1 : 4	96 : 4 : 0
Economic status (select categories)	Employees	93 : 5 : 2	95 : 1 : 4
	Employed pensioners	25 : 33 : 42	16 : 69 : 15
Profession (select types)	Blue-collar workers	76 : 18 : 6	88 : 6 : 6
	Workers in trade and services	90 : 5 : 5	96 : 2 : 2
	Clerical workers	93 : 5 : 2	97 : 3 : 0
	Creative professionals	96 : 2 : 2	96 : 4 : 0
	Entrepreneurs	85 : 4 : 11	80 : 2 : 18
Total		**91 : 6 : 3**	**92 : 4 : 4**

Source: Institute for Public Affairs, August 2006.

Part-time employment is a viable way of keeping elderly women and men on the labor market. It may be suitable particularly for people performing manual work that tends to have more harmful impact on their health and physical condition.

Working Hours

The working time of Slovak women and men is one of the longest in the European Union. Men work three hours longer and women six hours longer than the EU-27 average. In 2005, the average weekly workload in EU member states was 42 hours for men and 35 for women (see Graph 4.20). The longest was the working time of men in Greece (49 hours) and Romania (48 hours), and the working time of women in Romania (44 hours) and Belgium (43 hours). On the other hand, the shortest hours were spent at work by French (37) and Dutch (38) men, as well as Dutch (26) and British (29) women. The average weekly workload of Slovak men was 45 hours, which placed them third in the EU along with Polish and Belgian men. Slovak women with their 41 weekly hours also ranked third along with Polish and Portuguese women.

Graph 4.20
Average weekly working hours of women and men in EU member states (2005)

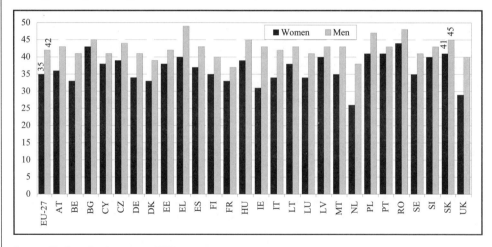

Source: *Working Conditions in...*, 2007.

The difference between the average weekly workload of Slovak women and men is only four hours, which is one of the smallest in the entire European Union. On the other hand, the greatest gender gap is in the Netherlands, Ireland (12 hours each) and Great Britain (11 hours). In all of these countries, many women are employed part time.

The *European Working Conditions Survey* also studied the share of women and men who work more than 48 hours per week. Such long working hours are most common in Romania, Greece, Poland and the Czech Republic. In Slovakia, 21% of men and 17% of women work more than 48 hours per week. The difference between Slovak women and men with long weekly hours was relatively small, at 4 percentage points. Gender gaps were smaller only in Italy and France (*Working Conditions in...*, 2007, p. 35).

A survey carried out in 2006 by the Institute for Public Affairs set out to outline the social profiles of women and men according to their weekly working hours (see Table 4.22). Respondents were asked to estimate the total number of hours per week spent at paid work, including second jobs and private business. Women estimated their total weekly workload at 44 hours and men at 48 hours.[8] The survey confirmed that Slovak men work four hours more per week than women.

In 2006, the busiest Slovak women and men were in the under-24 age group (46 and 50 hours, respectively) and in the 35 – 39 age group (45 and 49 hours, respectively). On the other hand, the shortest hours were in the age group of women and men over 55 (42 and 46 hours, respectively). The differences between the age groups were relatively small, which may be attributed to the dominance of full-time contracts in all age groups except employed pensioners.

Table 4.22
"How many hours per week do you spend doing paid work, including second jobs, private business, etc.?" (2006 – by age, profession and sector)

		Women	Men
	Under 24	46	50
	25 – 29	45	47
	30 – 34	43	47
Age	35 – 39	45	49
	40 – 44	43	47
	45 – 49	44	48
	50 – 54	44	48
	55 – 64	42	46
	Blue-collar workers	42	46
	Workers in trade and services	45	49
Profession (select types)	Clerical workers	44	43
	Creative professionals	41	46
	Executive professionals, managers	48	52
	Entrepreneurs	54	56
Ownership sector	Public	41	44
	Private	44	49
	Industry	43	46
	Construction	0	52
	Trade and services	47	42
Sector of economy	Hotels and restaurants	46	54
	Public administration and social security	41	43
	Education	38	42
	Health and social care	47	46
	Other services	47	50
Total		44	48

Source: Institute for Public Affairs, August 2006.

Table 4.22 also shows that entrepreneurs work the longest weekly hours (54 hours on average for women and 56 hours for men), followed by persons employed in trade and services (45 and 49 hours, respectively). High weekly hours were also common among executive professionals and managers, both women (48 hours) and men (52 hours). Women and men employed within the private sector spend more hours at work (44 and 49 hours, respectively) than those in the public sector (41 and 42 hours, respectively).

The average number of weekly working hours also differs by economic sector. In 2006, the longest hours were typical of men employed in hotels and restaurants, construction and other serv-

---

8   The longer working time of women and men found in the survey carried out by the Institute for Public Affairs (IVO) compared to the *European Working Conditions Survey* is due to the fact that the respondents in the IVO survey estimated not only hours spent in their main job, but the total number of working hours.

ices (over 50 hours), as well as of women employed in trade and services, health and social work, hotels and restaurants and other services (between 46 and 47 hours). On the other hand, the sectors with the shortest weekly hours of work included the education (38 hours for women and 42 for men) as well as public administration and social security (41 and 43 hours, respectively).

But it definitely pays to work longer hours. According to the same survey, incomes of women and men are closely tied to the extent of their working time. For instance, women and men whose monthly wages are less than Sk10,000 work 43 and 45 hours per week, respectively. On the other hand, women and men whose monthly incomes exceed Sk35,000 work 10 hours more on average.

Types of Work Schedule

In 2004, as many as 81.1% of Slovak women and 78.7% of men had a fixed work schedule while 18.9% of women and 21.3% of men used other types of work schedule (see Graph 4.21). Women slightly prevailed in using a flexible daily schedule (4.8% of women and 4.0% of men) and a flexible weekly and monthly schedule (7.3% vs. 5.8%). On the other hand, there were more men basing their work schedule on individual agreements with employers (2.1% of women and 5.1% of men) and other types of arrangements (2.7% and 4.9%, respectively).

Graph 4.21
Employed women and men by type of work schedule (2004 – in %)

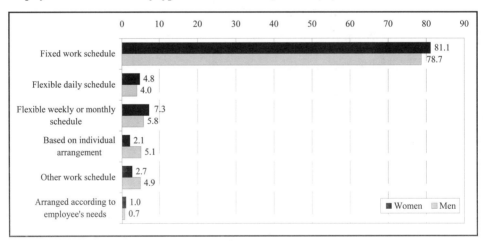

Note: The remainder of the 100% figure for women and men is made up of unidentified employees.
Source: *Štatistické..., 2005.*

Working from Home

Working from home is one of the most promising types of flexible work schedule. As Graph 4.22 shows, 9.1% of employed women used this model in 2005 (4.9% regularly and 4.2% occasionally). Among men, the percentages were a little lower.

However, the demand for this kind of work schedule among women and men is much higher. According to a survey conducted in 2006 by the Women in Business Association 32% of women and 20% of men would prefer to work from home. The same desire was expressed by people between 45 and 59 (30%); by parents (28%) as well as childless persons (25%),

Graph 4.22
Incidence of work at home among employed women and men (2005 – in %)

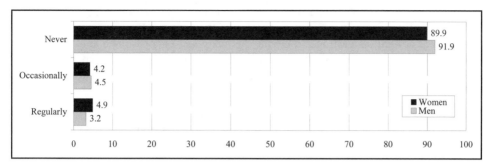

Note: The remainder of the 100% figure for women and men is made up of unidentified employees.
Source: *Výsledky...*, 2005.

residents of towns (29%) as well as villages (23%), people with higher (30%) as well as lower education (23%) (*Názory...*, 2006). Although more recent data are unavailable, we can assume that the total number of people working at home has increased since 2005. At the same time, the demand for this flexible work schedule is still far from being fulfilled.

Types of Work Regime

Although the diversity of work regimes in economically developed countries has increased in recent years, the standard five-day working week still prevails in the EU. Also, the regimes of women and men continue to show significant differences (*Working Conditions in...*, 2007).

Table 4.23
Work regimes of full-time employees in EU member states (2005 – in %)

	Women	Men
Average number of workdays per week		
Less than 5 days	5	4
5 days	71	71
6 or 7 days	24	25
10 or more working hours per day		
Never	**70**	52
One to four times per month	14	**20**
Five and more times per month	16	**28**
At least 2 working hours from 18.00 – 22.00		
One to five times per month	7	**12**
Six and more times per month	10	**15**
At least 2 working hours from 22.00 – 05.00		
One to five times per month	15	**19**
Six and more times per month	29	**34**
Saturday work		
Once or twice a month	24	**28**
Three and more times per month	28	29
Sunday work		
Once or twice a month	16	**18**
Three and more times per month	12	16

Note: Average values for 27 EU member states.
Source: *Working Conditions in...*, 2007.

According to Table 2.23, as many as 30% of women and 48% of men employed full time in the EU members states worked 10 or more hours per day at least once a month. Sixteen percent of women and 28% of men had five or more such long days. Seventeen percent of women and 27% of men worked in the evening at least once a month; 44% of women and 53% of men worked at night at least once a month. As many as 52% of women and 58% of men worked on Saturday and 28% of women and 30% of men worked on Sunday at least once a month. The greatest gender gaps are in the incidence of evening and night work as well as in overtime work.

How frequent are non-standard work regimes in Slovakia? As Table 4.24 shows, Slovak men work overtime twice as often as women: only 5% of all employed women and 9.1% of all employed men worked overtime in 2005. The share of women in the total number of employees working overtime was only 30.3%.

Table 4.24
Overtime work among employed women and men in Slovakia (2005 – in thousands and %)

	Women		Men		% of women
	in thousands	%	in thousands	%	
Working overtime	49,7	5,0	114,5	9,1	30,3
Not working overtime	933,7	94,8	1 114,6	89,1	45,6
Unidentified	1,2	0,2	22,0	1,8	5,1
Employed total	984,6	100,0	1 251,1	100,0	44,0

Source: *Výsledky...*, 2005.

As Graph 4.23 reveals, as many as 67% of women and 78% of men worked between 5 and 14 hours overtime per week. Lower and higher amount of overtime work was rather rare. Among women working overtime, 44% worked five to nine hours longer per week; 23% worked 10 to 14 hours more; 18% worked 15 hours and more and 15% worked less than five hours overtime per week. Among men working overtime, 40% worked 10 to 14 hours longer per week; 38% worked five to nine hours more; 12% worked over 15 hours more and 10% worked less than five hours overtime per week.

Graph 4.23
Employed women and men working overtime by number of hours (2005 – in %)

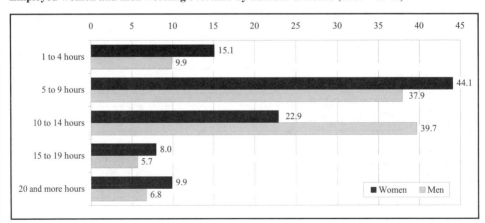

Source: *Výsledky...*, 2005.

In Slovakia, women and especially men work weekends relatively often. In 2005, as many as 43.8% of women and 57.6% of men worked on Saturday; 23.6% of women and 27.6% of men on a regular basis. Sunday work was less frequent but by no means rare: 28.7% of women and 41% of men spent their Sundays at work; 17.5% of women and 21.7% of men on a regular basis.

Evening work is relatively frequent in Slovakia, too: in 2005, as many as 28.1% of employed women and 39.4% of men worked in the evenings; 19.5% of women and 23.3% of men of them regularly. Night work is less frequent: 17.6% of women and 26.5% of men spent their nights at work; 12.5% of women and 18.6% of men did so regularly.

Table 4.25

Employed women and men in Slovakia by weekend, evening and night work (2005 – in %)

		Women	Men
Saturday work	Regularly	23.6	27.6
	Occasionally	20.2	30.0
	Never	55.3	42.0
Sunday work	Regularly	17.5	21.7
	Occasionally	11.2	19.3
	Never	70.3	58.6
Evening work	Regularly	19.5	23.3
	Occasionally	8.6	16.1
	Never	70.9	60.3
Night work	Regularly	12.5	18.6
	Occasionally	5.1	7.9
	Never	81.5	73.2

Note: The remainder of the 100% figure for women and men is made up of unidentified employees.
Source: *Výsledky...*, 2005.

All these data prove that there is a gender gap in non-standard work regimes, which are more frequent among men than women. A representative survey by the Institute for Public Affairs exposed also significant age specifics. According to Table 4.26, overtime work is more widespread among women and men under 45 (15% and 21%, respectively) than among women and men over 45 (10% and 17%, respectively). On the other hand, only 11% of women and 6% of men under 45 did not have this experience at all, while among women and men over 45 these numbers were higher (20% and 9%, respectively). Overtime work is thus more typical of younger generation.

Table 4.26
"How often do you work overtime, at night or on weekends?" (%)

		Women		Men	
		Under 45	Over 45	Under 45	Over 45
Overtime work	Very often	15	10	21	17
	Quite often	18	19	28	25
	Sometimes	36	32	29	28
	Rarely	21	19	16	21
	Never	11	20	6	9
Night work	Very often	5	5	9	8
	Quite often	5	4	16	7
	Sometimes	7	6	11	14
	Rarely	10	11	18	17
	Never	72	74	47	54
Weekend work	Very often	11	10	13	12
	Quite often	18	15	24	19
	Sometimes	23	19	22	25
	Rarely	23	21	23	31
	Never	25	36	19	14

Source: Institute for Public Affairs, August 2006.

Night work is rarer than overtime work, especially among women. Weekend work is also more common among younger employees and among men. All in all, non-standard types of work regime are more widespread among men and in the younger generation.

Finally, let us look at the incidence of shift work among women and men. According to Graph 4.24, there are no major gender differences. In 2005, approximately one in four employed women and men in Slovakia worked shifts (24.3% and 23.7%, respectively).

Graph 4.24
Employed women and men in Slovakia by shift work (2005 – in %)

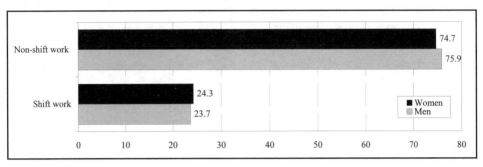

Note: The remainder of the 100% figure for women and men is made up of unidentified employees.
Source: *Výsledky...*, 2005.

We may conclude that Slovakia's labor market is dominated by traditional employment patterns. The vast majority of women and men work full time. Although part-time or fixed-term employment contracts have become more widespread in recent years, they are still much less common than in Western European countries. Flexible work schedules are more frequent among women than among their male counterparts. On the other hand, men are more often involved in overtime work and non-standard types of work regime.

4.1.7. QUALITY OF WORKING LIFE AND ITS IMPACT ON HEALTH

In this section, we examine four select dimensions of working life of women and men in Slovakia: first, autonomy at work; second, cognitive demands of work; third, physical risks at work; fourth, work-related health problems and overall impact of work on health.

The analysis is largely inspired by the studies by the Finnish expert on ageing and age management Juhani Ilmarinen (Ilmarinen, 1999; 2006; 2008). It is based on the findings of the *Fourth European Working Conditions Survey*, which was carried out in 31 European countries by the European Foundation for the Improvement of Living and Working Conditions in September 2005 (www.eurofound.eu.int/ewco/surveys/index.htm). Slovakia took part in this extensive comparative survey.[9] For the purposes of our book, the survey findings were submitted to a secondary analysis that distinguished between four major categories of employed persons – women and men under and over 45.

Autonomy at work

One of the key factors affecting people's job performance is the extent of autonomy at work. According to Juhani Ilmarinen, "the right to regulate one's own work is important to every-

---

[9] The sample was representative of Slovakia's entire employed population and includes respondents who worked at least one hour in one calendar week. The survey data were processed by Marián Velšic.

one, but especially to ageing workers. This need is generated by the increase in personal differences with age. Work experience refines work methods and habits of people, who adjust to working in ways that suit them best... If workers are able to make their own choices and adjust to their work according to their own resources, aptitudes, and routines, they will cope well with their work. On the other hand, heavily regulated work processes with a set pace and minimum room for individual variation will lead to an unsatisfactory result as ageing takes place." (Ilmarinen, 2006, p. 303).

> In terms of autonomy at work, Slovakia is near the bottom of the list of the 31 European countries that took part in the *Fourth European Working Conditions Survey* in 2005. Slovakia ranked 29th, and was trailed only by Greece and Bulgaria (*Fourth European...*, 2007, p. 51).

Important aspects of autonomy at work include the ability to choose or change speed of work; to choose or change methods of work, to choose or change order of tasks, to take a break when desired.

What is the autonomy of women as compared to men in Slovakia? As Table 4.27 shows, women enjoyed greater autonomy at work in 2005. In three of four examined indicators, they achieved higher values than men. It means that more women than men were able to choose or change speed of their work, to choose or change methods of work and to choose and change the order of tasks. Men, for their part, were more frequently able to take a break when desired. Gender differences were slightly more significant within the younger group than within the older group of workers. In other words, younger women were better off compared to younger men than older women were compared to older men.

As many as 68% of women over 45 were able to choose or change speed of their work; 65% were able to choose and change their work methods; 63% were able to choose or change order of their tasks; and 62% were able to take a break when desired. In two out of the four parameters examined, the autonomy of older women was greater than of their male counterparts; in the remaining two parameters, the autonomy of older women was about the same.

Table 4.27 also illustrates that the factor of age has a gender-specific impact. The autonomy at work among older women is lower than among the younger ones (in case of three from the four examined parameters). On the other hand, the situation among men is different: the extent of their autonomy at work does not decline with their age.

Table 4.27
Extent of work autonomy of women and men in Slovakia – by age (% of affirmative answers)

	Women			Men		
	Under 45	Over 45	Total	Under 45	Over 45	Total
Able to choose or change speed of work	72	68	71	64	67	65
Able to choose or change methods of work	72	65	65	62	61	62
Able to choose or change order of tasks	65	63	64	54	54	54
Able to take a break when desired	53	62	57	63	64	63

Source: *European Working Conditions Survey 2005* (secondary data analysis).

Cognitive demands of work

Let us now look at the cognitive dimensions of work. We will focus only on three basic demands: the ability to solve unforeseen problems independently, to carry out complex tasks, and to learn new things.

In the average of 31 European countries surveyed in 2005, women were less frequently solving unforeseen problems on their own; carrying out complex tasks; and learning new things. The lower cognitive demands of women's work applied in all age categories of workers (*Fourth European...*, 2007, p. 47).

What are the differences between the cognitive demands of the work performed by women and men in Slovakia? Table 4.28 provides a rather ambivalent picture. Out of three types of cognitive demands, two were more frequently expected of men and one of women. The ability to solve unforeseen problems on their own was required from 73% of women and 79% of men; the ability carry out complex tasks was expected from 61% of women and 65% of men. On the other hand, the ability to learn new things was demanded from 71% of women and 67% of men.

How do the cognitive demands of work change with changing age of people? In the older age category, 71% of women but 80% of men were expected to solve unforeseen problems independently; 63% of women but 67% of men were entrusted with carrying out complex tasks. On the other hand, 69% of women but only 62% of men were required to learn new things.

Thus cognitive demands of work tend to change with increasing age of women as well as of men. Compared to their younger colleagues, women over 45 scored lower values in two cognitive dimensions of work and higher values in one dimension. On the other hand, men over 45 scored higher values in two dimensions and lower values in one dimension compared to younger men. Women over 45 were required to solve unforeseen problems and learn new things less frequently than younger women. In other words, older women are less able to use their experience at work than younger women, as well as men of their own age. The gender gap in cognitive demands of work tends to grow deeper with age, and to the detriment of women.

Table 4.28
Cognitive demands of work of women and men in Slovakia – by age (% of affirmative answers)

	Women			Men		
	Under 45	Over 45	Total	Under 45	Over 45	Total
Solving unforeseen problems independently	75	71	73	78	80	79
Learning new things	72	69	71	70	62	67
Carrying out complex tasks	60	63	61	64	67	65

Source: *European Working Conditions Survey 2005* (secondary data analysis).

Physical Risks of Work

Physical risks at work in the broadest sense encompass exposure to ergonomic risks, biological or chemical risks as well as to ambient environmental risk factors (*Fourth European...*, 2007, p. 29). To what extent are working women and men in Slovakia exposed to such risks? As Table 4.29 shows, women are exposed to less physical risks at work than men, as they scored lower values on 13 out of 15 examined indicators. There were only two exceptions: compared to men, women are more frequently required to lift or move people and are to the same extent exposed to infectious materials.

Let us look at the exposure to psychical risks of women over 45. As for ergonomic risks, 56% of them are exposed to standing or walking for at least half of their working hours; 52% to repetitive movements of their hands or arms; 20% of them are working in tiring or painful positions; 11% are required to carry or move heavy loads and 4% to lifting or moving people.

As for environmental, biological and chemical risks, 16% of women over 45 are exposed to noise for at least half of their working hours; 12% to infectious materials; 10% are required to work in high temperatures, 8% must inhale smoke, fumes and dust, 7% handle chemical products or substances, 6% are exposed to the vibrations of hand tools and machinery, 6% work in low

> The marked gender gap in exposure to physical risks can be attributed to the gender segregation in specific sectors. For instance, the sectors of construction, as well as manufacturing and agriculture that are strongly masculinized are reporting higher-than-median exposure to each set of physical risks. On the other hand, there are specifically female types of risks as well, such as lifting or moving people or exposure to infectious materials (*Fourth European...*, 2007, p. 30 and following).

temperatures, 5% breath in tobacco smoke and 4% inhale vapors of chemical substances such as solvents and thinners.

A comparison of the situation of women and men over 45 shows that women are less frequently exposed to 13 out of 15 physical risk factors (see Graph 4.25).

How do women over 45 perceive their situation compared to the younger women? As Table 4.29 indicates, they are more critical of their work conditions; they feel more exposed to 11 out of 15 examined physical risks. On the other hand, men over 45 do not have such a strong feeling of deterioration. Compared to their younger colleagues, they believe they are more exposed to six physical risks, equally exposed to five risks, and less exposed to four physical risks.

These findings indicate that gender differences in perceived exposure to physical risks at work tend to decrease with age. Still, men over 45 assess their exposure to physical risks much more critically than their female counterparts.

Table 4.29
Exposure of Slovak working women and men to physical risks – by age (% of exposed half of the time or more)

	Women			Men		
	Under 45	Over 45	Total	Under 45	Over 45	Total
Standing or walking	54	56	55	66	63	64
Repetitive hand or arm movements	50	52	51	57	54	56
Tiring or painful positions	12	20	15	27	26	26
Noise so loud that you have to raise your voice to talk to people	14	16	15	35	30	33
Handling or being in direct contact with infectious materials	9	12	10	7	13	10
Carrying or moving heavy loads	6	11	8	26	25	25
High temperatures that make you perspire even when not working	6	10	8	19	22	20
Breathing in smoke, fumes, powder or dust	6	8	7	33	32	32
Handling or being in skin contact with chemical products or substances	7	7	7	12	11	12
Vibrations of hand tools, machinery etc.	6	6	6	24	25	25
Low temperatures whether indoors or outdoors	3	6	5	17	23	19
Tobacco smoke from other people	5	5	5	14	9	12
Lifting or moving people	4	4	4	1	5	3
Breathing in vapors, such as solvents and thinners	3	4	4	12	18	15
Radiation such as X rays, radioactive radiation, welding light, laser beams	1	0	1	4	7	5

Source: *European Working Conditions Survey 2005* (secondary data analysis).

Graph 4.25
Exposure of women and men over 45 to physical risks (% of exposed half of the time or more)

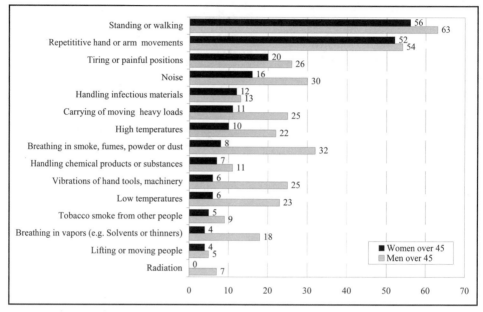

Source: *European Working Conditions Survey 2005* (secondary data analysis).

Work-related Health Problems

Are there any differences in health problems caused by work experienced by women and men in Slovakia? Data in Table 4.30 give an affirmative answer: negative health outcomes afflict men more frequently than women. Overall, men complained of nine types of health problems more frequently than women; they mentioned overall fatigue, backache, muscular problems in the back, neck and limbs, eyesight problems, injuries, breathing difficulties, skin problems, hearing problems and heart trouble). Other six health problems were reported as often by women as by men (i.e. the difference in their incidence was maximum one percentage point). Only headaches were mentioned more frequently by women than by men.

And what is the situation of women over 45? A significant proportion of them complained of overall fatigue (43%), backache (40%), stress (38%), muscular pain (34%); headaches (33%), irritability (21%) and eyesight problems (21%). A smaller, but still noteworthy proportion of older women also reported stomach pain (16%), sleeping problems (14%), allergies (11%), injuries (11%), breathing difficulties (10%), skin problems (10%), hearing problems (7%), anxiety (7%) and heart trouble (7%).

A comparison of women over 45 to their male counterparts shows that women complained of six types of health problems more frequently than men (particularly stress and headaches, but also allergies and muscular pain, sleeping problems and stomach pain); of five types less frequently than men (eyesight problems, injuries, breathing difficulties, hearing problems and heart trouble); and of five problems as frequently as men. These findings show that there are much smaller gender differences in the perception of work-related health problems in the older generation than in the younger one.

The data in Table 4.30 also illustrate that views of work-related health problems tend to change with age, and these changes are largely gender-specific. As they get older, women tend to feel negative health impact of their work more strongly than men. Women over 45 complained of all 16 examined types of health problems more frequently than younger women. This is particularly true of overall fatigue, muscular pain, but also of stress, backache, headaches and

Table 4.30
Women and men in Slovakia experiencing work-related health problems (%)

	Women			Men		
	Under 45	Over 45	Total	Under 45	Over 45	Total
Overall fatigue	25	43	37	38	44	41
Backache	31	40	35	42	39	41
Stress	28	38	32	29	32	31
Headaches	25	33	29	23	25	24
Muscular pain in back, neck or limbs	22	34	27	32	31	31
Irritability	18	21	19	20	21	20
Eyesight problems	15	21	17	20	26	22
Sleeping problems	10	14	12	11	12	11
Stomach pain	8	16	11	7	14	10
Allergies	7	11	9	8	8	8
Injury	7	11	8	25	25	25
Breathing difficulties	7	10	8	15	15	15
Skin problems	7	10	8	13	11	12
Hearing problems	4	7	6	17	21	19
Anxiety	5	7	6	3	6	5
Heart trouble	3	7	5	4	9	7

Source: *European Working Conditions Survey 2005* (secondary data analysis).

Graph 4.26
Women and men over 45 experiencing work-related health problems (%)

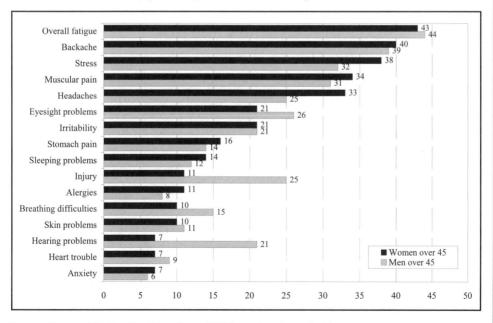

Source: *European Working Conditions Survey 2005* (secondary data analysis).

Compared to the European average, there is a much larger portion of people in Slovakia, who think that their health is affected by their work. In this regard, Slovakia ranked 9th among 31 European countries examined by the *European Working Conditions Survey* in 2005. (*Fourth European...*, 2007, p. 61).

Graph 4.27
"Do you think your health or safety is at risk because of your work?" (% of affirmative answers)

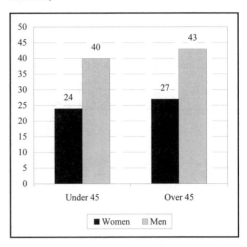

Source: *European Working Conditions Survey 2005* (secondary data analysis).

stomach pain. On the other hand, men over 45 complained only of 8 out of 16 examined health problems more often than younger men.

Let us now take a look at the overall perceived impact of work on health. Obviously, there are many factors affecting people's views of this impact. Among them are also cognitive demands and physical risks of work, autonomy at work, as well as individual experience with particular work-related health problems.

As many as 41% working men in Slovakia, but only 25% of women thought in 2005 that their work threatened their health and safety. Thus the gender gap is quite remarkable. Interestingly enough, this critical perception is only slightly more widespread among working women and men over 45 than among their younger counterparts (see Graph 4.27).

4.1.8. REMUNERATION OF WOMEN AND MEN[10]

Universal Character of Gender Differences in Remuneration[11]

The gender difference in remuneration for work, also known as the gender pay gap, is one of the three key indicators of the gender inequality on the labor market – along with gender differences in employment and unemployment rates.[12] The concept of equal pay for work of equal value has existed for over six decades in Europe (since the Rome Treaty of 1957), but it was not until the late 1990s that this issue attracted the interest of European institutions and their leaders (*Gender...*, 2003; *Report from...*, 2006; Määttä, 2007; *Opinion...*, 2007) and became the focus of regular statistical surveys (*Women Have...*, 1999; epp.eurostat.ec.europa.eu) as well as of sociological and economic research (Olsen – Walby, 2004; Farell, 2005).

The research gradually exposed an entire complex of interrelated factors affecting the gender gap in the remuneration of women and men. These factors include:

---

[10] This section is a continuation of analyses by Jarmila Filadelfiová in Filadelfiová – Bútorová, 2007b and in Cviková, 2008.
[11] In this section, the wages are expressed in Slovak crowns (koruna – Sk). On 1 January 2009, Slovakia joined the European single currency and adopted the euro. The official conversion rate has been set at 30.1260 Slovak crowns to the euro.
[12] Since 2002, the gender pay gap has been included among structural indicators to measure progress in attaining the goals set by the Lisbon Strategy. It is also considered an important indicator of the quality of work (*Indicators...*, 2001).

- The gender segregation of economic sectors and professions, and lower remuneration in those sectors and professions where women prevail (Benassi, 1999; Barošová, 2006, Franco, 2007a; Cviková, 2008);

- Differences in human capital, particularly in terms of educational attainment, qualifications and work experience;

- Different job-seeking strategies used by women and men: since women have to pay more attention than men to balancing their professional and family obligations, they tend to prefer jobs closer to home even if they pay less;

- Different types of career: because they take care of children at a younger age and of other family members at an older age, women's professional careers are more frequently interrupted and shorter than those of men; also, their career advancement is generally slower;

- Women more frequently accept part-time employment contracts;

- System of wage calculation (particularly the division into a basic wage and flexible bonuses);

- Direct and indirect discrimination against women.

Women earn much less on average than men

According to the recent statistical data, the average wage of women in 2006 was 27% lower than the average wage of men in Slovakia (see Table 4.31). While the average gender pay gap in Europe closed over the past decade, in Slovakia it widened. On average, women earned 21.5% less than men in 1997, but by 2006 the difference had increased to 26.9%. In terms of the gender pay gap, Slovakia ranked third among all EU member states in recent three years, trailing only Cyprus and Estonia (*Tackling...*, 2007).

Table 4.31
Average gross monthly wage of women and men in Slovakia and the ratio of women's wages to men's wages (1997 – 2006, in Slovak crowns (Sk) and %)

	Women (Sk)	Men (Sk)	Women's wages/ men's wages (%)	Gender wage difference (%)
1997	8,793	11,202	78.5	21.5
1998	8,747	11,356	77.0	23.0
1999	9,050	12,066	75.0	25.0
2000	9,952	13,267	75.0	25.0
2001	10,623	14,332	74.1	25.9
2002	12,125	16,899	71.7	28.3
2003	12,899	17,706	72.8	27.2
2004	14,256	19,700	72.4	27.6
2005	15,394	21,503	71.6	28.4
2006	16,575	22,686	73.1	26.9

Source: *Výberové...*, 2007.

Gender gap in monthly wages is greater than in hourly earnings

The gender difference in monthly wages is generally greater than the difference in hourly earnings (see Table 4.32). The main reason is that monthly wages reflect the total number of hours worked, including overtime, as well as the type of employment contract and various bonuses, e.g.

13th or 14th salaries, etc. This was also the case in Slovakia in 2006, when women trailed men by 23% in terms of the average hourly earnings but by 26% in terms of the average monthly wage.

Graph 4.28
Average gross monthly wage of women and men in Slovakia (1997 – 2006, in Sk)

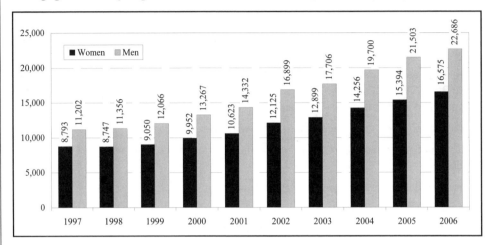

Source: *Výberové...,* 2007.

Table 4.32
Average hourly earnings of women and men (2001 – 2006, in Sk)

	2001	2002	2003	2004	2005	2006
Women	68.30	79.30	82.30	87.90	93.30	99.59
Men	92.90	107.20	111.00	118.90	127.30	129.75
Women's earnings /men's earnings (%)	73.5	74.0	74.1	73.9	73.3	76.7

Source: *Analýza...,* 2005; *Informačný...,* 2006.

As in other European countries, the gender pay gap in Slovakia is substantially larger in the private sector than in the public sector. In recent years, the average hourly earnings of women employed in the public sector were over 80% of the average hourly earnings of their male counterparts, while in the private sector they reached around 75% (see Table 4.33).

Table 4.33
Women's average hourly earnings as a percentage of men's average hourly earnings – by ownership sector (2001 – 2006, in %)

	2001	2002	2003	2004	2005	2006
Business sector	74.6	74.3	74.0	74.1	73.4	76.7
Non-business sector	85.4	85.8	85.4	86.1	81.4	NA

Note: NA = not available
Source: *Analýza...,* 2005; *Informačný...,* 2006.

Gender pay gap reflects horizontal segregation on the labor market

Foreign studies show that the gender pay gap clearly reflects the horizontal gender segregation on the labor market and the undervaluing of those sectors and professions in which women prevail (Franco, 2007b; Grimshaw – Rubery, 2007). As Table 4.34 shows, this factor applies in Slovakia as well. The average wage in most sectors dominated by women is lower in the long term than the average wage in Slovakia's national economy. This is true especially of the sectors of health and social work, education, hotels and restaurants and other public services. For instance, the average wage in health and social work, where over 80% of all employees were women in 2006, was 20% lower than the national average. In1997, the difference was only 10%. Similar trend can be seen also in the sector of hotels and restaurants, where the average wage in 2006 was almost 30% lower than the national average, although a decade earlier the difference was only 16%. The average wage in education was 20% less in 2006, although in 1997 it was only 16% less.

Table 4.34
Average gross monthly wage by sector and the ratio of average wages in various sectors to the average wage in the national economy (1997 and 2006 – in Sk and %)

	Average wage (Sk)		Ratio to the average wage in the national economy (%)	
	1997	2006	1997	2006
Agriculture and forestry	7,363	15,351	79.8	77.6
Mining and quarrying	10,485	20,917	113.6	105.8
Industry	9,197	19,959	99.7	100.9
Electricity, gas and water supply	12,212	27,236	132.4	137.7
Construction	9,970	19,050	108.1	96.3
Wholesale and retail trade	9,825	20,217	106.5	102.2
Hotels and restaurants	7,743	13,769	83.9	69.6
Transport, storage, post and telecommunications	10,089	22,001	109.3	111.2
Financial intermediation	17,886	38,409	193.9	194.2
Industry	10,710	25,532	116.1	129.1
Real estate, renting and business activities	11,240	19,965	121.8	101.0
Education	7,771	15,847	84.2	80.1
Health and social work	8,373	15,917	90.7	80.5
Other community, social and personal service activities	7,372	16,158	79.9	81.7
National economy total	9,226	19,776	100.0	100.0

Source: *Slovstat*, 2008.

The highest average wages were in sectors dominated by men, for instance electricity, gas and water supply, real estate, renting and business activities, transport, storage, post and telecommunications, and mining and quarrying.

The only two economic sectors with high average wages that employed more women than men were the financial intermediation and the wholesale and retail trade. The average wage in the former sector was the highest of all sectors, almost double the average in the national economy.

Gender wage gap is present also within individual sectors

As Table 4.35 shows, gender wage gap is present also within individual sectors. In the long term, it is the greatest in those sectors with the highest average wages. In other words, although women prevail in some sectors with high average wages, their actual economic benefit is lesser than that of men from the same sector.

In 2005, the greatest absolute difference between the average wages of women and men was in the banking and insurance sector (Sk16,480, or 37%); which after a large gap was followed by leasing and trading in real estate (Sk8,576, or 34%), trade and repairs (Sk7,859, or 37%) and indus-

Table 4.35
Gender wage gap (GWG) within the sectors (1996 and 2005 – in Sk and %)

	Absolute GWG(Sk)		Relative GWG (%)	
	1996	2005	1996	2005
Agriculture and forestry	1,976	2,971	25.5	19.7
Mining and quarrying	2,506	2,745	23.8	13.6
Industry	3,349	7,623	31.4	34.7
Electricity, gas and water supply	1,438	2,460	12.5	9.2
Construction	1,420	2,545	14.4	13.0
Wholesale and retail trade	2,387	7,859	26.4	37.1
Hotels and restaurants	1,227	4,978	17.4	29.3
Transport, storage, post and telecommunications	834	3,685	8.8	17.1
Financial intermediation	4,940	16,480	31.0	36.9
Industry	2,130	8,576	22.7	34.1
Real estate, renting and business activities	802	4,554	7.8	20.7
Education	1,624	4,311	18.5	22.1
Health and social work	2,056	4,180	22.5	23.8
Other community, social and personal service activities	493	2,188	5.9	13.4
National economy total	2,535	6,109	25.5	28.4

Note: The absolute gender wage difference is calculated as the average male wage minus the average female wage. The relative gender wage difference is calculated as the ratio of the absolute wage difference to the average male wage, multiplied by 100.
Source: Barošová, 2006, p. 70.

trial production (Sk7,623, or 35%). In all of these sectors, the gender pay gap exceeded one third of the average male wage (Barošová, 2006). On the other hand, the lowest gender differences were recorded in sectors such as the production and distribution of electricity, gas and water, construction, other public services and mining and the extraction of minerals.

Thus the gender pay gap is typical *of all economic sectors*, even strongly feminized ones. Table 4.35 also illustrates the increase in the gender pay gap between 1996 and 2005; in some sectors, the gender pay gap increased four or even five times in absolute terms.

Gender wage gap is present in all professions and education categories

A comparison of the monthly wages of women and men in 2007 shows that women earn less than men in all types of profession (see Table 4.36). For instance, female scientists and intel-

Table 4.36
Average gross monthly wages of women and men and the ratio of women's wages to men's wages – by profession (2007 – in Sk and %)

	Monthly wage (Sk)		Women's wages/ men's wages (%)
	Women	Men	
Legislators, senior officials and managers	39,111	57,549	68.0
Scientists and intellectual workers	24,788	33,601	73.8
Technical, medical and pedagogical professionals	21,258	28,790	73.8
Administrative workers (officials)	16,944	21,182	80.0
Workers in trade and services	12,518	16,398	76.3
Qualified workers in agriculture and forestry	14,053	15,453	90.9
Craftsmen and qualified producers, repairmen	13,704	20,511	66.8
Plant and machine operators	15,277	20,007	76.4
Supporting and non-qualified staff	10,935	14,409	75.9
Total	19,045	25,261	75.4

Source: *Informačný...*, 2007.

Table 4.37
Average gross monthly wages of women and men and the ratio of women's wages to men's wages – by education (2007 – in Sk and %)

	Monthly wage (Sk)		Women's wages/ men's wages (%)
	Women	Men	
Elementary school	12,403	16,435	75.5
Vocational without A levels	13,208	19,244	68.6
Secondary without A levels	14,487	18,755	77.2
Complete vocational	17,675	22,955	77.0
Complete secondary (academic schools)	19,008	24,393	77.9
Complete secondary (trade schools)	19,098	25,339	75.4
Higher vocational	21,048	28,594	73.6
Bachelor's degree	22,539	33,899	66.5
University	29,111	42,080	69.2
Scientist's degree	30,891	38,705	79.8
Total	**19,045**	**25,261**	**75.4**

Source: *Informačný...*, 2007.

lectual workers earned 26% less than their male counterparts; among technical, medical and pedagogical professionals, the gender wage gap exceeded also 26%, among administrative workers it reached 20%, etc.

Even in the best-paid professions – i.e. legislators, senior officials and managers – women are not automatically guaranteed equal pay to that of men; on the contrary, the gender pay gap is one of the largest here. In 2007, the average monthly wage of men in this type of profession was Sk57,549, while that of women was only Sk39,111 or 32% lower. The only category of jobs with a greater gender pay gap was that of craftsmen, qualified producers and repairmen, where the hourly wage of women was 33 % lower than that of men.

Gender gaps in hourly wages were also present among workers in trade and services (24%), qualified workers in agriculture and forestry (9%), plant and machine operators (24%) and supporting and non-qualified staff (24%).

Similarly, gender pay gaps persist in all education categories (see Table 4.37). Paradoxically, the greatest gender differences in remuneration are between women and men with the highest educational attainment. While the average monthly wage of women in Slovakia's national economy in 2007 was 25% lower than that of men, among persons with university diploma the gap was 31%.

Women's wages are lower than men's wages in all age groups

In every age group, women's wages are lower than men's wages. As Table 4.38 and Graph 4.29 show, gender pay gap is the smallest when women and men enter the labor market immediately after completing their education. Afterwards, it increases and peaks in the 35 – 39 age group, where women's wages lag behind men's wages by as much as one

Table 4.38
Average gross monthly wages of women and men and the ratio of women's wages to men's wages – by age (2007 – in Sk and %)

	Monthly wage (Sk)		Women's wages/ men's wages (%)
	Women	Men	
Under 20	11,615	13,630	85.2
20 – 24	15,338	17,366	88.3
25 – 29	19,954	23,446	85.1
30 – 34	20,252	28,120	72.0
35 – 39	19,337	28,439	68.0
40 – 44	18,968	27,694	68.5
45 – 49	19,018	26,209	72.6
50 – 54	19,202	24,524	78.3
55 – 59	18,823	23,495	80.1
Over 60	16,563	22,842	72.5
Total	**19,045**	**25,261**	**75.4**

Source: *Informačný...*, 2007.

third. While the gender pay gap narrows in the following age groups, it never comes anywhere near closing.

The gender pay gap in the age category over 45 fluctuates around 25%, except for the 55 – 59 age group where it is 20%.

Graph 4.29
Difference between average monthly wages of women and men – by age (2007 – in %)

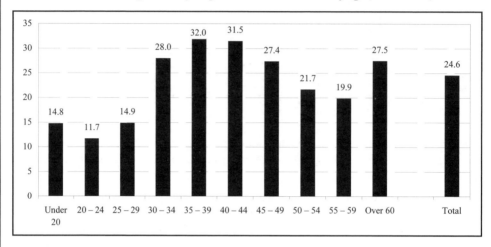

Source: *Informačný...*, 2007.

To sum up, the gender pay gap is universal in nature as it concerns all categories of women and men on the labor market. Regardless of sector of economy, ownership sector, type of profession, educational attainment or age, the hourly earnings and monthly wages of women are always lower than those of men.

Earned Incomes of Women Over 45 and Their Perception

The existence of a substantial gender pay gap in Slovakia was proved also by a representative survey carried out in 2006 by the Institute for Public Affairs (see Table 4.39). According to its findings, 38% of employed women, but only 17% of employed men earned less than

Table 4.39
"Which of the following categories would you place your net monthly earned income in?" (%)

Wage category (Sk)	Under 45		Over 45		Total	
	Women	Men	Women	Men	Women	Men
Under 10,000	39	16	37	18	38	17
10,001 – 20,000	52	61	50	61	52	61
20,001 – 30,000	7	15	11	17	8	15
Over 30,001	2	9	2	5	2	7

Note: All earned net monthly incomes of employed respondents. The answers "I don't know" and "didn't answer" were disregarded.
Source: Institute for Public Affairs, August 2006.

Sk10,000 net per month. On the other hand, only 10% of women, but 22% of men had an income of over Sk20,000. Most women (52%) and men (61%) fell into wage categories between Sk10,000 and Sk20,000.

The age of 45 did not represent an important limit in terms of gender pay gap, as differences in the remuneration of women and men under 45 and over 45 did not change. For instance, a net monthly earned income of less than Sk10,000 was declared by 39% of women and 16% of men in the under-45 age category and by 37% of women and 18% of men in the over-45 age category.

Let us now take a closer look at the income situation of women over 45. As Table 4.40 shows, 81% of these women earned less than Sk15,000 per month in 2006. As women get older, the disproportion between those who earn less than Sk15,000 and those who earn more than Sk15,000 grows (from 80% vs. 20% among women aged 45 – 49 to 84% vs. 16% among women over 55). This is probably the result of two factors: first, for many women from the oldest age group earned income as merely an addition to their pensions; second, there are more women with only elementary education in this age group.

Table 4.40
Net earned monthly income of women between 45 and 64 – by age (%)

Wage category (Sk)	45 – 49	50 – 54	55 – 64	Total
Under 5,000	2	6	8	5
5,001 – 10,000	42	41	35	40
10,001 – 15,000	36	33	41	36
15,001 – 20,000	11	12	8	11
20,001 – 25,000	6	4	2	4
25,001 – 30,000	3	1	4	2
Over 30,001	0	3	2	2

Note: All earned net monthly incomes of employed women. Due to the low number of employed women over 55, the 55 – 59 and 60 – 64 age groups were merged together.
Source: Institute for Public Affairs, August 2006.

Educational attainment is a much more important factor affecting the pay of women over 45 (see Table 4.41 and Graph 4.30). As many as 92% of women with elementary education, but only 5% of women with university education earned less than Sk10,000 per month. As many as 59% of women with university education, but only 19% of women with secondary education had a net monthly income exceeding Sk15,000. Such an income was rather exceptional among women with vocational education (9%) and non-existent among those with elementary education.

Table 4.42 shows that women are generally less satisfied with their pay than men (39% of women vs. 44% of men). This difference is typical of women and men under 45 as well as over 45. At

Table 4.41
Net earned monthly income of women between 45 and 64 – by education (%)

	Elementary	Secondary without A levels	Complete secondary	University	Total
Under 5,000	5	5	5	0	5
5,001 – 10,000	87	46	35	5	40
10,001 – 15,000	8	40	41	36	36
15,001 – 20,000	0	8	12	26	11
20,001 – 25,000	0	1	5	12	4
25,001 – 30,000	0	0	1	14	2
Over 30,001	0	0	1	7	2

Note: All earned net monthly incomes of employed women.
Source: Institute for Public Affairs, August 2006.

Graph 4.30
Net earned monthly income of women between 45 and 64 – by education (%)

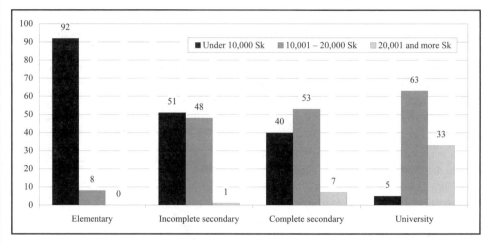

Note: All earned net monthly incomes of employed women.
Source: Institute for Public Affairs, August 2006.

Table 4.42
Satisfaction of younger and older women and men with remuneration (% of answers "certainly and rather satisfied" : "definitely and rather unsatisfied")

	Women	Men
Under 45	41 : 59	47 : 53
Over 45	35 : 63	40 : 60
Total	39 : 60	44 : 56

Note: Data for employed respondents only. The remainder of the 100% figure comprises the answer "I don't know".
Source: Institute for Public Affairs, August 2006.

the same time, older generation – both women and men – was more critical of their incomes than the younger generation.

But let us examine the satisfaction of older women and men with their income from the more detailed viewpoint of five-year age intervals. As Graph 4.31 suggests, women between 50 and 54 are much less satisfied with their incomes (15% satisfied) than women from the previous 45 – 49 age group (38% satisfied). At the same time, they are less satisfied than women from the two subsequent age groups (60% each). The same declining trend can be seen also among men, but here the lowest satisfaction was recorded in the 55 – 59 age group (29% satisfied). Women and men thus seem least happy with their pay in the age preceding the five-year interval in which most of them become eligible for retirement. There are three plausible explanations why those who decide to work past their retirement age are more satisfied with their pay than their younger counterparts: first, their pensions increase by their remaining at work; second, they can rely on their pensions to boost their earned income; third, they appreciate also other, non-financial aspects of their work.

Let us conclude. There are significant differences between women and men in Slovakia in terms of earned incomes as well as satisfaction with them. The long-term gender pay gap has persisted and even widened in recent years. This discrepancy affects not only the social situation of working women, but also their economic chances in post-productive years. It is particularly alarming in the context of the long-term trend toward the feminization of ageing. The lower incomes of women throughout their professional career are subsequently reflected in their lower old-age pensions. In a broader context, this trend contributes to the feminization of poverty (Filadelfiová – Guráň – Šútorová, 2002; Bednárik, 2004).

Graph 4.31
Satisfaction of women and men over 45 with their pay (% of affirmative answers)

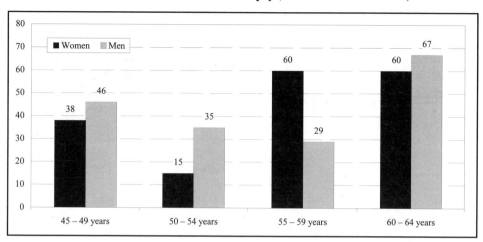

Note: Data for employed respondents only.
Source: Institute for Public Affairs, August 2006.

It is important to realize that the gender pay gap can be reduced or even closed only if the equality of opportunities for women and men in the whole society increases – not only on the labor market but also in the private sphere, which requires more effective harmonization of work and family life. Another challenge is setting such parameters of the pension system that would alleviate the existing gender differences in pensions, instead of deepening them.[13]

4.1.9. UNEMPLOYMENT OF WOMEN AND MEN
Development after 1989

In Slovakia, unemployment re-emerged in the early 1990s as an almost new phenomenon. Before 1989, the country under communism had officially claimed full employment, and there was only hidden unemployment or over-employment. In less than two decades, unemployment changed dynamically. Following the record-breaking years of 2000 to 2004, when the unemployment rate repeatedly approached 20%, unemployment declined rapidly (see Graph 4.32). By 2007, the overall unemployment rate had fallen to 11.0%; without work were 12.5% of women compared to 9.8% of men.

Nevertheless, Slovakia's unemployment is still relatively high compared to most EU member states. In 2006, the average unemployment rate in the EU-27 was 7.9%; the unemployment rate of women was 8.8% and that of men was 7.2%. In the Czech Republic, 8.8% of women and 5.8% of men were unemployed (*Employment in...*, 2007).

---

[13] The risk of deepening gender gaps in pensions was highlighted by Oľga Pietruchová, who pointed out that the pension reform in 2004 had not been preceded by a thorough analysis of its different impacts on women and men. She argued that the introduction of two "savings" pillars (i.e. the capitalization and voluntary pillars) gives women less chances to save enough funds for the period following their retirement compared to men. This ensues from the fact that most women interrupt their professional careers because of childcare (Pietruchová, 2006; 2008).

Graph 4.32
Unemployment rate of women and men in Slovakia (1994 – 2007, in %)

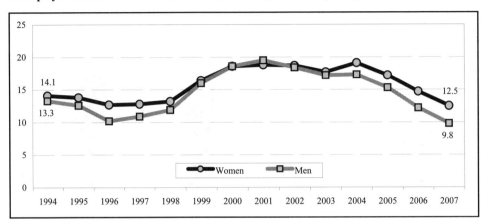

Note: The unemployment rate is calculated as the ratio of unemployed to the total number of economically active persons. The methodology used by labor force surveys was applied.
Source: *Slovstat*, 2008.

As Graph 4.32 illustrates, the gender gap in unemployment disappeared during the peak period between 2000 and 2004, but resurfaced as soon as unemployment began to decline. By 2007, the unemployment rate of women was almost three percent higher than that of men.

Unemployment of Women and Men by Educational Attainment

The unemployment of women and men depends largely on their education. As Graph 4.33 documents, the lower the educational attainment, the higher the incidence of unemployment.

Graph 4.33
Unemployment rate of women and men – by education (2007 – in %)

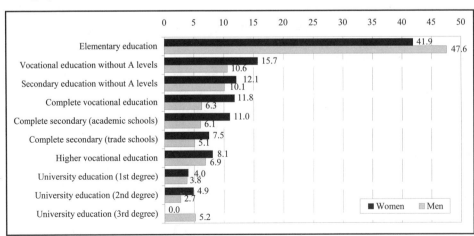

Note: The unemployment rate is calculated as the ratio of unemployed to the total number of economically active persons. The methodology used by labor force surveys was applied.
Source: *Slovstat*, 2008.

In 2007, the unemployment rate was 41.9% among women with elementary education and 47.6% among their male counterparts; in other words, only 58.1% of economically active women and 52.4% of economically active men from this education category were employed. The unemployment rate declines as people become more educated, at first sharply and then moderately but steadily. Among women and men with all three degrees of university education, unemployment is usually under 5%.

Graph 4.33 also shows that at 8 from 10 levels of education – except for the lowest and highest ones – the unemployment of women was higher than that of men.

Unemployment of Women and Men by Age

In ten out of eleven age groups, the share of unemployed women is higher than that of men (see Table 4.44). The unemployment rate is by far the highest in the youngest age categories of women and men. In 2007, 49.8% of economically active women and 42.7% of economically active men between 15 and 19 were unemployed. In the next age group of 20 – 24 year olds, the unemployment rate dropped to 16.1% among women and 17.4% among men. This is the only age group where the unemployment rate of women is lower than that of men.

Let us now look at the differences in the age structure of unemployed women and men (see Graph 4.34). In 2007, 18% of all unemployed men and 12.1% of all unemployed women were between 20 and 24. The age

Table 4.44
Unemployment rate of women and men – by age (1995, 2000 and 2007 – in %)

	Women			Men		
	1995	2000	2007	1995	2000	2007
15 – 19	37.5	62.2	49.8	47.8	56.6	42.7
20 – 24	16.6	24.9	16.1	18.6	31.3	17.4
25 – 29	21.4	19.9	13.8	13.1	18.3	9.3
30 – 34	14.2	20.1	12.4	10.8	15.0	8.6
35 – 39	13.6	17.6	11.0	9.9	15.8	7.6
40 – 44	8.4	13.1	10.7	9.3	14.3	9.8
45 – 49	6.9	13.3	11.1	7.4	13.6	7.9
50 – 54	7.8	10.6	12.5	8.8	13.2	7.9
55 – 59	10.3	8.7	9.1	6.5	14..4	8.3
60 – 64	13.8	6.1	9.4	6.6	6.8	5.0
Over 65	6.7	29.9	3.2	6.9	8.1	1.8
Total	13.8	18.6	12.5	12.6	18.6	9.8

Source: *Slovstat*, 2008.

Graph 4.34
Age structure of unemployed women and men in Slovakia (2007 – in %)

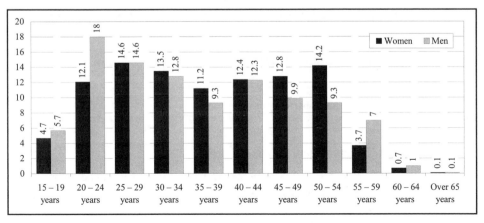

Note: The methodology used was from labor force surveys.
Source: *Slovstat*, 2008.

group of unemployed between 25 and 29 reached 14.6% of all unemployed women, as well as men. The percentage of unemployed in each of the next five age groups (i.e. between 30 and 54) among all unemployed women was higher than that of unemployed men of the same age (except for the 40 – 44 age group). On the other hand, the share of unemployed men in the 55 – 59 age group was almost double in comparison with that of unemployed women.

How did women and men participate in the overall decline in unemployment between 2000 and 2007? As Graph 4.35 shows, the unemployment rate of men declined more rapidly than that of women: by 2007, the male unemployment rate dropped to 52.7% of the level from 2000, while the unemployment rate for women declined to 67.2%.

In all age groups, the index of change in the unemployment rate was lower for men than for women. While the difference between women and men was not significant in younger age groups, it increased with age. Moreover, the index exceeded 100 for all three age groups of women older than 50, which means that the unemployment rate between 2000 and 2007 actually increased in all of these age groups.

Graph 4.35
Index of change in the unemployment rate of women and men – by age (2007; 2000 = 100)

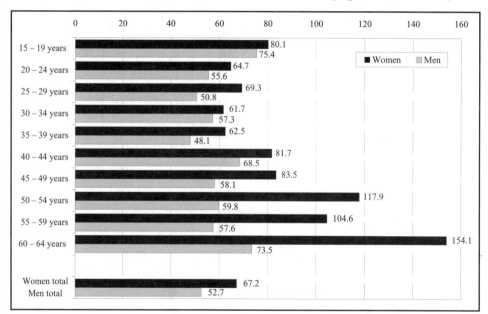

Note: The methodology used was from labor force surveys.
Source: *Slovstat*, 2008.

Long-Term Unemployment of Women and Men

A negative trend of the last decade has been the growth in the long-term unemployment of women and men. Between 1998 and 2006, the share of long-term unemployed increased from 7.1% to 11.2% among women and from 6.0% to 9.4% among men.

The long-term unemployment of Slovak women and men is substantially higher than the EU-27 average (see Graph 4.36). In 2006, the share of women unemployed over the long term

Table 4.45
Long-term unemployment of women and men (1998 – 2006, in %)

		1998	1999	2000	2001	2002	2003	2004	2005	2006
Long-term unemployment	Women	7.1	8.3	10.2	11.3	12.5	11.7	12.4	12.3	11.2
	Men	6.0	7.4	10.3	11.3	11.9	11.3	11.3	11.2	9.4
	Total	6.5	7.8	10.3	11.3	12.2	11.4	11.8	11.7	10.2
Overall unemployment	Women	13.2	16.4	18.6	18.8	18.7	17.7	19.1	17.2	14.7
	Men	11.9	16.0	18.6	19.5	18.4	17.2	17.3	15.3	12.2
	Total	12.6	16.4	18.8	19.3	18.7	17.6	18.2	16.3	13.4

Note: The unemployment rate is calculated as the ratio of unemployed to the total number of economically active persons. The long-term unemployment rate is calculated as the percentage of those who have been unemployed longer than 12 months out of the total number of economically active persons. The methodology used by labor force surveys was applied.
Source: *Slovstat*, 2008.

was almost three times higher in Slovakia than in the EU-27 (11.2% vs. 4.0%); the same goes for Slovak men (9.4% vs. 3.3%).

Graph 4.36
Long-term unemployment rate in Slovakia and EU member states (2006 – in %)

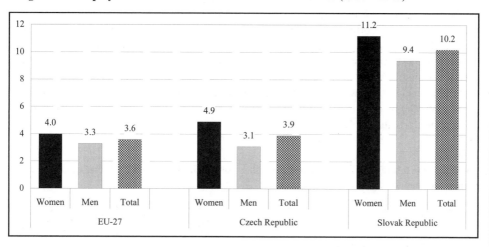

Source: *Employment in...*, 2007.

Table 4.46
Structure of unemployed women and men in Slovakia – by length of unemployment (1996 – 2007, in %)

	1996		1998		2000		2004		2007	
	Women	Men	Women	Men	Women	Men	Women	Men	Women	Men
Under 3 months	20.2	16.4	20.4	17.4	11.1	13.1	12.8	14.2	11.1	10.9
3 – 6 months	17.2	11.9	17.9	15.6	13.8	12.3	9.6	9.4	7.0	6.4
6 – 12 months	16.8	17.4	19.8	17.2	19.4	19.6	17.4	15.6	12.5	10.4
Over 12 months	45.8	51.7	41.9	48.5	54.7	53.3	60.2	60.8	69.4	72.3

Note: The methodology used by labor force surveys was applied. The remainder of the 100% figure is made up of people whose length of unemployment was not identified.
Source: *Slovstat*, 2008.

The increase in long-term unemployment is also reflected in the structure of unemployed women and men (see Table 4.46). While in 1996, those unemployed for 12 months or longer made up 45.8% of the total number of unemployed women and 51.7% of the total number of unemployed men, by 2007 their shares increased to 69.4% and 72.3%, respectively. On the other hand, the percentages of persons who had been unemployed for shorter periods declined substantially.

4.2. WORK IN THE PERCEPTION OF WOMEN AND MEN
4.2.1. WORK AND PRIVATE LIFE

One of the factors that shape the lives of employed women and men is the relationship between their work and private life.[14]

As Table 4.47 shows, 39% of employed women and 55 % of men in Slovakia view their work primarily as a way to make money. One in three women (33%) and almost one in four men (23%) are emotionally more identified with their work, but are still able to draw a clear line between work and private life. While these people like to work, they also make sure that their work does not interfere with their private life.

On the other hand, 24% of women and 20% of men consider their work to be important, and even if they try, they often can't prevent their work from interfering with their private life. The fact that there is a slightly higher share of these attitudes among women than among men may indicate a stronger pressure of traditional gender expectations. In other words, a woman, even if she might work less overtime than a man, can have a stronger feeling that her long working hours interfere with her family commitments. Last, but not least, 4% of women and 2% of men may be described as true workaholics, as work is the centre of their universe and ordains their private lives as well.

Table 4.47
"Which of the following assertions best describes your attitude to work?" (views of employed women and men in %)

	Views of women			Views of men		
	Under 45	Over 45	Total	Under 45	Over 45	Total
To me, work is primarily a way of making money.	38	39	39	58	49	55
I like to work but I don't let work interfere with my private life.	35	31	33	20	29	23
Work is rather important to me and it often interferes with my private life even if I don't want it to.	25	24	24	20	19	20
Work is so important to me that it takes precedence over my private life – I live my job.	2	6	4	2	3	2

Note: The answers "I don't know" and "didn't answer" were disregarded. The percentages in the columns add up to 100%.
Source: Institute for Public Affairs, August 2006.

Table 4.47 also illustrates that after they reach the age of 45, men tend to grow more emotionally identified with their work, but not at the expense of their private lives. Among women,

---

[14] In Slovakia there is a shortage of generally available findings of sociological surveys that map the current attitudes of women and men of various ages to work in the broader context of their personal preferences. In 2006, the Institute for Public Affairs tried to fill this gap by carrying out a representative survey. Its findings have provided the basis for this chapter.

the effect of age shows up in a moderate increase in the share of workaholics who are fully devoted to their work. This may ensue from the fact that among older employed women, there is a higher percentage of lonely women, widows or women with grown-up children who fill up or even replace their private lives with work.

As Table 4.47 shows, views of women and men over 45 are more alike than those of younger people.

The relationship that people develop between work and their private life is influenced by their educational attainment. The higher it is, the stronger is the interference of the work with their private life: people with higher education often have more interesting jobs and higher positions in the workplace, which require from them greater commitment to work.

The impact of education is especially strong among employed women in their mature years (see Graph 4.37). As many as 60% of women with lower education, but only 28% of women with higher education view work primarily as a means to earn their living. On the other hand, 35% of women with higher education but only 12% of women with lower education admit that work interferes with their private lives.

Graph 4.37
"Which of the following assertions best describes your attitude to work?" (views of women over 45 by education – in %)

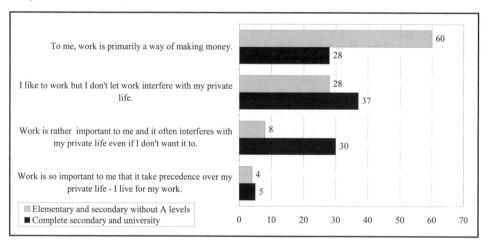

Note: The answers "I don't know" and "didn't answer" were disregarded.
Source: Institute for Public Affairs, August 2006.

4.2.2. WHAT WOMEN AND MEN APPRECIATE ABOUT THEIR WORK

How do women and men see the value of their work? Table 4.48 shows some gender similarities as well as differences. Sixty percent of women and 73% of men appreciate their work primarily because it allows them to provide financially for their families. Thirty percent of women and 32% of men appreciate the chance to reach financial independence. The following four benefits of work in the eyes of women are: being in contact with other people (31%), doing what they like to do (23%), using their education and skills (17%) and being useful to others (13%). Finally, 12% of women appreciate that their work allows them to earn security for the old age, while 9% appreciate the social status acquired thanks to their work.

Compared to men, women see themselves as breadwinners less frequently. They also put lower emphasis on the importance of work for earning security for the old age – despite (or because of?) the fact that their pensions are lower than those of men. On the other hand, women more frequently mention social dimensions of work such as maintaining contact with other people, a feeling of usefulness with respect to others and the possibility to earn social status through work.

Table 4.48
"What do you appreciate most about your work?" (views of employed women and men under 45 and over 45 – in %)

	Views of women			Views of men		
	Under 45	Over 45	Total	Under 45	Over 45	Total
Being able to support my family financially	57	65	60	69	81	73
Being in contact with other people	33	28	31	17	14	16
Being financially independent	38	19	30	37	23	32
Being able to do what I like to do	22	25	23	14	26	23
Being able to use my education and skills	16	18	17	18	17	18
Being useful to other people	11	15	13	6	8	7
Being able to earn security for old age	7	20	12	14	26	18
Being able to earn social status	12	6	9	5	5	5

Note: This table features the sums of the first and second most important options.
Source: Institute for Public Affairs, August 2006.

Table 4.48 also illustrates that women's views of the value of their work tend to change as they grow older. Women in their mature years appreciate more the chance to provide financially for their families and to earn security for their old age, as well as the chance to do what

Graph 4.38
"What do you appreciate most about your work or profession?" (views of women over 45 by education in %)

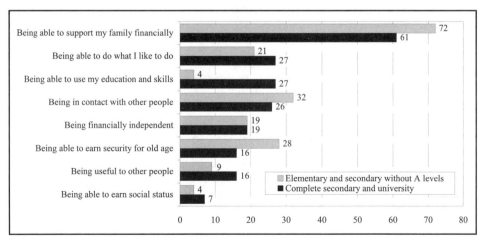

Note: This graph features the sums of the first and second most important options.
Source: Institute for Public Affairs, August 2006.

they like to do and to be useful to others. Younger women, for their part, emphasize financial independence and the chance to maintain social contacts and earn social status. Similar differences are characteristic also of the views of older and younger men.

Education is an important factor, too. It plays a strong role particularly in the group of women between 45 and 64. While less educated women accentuate that their work gives them a chance to provide for their households and earn security for their old age, more educated women appreciate the chance to use their education and skills. They also more frequently emphasized the self-fulfillment and status-building dimensions of work.[15]

4.2.3. SATISFACTION WITH SPECIFIC ASPECTS OF WORK

The value people attribute to their work largely depends on its specific nature, i.e. on job description, working conditions, employer's approach, remuneration, etc. Let us therefore examine how women and men perceive key aspects of their concrete work.

As Table 4.49 indicates, the views of women and men are similar in many respects. Both groups strongly emphasize those aspects of work that are related to the atmosphere in the workplace. For instance, they appreciate having good friends at work (90% of women and 87% of men), feeling at home in their organizations (77% of women and 73% of men), having a good boss (76% of women and 74% of men) and having an employer that understands the needs of their employees (70% of women and 72% of men). The vast majority of women and men are satisfied with their working time (84% of women and 81% of men), despite the

Table 4.49
"To what degree do the following assertions characterize particular aspects of your work?"
(% of answers "certainly and rather yes" : "definitely and rather no")

	Views of women			Views of men		
	Under 45	45 – 64	Total	Under 45	45 – 64	Total
I have very good friends at work.	89 : 10	90 : 10	90 : 10	90 : 10	84 : 14	87 : 11
Hours of work suit me fine.	82 : 18	88 : 11	84 : 15	80 : 20	82 : 19	81 : 19
I feel at home in this organization.	77 : 22	77 : 23	77 : 23	73 : 26	75 : 22	73 : 25
I have a good boss.	78 : 21	72 : 25	76 : 22	76 : 22	70 : 28	74 : 24
My employer understands the needs of employees like myself.	74 : 25	66 : 31	70 : 27	71 : 27	73 : 25	72 : 27
Work allows me to use my education, qualifications and experience.	71 : 29	68 : 32	70 : 30	71 : 29	72 : 27	72 : 28
In my job I can learn new things and grow professionally.	63 : 37	51 : 49	58 : 41	63 : 37	55 : 44	60 : 40
I am satisfied with my remuneration.	41 : 59	35 : 63	39 : 60	47 : 53	40 : 60	44 : 56
My work gives me good prospects for promotion.	31 : 66	15 : 81	25 : 72	34 : 63	18 : 79	28 : 69
My work gives me various social benefits.	20 : 78	23 : 75	22 : 77	29 : 71	30 : 69	29 : 70
I might well lose my job within a year.	12 : 69	20 : 59	15 : 65	12 : 67	15 : 64	13 : 66
I am satisfied with my current job.	87 : 13	86 : 14	87 : 13	86 : 14	89 : 11	87 : 13
I would change my job if I had a chance.	43 : 50	42 : 57	43 : 53	44 : 49	36 : 58	41 : 52

Note: The remainder of the 100% figure comprises the answer "I don't know".
Source: Institute for Public Affairs, August 2006.

---

[15] With this attitude toward work, educated women and men over 45 find it difficult to put up with those employers who underrate or even disparage them because of their age. Age discrimination of employees is often counterproductive to the mission of an institution, but it can serve the interests of managers: younger employees are less experienced, and often are easier to control and less critical of the professional performance of their manager. One of the domains where employees in their mature years are quite frequently exposed to age discrimination is the media.

fact that it is longer and less flexible than is the EU average (see Section 4.1.6. of this publication). Most of women and men (70% and 72%, respectively) also appreciate that their work allows them to use their education, qualifications and experience, as well as the opportunity to learn new things and grow professionally (58% and 60%, respectively).

However, only two thirds of employed women and men (65% and 66%, respectively) feel secure in their work. The remaining one third explicitly admitted or did not exclude the possibility of losing their job.

People are much more critical of other aspects of their employment. Only 39% of women and 44% of men were satisfied with their wages. Only 25% of women and 28% of men saw good prospects for promotion in their current jobs, while 72% of women and 69% of men did not. Respondents were even more critical of the social benefits provided by their jobs: as many as 77% of women and 70% of men did not see any. The fact that women are more critical about all these aspects of their work than men corresponds with their weaker position on the labor market (see Section 4.1. of this book).

Graph 4.39
Share of women and men who are satisfied with their work and stable in their jobs (%)

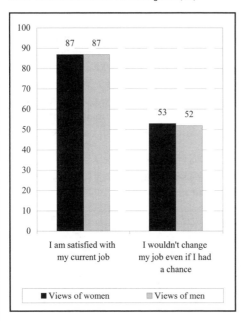

Note: The remainder of the 100% figure comprises negative answers and the answer "I don't know".
Source: Institute for Public Affairs, August 2006.

So far, we have examined how women and men see specific aspects of their work. But how strong is their overall satisfaction? On the one hand, a huge majority of women and men (87% each) expressed general satisfaction with their work (see Graph 4.39). On the other hand, this very positive finding should be taken with some reservations, as 43% of women and 41% of men also said they would change jobs if they had a chance. Only a narrow majority of women (53%) and men (52%) would keep their current job even if they were offered another.

What aspects of work motivate women and men to keep the current jobs or to switch them? Women are particularly sensitive to three factors: satisfaction with their pay, "feeling at home" in the workplace, and a conviction that their employer understands their needs. The same three factors are also most important for men, albeit in a different order.

Let us now compare attitudes of people belonging to various age groups. As Table 4.49 shows, women over 45 were less satisfied with 7 out of 13 aspects of their work than younger women. This difference was the most apparent in their evaluation of job security (positive evaluation was expressed by 59% of women over 45 compared to 69% of younger women), of prospects for promotion (15% and 31%, respectively) and of chance to learn new things and grow professionally (51% and 63%, respectively). Younger women were more critical of only two aspects of work: the social benefits ensuing from employment and the working time.

At the same time, women over 45 expressed overall satisfaction with their current jobs almost exactly as often as younger women (86% and 87%, respectively). Older women were also more reluctant to contemplate switching jobs (57% : 50%). This indicates that they have accepted their current employment situation. They may also be discouraged from considering a career change because they are aware that women of their age face poorer chances on the labor market (see Section 5.2. of this book).

And how does the satisfaction with work evolve with age among men? According to Table 4.49, older men are more critical of 6 out of 13 aspects of their work than younger men. Their views do not grow as negative with age as they do among older women. Similarly to their female counterparts, men over 45 were particularly critical of their prospects for promotion (18% of men over 45 saw good chances of promotion compared to 34% of younger men), remuneration (40% and 47%, respectively), the possibility to learn new things and grow professionally (55% vs. 64%) and employment security (64% vs. 67%). Despite all that, men in their mature years felt more satisfied with their current jobs (89% vs. 86%) and more reluctant to contemplate switching jobs (58% vs. 49%) than their younger colleagues.

A comparison of the views of women and men over 45 shows that women feel generally less satisfied with their jobs than their male counterparts; they evaluated 8 out of 13 aspects of work more critically than men, while only in four cases they expressed felt satisfaction.

As one would expect, people's satisfaction with particular aspects of their work are significantly affected by their education. Table 4.50 shows the impact of the educational attainment on the views of women and men between 45 and 64. Both mature women and men who have a higher education are much more satisfied with their jobs, feel more at home in their workplace, and are more satisfied with the use of their education, qualifications and experience. They also see better chances to learn new things and grow professionally. They are more satisfied with their pay, they feel more secure in their current job, and are less tempted to switch jobs.

Table 4.50
Views of women and men between 45 and 64 regarding select aspects of their work (% of answers "certainly and rather yes" : "definitely and rather no" – by education)

	Views of women		Views of men	
	Elementary and secondary without A levels	Complete secondary and university	Elementary and secondary without A levels	Complete secondary and university
I have very good friends at work.	89 : 11	87 : 13	81 : 17	86 : 11
Hours of work suit me fine.	84 : 12	85 : 15	80 : 20	87 : 14
I feel at home in this organization.	70 : 30	77 : 23	72 : 25	79 : 17
I have a good boss.	70 : 26	71 : 28	71 : 26	73 : 25
My employer understands the feelings of employees like myself.	62 : 32	64 : 34	74 : 25	78 : 20
Work allows me to use my education, qualifications and experience.	49 : 51	78 : 22	62 : 36	79 : 21
In my job I can learn new things and grow professionally.	33 : 65	62 : 38	51 : 49	64 : 36
I am satisfied with my remuneration.	30 : 70	41 : 57	35 : 64	47 : 53
My work gives me good prospects for promotion.	9 : 89	18 : 74	18 : 79	20 : 74
My work gives me various social benefits.	25 : 76	25 : 73	32 : 68	27 : 71
I may well lose my job within a year.	27 : 47	18 : 64	21 : 53	9 : 72
I am satisfied with my current job.	76 : 24	90 : 10	89 : 11	89 : 11
I would change my job if I had a chance.	47 : 49	42 : 58	44 : 47	30 : 64

Note: The remainder of the 100% figure comprises the answer "I don't know".
Source: Institute for Public Affairs, August 2006.

Table 4.50 also permits a comparison of gender differences. Women with complete secondary and university education are more critical of their remuneration and the approach of their employers than their male counterparts. They also feel less secure in their jobs and more frequently think about switching jobs. Needless to say, their more critical views reflect their weaker position on the labor market (See Sections 4.1.8. and 4.1.9. of this book).

4. 2.4. PROFILE OF THE WORK TEAM

Gender Composition of Work Teams

One of the hallmarks of Slovakia's labor market is its strong gender segregation. It shows up not only on the level of economic sectors or types of profession, but also in the make-up of

Graph 4.40
"What is your work team like in terms of gender make-up? And what kind of work team would you prefer?" (views of employed women and men – in %)

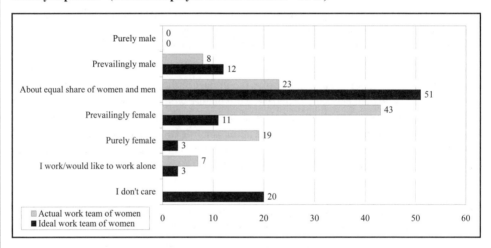

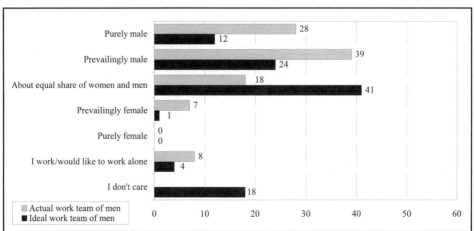

Note: The answers "I don't know" and "didn't answer" were disregarded.
Source: Institute for Public Affairs, August 2006.

work teams (Graph 4.40). As for women, 19% of them work in a purely female team and 43% in a prevailingly female work team. A further 23% of women work in teams that have approximately the same portion of women and men. Only 8% of women work in prevailingly male teams. The remaining 7% work alone.

The composition of teams is which the men work is even more one-sided: 28% of them work in purely male environments and 39% work in prevailingly male workplaces. Only 18% of men work in teams that are balanced in terms of gender, and 7% work in prevailingly female workplaces. The remaining 8% of men work alone.

Let us now examine the notions of women and men about the ideal gender profile of their work teams. A Graph 4.40 shows, they differ significantly from reality. Both women and men favor gender-balanced work teams: 51% of women and 41% of men would like to work in such teams. Twenty percent of women and 18% of men do not attach special importance to the gender profile of their work team. Small portions of women and men (3% and 4%, respectively) prefer to work alone.

Remaining 26% of women would choose either prevailingly male (12%) or predominantly or purely female (14%) work teams. On the other hand, the remaining 36% of men would prefer prevailingly (24%) or purely male (12%) workplaces. In other words, women are more ready to work in gender-balanced teams or in workplaces with a stronger presence of men. [16] On the other hand, men tend to prefer male colleagues.

Graph 4.40 also shows that women find predominantly or purely female teams generally less attractive than men find prevailingly or purely male workplaces. A comparison of the actual and ideal gender make-up of teams shows that women experience a greater discrepancy between the actual and ideal make-up of their work teams than men.

How does the gender make-up of women's work teams change, as they get older? According to Table 4.51, these changes are minor, as most women under 45, as well as women over 45 work in prevailingly female teams. This experience is slightly more frequent among women over 45 (45%) than among younger women (42%), while working in gender-balanced work teams is less common (18% and 27%, respectively).

As for the notions of mature women about the ideal gender profile of their work team, they differ from those of younger women in two respects: first, women 45+ place less

Table 4.51
"What is your work team like in terms of gender make-up? And what kind of work team would you prefer?" (views of employed women by age – in %)

	Views of women		Views of men	
	Actual team	Ideal team	Actual team	Ideal team
Prevailingly male	8	14	8	10
About equal share of women and men	27	55	18	43
Prevailingly female	42	10	45	13
Purely female	18	3	20	2
I work/would like to work alone	5	3	9	3
I don't care	–	15	–	29

Note: The answers "I don't know", "didn't answer" and "other answer" were disregarded. The percentages in the columns add up to 100%.
Source: Institute for Public Affairs, August 2006.

---

[16] This is especially typical of women with higher education. On the other hand, women with lower education favor predominantly or purely female teams.

emphasis on a balanced gender make-up (43% of women over 45 compared to 55% among younger women); second, they do not seek prevailingly male workplaces to the same extent (10% and 14%, respectively). Also, they are more frequently indifferent about the issue (29% and 15%, respectively). One may conclude that the discrepancy between the actual and ideal gender profile of the work team is slightly weaker among older than among younger women.

Age Composition of Work Teams

Age diversity on the labor market is reflected in the age composition of work teams. In Slovakia, 44% of working women and 51% of men are part of mixed work teams consisting of colleagues in their young, middle and older years. Further 29% of women and

Graph 4.41
"What is your work team like in terms of age composition? And what kind of work team would you prefer?" (views of employed women and men – in %)

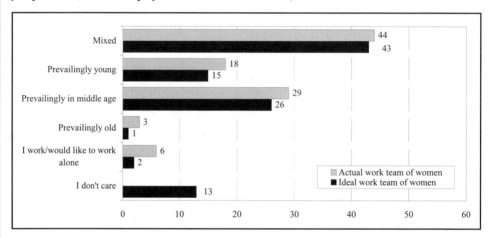

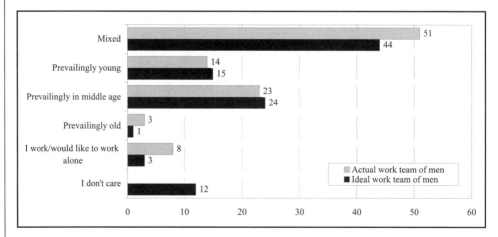

Note: The answers "I don't know", "Didn't answer" and "Other answer" were disregarded.
Source: Institute for Public Affairs, August 2006.

23% of men work in middle-aged teams while 18% of women and 14% of men have mostly young colleagues. Only 3% of women and men work in prevailingly older teams. Women's experience of age diversity in the workplace is very similar to that of men (Graph 4.41).

And how do women and men view the age composition of their ideal work teams? Their ideals are very similar, and very close to reality. Forty three percent of women and 44% of men believe it is best to work in a mixed work team. Twenty six percent of women and 24 % of men would prefer a middle-aged work team. Fifteen percent of women and men wish their colleagues were mostly young, while only 1% of them would rather be part of an older work team. Thirteen percent of women and 12% of men do not care about the age composition of their workplaces.

4.2.5. PROFILE OF THE MANAGER

Gender inequality in filling management posts has long been present on Slovakia's labor market. According to the survey carried out in 2006 by the Institute for Public Affairs, 62% of employed persons said their immediate boss was a man, while only one 26% said it was a woman (See Graph 4.42).

In terms of age, most people's immediate bosses are middle-aged (56% of all managers – 39% are men and 17% are women), followed by managers in their older years (18% of all managers – 14% are men and 4% are women) and young managers or those in their prime (14% of all managers – 9% are men and 5% are women).

The experience of women and men is substantially different. As many as 80% of men, but only 46% of all women said their immediate boss was a man, regardless of age. On the other hand, 46% of women, but only 6% of men had women as their immediate manager. While the share of women managed by men and by women is equal (46%), the share of men managed by men (80%) is vastly greater than the share of men managed by a woman (6%). In other words, the ratio of men whose immediate managers are men and those whose bosses are women is 13:1.

How do women and men view the ideal profile of their manager? About one fourth of women and men (28% and 24%, respectively) said they did not attach importance to their manager's age or gender.

But the ideals of the remaining three quarters of respondents are quite different. Men strongly prefer male managers (70%) to female managers (6%); according to them, the ideal manager is a middle-aged man (52%).

Women are slightly more divided, showing a preference for male managers (45%) over female bosses (27%); in both cases, they prefer managers in their middle years.

As these findings show, public opinion reproduces the disproportion between the actual representation of women and men in management posts, which is strongly in favor of men. It is noteworthy that women themselves contribute to reinforcing the image of men as ideal managers.[17]

---

[17] People's preferences regarding their managers were also examined in a survey carried out by the FOCUS agency in 1995. Both men and women preferred male managers to female ones (Bútorová, 1996, pp. 90 – 91).

Graph 4.42
"Who is your immediate boss? And who would you like to have as your immediate boss?"
(views of employed women in %)

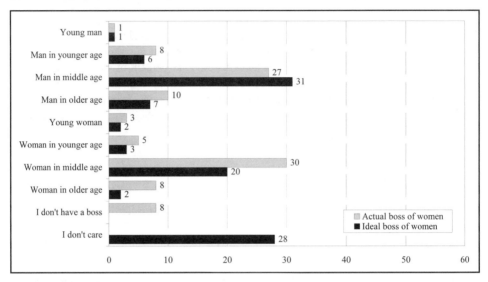

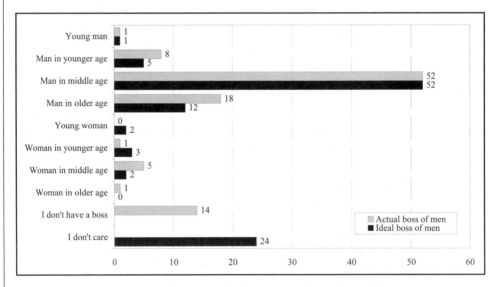

Note: The answers "I don't know", "didn't answer" and "other answer" were disregarded.
Source: Institute for Public Affairs, August 2006.

4.2.6. WHAT PRICE ARE WOMEN AND MEN PREPARED TO PAY TO KEEP THEIR JOB

How would women and men react if their job were in jeopardy? What concessions would they be willing to make in order to keep it?

As Table 4.52 shows, the least acceptable alternative for women as well as for men is to accept worse jobs, i.e. jobs that would be more strenuous, in a more harmful environment, etc. Almost three in four women (73%) and over two in three men (68%) rejected such an option.

The second least acceptable alternative is working for a lower wage. This option is less acceptable for men (67%) than for women (54%). Needless to say, this difference reflects the stronger emphasis men put on the financial aspects of work and their greater identification with the role of the breadwinner.

The third option – to work longer hours at the expense of family and private life – was acceptable for 59% of men, but only 45% of women. Longer absence from home would mean for many women more difficulties in fulfilling their role of the homemaker.

Finally, 66% of women and 75% of men declared their willingness to commute to work from a greater distance. Again, the lower inclination of women to accept this option has to do with their greater participation in taking care of family members and of the household.

Table 4.52
"Imagine your job is in jeopardy. What would you be willing to do to keep your job?" (% of answers "certainly and rather yes" : "definitely and rather no")

	Views of working women			Views of working men		
	Under 45	Over 45	Total	Under 45	Over 45	Total
Accept worse work	15 : 80	30 : 64	21 : 73	26 : 71	32 : 64	28 : 68
Work for a lower wage	33 : 60	49 : 45	40 : 54	29 : 70	34 : 62	31 : 67
Work more hours at the expense of family or private life	42 : 49	50 : 45	45 : 48	60 : 35	57 : 38	59 : 36
Commute to work from a greater distance	69 : 28	61 : 35	66 : 30	79 : 19	67 : 30	75 : 23

Note: The remainder of the 100% figure comprises the answer "I don't know".
Source: Institute for Public Affairs, August 2006.

Graph 4.43
"Imagine your job is in jeopardy. What would you be willing to do to keep your job?" (% of affirmative answers of employed women and men over 45)

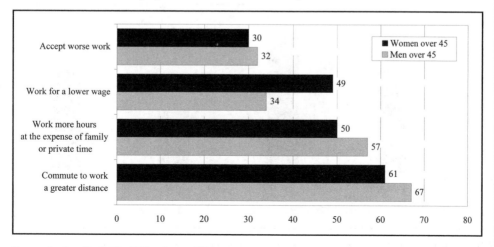

Source: Institute for Public Affairs, August 2006.

Table 4.52 shows also the impact of the age. Women over 45 are more prepared to accept worse work, a lower wage, and longer working hours than younger women. At the same time, they are less willing to commute to work from a greater distance.

Almost one half of women over 45, but only one third of men of the same age would accept a lower wage – a much greater gender gap than in the younger group. On the other hand, women over 45 are slightly more negative than their male counterparts about all three other job-keeping strategies, particularly those that would make the fulfillment of their family responsibilities more difficult.

Finally, let us examine the role of education in the job-keeping strategies of women over 45. Table 4.53 illustrates that women with higher education, who tend to perceive work more as a source of self-fulfillment, would be more prepared to accept working for a lower wage, working longer hours and commuting to work from a greater distance. Women with lower education, for their part, would be more willing to accept worse work.

Table 4.53
"Imagine your job is in jeopardy. What would you be willing to do to keep your job?" (% of affirmative : negative answers of employed women and men over 45 – by education)

	Views of women		Views of men	
	Elementary and secondary without A levels	Complete secondary and university	Elementary and secondary without A levels	Complete secondary and university
Accept worse work (e.g. more strenuous, in a harmful environment, etc.)	34 : 62	27 : 64	35 : 62	29 : 68
Work for a lower wage	43 : 53	52 : 41	29 : 67	40 : 56
Work more hours at the expense of family or private time	48 : 50	51 : 42	61 : 33	52 : 36
Commute to work from a greater distance	36 : 60	74 : 20	67 : 30	68 : 29

Note: The remainder of the 100% figure comprises the answer "I don't know".
Source: Institute for Public Affairs, August 2006.

Graph 4.44
"Would you be willing to work for a lower wage in order to keep your job?" (% of affirmative answers among women and men – by age and education)

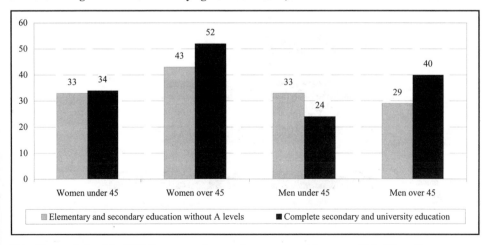

Note: The remainder of the 100% figure comprises negative answers and the answer "I don't know".
Source: Institute for Public Affairs, August 2006.

Higher education is associated with greater preparedness to work for less money among men over 45, too. However, this is not the case of other three job-keeping alternatives.

And what are the attitudes of younger women with higher education? Compared to their less educated counterparts, they are more reluctant to work for a lower wage, to work longer hours, or to accept worse work. The only exception is the option to commute to work from a greater distance.

Compared to their male counterparts, educated women under 45 are slightly more willing to accept a lower wage (Graph 4.44). Educated men under 45, for their part, are more prepared to make all three remaining concessions – to accept worse work, to work longer hours, and to commute from a greater distance.

4.2.7. COPING WITH THE PHYSICAL AND MENTAL DEMANDS OF WORK

How do women and men perceive two key dimensions of their work ability, i.e. the ability to cope with the physical and mental demands of their work? A glance at Graph 4.45 reveals that within both examined groups positive evaluations prevail by a wide margin over ambivalent and negative ones. Few women and men think that they handle either type of demands very poorly or rather poorly. Thirty eight percent of women and 46% of men believe they cope with the physical demands of their work very well; a further 48% of women and 45% of men find it rather good. As for the mental demands, 31% of women and 37% of men evaluated their performance as very good; a further 54% of women and 51% of men as rather good.

If we project these evaluations onto a scale from 1 to 5, where 1 means the best performance and 5 stands for the poorest one, then the average grade for copying with physical demands is 1.79 among women and 1.63 among men. The average grade for handling of mental challenges is 1.86 among women and 1.76 among men. To sum up, both women and men awarded themselves an average grade of "B+" on the "school scale" for copying with the physical and mental challenges of their work.

Besides the aforementioned similarities, there are also two differences in these perceptions. First, women are slightly more critical of their physical and mental performance at work than men. Second, both women and men believe that they handle the physical challenges of their work slightly better than the mental ones.

Let us now examine Table 4.54 illustrating the effect of various factors. It documents that women and men feel the physical and mental load of their work more as they grow older.[18] Women between 45 and 54, and especially women between 55 and 64, are particularly critical. Among men, the feeling of the mental load of their work peaks between 45 and 54 years and then slowly subsides; on the other hand, the sensation of the physical load increases until the 55 – 64 age group.

Table 4.54 also shows that women over 45 assess their ability to cope with the physical and mental challenges of their work more critically than younger women, as well as men over 45.

---

[18] The only exception is the youngest women under 24, who evaluated their ability to cope with the physical and mental challenges of their work as critically as women over 55.

Graph 4.45
How women and men assess their ability to cope with the physical and mental demands of their work (%)

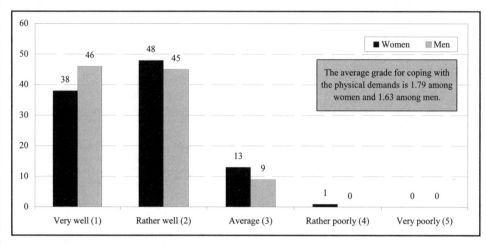

The average grade for coping with the physical demands is 1.79 among women and 1.63 among men.

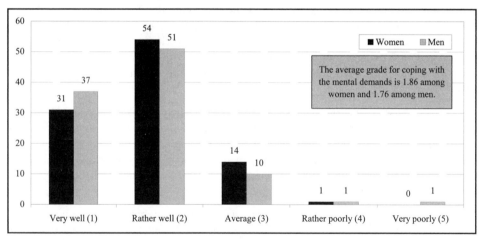

The average grade for coping with the mental demands is 1.86 among women and 1.76 among men.

Note: The answers "I don't know" and "didn't answer" were disregarded.
Source: Institute for Public Affairs, August 2006.

Education is an important factor, too. Both women and men with higher education tend to be more satisfied with handling the physical and mental demands of their work than their less-educated counterparts.

Finally, the assessment of the ability to cope with the physical and mental demands of work depends on the type of profession. As we have seen above, women are generally more critical of their work performance than men. However, as Table 4.54 documents, this applies only to blue-collar professions and administrative jobs. On the contrary, women who work as executives or creative professionals evaluate their ability to cope with the physical and mental challenges of their work better than men.

Table 4.54
"How do you cope with the physical and mental demands of your work?" (average grades among women and men – by age, education and profession)

		Women's self-evaluation		Men's self-evaluation	
		Physical demands	Mental demands	Physical demands	Mental demands
Age	18 – 24	2.04	2.04	1.46	1.71
	25 – 34	1.56	1.72	1.49	1.61
	35 – 44	1.75	1.79	1.56	1.78
	45 – 54	1.88	1.94	1.78	1.88
	55 – 64	1.97	2.06	1.95	1.82
	Under 45	1.71	1.79	1.51	1.70
	45 – 64	1.91	1.97	1.84	1.87
Education	Elementary and secondary without A levels	1.96	1.97	1.71	1.77
	Compete secondary and university	1.69	1.80	1.56	1.75
Profession (select types)	Supporting and non-qualified staff	1.97	1.97	1.81	1.81
	Plant and machine operators	1.92	1.96	1.57	1.67
	Administrative workers	1.62	1.82	1.40	1.50
	Technical, medical and pedagogical professionals	1.70	1.86	1.71	2.13
	Scientists and intellectual workers	1.50	1.67	1.44	1.74
Total average grade		1.79	1.86	1.63	1.76

Note: Evaluations on a scale ranging from 1 (very well) to 5 (very poorly). The answers "I don't know" and "didn't answer" were disregarded.
Source: Institute for Public Affairs, August 2006.

4.2.8. OVERALL WORK ABILITY

Let us now examine how people in Slovakia assess their overall work performance. As Graph 4.46 shows, most women and men evaluate it very positively. When asked to compare their

Graph 4.46
"How would you evaluate your current performance at work compared to your performance in the prime of your career?" (%)

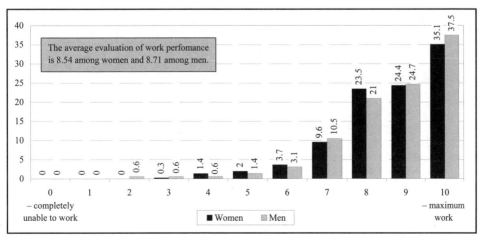

Note: Evaluation on a scale ranging from 0 (completely unable to work) to 10 (maximum work performance). The answers "I don't know" and "didn't answer" were disregarded.
Source: Institute for Public Affairs, August 2006.

Table 4.55
"How would you evaluate your current performance at work compared to your performance in the prime of your career?"
(average grades of women and men – by age)

Age	Women	Men
25 – 34	8.84	9.00
35 – 44	8.68	8.97
45 – 54	8.46	8.42
55 – 64	7.79	7.92
Total average grade	8.54	8.71

Note: Evaluation on a scale ranging from 0 (completely unable to work) to 10 (maximum work performance). The answers "I don't know" and "didn't answer" were disregarded.
Source: Institute for Public Affairs, August 2006.

actual performance at work to their perform-ance in the prime of their careers, 83% of women and men awarded themselves 8 or more points on a 10-point scale. The average grade was 8.54 among women and 8.71 among men. Again, employed women viewed their actual performance at work slightly more critically than men.

The evaluation of the overall performance at work is influenced by the age of workers (see Table 4.55). In general, women and men tend to be more critical as they get older.[19] At the same time, women in almost all age categories evaluate their own overall work performance more critically than men. The difference between women and men was the largest in the 35 – 44 age group. The only exception was the 45 – 54 age group, where the self-perception of women was slightly better than that of men.

Women's evaluation of their performance at work is strongly affected by their educational attainment. Women with higher education assess their performance more positively, which is especially the case of women over 45. On the other hand, education was not a significant factor in any age category of men (see Table 4.56).

Table 4.56
"How would you evaluate your current performance at work?" (average grades of women and men – by age, education and profession)

		Women's self-evaluation			Men's self-evaluation		
		Under 45	Over 45	Total	Under 45	Over 45	Total
Education	Elementary and secondary without A levels	8.57	7.76	8.22	8.98	8.24	8.68
	Complete secondary and university	8.75	8.64	8.71	8.99	8.26	8.75
Profession (select types)	Supporting and non-qualified staff	8.85	7.44	8.03	9.06	7.40	8.28
	Plant and machine operators	8.59	7.50	8.26	9.00	8.31	8.81
	Administrative workers	8.57	8.65	8.60	8.63	8.75	8.65
	Technical, medical and pedagogical professionals	8.71	8.82	8.75	9.27	8.25	8.95
	Scientists and intellectual workers	8.88	9.00	8.92	8.58	8.87	8.74
Total average grade		8.69	8.31	8.54	8.99	8.25	8.71

Note: Evaluation on a scale ranging from 0 (completely unable to work) to 10 (maximum work performance). The answers "I don't know" and "didn't answer" were disregarded.
Source: Institute for Public Affairs, August 2006.

As one would expect, people's views of their performance at work differ according to the type of their profession. Among women, unskilled manual workers are most critical of their performance (8.03 points on average), followed by plant and machine operators (8.26). On the other hand, women in intellectually challenging professions such as executive and crea-tive professionals evaluate their own performances rather positively (8.75 and 8.92, respec-tively). Among men, the differences in views are similar.

---

[19] Due to the wording of the question, the under-24 age group was excluded from the analysis.

In the age group of women over 45, these differences deepen. For instance, unqualified workers over 45 evaluated their work performance far more critically (7.44) than their younger colleagues (8.85). On the other hand, older women in mentally challenging professions see their performance even more positively than their younger colleagues (9.00 vs. 8.88 among scientists and intellectual workers of older and younger age).

These findings indirectly warn against overgeneralizations and stereotypical judgments about the same (negative) impact of age on the work ability of all women and men. They urge us to respect the increasing diversity of work performance, which is corroborated also by longitudinal research (Ilmarinen, 2006, pp. 134 – 136). A closer look at the generally more critical self-evaluation of work performance among older women and men reveals specific differences caused particularly by education and type of profession. In other words, the work ability of older people tends to vary according to the type of work they perform.

4.2.9. HOW WOMEN AND MEN ASSESS THEIR ABILITY TO WORK UNTIL RETIREMENT

The question in the title of this section is particularly important for women in Slovakia whose retirement age is gradually being increased.

According to estimates, due to the pension reform launched in 2004, approximately 200,000 women should remain on the labor market longer than they originally expected. As a qualitative survey carried out by the Institute for Public Affairs in spring 2006 revealed, many of them experience anxiety and fear that they may lose their jobs before they reach their retirement age. But do they feel fit enough to carry out their current work until retirement? And how do they see their chances, compared to men at the same age?

As Table 4.57 shows, only 53% of employed women over 45 believed they would be able to do their current work until retirement. On the other hand, 19% did not believe in it, and 28% did not dare to give a prediction. In this respect, women in their mature years are less optimistic than their male counterparts. Among men, 61% expressed the hope that they would be able to carry out their current work until their retirement, while only 10% were pessimistic. The share of ambivalent answers was similar as among women (29%).

The data in the Table 4.57 also document that the confidence of women and in their ability to carry out the work until retirement tends to increase with age. At the same time, women of all ages are slightly less optimistic than men. However, the gender difference in expectations becomes gradually smaller.

The fact that optimism increases as people grow older may seem paradoxical at first glimpse. How-

"I have eight years to go before retirement… I'm afraid of losing my job… What if the school is closed? I love my students and my job immensely. I think that's why I lasted for so long there… I always wake up thinking what will happen 'if'…" (Mária, 52, an elementary school teacher from Banská Bystrica)

"I can't last that long. There's no way." (Eva, 52, a seamstress from Rožňava)

"I can imagine it. If I stay healthy, it's possible." (Dana, 52, an art schoolteacher from Banská Bystrica)

ever, it becomes less surprising when we realize that a substantial majority of women and men in all three age brackets within the 45 – 59 age group view their health as very good, good or at least satisfactory. This explains why the feeling of uncertainty gradually subsides and women and men become more confident in their ability to carry out their work until retirement. More optimistic are those women and men who evaluate well their coping with the physical and mental demands of their work and who do not see major health risks associated with their jobs.

Table 4.57
"Do you think you will be able to carry out your current work until you reach retirement age?"
(% of answers "certainly and probably yes" : "definitely and probably no" : "I don't know")

		Views of women			Views of men		
		Yes	No	Yes	No	Yes	No
Age	45 – 49	46	24	30	54	13	33
	50 – 54	55	19	26	61	9	30
	55 – 59	67	6	27	70	6	24
Effects of work on health	Major	21	43	36	27	27	46
	Minor	54	25	21	60	7	34
	None	61	10	29	74	9	17
Profession (select types)	Supporting and non-qualified staff	39	23	38	55	18	27
	Administrative workers	63	11	26	100	0	0
	Technical, medical and pedagogical professionals	58	31	11	75	8	17
	Scientists and intellectual workers	56	17	27	85	15	0
Total		53	19	28	61	10	29

Note: Answers of employed women and men between 45 and 59 that do not receive old-age pensions.
Source: Institute for Public Affairs, August 2006.

As one would imagine, the expectations of women and men depend on the type of their profession. Optimism is rarer among blue-collar workers and more frequent among people with white-collar professions, regardless of their qualifications. As for women, their belief in preserving work ability until retirement is relatively rare among unskilled manual workers (39%), but much more widespread among clerks (63%); executive professionals (58%) and scientists and intellectual workers (56%). Similar differences are typical of men.

At the same time, women in every type of profession demonstrate slightly less optimism and self-confidence than men. Their greater uncertainty may reflect not only their conviction about the weaker position of women on labor market, but also their awareness of the challenges connected with a substantial increase in the retirement age of women.

5. GENDER EQUALITY IN PUBLIC PERCEPTION

Zora Bútorová

5. GENDER EQUALITY IN PUBLIC PERCEPTION

5.1. STATUS OF WOMEN AND MEN IN SOCIETY

5.1.1. HOW WOMEN AND MEN SEE THEIR STATUS

A majority of the Slovak public believes that women have a lower status in society and fewer opportunities than men (see Table 5.1). In a survey from August 2006 carried out by the Institute for Public Affairs, 71% of women and 55% of men held this opinion. Only 24% of women, but 41% of men believed that women had an equal status and opportunities. A marginal of women and men (3% of each) thought that women had better opportunities than men.

These figures indicate that for people in Slovakia, gender inequality is primarily the issue of the disadvantaged position of women.[1]

Table 5.1
"How do you perceive the status and opportunities of women in our society compared to those of men?" (%)

	Views of women					Views of men				
	2003	2004	2005	2006	2007	2003	2004	2005	2006	2007
Worse	74	71	64	66	71	54	50	47	46	55
Equal	20	25	30	30	24	38	43	45	47	41
Better	4	4	4	3	3	5	5	5	5	3
I don't know	2	0	2	1	1	3	2	2	2	1

Source: Institute for Public Affairs, September 2003, November 2004, November 2005, August 2006.

Do Slovak women try hard enough to improve their position in society and exercise their rights? As Table 5.2 shows, women are rather self-critical. According to a survey carried out in 2006 by the Institute of Sociology of the Slovak Academy of Sciences, 69% of female respondents believed that women defend their rights insufficiently while only 26% consid-

Table 5.2
"Do women in Slovakia sufficiently stand up for their rights?" (%)

	Views of women			Views of men		
	2000	2002	2006	2000	2002	2006
Yes	16	19	26	28	33	47
No	65	74	69	40	51	43
I don't know	20	8	5	32	17	10

Source: Institute for Public Affairs, March 2000 and June 2002; Institute of Sociology of the Slovak Academy of Sciences, May – June 2006.

---

[1] It should be noted that people in Slovakia do not interchange the concepts of "worse status and opportunities of women" and of "discrimination against women", as they view the latter concept as much more radical. According to the *Eurobarometer* survey carried out in June and July 2006, only 32% of respondents believed that discrimination against women was prevalent in Slovakia (*Discrimination...*, 2007). In other words, those who criticized discrimination against women were significantly fewer than those who pointed out women's worse status and opportunities in society.

Table 5.3
"Which institutions in Slovakia best promote the equal status of women in society?" (%)

	Views of women	Views of men
Non-governmental organizations	46	44
European Commission	38	36
Trade unions	19	17
Education system	15	16
Ombudsman for human rights	12	15
Parliament	11	16
Cabinet	11	15
Churches	10	11
Courts of justice	9	11
Police	4	5
Slovak Army	2	4

Note: Respondents were free to choose three answers, which is why the percentages in the columns exceed 100%.
Source: Institute of Sociology of the Slovak Academy of Sciences, May – June 2006.

ered their efforts adequate. Men were much more benevolent, as more of them considered women's efforts sufficient than otherwise (47% vs. 43%). Compared to similar surveys conducted by the Institute for Public Affairs in 2000 and 2002, the gap between the views of women and men became wider.

A more positive evaluation of women's ability to defend their rights was probably caused by the attention that media paid to the issue of gender equality at the turn of the 21st century, largely due to several campaigns organized by women's non-governmental organizations, for instance *Piata žena* [One Woman in Five] or *Urobme to!* [Let's Do It!].[2] In recent years, the issue of gender equality was highlighted particularly by projects within the framework of the EQUAL Community Initiative as well as other schemes supported by the European Union.

This explanation is further supported by the fact that public opinion in Slovakia sees non-governmental organizations and the European Commission as the institutions that promote the equal status of women in society most effectively (Bahna, 2006, p. 48). According to the aforementioned survey by the Institute of Sociology of the Slovak Academy of Sciences, other political or social institutions do not have nearly as positive an impact in the eyes of Slovak population. Symptomatically, 23% of women and 21% of men were unable to take a stand on the issue.

Thus it can be stated that public opinion largely corresponds to reality: in Slovakia, ideals of gender equality have remained mostly "on paper" and have not been fully embraced even by the institutions that should be the most concerned with their implementation (Debrecéniová – Očenášová, 2005; Filadelfiová – Bútorová, 2007a). Particularly noteworthy is the low recognition of the role of trade unions, the education system, parliament, cabinet, as well as of the contribution of the ombudsman for human rights, courts of justice and the police. Although these findings date back to 2006, it can be assumed that they remain pertinent.

5.1.2. HIERARCHY OF WOMEN'S ISSUES

What are the main reasons behind the prevailing public opinion that women in Slovakia are disadvantaged compared to men? To answer this question, it is useful to know which problems of women people in Slovakia consider most urgent.

The spontaneous answers to an open-ended question indicate that for Slovak public, women encounter the most pressing problems on the labor market. In 2007, they were cited by 87%

---

[2] Although both campaigns met with a vivid public response, they were essentially different in terms of focus as well as effects. While the *Piata žena* campaign managed to increase sensitivity of ordinary citizens and politicians to the problem of violence against women (www.piatazena.sk; Bútorová – Filadelfiová, 2006), the *Urobme to!* campaign was rather controversial and caused also certain unintended negative effects (Filadelfiová, 2003).

of female and 85% of male respondents (see Table 5.4). People's sensitivity to these problems was significantly higher than in 2000, when they were spontaneously singled out by 31% of women and 17% of men. While in 2000, women considered their problems on the labor market far more urgent than did men, the situation became quite different seven years later.

A detailed analysis revealed that most frequently cited problems of women on the labor market included inadequate remuneration as well as problems in applying for jobs or during the dismissal of employees; women returning from maternity leave and mature women were described as the most disadvantaged categories in this respect. Another serious problem was the overall shortage of labor opportunities on the labor market. Fewer respondents mentioned inconvenient working conditions and work regimes, for instance night or double-shift work, the absence of flexible working hours, overtime work, harmful environment, and limited opportunities for women to participate in training programs. Some criticism was also aimed at the unaccommodating approach taken by employers, particularly towards mothers with dependent children, handicapped women and older women.

Table 5.4
"Think of the most urgent problems women face in Slovakia. Which should be addressed first?" (%)

	Views of women		Views of men	
	2000	2007	2000	2007
Women's problems on the labor market. Of those:	31	87	17	85
• Inadequate remuneration of women	10	32	5	31
• Discrimination against women when recruiting and laying off workers	6	22	2	21
• Unemployment	6	18	6	17
• Discrimination against women at work in general	4	8	2	8
• Unsuitable work regime and working conditions for women	5	7	2	8
Problems related to family care and household duties. Of those:	22	39	11	40
• Unsatisfactory social policy and state care for families with children	15	25	9	25
• Double burden of women	6	13	2	13
• Unequal status of women in families, unjust division of family duties	1	1	0	2
Increasing retirement age for women	2	15	2	11
Unequal status of women in society	7	13	3	18
Violence against women; trafficking in women; sexual harassment	4	9	1	7
Women's low participation in decision-making processes	4	7	2	7
Health and health care issues	2	5	2	4
Problems of female pensioners and lonely women	0	4	0	2
Reproductive behavior and family planning issues	0	2	0	0

Note: This was an open-ended question. Respondents could give three answers, which is why the total sum in columns exceeds 100%.
Source: Institute for Public Affairs, March 2000 and November 2007.

After a significant gap, second on the list of the most pressing issues facing women were problems related to childcare, family care and household duties; these were cited by 39% of women and 40% of men. Here, most respondents criticized the government's social policy towards families with children, particularly those with many children, those with handicapped children, and single-parent families. Fewer respondents mentioned the double burden experienced by employed women, which is aggravated by the insufficient availability of pre-school education facilities and housework services.

Special attention should be paid to the fact that almost no women and men (1% and 2%, respectively) cited the unsatisfactory quality of partnership relations within the family, i.e. the unjust division of responsibilities for running household and taking care of children, the

Graph 5.1
"Think of the most urgent problems women face in Slovakia. Which should be addressed first?" (views of women and men in 2000 and 2007 – in %)

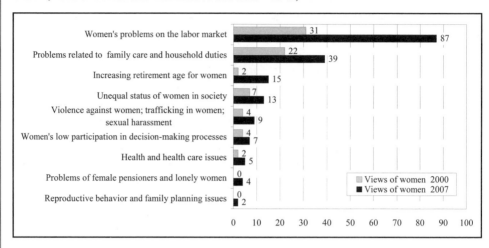

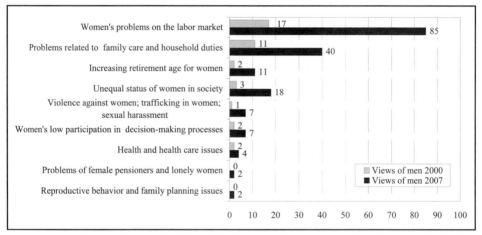

Source: Institute for Public Affairs, March 2000 and November 2007.

accumulation of decision-making powers in the hands of the father, etc. This indicates that the country's traditional cultural standards favoring the patriarchal family still hold sway. The public in Slovakia does not realize that women cannot be relieved of their double burden solely through state-of-the-art service infrastructure or generous state financial subsidies for families. It is impossible to attain this goal without bringing partnership relations to a different level.

The remaining problems of women were not viewed as urgent by female and male respondents. The issue of women's increasing retirement age ranked third on women's list and fourth on men's list (15% and 11%, respectively). The greater sensitivity of women and men to this problem in 2007 compared to 2000 was largely a reaction to the legislative change that took effect in 2004 (see Section 3.3. of this book). The increase in the retirement age for women affects entire families because it postpones the point when women become available to take full care of "the family hearth"; hence the increase in men's sensitivity to this issue.

Thirteen percent of female respondents and 18% of male respondents expressed the view that women in Slovakia are generally disadvantaged. Men seem to be more prepared to admit that women are not treated equally in Slovakia, but prefer not to put a tag on it. This different reaction of male respondents may indicate their desire to present themselves as politically correct.

Fifth on the list of women's problems presented by women as well as men was violence against women, trafficking in women and sexual harassment. This problem was cited by 9% of women and 7% of men, which in both cases indicates an increase in sensitivity compared to 2000.[3]

As the sixth most pressing problem, female and male respondents picked the low participation of Slovak women in decision-making processes (7% each). This persisting low position corroborates the seemingly paradoxical, but deeply rooted reality that few women and men in Slovakia see the way toward solving the most pressing women's issues in increasing their participation in decision-making processes. While most women and men say they support women's greater participation in public life (see Section 7.3.3. of this book), neither seem to expect too much of it. In this context, we can understand why top politics in Slovakia does not include a single woman who built her political career on successfully promoting the agenda of women. This only strengthens the syndrome of learned helplessness, which encourages women to believe that they do not need to tackle their problems themselves as long as they delegate the responsibility to men. Needless to say, this approach fails to apply effective pressure to address women's issues.

Seventh on the women's list as well as on the men's list were issues related to health and health care (5% of women and 4% of men); eighth were the problems facing two specific categories of women – pensioners and lonely women (4% of women and 2% of men).

It is particularly noteworthy that reproductive behavior and family planning issues ranked last on the list of the most pressing problems of Slovak women, as they were cited by only 2% of women and 0% of men. These correspond to the objective increase in the responsibility of reproductive behavior of people, as well as to their general satisfaction with the abortion law (see Section 2.3.2. of this book).

Overall, we may conclude that the sensitivity of Slovak women and men to women's problems increased between 2000 and 2007. While men showed less sensitivity than women at the beginning of the period examined, their views changed more rapidly and the gap between the views of women and men had closed almost completely by the end of the period.

In the long run, people in Slovakia believe that women face their most serious problems on the labor market. The ranks of women and men who demand solutions in this sphere have grown most rapidly. The increase in sensitivity to the problems of women in other spheres, such as in politics or the health care, was far less significant. Compared to 2000,

---

[3] On the other hand, it represents a decline in sensitivity compared to 2002 when this issue was cited by 14% of female and 9% of male respondents (Bútorová – Filadelfiová – Gyárfášová – Cviková – Farkašová, 2002). However, this decline may hardly be interpreted as a reaction to objectively reduced occurrence of violence against women. It rather reflects the fact that neither politicians nor the media paid sufficient attention to the problem during the recent years. This period differed from the years at the turn of the century when women's non-governmental organizations launched the *Každá piata žena* [One Woman in Five]campaign and in cooperation with members of parliament managed to introduce legislative changes aimed at improving protection of violence victims (www.piatazena.sk; Bútorová – Filadelfiová, 2005). In this respect, we can only welcome a nationwide campaign called *Zastavme domáce násilie na ženách* [Stop Domestic Violence against Women] organized between November 2007 and May 2008 by the Ministry of Labor, Social Affairs and Family in cooperation with the Information Office of the Council of Europe and women's non-governmental organizations associated in the Piata žena initiative (www.zastavmenasilie.sk).

Slovak women and men also have grown more sensitive to the conditions in which women take care of family and household, especially to the inadequate assistance provided by the central government and local governments. Unfortunately, a very low proportion of Slovak women and men realize the importance of a more balanced division of family responsibilities.

5.1.3. CHANCES OF WOMEN AND MEN IN SELECT AREAS

The previous section outlined the most pressing problems of women in Slovakia as perceived by the public. However, the findings do not clearly indicate whether people view these problems in the context of gender inequality. Let us therefore look at the perception of women's and men's opportunities in concrete areas of society, i.e. on the labor market, in politics, in the health service and in the education system (Table 5.5). The following analysis is based on the findings of two successive surveys conducted by the Institute for Public Affairs in 2000 and 2002, as well as on a follow-up survey carried out by the Institute of Sociology of the Slovak Academy of Sciences in 2006.

Table 5.5
"Do women in Slovakia have opportunities equal to men?" (% of answers "men are privileged" : "women and men have equal chances" : "women are privileged" : "I don't know")

		2000	2002	2006
When it comes to remuneration for work	Views of women	80 : 15 : 0 : 5	83 : 14 : 1 : 2	84 : 12 : 0 : 4
	Views of men	59 : 31 : 2 : 8	62 : 30 : 2 : 6	65 : 28 : 2 : 4
When it comes to promotion at work	Views of women	70 : 20 : 2 : 8	82 : 12 : 1 : 5	83 : 12 : 2 : 4
	Views of men	45 : 38 : 5 : 12	61 : 28 : 2 : 9	64 : 27 : 4 : 5
When applying for jobs	Views of women	74 : 20 : 1 : 5	79 : 16 : 1 : 4	75 : 20 : 1 : 4
	Views of men	51 : 38 : 3 : 8	57 : 32 : 4 : 7	53 : 38 : 4 : 5
When it comes to keeping a jobs during layoffs	Views of women	63 : 24 : 4 : 9	62 : 26 : 3 : 9	60 : 27 : 5 : 8
	Views of men	45 : 38 : 5 : 12	44 : 41 : 5 : 10	43 : 41 : 9 : 7
When it comes to placement on the candidates lists of political parties and running for political posts	Views of women	56 : 18 : 0 : 26	69 : 16 : 1 : 14	72 : 15 : 1 : 12
	Views of men	40 : 33 : 3 : 24	55 : 26 : 3 : 16	58 : 28 : 3 : 12
When applying for secondary and university studies*	Views of women	17 : 67 : 0 : 16	12 : 77 : 1 : 10	11 : 79 : 2 : 11
	Views of men	10 : 73 : 1 : 16	8 : 80 : 3 : 9	5 : 82 : 5 : 8
When in need of a complex medical examination	Views of women	–	5 : 83 : 3 : 9	–
	Views of men	–	4 : 82 : 7 : 7	–

Note: * In 2000, the question examined only the access of women and men to university education.
NE – was not examined.
Source: Institute for Public Affairs, March 2000 and June 2002; Institute of Sociology of the Slovak Academy of Sciences, May – June 2006.

Let us begin with the analysis of the areas that people in Slovakia see as the least problematic. A substantial majority of women and men agree that when in need of a complex medical examination and when applying for studies, the chances of women and men are equal.[4]

---

[4]   It should be noted however that public opinion might not adequately reflect actual chances of women and men in these areas. A comprehensive analysis of gender equality cannot be limited to what people think but must also rely on other, more objective indicators. Such an analysis in the field of health service is till lacking in Slovakia. Truly inspirational is the book *Megatrends for Women* published by Patricia Aburdene and John Naisbitt in 1992, which brought a whole range of facts on preferential treatment of men in American medical research and medical care (Aburdene – Naisbitt, 1992, pp. 128 – 164). Similarly, chances of women and men when applying for secondary or university studies may not be as equal as they look according to public opinion. For instance, schools heavily dominated by women may give preference to male applicants and

In other words, the public does not perceive the health service and the education system as very problematic in terms of gender equality.

However, according to public perception, the chances of women and men are not equal in the next two areas, i.e. in politics and on the labor market. Most respondents expressed the opinion that women are disadvantaged when aspiring to be placed on the candidate list of a political party or to be elected to a post. Moreover, the share of people who believe that women's chances in politics are worse than those of men increased between 2000 and 2006.

The most critical are views of the chances of women on the labor market. Eighty four percent of women and 65% of men state gender inequality in remuneration and promotion at work. The hiring of employees is perceived also as quite problematic, because 75% of women and 53% of men believe that women stand a worse chance than men. Gender inequality is slightly less apparent when employees are being laid off: 60% of women but only 43% of men think that women are more likely than men to lose their jobs.

Table 5.5 shows a particularly strong increase in the number of people who believe that women have lower chances when it comes to their promotion at the workplace or within the political party. In other words, the public has grown more aware of the glass ceiling that women encounter when they strive for vertical mobility in the labor market and in politics.

5.1.4. ATTITUDES TOWARD PREFERENTIAL TREATMENT OF MEN ON THE LABOR MARKET

How does the public perceive gender equality on the labor market in general? The most widespread view is that men are privileged. In a survey carried out in 2005 by the Institute for Public Affairs, 75% of women and 58% of men shared this opinion. The opposite view, i.e. that women are the privileged ones, was quite marginal (2% of female and 3% of male respondents).

Let us now have a closer look at the attitudes toward the preferential treatment of men on the labor market: do people condemn it, or do they support it? This question is crucial because moral condemnation of gender inequality is an indispensable (though not sufficient) prerequisite for introducing the needed change within society.

As Table 5.6 shows, 70% of women not only think that men are privileged on the labor market, but also condemn it as wrong. Only 3% of women admit the privileged status of men and approve of it. The rest of 25% of women do not share the view that men are privileged on the labor market.

Men's views are quite different, as only 44% of them condemn the preferential treatment of men while 11% approve of it and 42% deny the very existence of gender inequality on the labor market.

---

vice versa. Besides, gender equality in the field of education must be examined in a more comprehensive way, i.e. not solely from the viewpoint of admission process. A survey carried out by the Institute of Sociology of the Slovak Academy of Sciences in 2006 brought interesting findings about equal opportunities at schools. Twenty percent of women and 14% of men repeatedly witnessed the preferential treatment of persons of the opposite sex, while 27% of women and 23% of men occasionally witnessed such a discriminatory behavior (*Slovensko na ceste...*, 2006, pp. 70 and 76). According to the qualitative survey conducted by the Institute for Public Affairs for Aspekt, a feminist civic association and think-tank, teachers at elementary schools in Slovakia tend to apply gender stereotypes when approaching girls and boys in class (Filadelfiová, 2008b). These findings indicate that the area of education is not free of gender inequality. For further details on gender equality in the field of education system, please see Kiczková – Szapuová – Zezulová, 2006; Bitušíková, 2004; *Waste...*, 2004.

Graph 5.2
"Do women and men have equal chances on the labor market (when it comes to remuneration, promotion at work, hiring and firing, etc.)?" (%)

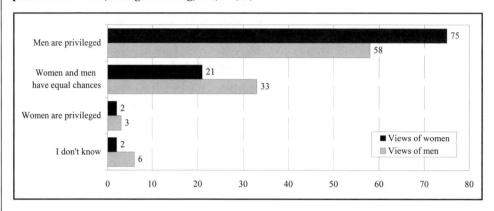

Source: Institute for Public Affairs, September 2005.

Table 5.6
Attitudes of women and men to the preferential treatment of men on the labor market (%)

	Attitudes of women	Attitudes of men
I think that men are privileged and I don't approve of it.	70	44
I think that men are privileged and I find it justified.	3	11
I think that men are privileged but I don't know whether it is right or wrong.	2	3
I don't think that men are privileged.*	25	42

Note: * This category comprises the answers "Women and men have equal chances", "Women are privileged" and "I don't know" from Graph 5.2.
Source: Institute for Public Affairs, September 2005.

The findings of a survey carried out in 2002 by the Institute for Public Affairs give us closer insight into the views of people who disapprove of the preferential treatment of men on the labor market (Bútorová – Filadelfiová – Gyárfášová – Cviková – Farkašová, 2002). This category of people may be divided into two subgroups: those who condemn the unequal treatment and emphasize the need of its elimination; and those who condemn it but believe that it is natural and has existed for ages, and therefore it cannot be removed. Among those women who criticize unequal treatment, advocates of active change prevail strongly over those who have accepted it as given (70% vs. 30%). Among men, advocates of active change constitute a less commanding majority of about 60% vs. 40%.

These findings offer two basic conclusions. First, men are not only less aware of gender inequality on the labor market, but they also more often tend to view the *status quo* as unchangeable and based on the "natural" gender order of society. Second, the share of women and men who not only disapprove of gender inequality but also want to eliminate it is lower than the percentages in Table 5.6 suggest. We estimate that only around 50% of women (as opposed to 70% in Table 5.6) and only 26% of men (as opposed to 44% in Table 5.6) would be willing to actively endorse gender equality on the labor market.

5.1.5. ARGUMENTS FOR AND AGAINST PREFERENTIAL TREATMENT OF MEN

What are the strongest arguments against the preferential treatment of men on the labor market? Spontaneous answers of both female and male respondents indicate that almost two in three of them (64% of women and 66% of men) have ethical objections. They condemn discrimination against women as unjust, unnatural, demeaning and old-fashioned.

The second strongest argument (shared by 46% of women and 37% of men) is that women perform equally well or even better than men at work. This argument is particularly prevalent among more educated and younger respondents.

The remaining two arguments were less frequent. Nine percent of women and 7% of men demanded equalization measures to improve women's chances on the labor market so that they are not disadvantaged for fulfilling their role in the family. Finally, 6% of women and 4% of men emphasized that women are also breadwinners, which is why men should not be privileged.

Table 5.7
"Why do you condemn the preferential treatment of men on the labor market?" (%)

	Views of women	Views of men
Because it violates the principle of equality; it is discriminatory; unjust, demeaning, unnatural, old-fashioned.	64	66
Because the work performance of women is equal to and sometimes even better than that of men.	46	37
Women should not be disadvantaged for being mothers. On the contrary, equalization measures should be introduced to strengthen women's chances on the labor market.	9	7
Because women are also breadwinners for their families.	6	4
Other reasons	0	3

Note: This was an open-ended question. Respondents who approved of the preferential treatment of men were not included. Respondents could give three answers, which is why the total sum exceeds 100%.
Source: Institute for Public Affairs, September 2005.

Let us now examine the arguments of those who endorse the preferential treatment of men on the labor market. According to Table 5.6, this group is much smaller than the group of advocates of gender equality. Their attitudes are based primarily on the conviction that the traditional division of labor between women and men is natural and should be preserved. They see men as the principal breadwinners whose work is not limited by family obligations (100% of female respondents and 87% of male respondents). A considerably smaller percentage of respondents (14% of women and 23% of men) believe that men are physically and mentally predisposed to better work performance.

Table 5.8
"Why you approve of the preferential treatment of men on the labor market?" (%)

	Views of women	Views of men
Because men have fewer family obligations and therefore a greater capacity to devote fully to their work.	100	87
Because men are physically and mentally predisposed to perform better at work.	14	23
Other reasons	1	0

Note: This was an open-ended question. Respondents who disapproved of the preferential treatment of men were not included. Respondents could give three answers, which is why the total sum exceeds 100%.
Source: Institute for Public Affairs, September 2005.

Let us now look at the support of gender equality in particular socio-economic environments. We will use the data of a survey by the Institute for Public Affairs in which respondents were asked to endorse one of two diametrically opposed assertions about gender equality. As Table 5.9 shows, 70% of women, but only 51% of men advocated gender equality. On the other hand, 14% of women and 24% of men openly endorsed preferential treatment of men and another 15% of women and 23% of men took ambivalent positions. It is clear that the advocates of gender equality do not have a majority among men.

Table 5.9
"Which of the following statements do you support?
A. Men are entitled to better positions at work as well as better pay.
B. Women and men are entitled to equal positions at work as well as equal pay."
(support of A : undecided : support of B – in %)

		Views of women	Views of men
Education	Elementary	18 : 16 : 60	28 : 22 : 45
	Secondary without A levels	14 : 18 : 67	24 : 26 : 60
	Complete secondary	14 : 13 : 74	22 : 20 : 56
	University	11 : 13 : 76	14 : 24 : 61
Economic status (select categories)	Non-qualified manual workers	13 : 17 : 70	23 : 35 : 35
	Scientists and intellectual workers	7 : 18 : 75	19 : 16 : 66
	Entrepreneurs	17 : 3 : 80	26 : 18 : 52
	Unemployed	12 : 18 : 69	35 : 27 : 31
	Students	24 : 15 : 61	22 : 28 : 45
Total		**14 : 15 : 70**	**24 : 23 : 51**

Note: The remainder of the 100% figure comprises the answer "I don't know".
Source: Institute for Public Affairs, November 2007.

Table 5.9 also shows the significant opinion differences within the group of women and men based on their educational attainment, economic status and profession.

The idea of gender equality has a stronger support among women and men with higher education. It is embraced by unskilled female workers, but not by their male counterparts (assertion B was endorsed by 70% of women but only by 35% of men). Similar differences in opinions are also between unemployed women and men (69% vs. 31%).

Within the group of entrepreneurs, gender equality is endorsed by 80% of women but only 51% of men. A stronger emphasis of women comes as no surprise, if one realizes how much courage, determination and perseverance it takes for women to embark on the challenging and risky path of self-employment. Female entrepreneurs in Slovakia continue to represent a minority, not only among employed women but also within the group of entrepreneurs (See Section 4.1.5. of this book). To them, the preferential treatment of men represents one of the obstacles of their economic success. What they need instead is support from their relatives and friends (Šumšalová, 2007).

The smallest, yet significant difference is between the opinions of women and men who work as creative professionals. Among them, the principle of gender equality was endorsed by 75% of women and 66% of men.

The opinions of students present a truly unpleasant surprise. A below-average endorsement of gender equality among female students (61%, compared to 70% for all women) as well as among male students (45%, compared to 51% for all men) has to be interpreted as a warning that Slovak society will not automatically embark on a road toward gender equality – just because a younger generation has arrived. Such a spontaneous value shift is not probable even among the most educated young people. If the country fails to introduce gender sensitive education at all levels of the education system as well as in the media, and does not "inoculate" young people with the values and ideals of gender equality, Slovak society may experience a backlash leading to even lower chances of women.

5.1.6. "IF A PERSON OF THE OPPOSITE SEX HELD MY JOB..."

So far, we have analyzed the general views regarding opportunities of women and men on the labor market. Now we will get closer to the concrete situation and experience of women and men. First, we will show how they see the situation in their current workplace, and then we will examine their long-term experience with discrimination.

We examined the situation of women and men in their own workplace by means of a hypothetical question exploring two cases: a woman replaced in her job by a man and vice versa (see Table 5.10).

Table 5.10
"Imagine that your current job was held by a person of the same age but opposite sex.* What would be his/her position?" (views of employed women and men – 2006 and 1995, in %)

Views of women	2006 (1995)	Views of men	2006 (1995)
In terms of work performance:		In terms of work performance:	
A man would work more	5 (4)	A woman would work more	4 (5)
A man would work equally	74 (60)	A woman would work equally	48 (44)
A man would work less	16 (20)	A woman would work less	39 (36)
I don't know	5 (15)	I don't know	9 (15)
In terms of wage:		In terms of wage:	
A man would earn more	29 (34)	A woman would earn more	0 (0)
A man would earn equal wage	60 (50)	A woman would earn equal wage	48 (50)
A man would earn less	1 (2)	A woman would earn less	39 (36)
I don't know	10 (15)	I don't know	13 (13)
In terms of colleagues' respect:		In terms of colleagues' respect:	
A man would enjoy greater respect	21 (22)	A woman would enjoy greater respect	4 (5)
A man would enjoy equal respect	64 (51)	A woman would enjoy equal respect	53 (42)
A man would enjoy less respect	4 (4)	A woman would enjoy less respect	31 (39)
I don't know	11 (18)	I don't know	12 (14)

* The survey from 1995 did not specify that the employee of the opposite sex would be the same age.
Note: Figures in brackets are from the 1995 survey.
Source: FOCUS, June 1995; Institute for Public Affairs, August 2006.

In the survey from 2006, a majority of female respondents assumed that a man doing their job would perform equally (74%), earn an equal wage (60%) and enjoy equal respect (64%). A far smaller proportion of employed women believed that a man in their place would make more money (29%) and get greater respect (21%). Only 5% guessed that he would work more, while 16% expected that he would work less. Compared to a similar survey from 1995, there was an increase in the share of women who believed in gender equality in their workplace.

The views of men are significantly different. In 2006, only one in two male respondents believed that a woman doing their job would carry an equal workload (48%), earn an equal wage (48%), and enjoy the same prestige (53%). On the other hand, a relatively significant proportion of them expected she would earn a lower wage (39%) and get less respect (31%). Thirty nine percent of men believed that a woman would not be able to handle their workload. A subsequent analysis revealed that men who expected their female replacements would do less work also expected them to earn less and enjoy less respect, which they apparently considered just. Men's views of the chances of women in their workplaces are remarkably stable compared to 1995.

These findings indicate an interesting paradox. Although women generally perceive their opportunities on the labor market much more critically than men (see Graph 5.2 in this chapter), most of them still believe that if a man replaced them in their jobs, he would perform equally well and receive equal treatment in terms of remuneration and prestige. On the other hand, only about one in two men expect the same of their potential female replacements.

This asymmetry can be explained by means of two hypotheses. First, due to gender segregation on the labor market, women more frequently fill some jobs not because they succeeded in competition with men but because these jobs were available. Second, some men are convinced that their jobs are more demanding (either physically or mentally) and believe that coping with these challenges requires a performance that only a man can deliver; consequently, they expect a higher wage and greater respect. This widespread belief of men may rest on the stereotypical expectation that the performance of a woman would be hampered by her family obligations, limiting her ability to compete with men.

5.1.7. EXPERIENCE OF UNEQUAL TREATMENT IN THE WORKPLACE

In the previous section, respondents expressed their views about a hypothetical situation that could happen in their current workplaces. But what is their personal experience with the preferential treatment of the opposite sex? Have they encountered it during their professional lives?

A partial answer to this question was provided by a survey of the Institute of Sociology of the Slovak Academy of Sciences, which studied the lifetime experience of women and men with unequal treatment (see Graph 5.3). The survey found that during their professional careers women far more frequently encountered such discriminatory behavior than their male colleagues. One in three employed women (34%) but only one in ten employed men (10%) said they had repeatedly witnessed preferential treatment of their colleague of the opposite sex; another 32% of women and 22% of men cited occasional experience with this phenomenon.

However, if we really want to find out how women and men perceive their status and opportunities on the labor market and whether they feel that they are being treated justly and with respect, we should not limit our analyses only to their experience of gender inequality. We should include also experience with other types of discrimination and other negative situations in the workplace.

Such a broader insight was provided by a survey by the Institute for Public Affairs, which resulted in the identification of a list of negative situations that women and men had directly experienced in their workplaces over the past decade. While 25% of women complained of teasing, gossip or mockery from their colleagues, only 11% of men mentioned this experience. Second on the list of women's experience was discrimination by their boss and injustice in pay or work assignments (18%). While this type of negative experience was the most frequent among men, it still occurred less frequently than among women (14%).

Graph 5.3
"Have you ever personally experienced a situation where a colleague of the opposite sex was given preferential treatment at work?" (%)

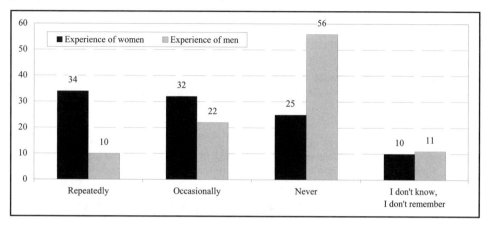

Note: Answers of respondents who never worked in mixed work teams were disregarded.
Source: Institute of Sociology of the Slovak Academy of Sciences, May – June 2006.

Less common negative experiences in the workplace included bullying or mobbing by a boss (7% of women and 3% of men), unwanted sexual attention in the form of sexual jokes, comments, proposals for sex, etc. (7% of women and 4% of men), bullying or mobbing by colleagues (5% of women and 1% of men), sexual harassment (4% of women and 0% of men) and physical conflicts or assaults(1% of women and men).

As Graph 5.4 shows, women reported personal experiences of all of these negative situations – except for physical conflicts or assaults – more frequently than men.

Graph 5.4
"Have you personally experienced one of the following situations over the past 10 years?"
(% of affirmative answers of employed women and men)

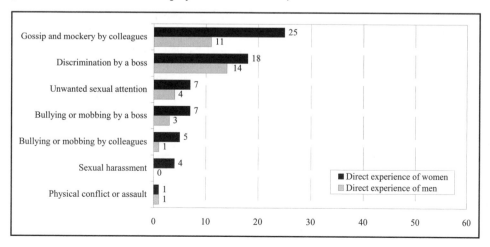

Source: Institute for Public Affairs, August 2006.

Let us now take a look at the overall – i.e. direct and indirect –experience of women and men of discriminatory or otherwise harmful behavior in the workplace. In other words, we are interested in the personal experience of female respondents as well as their female colleagues and in the personal experience of male respondents as well as their male colleagues. This broader perspective reveals a different picture. As Graph 5.5 shows, women encounter three types of negative situations more frequently than men: gossip and mockery within a work team, displays of unwanted sexual attention and sexual harassment. Men, for their part, are more frequently confronted with physical conflicts and assaults. Discrimination and bullying from bosses as well as from colleagues were equally reported by female and male respondents.

Graph 5.5
"Have you or any of your colleagues personally experienced one of the following situations over the past 10 years?" (% of affirmative answers of employed women and men)

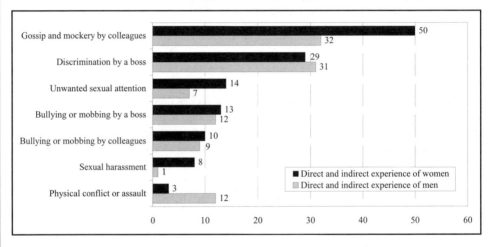

Source: Institute for Public Affairs, August 2006.

A more detailed analysis of the experience of women has revealed that the occurrence of all negative situations does not depend on their educational attainment. On the other hand, women's age is a significant factor. A comparison of women under 45 and over 45 shows that mature women more frequently encounter discrimination and bullying from bosses and colleagues. Younger women, for their part, more often become targets of unwanted sexual attention and sexual harassment as well as targets of gossip, teasing and mockery.

5.2. STATUS OF WOMEN OVER 45 ON THE LABOR MARKET
5.2.1. REASONS FOR DISCRIMINATION ON THE LABOR MARKET

Let us examine gender inequality in the context of other inequalities on the labor market. People in Slovakia see various reasons for the discrimination on the labor market. A survey carried out by the Institute for Public Affairs ranked them by their occurrence. According to public opinion, the most frequent reasons are age (93% of respondents believed that age discrimination happens very often or quite often), health condition or disability (88%), pregnancy or maternity (77%), racial or ethnic background (67%), obligations to other family members (64%) and sex (52%).

Table 5.11
"Are people in Slovakia disadvantaged or discriminated against on the labor market for the following reasons?" (views of the entire population – in %)

	Very often	Quite often	Rarely	Exceptionally or never	I don't know
Age	65	28	4	2	1
Health condition or disability	49	39	8	2	3
Pregnancy or maternity	37	40	13	4	6
Racial or ethnic origin	32	35	18	9	5
Obligations to other family members	22	42	21	10	6
Sex	18	34	28	15	4

Source: Institute for Public Affairs, September 2005.

Graph 5.6
"Are people in Slovakia disadvantaged or discriminated against on the labor market for the following reasons?" (% of answers "very and quite often")

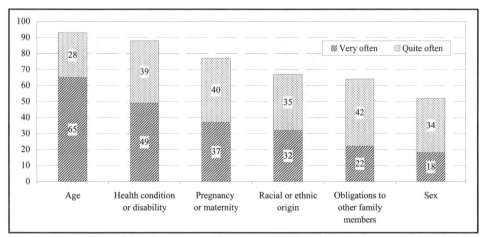

Source: Institute for Public Affairs, September 2005.

Each of the forms of discrimination described on the labor market were cited more frequently by people from more "vulnerable" environments, who are therefore more familiar with particular disadvantages, i.e. women, old people, less educated people, people with lower income, and residents of regions outside the capital Bratislava.

The first situation on the labor market in which people may encounter discrimination is in applying for a job. In a survey by the Slovak National Centre for Human Rights (SNSĽP), 84% of respondents believed that "in the process of hiring new employees, employers should be interested solely in the qualifications and abilities of the applicants and should ignore personal details such as sex, age, nationality, sexual orientation, health or religion" (*Empirical Data...*, 2005d). Unfortunately, this ideal is far from reality: 95% of respondents in the same survey said that when hiring new employees, employers often take into account the age, health (81% each), sex (77%) and racial or ethnic origin (53%) of job applicants.[5] In case of some job applicants, these reasons may have a cumulative effect.

According to these findings, people in Slovakia perceive the age of employees or job applicants to be the main reason for their discrimination on the labor market. That goes against the widespread support for the principle of equal opportunities for people of all ages (see Graph 5.7). In a survey carried out by the Institute for Public Affairs, almost two thirds of respondents (63%) agreed with the statement that "despite of a shortage of jobs, people of all ages should have an equal chance". On the other hand, 16% of respondents agreed with the opposite – openly discriminatory or ageist statement that "in case of a shortage of jobs, younger people should take precedence over older people". There are more advocates of equal opportunities for all age categories among women; people in their middle or older years; and people with higher education.

Graph 5.7
"Which of the following statements do you support?
A. In case of a shortage of jobs younger people should take precedence over older people.
B. Despite a shortage of jobs, people of all ages should have an equal chance."
(support of A : undecided : support of B – in %)

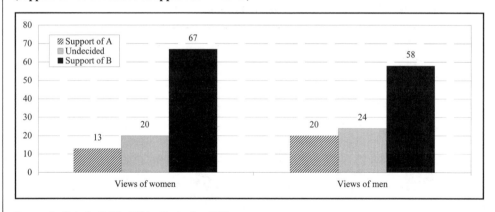

Source: Institute for Public Affairs, September 2005.

5.2.2. ATTRACTIVENESS OF JOB APPLICANTS OF DIFFERENT AGE AND SEX

Obviously, every person has several qualities that can increase or reduce his or her chances on the labor market. The following analysis will focus on the combination of sex and age. We will take into account six categories: women in their young, middle and older years, as well as their male counterparts.

What is the attractiveness of these categories of job applicants? To answer this question, we will focus on the private sector, which employs most people in Slovakia. We should note that

---

5   Only a marginal share of respondents (6%) said that employers very often or quite often take into account the religious beliefs and sexual orientation of job applicants (*Empirical Data...*, 2005d).

according to public opinion, private companies most frequently discriminate against employees and job applicants.[6]

Table 5.12
"Imagine that you are the manager of a private company. You are hiring new employees and have several job applicants to choose from. All have the required qualifications and differ only by age and sex. Which of the following job applicants would be your first, second and third choice?" (views of the entire population – in %)

	1st place	2nd place	3rd place	Overall position*
Man in middle age	22	15	16	53
Woman in middle age	17	15	13	45
Young woman	13	16	13	42
Young man	13	14	14	41
Woman in older age	4	7	6	17
Man in older age	4	5	6	15
I wouldn't make any of those choices because I don't distinguish people by age and sex	22	–	–	22
I don't know	5	–	–	5

* The sum of 1st, 2nd and 3rd place rankings. Percentages in columns exceed 100%.
Source: Institute for Public Affairs, September 2005.

As Table 5.12 shows, middle-aged men are generally considered to be the most attractive workers (53%), followed by middle-aged women, young women and young men, whose overall ranking ranges between 45% and 41%. Workers in their older years are perceived as far less attractive, with the fewest respondents choosing to employ older women (17%) and older men (15%).

Table 15.2 shows that only 22 % of respondents spontaneously refused to distinguish between job applicants on the basis of age and sex. In other words, the actual share of respondents who spontaneously subscribed to the principle of equal opportunities for people of all ages is much smaller than the nearly two-thirds (63%) who subscribed to that principle on a declarative basis (see Graph 5.7). A deeper analysis revealed that women, as well as individuals with a higher education more frequently refused to use the criteria of age and sex to distinguish between job applicants.

On the other hand, 73% of respondents openly acknowledged their sex and age preferences. Let us now take a closer look at them and try to establish whether there are any gender differences in assessments of the attractiveness of job applicants.

Table 5.13 shows that women and men tend to prefer middle-aged and young job applicants to those in their older years. This tendency is slightly more apparent among men.

At the same time, women tend to prefer women to men in every age category, while men likewise tend to prefer men to women. In other words, both women and men show a sort of "gender solidarity".[7]

---

[6] Such was the opinion of 73% of respondents in the SNSĽP survey. According to 7%, discrimination was most frequent in government organizations, while 6% said it was in the public sector, and 6% saw discrimination as equally spread in all sectors (*Terénny výskum...*, 2006).

[7] The only exception is the relatively favorable attitude of men to young women. Hypothetically, this attitude may also be affected by the physical attractiveness of young women, their greater pliability, or the chance of saving money on their wages. On the other hand, this may also affected by an attempt of respondents to distance themselves verbally from discrimination against young women, particularly mothers of small children, which was recently the target of strong public criticism (Marošiová – Šumšalová, 2006).

Table 5.13
"Imagine that you are the manager of a private company. You are hiring new employees and have several job applicants to choose from. All have the required qualifications and differ only by age and sex. Which of the following job applicants would you prefer?" (%)

	Preferences of women		Preferences of men	
	%	Ranking	%	Ranking
Woman in middle age	53	1	38	4
Man in middle age	47	2	60	1
Young woman	42	3	45	3
Young man	30	4	52	2
Older woman	23	5	9	6
Older man	12	6	18	5
I wouldn't make any of those choices because I don't distinguish people by age and sex	26	–	19	–
I don't know	4	–	5	–

Note: The sum of 1st, 2nd and 3rd place rankings. Percentages in columns exceed 100%.
Source: Institute for Public Affairs, September 2005.

We should not forget, however, that in the real functioning of the private sector in Slovakia, men have far greater opportunities to exercise their gender preferences because they more frequently hold managerial posts.

5.2.3. CHANCES OF JOB APPLICANTS OF DIFFERENT AGE AND SEX

What are the chances of job applicants from the six aforementioned categories in private companies in Slovakia?

According to Table 5.14 and Graph 5.8, people in Slovakia believe that older women and men stand the least chance of getting hired. The position of older women is significantly weaker: the percentage of respondents who named older women in the first place was far greater than the share of those who named older men (53% and 15%, respectively).

The third most disadvantaged category of job applicants is women in their middle years. Their chances are seen as far lower than those of their male counterparts. The position of young women is perceived as slightly worse than that of middle-aged men. According to public perception, young men have the best chances.

People in Slovakia suppose that with the increasing age of women and men, their chance on the labor market shrinks. However, age is a much greater handicap for women than for men. While the chances of men in their middle years are perceived as only slightly worse than those of young men, age is already a factor for the middle-aged women, whose chances fall off steeply in this age already.

According to public opinion, female job applicants of every age stand less chance of being hired than their male counterparts. The gap between women and men opens wider in the middle and especially the old years.[8]

---

[8] Public opinion adequately reflects the unequal chances of female and male job applicants of various ages. Also the analysis by Profesia, the country's largest on-line employment agency, has proved substantially lower interest of employers in female and male job applicants of mature and older age (Jakuš, 2007).

Table 5.14
"Given common hiring policies at Slovak private companies, which three categories of job applicants have the lowest chance to get a job?" (2007 and 2005 – views of the entire population, in %)

	1st place	2nd place	3rd place	Overall position*
Young man	7 (9)	7 (8)	6 (5)	20 (22)
Man in middle age	9 (7)	6 (7)	11 (11)	26 (24)
Young woman	8 (9)	9 (10)	13 (12)	29 (31)
Woman in middle age	7 (5)	15 (14)	35 (35)	56 (53)
Older man	15 (15)	40 (39)	20 (18)	75 (72)
Older woman	53 (51)	20 (18)	6 (5)	78 (74)

Note: The remainder of the 100% figure comprises the answer "I don't know". Figures in brackets are from 2005.
* The sum of 1st, 2nd and 3rd place rankings.
Source: Institute for Public Affairs, September 2005 and November 2007.

Graph 5.8
"Given common hiring policies at Slovak private companies, which three categories of job applicants have the lowest chance to get a job?" (2007 – in %)

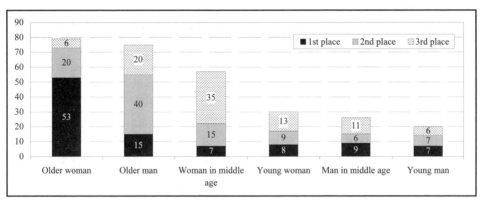

Note: The sum of 1st, 2nd and 3rd place rankings without distinction.
Source: Institute for Public Affairs, November 2007.

Let us now examine whether the gender of the respondents affects their views of the chances of women and men of various ages on the labor market. On the one hand, women and men agree that older women and men are the most disadvantaged, and that women in their middle years are also significantly disadvantaged (see Table 5.15).[9] On the other hand, women are more critical of the chances of women in their middle and older years, while men are more critical of the chances of younger and middle-aged men. The difference between the chances of young women and young men is far more significant according to female respondents than according to their male counterparts. The gender gap is the greatest when respondents evaluate the chances of middle-aged women; female respondents see them in far more critical light than male respondents.

---

[9]   Women and men with higher education are more aware of the disadvantages on the labor market faced by women in older and middle years.

Table 5.15
"Given common hiring policies at Slovak private companies, which three categories of job applicants have the lowest chance to get a job?" (2005 and 2007 – in %)

	Views of women		Views of men	
	2005	2007	2005	2007
Young man	20	16	24	25
Man in middle age	22	23	27	29
Young woman	32	29	30	29
Woman in middle age	58	62	48	50
Older man	71	75	72	75
Older woman	75	80	73	76

Note: The sum of 1st, 2nd and 3rd place rankings.
Source: Institute for Public Affairs, September 2005 and November 2007.

To summarize: while most people in Slovakia declare that they support the principle of equal opportunities for persons of all ages, in reality they subscribe to deeply rooted age stereotypes and attribute different attractiveness to female and male workers of various ages. The public views older men and especially older women as the least attractive job applicants.

Public opinion views middle-aged women as one of the most attractive categories of job applicants, second only to men in their middle years. However, this does not correspond to the actual attitudes of most employers to middle-aged women as job applicants. According to public opinion, women in their middle years are the third most disadvantaged category on the labor market, following older women and men. Their situation is far worse than that of young women, and especially than that of young and middle-aged men.

These findings show that people in Slovakia realize that there are age inequalities on the labor market and see a discrepancy between the legal ban on discrimination based on age and sex and the common practices of employers. This is why eighty nine percent of respondents in a survey by the SNSĽP in 2005 expressed the belief that this issue should be addressed with greater vigor than it has been so far (*Empirical Data...*, 2005d).

5.2.4. CHANCES OF WOMEN AND MEN OVER 45

Let us now have a closer look the situation of women and men over 45 on the labor market. How does public opinion perceive gender equality within this specific age category? According to Graph 5.9, two in three women (65%) and one in two men (49%) are convinced that men are privileged, while only 1% of female and 2% of male respondents think the opposite.

When we compare these views with opinions about the overall opportunities of women and men regardless of age, we see that people are less aware and /or critical of gender inequalities within the age category over 45. This may be the impact of the age factor: when respondents evaluate the situation of older people, their gender-sensitiveness tends to be overshadowed by their general perception that older people face greater disadvantages than younger people. In other words, gender-sensitiveness becomes weaker, while age-sensitiveness become stronger.

How do people over 45 see the issue of equality among women and men of their age? The views presented by women over 45 are virtually identical to those of all women. However, the views of men over 45 differ slightly from those presented by all men, as men over 45 are

Graph 5.9
"Do women and men over 45 have equal chances on the labor market (when it comes to remuneration, promotion at work, hiring and firing, etc.)?" (%)

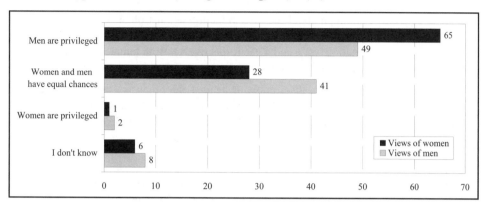

Source: Institute for Public Affairs, August 2006.

less aware of their privileged position. Thus the gap in views on gender equality held by women and men tends to increase after the age of 45.[10]

How do people evaluate the preferential treatment of men over 45 on the labor market? As Graph 5.9 and Table 5.16 illustrate, there are marked differences between the views of women and men. As for women, 65% of them believe that men over 45 are privileged and 58% disapprove of it. As for men, only 49% admit that women over 45 are disadvantaged and only 36% disapprove of it. The distribution of views presented by women and men over 45 is quite similar.

Table 5.16
Attitudes of women and men to the preferential treatment of men over 45 on the labor market (%)

	Attitudes of women	Attitudes of men
I think that men are privileged and I don't approve of it.	58	36
I think that men are privileged and I find it justified.	5	10
I think that men are privileged but I don't know whether it is right or wrong.	2	3
I don't think that men are privileged.*	35	51

Note: * This category comprises the answers "Women and men have equal chances", "Women are privileged" and "I don't know" from Graph 5.9.
Source: Institute for Public Affairs, September 2006.

5.2.5. DISCRIMINATION AGAINST OLDER WOMEN AND MEN

In this section, we will outline what people think of discrimination against older women and men on the labor market, and then we will explore whether their views are based on their own personal experience. Table 5.17 comprises the findings of a survey by the Institute for Public Affairs. The wording of the question did not explicitly specify the reasons for discrimination,

---

10 The views of men over 45 are affected by their educational attainment. Only 35% of men with elementary education, but 61% of men with university degrees admit that women are disadvantaged.

so respondents were not limited to discrimination based on age or sex but could take into consideration other reasons as well (e.g. race, ethnicity, disability, social situation, sexual orientation, religion, etc.).

The views of women and men about the discrimination against older women and men are different. A clear majority of women, but only a minority of men believe that older women frequently face discrimination (60% and 43%, respectively). Both female and male respondents in their older years are slightly more critical (66% and 50%, respectively).

On the other hand, the public sees discrimination against older men as a far less urgent social problem, as only 31% of women and 32% of men stated its frequent incidence. Again, older women and men are slightly more critical than the overall population (33% and 37%, respectively).

Table 5.17
"How often in your opinion do older women and men encounter discrimination on the labor market in Slovakia?" (% of answers "very and quite often" : "sometimes" : "rarely and never")

	Discrimination against older women	Discrimination against older men
Views of all women	60 : 27 : 9	31 : 35 : 25
Views of women over 45	66 : 22 : 9	33 : 35 : 23
Views of all men	43 : 34 : 13	32 : 35 : 24
Views of men over 45	50 : 30 : 12	37 : 19 : 8

Note: The remainder of the 100% figure comprises the answers "I don't know".
Source: Institute for Public Affairs, August 2006.

To what extent are people's views about discrimination against older women based on their personal contact with women who have become victims of discrimination on the labor market? As Graph 5.10 documents, 49% of female respondents and 37% of male respondents had encountered a victim of such discrimination in their closest environment (i.e. among relatives, neighbors or friends). Older women as well as older men have come across such cases more frequently than their younger counterparts.

Graph 5.10
"Do you personally know of any case of discrimination against a woman over 45 on the labor market?" (% of affirmative answers)

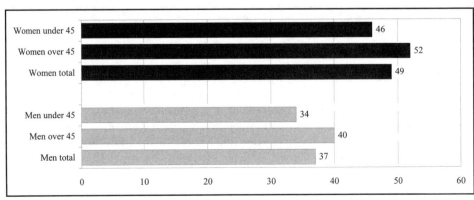

Source: Institute for Public Affairs, August 2006.

Obviously, the share of women over 45 who personally experienced discrimination on the labor market is much smaller. According to Graph 5.11, approximately one in five women of this age (21%) have had such type of negative personal experience. The incidence of victims of discrimination is more frequent among women working in the private sector (27%) and among employees of companies owned or managed by foreigners (32%) and less frequent among women employed in the public sector (14%). The feelings of discrimination are particularly widespread among unemployed women (55%).

Graph 5.11
"Have you personally encountered discrimination on the labor market since you reached the age of 45?" (% of affirmative answers in select categories of women over 45)

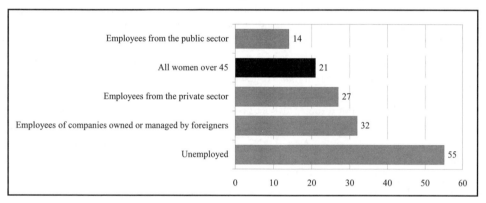

Source: Institute for Public Affairs, August 2006.

Graph 5.12
"Have you personally experienced any of the following situations over the past ten years?" (% of affirmative answers of employed women and men over 45)

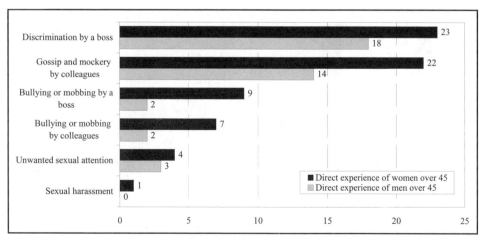

Source: Institute for Public Affairs, August 2006.

Finally, let us look at the personal experience of employed women and men over 45 with concrete forms of discrimination and other negative situations in the workplace. Graph 5.12

illustrates that this kind of experience is not rare, particularly among women. Twenty three percent of them have been discriminated against by their bosses and 9% have even been bullied or mobbed by them. Twenty two percent of women over 45 feel victimized by gossip and mockery from their colleagues, while 7% experienced even bullying or mobbing from their colleagues. Some 4% of women were the targets of unwanted sexual attention and 1% reported sexual harassment. Men over 45 had far less direct personal experiences with all of these negative situations.

5.2.6. CONCEPTS OF COMBATING DISCRIMINATION

The foregoing analysis showed that women in Slovakia, especially the older ones, experience considerable discrimination on the labor market. To what extent are they able to resist and combat discriminatory behavior?

People in Slovakia are rather skeptical on this matter. According to Graph 5.13, two thirds of female respondents (65%) thought that women over 45 cannot stand up for their employment rights effectively.[11] Critical opinions are less widespread among men, which can be explained by the fact that they are not directly afflicted by violations of women's rights (48%). At the same time, women feel more qualified to comment on the issue than men, as 13% of female but 23% of male respondents were unable to give an opinion.

Graph 5.13
"Do women over 45 sufficiently stand up for their employment rights?" (%)

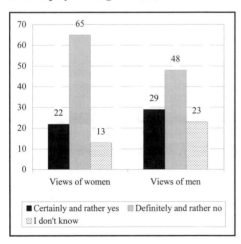

Source: Institute for Public Affairs, August 2006.

The key question is what exactly the victims of discrimination can do to exercise their rights. The existence of anti-discrimination legislation is an important prerequisite; however, it does not automatically guarantee restriction of discrimination or its elimination from the labor market. Victims of the discrimination, as well as general public have to take an active approach, so that discriminators feel the pressure and are forced to change their behavior.

The passage of the Anti-Discrimination Act in 2004 was welcomed wholeheartedly by 85% of Slovak citizens (Bútorová – Gyárfášová – Velšic, 2005). However, a survey carried out by the Slovak National Center for Human Rights one year later gave a less optimistic picture (*Terénny výskum...*, 2006). Only 40% of respondents were aware that an Anti-Discrimination Act had been passed, while 54% had no knowledge of it and 6% believed that such a law had not yet been passed. Given these findings, the amendment to the Anti-

---

[11] Women over 45 are more critical of their own ability to defend employment rights than younger women. The dissatisfaction is particularly strong about women with higher education. The most critical were female respondents with university degrees (76% of critical answers). On the other hand, male respondents with university degrees evaluated the defense of women's rights the most favorably (41% of critical answers).

Discrimination Act passed in February 2008, which was another important step towards strengthening legal protection of citizens against discrimination, will clearly not automatically curtail its occurrence on the labor market. Legislative standards have to be internalized by citizens and become social norms backed up by a set of positive and negative sanctions applied by the society.

When combating discrimination on the labor market, a lot depends on the attitudes of the direct or indirect victims of discrimination. Table 5.18 presents telling figures on the preparedness of working women and men to oppose discrimination.

Table 5.18
"What advice would you give to someone who has suffered discrimination in the workplace? How should he or she react?" (views of employed women and men – in %)

	Women under 45	Women over 45	Women total	Men total
Vague advice to use active defense strategies (e.g. "rebel"; "stand up for your rights"; "fight"; "look for possible solutions" etc.)	27	31	28	29
Vague advices to seek assistance outside the employer's organization, without specifying the institution (e.g. "complain to the appropriate authorities"; "turn to a civic association" etc.)	11	9	10	7
Resignation, feeling of helplessness, coming to terms with the discrimination (e.g. "be quiet or you could lose your job"; "you have no chance, the employer is always right"; "older people have no choice"; "women stand no chance"; "you won't get justice in this country"; "if you fight back, they will wear you down and you will have to quit" etc.)	12	20	15	8
Escapist solutions such as quitting or changing jobs (e.g. "give notice"; "ask to be transferred to another department"; "start up a business" etc.)	14	6	11	13
Active solutions within the employer's organization (e.g. "turn directly to the boss who discriminates"; "turn to a higher level boss"; "turn to the trade union organization in the workplace"; "turn to colleagues for help" etc.)	22	20	21	22
Addressing a specific institution outside the employer's organization and asking for help	10	9	10	14
Advice to improve work performance and appearance ("step up your work"; "prove your professional qualities"; "attend assertiveness training" etc.)	1	1	1	3
Advice to seek emotional support and guidance from relatives and friends	3	2	3	1
Advices to apply aggressive, non-constructive defense strategies (e.g. "take revenge, regardless of all negative consequences"; "have discriminator beaten up" etc.)	0	0	0	2

Note: This was an open-ended question. The remainder of the 100% figure comprises other answers.
Source: Institute for Public Affairs, August 2006.

Many employed women and men in Slovakia believe that it is important to combat discrimination actively. Unfortunately, a substantial part of them has only a vague idea of the effective ways of doing so, which is why they limit themselves to general remarks about the need to fight back (28% of women and 29% of men) or about the need to seek unspecified assistance outside the employer's organization (10% and 7%, respectively). Such vague recipes for combating discrimination were presented by 38% of women and 36% of men.

As for concrete ideas about active solutions, people believe that assistance should be sought within the employer's organization (21% of women and 22% of men) rather than from external institutions (10% and 14%, respectively). Concrete thoughts about the ways of combating discrimination were presented by 31% of women and 36% of men.

What are the concrete ways of combating discrimination within the employer's organization? Most respondents would turn directly to the boss who was the source of the discrimination and would demand an explanation and a remedy (10% of women and men); fewer respondents would seek help from a higher level boss (5% each), turn to the trade union organization in the workplace (5% each) or ask their colleagues for support (1% of women and 2% of men). The views of women and men are virtually identical.

What external institutions would employed women and men seek to protect them against discrimination in their own workplace? According to the respondents' answers, the list of such institutions includes lawyers and courts of justice, the police, the ombudsman, the labor inspectorate, the Ministry of Labor, Social Affairs and Family, and employment agencies.[12]

However, Table 5.18 also shows that a significant proportion of respondents advised the victims to resign and to adapt to discrimination. It is noteworthy that women recommended such passive solutions almost twice as often as men (15% and 8%, respectively).

The conviction of many women and men that it is futile to fight discrimination in the workplace gives rise to escapist solutions preferring departure from the workplace to seeking a true improvement. Men seem to prefer these solutions slightly more frequently than women (13% and 11%, respectively), probably because they are more confident they will be able to find another job.

Let us now take a closer look at the attitudes of women over 45 and compare them to those of younger women. Older women are clearly more likely to passively adapt to discrimination than their younger counterparts.[13] Twenty percent of women over 45, but only 12% of younger women prefer passive reaction. Along the same lines, older women are less considering the quitting of the workplace, due apparently to their awareness that it would be challenging for them to find another job (6% and 14%, respectively). Moreover, women over 45 have less clear ideas than younger women about the concrete ways of active defense against discrimination, and are less likely to seek solutions within the employer's organization.

These findings support the thesis that women over 45 present a more vulnerable group on the labor market than their male counterparts, as well as younger women.

---

[12] The Slovak National Centre for Human Rights was not mentioned at all by respondents. Its public visibility was very low, despite its 12-year existence. The Office of the Public Defender of Rights, which is the country's official term for the ombudsman's office, was more visible (*Reprezentatívny výskum...*, 2007).

[13] Similarly, older men differ from the younger ones by their greater inclination to passive adaptation and unwillingness to leave the workplace where discrimination is taking place.

6. WOMEN, MEN AND THE PRIVATE SPHERE

Jarmila Filadelfiová

6. WOMEN, MEN AND THE PRIVATE SPHERE

Differences between women and men can be found not only in the sphere of paid labor but also in the sphere of domestic or unpaid labor. Under the pre-industrial model, the former sphere was reserved for men as breadwinners and the latter for women as homemakers. Although this model has been substantially modified in modern societies, many of its original features have been preserved (Beck, 1986; Možný, 1990 and 1999; Gauthier, 1996; Crompton, 1999; Bauman, 2004). While "gender boundaries" between the private and the public sphere have become more permeable, gender differences within both spheres remain, as do problems in harmonizing work and family obligations.[1]

What about gender equality in the domestic sphere in Slovakia? To what degree does the conflict between professional and family obligations affect the professional careers and family lives of women and men? Before analyzing gender division of labor within the private sphere, let us outline the differences in the family situation of Slovak women and men.

6.1. FAMILY SITUATION IN TERMS OF GENDER AND AGE

Before 1989, Slovakia was a country where traditional behavioral patterns dominated in family life (see also Chapter 2 of this publication). A majority of women and men got married and became parents at least once in their lives. Already at that time, Slovakia witnessed a trend towards the atomization of families, i.e. a shift from the cohabitation of several generations towards young families living separately, as well as towards smaller families and more single-parent families. In the 1990s, the two-child family model prevailed over the multiple-child model. Along with these trends came changes in the structure of households. The overall share of two-parent families with children declined, while that of one-parent families and single individual households increased (Filadelfiová – Guráň, 1997; *Recent...*, 2000 and 2003; Filadelfiová – Cuperová, 2000; Vaňo, 2003 and 2007).

6.1.1. MARITAL STATUS OF WOMEN AND MEN

In terms of marital status, the structure of women in Slovakia differs from that of men. In 2006, the share of divorced and widowed individuals was higher among women over 15, while the share of single and married individuals was higher among men (see Graph 6.1). This is largely

---

[1] In the 1990s, these problems began to attract the attention of decision-makers. The increasing number of women entering the labor market and their growing employment highlighted the issue of gender inequalities in the public and private sphere, as well as the need to balance work and life. The public discourse criticized "gender-blind" theories of the welfare state, reproaching them for ignoring society's gender order (Lewis, 1992; Orloff, 1993). This criticism was reflected not only in welfare state theories (Esping-Andersen, 2000 and 2002; Korpi, 2001), but also in politics (*The Future...*, 2003; *Working...*, 2005a; *Integrated...*, 2005; *A Roadmap...*, 2006). In recent years, issues of gender equality in the private and public spheres as well as the issues of work-life balance have become the focus of EU policies. This new emphasis is also due to the population ageing and the declining birth rate (*Reconciling...*, 2001; *Confronting...*, 2005; *Changes...*, 2006; *Demographic...*, 2006; *Statistics...*, 2007).

Graph 6.1
Women and men over 15 by marital status (2006 – in %)

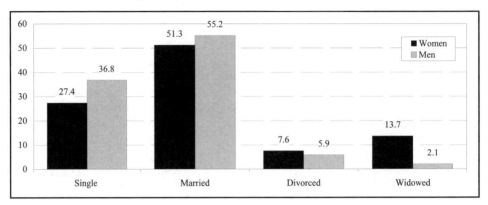

Source: *Štatistické...*, 2007.

the result of basic demographic processes, which differ among men and women. Men have a higher average age at marriage, a higher marriage rate due to repeat marriages and higher mortality.

These gender differences are even more pronounced in the over 45 age category, where 57% of women were married and 4% were single, compared to 70% and 9% of men, respectively (see Table 6.1). Two in five women over 45 reported a different marital status (13% were divorced, 26% were widowed and 1% cohabited), while among men, the share of such individuals was approximately one in five.

Table 6.1
Marital status of women and men under 45 and over 45 (2006 – in %)

	Women			Men		
	Under 45	Over 45	Total	Under 45	Over 45	Total
Single	33	4	20	53	9	34
Married	57	57	57	38	70	52
Divorced	6	13	9	5	6	5
Widowed	1	26	13	0	13	6
Cohabiting partner	3	1	2	4	2	3

Note: The percentages in the columns should add up to 100%.
Source: Institute for Public Affairs, August 2006.

6.1.2. PARENTHOOD MODELS

The overall structure of women and men in terms of the number of children is different. In all age categories, the share of childless men is higher than that of childless women (Graph 6.2 and Table 6.2). This is mostly because men become parents at a higher age than women, and because the share of men who never become parents is higher than that of women.

Let us compare the different age categories of married women and men. As Table 6.2 shows, 6% of all married women and 9% of all married men are childless.[2] More women as well as

Graph 6.2
Percentage of childless women and men by age (2006)

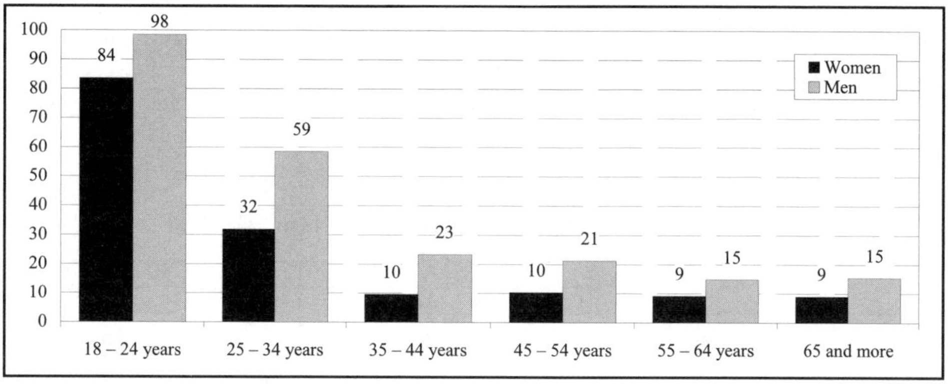

Source: Institute for Public Affairs, August 2006.

men have two children (49% of married women and 53% of married men) than one child (20% of women and 14% of men), three children (16% each) and four or more children (9% and 8%, respectively). This applies to women and men from both age categories, i.e. under 45 and over 45. The one-child family model was much more frequent among women and men under 45 than among older women and men (28% of women under 45, but only by 11% of their older counterparts). On the other hand, the share of women and men who had three and more children was significantly lower in the younger age category.

Table 6.2
Number of children of married women and men under 45 and over 45 (2006 – in %)

	Women			Men		
	Under 45	Over 45	Total	Under 45	Over 45	Total
No children	6	6	6	9	8	9
1 child	28	11	20	27	6	14
2 children	50	48	49	54	52	53
3 children	12	20	16	5	24	16
4 or more children	4	15	9	5	10	8

Source: Institute for Public Affairs, August 2006.

These age differences indicate that reproductive activity of women over 45 was higher than that of younger women, which also implied more interruptions during their professional careers and a heavier burden with childcare.

The category of women over 45 is quite diverse, not only in terms of the number of children but also in terms of the age at which women terminated their reproductive activity. The average age of these women's youngest children was 30.2; however, 11% of them still had at least one child younger than 18.

---

2   Census data only allow establishing the structure of married women according to the number of children. In 2001, 4.3% of them were childless; 17% had one child, 47% of them had two children, 21% had three children and 11% had four or more children (Pilinská 2005, p. 33). The structure of married women according to the survey by the Institute of Public Affairs was virtually identical to the census data.

6.1.3. STRUCTURE OF HOUSEHOLDS OF WOMEN AND MEN

The structure of households inhabited by women and men is also different. In 2006, women more frequently lived in one-parent family households and three-generation households, while men more frequently lived in two-parent family households with or without children (see Table 6.3). The share of women and men who lived as single individuals was more or less identical.

Table 6.3
Structure of households of women and men under 45 and over 45 in 2006 (%)

	Women			Men		
	Under 45	Over 45	Total	Under 45	Over 45	Total
Alone	4	22	12	6	20	12
Childless couple (married or cohabiting)	6	28	17	4	40	20
Two parents and dependent child/ren	65	23	46	68	28	50
One parent and dependent child/ren	10	15	12	10	3	7
Two parents, child/ren and grandparent/s	11	7	9	7	5	6
One parent, child/ren and grandparent/s	2	1	1	2	1	2
Other type of household	2	4	3	3	3	3

Note: The percentages in the columns should add up to 100%.
Source: Institute for Public Affairs, August 2006.

Table 6.3 also shows greater differences between the structure of households inhabited by older women and men compared to households inhabited by their younger counterparts. The greatest differences are in the share of women and men over 45 who live in one-parent families (15% of women compared to 3% of men) and the share of those who live in complete family households without children (28% of women compared to 40% of men). The share of women over 45 who live alone was only slightly higher than that of their male counterparts (22% and 20%, respectively). However, this share is lower only until the age of 64. In older age categories, the percentages of women living alone increase dramatically. While most men living alone are single or divorced, most women living alone are widows.

The differences described are due to several factors. The higher share of single young men is a result of their ability to become independent financially and in terms of housing, as well as of their tendency to marry later. The higher share of older men living in complete families is the result of their tendency to remarry if divorced or widowed, as well as their higher and earlier mortality. The fact that most dependent children are entrusted to their mothers after a divorce, along with the lower rate of remarriage among divorced or widowed women is the main reason for the higher share of one-parent families led by women. The lower and later mortality of women together with their lower rate of remarriage and their greater ability to take care of themselves are the main reasons of a higher share of women than men over 65 who live alone.

Households inhabited by women and men over 45 are generally more diverse than households inhabited by younger women and men. The main reason is that the share of women and men who live alone as well as the share of childless couples and one-parent families is increasing at the expense of the share of two-generation families comprising two parents and dependent children.

The family situation of women over 45 is quite diverse. Their marital status ranges from singles to widows, although married women remain dominant (58%). In terms of their children's age, there are women whose children still attend elementary school, although the average age of their youngest child is just above 30. Almost two in five of these women (38%) share a household with their unmarried children; however, approximately half of them live together with their partner only (i.e. in the "empty nest" type of family) or alone.

The diverse structure of families and households implies a broad spectrum of family obligations as well as different needs and expectations with respect to work and employment. Let us look first at family obligations.

6.2. IDEAL AND ACTUAL GENDER DIVISION OF DOMESTIC LABOR

The double burden of family and professional obligations is a chronic problem for women in Slovakia as well as abroad (Možný, 1990 and 1999; Matoušek, 1993; Čermáková – Maříková – Tuček, 1995; Silva – Smart, 1999; Inglehart – Baker, 2000; *The Life...*, 2008). Although the Communist regime strongly encouraged and significantly increased the participation of women on the labor market, taking care of the household chores and family members remained largely women's work (Provazník, 1989). The situation has not changed much since 1989. According to the authors of the book *She and He in Slovakia: Gender Issues in Public Opinion*, published by the Institute for Public Affairs in 1996, "the majority of women of productive age fulfill both roles, i.e. the role of an employed worker and the role of a homemaker and a mother" (Bútorová, 1996, p. 73). Since then, women have continued to carry a double burden, as confirmed by a number of surveys (*Úloha...*, 2006; *Ženy...*, 2006).

Similar conclusions can be made from the findings of a survey carried out by the Institute for Public Affairs in 2006, which examined the gender division of domestic labor in case of fifteen activities – eight of them related to managing the household, and seven related to looking after family members. The activities comprised everyday chores and less frequent duties. The survey examined the actual model of the division of labor as well as ideas of women and men about the ideal division of obligations.

6.2.1. HOUSEHOLD CHORES

Let us first look at the participation of women and men in the everyday chores related to managing the household. We will focus on those women and men who live in joint households, as either married or cohabiting couples.

As Table 6.4 shows, everyday household chores primarily fall on women's shoulders. They are the ones to do the laundry and ironing (as stated by 94% of women and 92% of men), cooking (80% of women and 75% of men), cleaning (73% and 66%, respectively) and washing the dishes (72% and 67%, respectively). These duties are the joint responsibility of women and men only in one third of all households. Households in which these chores are performed primarily by men are virtually unheard of. Shopping for groceries is the only regular household chore that men are more willing to accept; their overall participation in the "dirty household chores" is very low.

Table 6.4
"Who in your household does perform, and who in your opinion should perform, the following chores?" (% of answers "exclusively and mostly the man" : "man and woman about equally" : "exclusively and mostly the woman")

	Views of women		Views of men	
	Reality	**Ideal**	**Reality**	**Ideal**
Laundry and ironing	0 : 6 : 94	1 : 15 : 84	1 : 7 : 92	0 : 9 : 91
Cooking	2 : 18 : 80	0 : 31 : 69	2 : 23 : 75	1 : 24 : 75
Everyday cleaning and tidying up	1 : 26 : 73	0 : 45 : 54	2 : 33 : 66	1 : 37 : 62
Washing the dishes	1 : 27 : 72	1 : 55 : 44	5 : 28 : 67	1 : 38 : 61
Shopping for groceries	4 : 45 : 51	3 : 74 : 23	10 : 43 : 47	3 : 64 : 33
Taking care of administrative matters	25 : 47 : 28	25 : 70 : 5	24 : 48 : 28	23 : 65 : 12
Keeping the homestead	32 : 61 : 7	35 : 64 : 1	48 : 47 : 5	48 : 50 : 2
Household repairs and car maintenance	93 : 6 : 1	92 : 8 : 0	95 : 4 : 1	96 : 3 : 1
Everyday care of dependent children	1 : 25 : 75	0 : 40 : 60	6 : 28 : 66	0 : 30 : 70
Looking after sick children	2 : 26 : 72	1 : 47 : 53	4 : 22 : 74	2 : 31 : 67
Learning with children and helping with their homework	4 : 39 : 57	2 : 75 : 23	2 : 32 : 66	2 : 56 : 42
Looking after grandchildren in pre-school or in school age	0 : 47 : 53	0 : 69 : 31	2 : 56 : 42	0 : 61 : 39
Looking after adult family members (i.e. parents, parents-in-law, siblings)	2 : 58 : 40	0 : 85 : 15	3 : 74 : 23	1 : 76 : 22
Taking children to day care, kindergarten, school, activities clubs, etc.	3 : 49 : 48	1 : 79 : 20	5 : 51 : 44	0 : 68 : 32
Playing with children and taking them out	1 : 74 : 25	1 : 90 : 9	2 : 68 : 30	1 : 82 : 16

Note: This table features the answers of women and men who live in a partnership; the "Reality" column features only the answers of respondents to whom particular chores apply. The answers "I don't know" were disregarded.
Source: Institute for Public Affairs, August 2006.

Graph 6.3
Percentage of women and men who perform regular household chores – by marital status
(% of answers "exclusively or always")

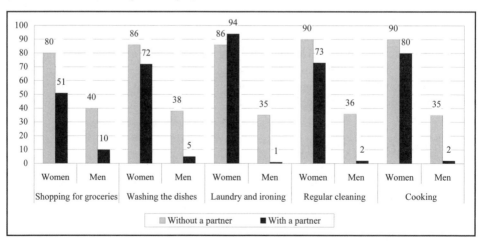

Note: The category "without a partner" comprises single, divorced and widowed women and men; the category "with a partner" comprises women and men living in matrimony or cohabitation.
Source: Institute for Public Affairs, August 2006.

And it is not because men do not know how to do those chores. As Graph 6.3 shows, 35% to 40% of men who live alone perform these duties always or usually. However, among men living in joint households with women, that share is only 1% to 10%. In other words, entering a partnership with a woman means for many men an opportunity to get rid of their responsibilities for the regular household chores and to delegate them largely or completely to the woman. Women, for their part, are used to performing these chores themselves regardless of their marital status.

So in everyday reality, men are largely "excused" from sharing responsibility for the regular household chores. As Table 6.4 indicates, this situation is largely in accordance with the normative expectations of Slovak population. On the one hand, very few women and men living in partnership (0 – 3%) believe that these duties should be performed primarily by men. On the other hand, there are certain dissimilarities between the views of women and men. Compared to women, men more frequently see the regular household chores as exclusively or mostly women's duties, particularly the laundry and ironing (91% of men and 84% of women), cooking (75% and 69%, respectively), cleaning (62% and 54%, respectively), washing the dishes (61% and 44%, respectively) and shopping for groceries (33% and 23%, respectively). Women, for their part, more frequently argue that these chores should be performed equally by both partners. The greatest difference was in respondents' opinions on washing the dishes, which 55% of women viewed as a job suitable equally for women and men, whereas 61% of men described it as a woman's responsibility. And what household chore inspired the greatest agreement between women and men? Clearly it was the laundry and ironing, which was viewed as "a woman's job" by 91% of men and 84% of women.

A comparison of the ideal and actual models of labor division within the household indicates that men can be more satisfied with the *status quo* than women; in the case of cooking, cleaning, laundry and ironing, their ideal notion is almost identical to the actual state of affairs. When it comes to washing the dishes, they admit that they should help more; on the other hand, they would like to transfer more responsibilities for the shopping to women.

Let us now look at the division of labor between women and men id case of three other activities related to the running of the household: taking care of administrative matters, performing household repairs and maintaining the car, and tending the homestead, i.e. looking after the house, garden, animals and fields.

Men participate in these activities to a far greater extent than in regular household chores. Doing household repairs and car maintenance is almost exclusively in the competence of men, as stated by 93% of female and 95% of male respondents. About one in four women and men stated that taking care of administrative matters was completely or mostly the duty of men; an equal share said it was the woman's job, and almost half said they shouldered this responsibility equally. As for tending the homestead, the views of women and men regarding the actual division of labor differed, as men saw their own participation as more intensive than did women. Almost one in two men (48%) claimed that they performed these activities by themselves, and about an equal proportion (47%) said they shared them with women; however, only one in three women (32%) credited men with greater responsibility for tending the homestead, while 61% felt that they performed these chores equally.

A comparison of the actual and ideal labor division indicates that most women and men are satisfied with the current state of affairs when it comes to tending the homestead, the upkeep of cars and doing household repairs. But neither women nor men seem completely happy about attending to administrative chores, as they wish to share this responsibility more than they actually do. The participative model, which is in fact practiced by less than half of all households (47% of women and 48% of men), was seen as ideal by 70% of women and 65% of men.

6.2.2. LOOKING AFTER FAMILY MEMBERS

Another category of domestic responsibilities is related to looking after children or other family members. All seven activities from this category are typically performed by women or are shared by both partners. Generally speaking, there are three basic models of sharing responsibility for these duties.

The first model may be described as strongly feminized because men rarely participate in these activities – not more than one third of them, in fact – and if they do, then only together with women. This applies mostly to the everyday care of the children, staying home with sick children, and helping children with their school obligations.

The second model is approximately evenly divided between equal participation by both partners and between women carrying the prevailing responsibility. Such is the case with taking children to day care, kindergarten, school and activities clubs, or looking after grandchildren.

In the third model, responsibility for performing various duties is mostly shared equally by both partners, and then shouldered primarily by women. Such a division of labor is typical of playing with the children or taking them out, as well as of looking after other adult family members.

This indicates that men prefer to help when it comes to playing with the children or taking them out, looking after adult family members and grandchildren, and taking children to day care, kindergarten, school or and activities clubs. On the other hand, they participate less in taking everyday care of the children, helping them with their school obligations, and attending to sick children.

Interestingly, men tend to believe that they participate more in these activities than women admit. For instance, 77% of men said they took part in looking after adult family members, but only 60% of women agreed that it was so; similarly, 58% of men claimed credit for looking after grandchildren, but only 47% of women concurred.

Does the actual division of labor in looking after family members correspond to the ideal notions of women and men? Table 6.4 tells us clearly that it does not. The share of women and men who believe that these activities should be equally performed by both partners is significantly higher than the share of women and men who actually perform them together. Women prefer such a participative model more frequently than men. On the other hand, men tend to share the traditional opinion that looking after other family members is the exclusive role of women.

So what is the overall picture of the actual and ideal division of labor in families and households? A substantial majority of the activities examined (12 out of 15) tend to lie on the shoulders of women far more than men. Such an unbalanced division of responsibilities is not in accordance with the ideal of equal participation by both partners.

Women are more pronounced advocates of a just division of domestic labor than men, who more frequently endorse the opinion that the principal responsibility for performing household chores and looking after other family members should be primarily borne by women. Such traditional notions are more widespread among men with lower education; blue-collar workers; and inhabitants of rural areas.

6.2.3. DIVISION OF LABOR IN THE YOUNGER AND OLDER GENERATIONS

A comparison of the gender division of labor between the younger and older generation offers a surprising picture. As Table 6.5 shows, in case of seven out of the fifteen domestic activities there was no significant difference between the group under 45 and over 45. These were the following activities: washing the dishes, everyday cleaning; laundry and ironing; taking care of administrative matters, doing household repairs and car maintenance; tending to the homestead; and looking after adult family members.

As for the remaining eight activities, the survey revealed that younger women carry a heavier burden than their older counterparts, while younger men participate in them less frequently than older men. Besides cooking and shopping, this applies to all ways of looking after younger family members: everyday care of the children, learning with them and helping them with their homework; taking them to day care, kindergarten, school, etc.; staying home with sick children; playing with them and looking after grandchildren.

Even greater differences between the two generations are in their normative notions of the ideal division of domestic labor. While younger women emphasize the participative model much more frequently than older women, no such opinion shift has occurred among younger men, whose views are virtually identical to those of older men. In some areas, younger men are even slightly more conservative. For instance, the opinion that doing the laundry and ironing, taking everyday care of the children, or taking them to day care, kindergarten, school or activities clubs is primarily a woman's job was more frequent among younger men than among older ones.

Table 6.5
"Who in your household does perform, and who in your opinion should perform, the following chores?" (% of answers "exclusively and mostly the man" : "man and woman about equally" : "exclusively and mostly the woman")

	Views of women		Views of men	
	Under 45	Over 45	Under 45	Over 45
Laundry and ironing	1 : 19 : 80	0 : 16 : 84	0 : 11 : 89	1 : 14 : 85
Cooking	1 : 41 : 58	0 : 27 : 73	1 : 26 : 73	1 : 28 : 71
Everyday cleaning and tidying up	0 : 54 : 46	0 : 42 : 58	1 : 39 : 60	0 : 41 : 59
Washing the dishes	1 : 62 : 37	1 : 53 : 46	1 : 44 : 55	1 : 42 : 57
Shopping for groceries	2 : 76 : 22	4 : 71 : 25	3 : 68 : 29	5 : 64 : 31
Taking care of administrative matters	20 : 74 : 6	29 : 66 : 5	22 : 65 : 13	25 : 65 : 10
Keeping the homestead	24 : 65 : 1	38 : 61 : 1	49 : 48 : 3	48 : 51 : 1
Household repairs and car maintenance	90 : 10 : 0	94 : 6 : 0	95 : 4 : 1	93 : 7 : 0
Everyday care of dependent children	1 : 45 : 54	0 : 39 : 61	0 : 31 : 69	0 : 33 : 67
Looking after sick children	1 : 54 : 45	1 : 42 : 57	1 : 36 : 63	1 : 32 : 67
Learning with children and helping with their homework	1 : 80 : 21	2 : 73 : 25	2 : 58 : 40	2 : 56 : 42
Looking after grandchildren in pre-school or in school age	0 : 76 : 24	1 : 67 : 33	1 : 61 : 38	0 : 64 : 36
Looking after adult family members (i.e. parents, parents-in-law, siblings)	1 : 88 : 12	0 : 80 : 20	1 : 76 : 23	2 : 75 : 23
Taking children to day care, kindergarten, school, activities clubs, etc.	2 : 84 : 14	1 : 78 : 21	1 : 67 : 32	1 : 71 : 28
Playing with children and taking them out	1 : 94 : 5	2 : 87 : 11	2 : 84 : 14	1 : 80 : 19

Note: This table features only the answers of respondents to whom particular chores apply. The answers "I don't know" were disregarded.
Source: Institute for Public Affairs, August 2006.

Table 6.5 shows also another interesting phenomenon: the differences between the views of younger women and men are more pronounced than between those of their older counterparts. In other words, younger women are much stronger advocates of a balanced division of labor than younger men, who in line with traditional gender stereotypes consider it right to delegate responsibility for performing household chores and looking after family members to women. The more educated women are, the more they demand that men participate more in domestic tasks.

6.2.4. SHIFTS WITHIN A DECADE

Let us now look at the continuity and changes in the gender division of domestic labor between 1995 and 2006. [3] As for the actual division of labor, Table 6.6 gives a surprising picture. There has been virtually no change in three types of activities: laundry and ironing (which has remained almost exclusively the domain of women); washing the dishes (which continues to be primarily a woman's responsibility); taking children to kindergarten, school and activities clubs (which remains split about evenly between both partners on the one hand, and primarily women on the other). The other three household chores – namely cooking, cleaning and shopping – have seen a moderate shift towards the participative model, which has relieved women although they continue to bear the principal burden. Taking care of administrative matters and dealing with the authorities has also become an obligation that is shared equally by both partners, but in this case it has reduced the burden on men rather than on

Table 6.6
"Who in your household does perform, and who in your opinion should perform, the following chores?" (% of answers "exclusively and mostly the man" : "man and woman about equally" : "exclusively and mostly the woman" – situation in 1995 and 2006)

		Views of women		Views of men	
		Reality	Ideal	Reality	Ideal
Laundry and ironing	1995	0 : 6 : 93	4 : 6 : 90	4 : 6 : 90	2 : 10 : 89
	2006	0 : 6 : 94	1 : 15 : 84	1 : 7 : 92	0 : 9 : 91
Cooking	1995	2 : 16 : 82	0 : 28 : 72	5 : 17 : 78	1 : 23 : 76
	2006	2 : 19 : 79	0 : 31 : 69	2 : 23 : 75	1 : 24 : 75
Everyday cleaning and tidying up	1995	1 : 21 : 78	1 : 44 : 55	5 : 25 : 70	1 : 37 : 62
	2006	1 : 26 : 73	0 : 45 : 54	2 : 33 : 66	1 : 37 : 62
Washing the dishes	1995	2 : 23 : 76	1 : 50 : 49	6 : 27 : 68	2 : 31 : 67
	2006	1 : 27 : 72	1 : 55 : 44	5 : 28 : 67	1 : 38 : 61
Shopping for groceries	1995	5 : 30 : 65	4 : 60 : 36	9 : 40 : 51	3 : 48 : 49
	2006	4 : 44 : 52	3 : 74 : 23	10 : 43 : 47	3 : 64 : 33
Taking care of administrative matters	1995	30 : 40 : 31	37 : 57 : 6	44 : 39 : 18	43 : 51 : 7
	2006	25 : 47 : 28	25 : 70 : 5	24 : 48 : 28	23 : 65 : 12
Learning with children and helping with their homework	1995	6 : 33 : 61	3 : 81 : 16	6 : 46 : 48	4 : 67 : 29
	2006	4 : 39 : 57	2 : 75 : 23	2 : 32 : 66	2 : 56 : 42
Taking children to day care, kindergarten, school, activities clubs, etc.	1995	5 : 49 : 46	3 : 79 : 19	6 : 52 : 41	3 : 69 : 28
	2006	3 : 49 : 48	1 : 79 : 20	5 : 51 : 44	0 : 68 : 32

Note: This table features the answers of women and men who live in a partnership. The "Reality" column features only the answers of respondents to whom particular chores apply. The answers "I don't know" were disregarded.
Source: FOCUS, June 1995; Institute for Public Affairs, August 2006.

---

[3] Since the list of activities examined in 1995 and 2006 was not identical, Table 6.6 features only eight of the fifteen previously discussed activities.

women. Finally, it was difficult to identity what shift has occurred in sharing the responsibility for supervising the children's school obligations, because the participation of men has increased according to women, but has declined according to men themselves. Whatever the case, the main responsibility still remains on women's shoulders.

And how did normative ideas of Slovak population evolve between 1995 and 2006? The changes in men's and women's minds were different.

Men's views of four from eight activities have changed very little. Most continue to regard cooking, cleaning, doing the laundry and ironing as the principal responsibility of women, and taking children to kindergarten, school or activities clubs as the joint responsibility of both partners. On the other hand, there are more men than a decade ago who see three other activities – shopping, washing the dishes and taking care of administrative matters – as joint tasks. At the same time, there are more men than before demanding that women assume greater responsibility for supervising children's school obligations.

The development of women's views about the ideal gender division of domestic labor was more significant; their emphasis on equal participation of both partners intensified. Women demand bringing responsibility for five household chores – namely doing the laundry and ironing, cooking, washing the dishes, shopping and dealing with the authorities – into a gender balance, what would alleviate the burden on them. On the other hand, their views regarding the participation of both partners in two other activities – cleaning and taking children to kindergarten, school or activities clubs – did not change much. The position of women on helping children with their homework changed in the same direction as that of men; nevertheless, shared involvement of both partners remained the ideal solution in women's eyes.

To summarize: the stereotypical division of labor in Slovak families and households into female and male chores has not changed much during the last decade. Not only is this traditional model reflected in the actual unbalanced actual participation of women and men in domestic labor, but it also persists in the normative ideas of the Slovak population. Although women advocate the just division of domestic labor far more frequently than men, there is still a substantial portion of them preferring traditional gender patterns. Generally speaking, the findings from 2006 corroborated those from 11 years ago: both women and men call for the model that suits them best: women more frequently prefer the partnership model, while men advocate the patriarchal model (Bútorová, 1996, p. 76).

6.3. NON-WORKING TIME OF WOMEN AND MEN
6.3.1. TIME DEMANDS OF DOMESTIC WORK

So far, we have discussed the gender division of labor in the family and the household. Now, let us take a closer look at the amount of time that women and men actually spend on domestic work.

Unfortunately, we cannot use data from a time use survey because it has not been carried out in Slovakia in recent decades.[4] In 2006, the Institute for Public Affairs tried to make up for this information deficit by carrying out a survey in which respondents were asked to estimate

---

[4] According to the Statistical Office of the Slovak Republic, time use survey is expected to be carried out in Slovakia between 2008 and 2010 (http://portal.statistics.sk/showdoc.do?docid=2857).

the total number of hours per week they spend performing household chores and look-ing after other family members, as well as the total number of hours they spend doing their paid job.[5]

Women in Slovakia are burdened with unpaid domestic work to a far greater extent than men (see Table 6.7). On average, women spend 21 hours per week performing household chores (compared to 13 hours spent by men) and 18 hours per week looking after other family mem-bers (compared to 8 hours spent by men). Every week, women spend a total of 39 hours on unpaid domestic work while men spend 21 hours on the same. Per day, this comes to about 5.5 hours for women and 3 hours for men.[6]

Table 6.7
Average weekly estimated number of hours spent on unpaid domestic work – by age

	Women			Men		
	Under 45	Over 45	Total	Under 45	Over 45	Total
Household chores	19	23	21	10	16	13
Looking after family members (children and adults)	22	13	18	8	7	8
Total amount of unpaid domestic work	41	36	39	18	23	21

Note: The answers "I can't estimate it" were disregarded.
Source: Institute for Public Affairs, August 2006.

Table 6.7 also illustrates that women under 45 spend 9 hours more on average per week looking after other family members than older women. Women over 45, for their part, spend 4 hours more on average per week doing household chores. Compared to men over 45, younger men spend 1 hour more per week looking after other family members but 6 hours less per week doing household chores.

Obviously, the volume of unpaid domestic work largely depends on people's marital sta-tus.[7] People who live in marriage or cohabitation spend the most time on it: every week, women spend 23 hours looking after other family members and 23 hours performing house-hold chores (46 hours total); men, for their part, spend 11 hours per week doing the former and 14 hours per week doing the latter (25 hours total). On the other hand, single women and men spend the least time on domestic work (19 hours and 12 hours total per week, respectively).

Although the volume of unpaid domestic work does depend on the marital status, the differ-ence between women and men is large in all categories. The greatest gender gap is in the category of married or cohabiting couples. Compared to men, women spend 12 hours more looking after family members and 9 hours more performing household chores, for a total difference of 21 hours. The total difference in the category of divorced or widowed women and men is 14 hours, while in the category of single women and men it is 7 hours.

Women with university degrees spend about 2 hours more per week looking after other fam-ily members and 2 hours less performing household chores than the average. On the other hand, women and men with only elementary education spend approximately 3 hours more

---

5 For more details on the working time of women and men, see Section 4.1.6. of this book.
6 Surveys from other European countries (e.g. Germany, Bulgaria, Estonia or Lithuania) also indicate that women spend approximately twice as much time as men doing unpaid domestic work (*Harmonized...*; https://www.testh2.scb.se/tus/tus/StatMeanMact1.html).
7 Another important factor is the number and age of children in the household. Generally speaking, the more and the younger the children in the family, the more care and time they require.

doing household chores than average, which probably has to do with the fact that they more frequently live in family houses and therefore have to take care of a homestead or a garden. Residents of small villages, which are inhabited largely by older people with lower educational attainment, generally spend more time on household chores.

What is the situation of employed women and men? Compared to men, their female counterparts spend much more time performing household chores as well as looking after other family members (see Table 6.8). Active participation of women on the labor market does not significantly alleviate their domestic burden. Employed women spend a total of 36 hours on unpaid domestic work, which is only 3 hours less than the average for all women, including unemployed ones.

Table 6.8
Average weekly estimated number of hours spent on paid work and unpaid domestic work – by age

	Employed women			Employed men		
	Under 45	Over 45	Total	Under 45	Over 45	Total
Unpaid domestic work. Of this:	36	36	36	21	19	20
• Household chores	17	21	19	10	11	10
• Looking after family members	19	15	17	11	8	10
Paid work	44	44	44	48	48	48
Paid and unpaid work total	80	80	80	69	67	68

Note: The answers "I can't estimate it" were disregarded.
Source: Institute for Public Affairs, August 2006.

Compared to men, women spend 4 hours less on paid work per week, but 16 hours more on unpaid domestic work. Altogether, women spend 80 hours a week on paid and unpaid work while men only spend 68 hours. In other words, the average woman in Slovakia works per week 12 hours more than the average man.

The differences between employed women and men under 45 and over 45 in terms of the total time spent at work are not large. The weekly workload at paid jobs averages 44 hours for women and 48 hours for men. However, younger women and men spend 4 and 3 hours more, respectively, looking after other family members. Older women and men, for their part, spend 4 and 1 hour more, respectively, doing household chores. While the total time spent on unpaid domestic work remains the same for employed women under and over 45 (36 hours for younger as well as older women), it tends to decline with age for employed men (from 21 hours for men under 45 to 19 hours for men over 45).

According to Graph 6.4 that presents the situation of various age groups in more detail, employed women between 35 and 44 are the most burdened of all, spending 44 hours on paid work and 42 hours on unpaid domestic work. Their total of 86 hours is 6 hours longer in comparison to the average employed woman. Men from the same age group spend 48 hours at paid work and 23 hours on unpaid domestic work; their total of 71 hours is 3 hours longer than in comparison to the average employed man, but 15 hours shorter in comparison to the average employed woman between 35 and 44.

The second most burdened category is women and men between 45 and 54 (80 hours for women and 66 hours for men), followed by women and men between 55 and 64. Employed women and men from the youngest age category spend the least time on unpaid domestic work and the most time on paid work.

Graph 6.4
**Average weekly estimated number of hours spent on paid work and unpaid domestic work –
by age**

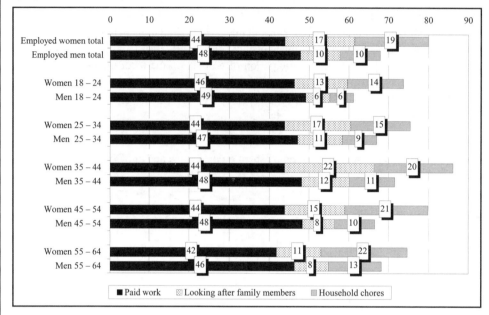

Note: The answers "I can't estimate" were disregarded.
Source: Institute for Public Affairs, August 2006.

Graph 6.5
**Average weekly estimated number of hours spent on paid work and unpaid domestic work –
by marital status**

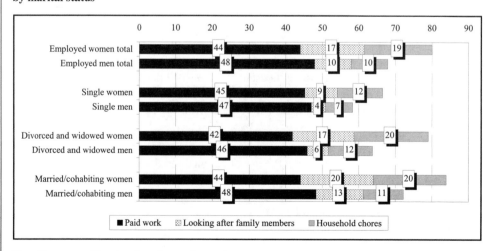

Note: The answers "I can't estimate" were disregarded.
Source: Institute for Public Affairs, August 2006.

Similarly to the entire population, the total workload of employed women and men largely depends on their marital status (see Graph 6.5). Women and men who live in a partnership are the most burdened. The average married or cohabitating woman spends 44 hours on her paid work and 40 hours on unpaid domestic work (84 hours total), while the average married or cohabitating man spends 48 hours on his paid work and 24 hours at home (72 hours total). The total workload of employed married women is thus 12 hours greater than that of employed married men.

On the other hand, the combined workload of paid and unpaid work is the lowest for single men (58 hours total) and single women (66 hours total). The total workload of divorced and widowed women is 79 hours and men 64 hours.

All these findings confirm the universal nature of gender differences in terms of the total amount of time spent on paid work and unpaid domestic work. Regardless of their age and marital status, employed women carry a much heavier load of household and family obligations than employed men.

6.3.2. FREQUENCY OF EXTRA-WORK ACTIVITIES

Let us now examine household chores and care for family members as part of a broader spectrum of extra-work activities. While the previous analysis was based on respondents' estimates of the weekly number of hours spent on unpaid domestic work, the following analysis will compare the frequency of various activities.

As Table 6.9 indicates, the most common type of extra-work activities are household chores, which are frequently – i.e. every day or at least several times a week – performed by almost all women (95%) and three in four men (75%).

Obviously, not everybody has other family members to take care of. Of those parents who have dependent children requiring care, 74% of women and 63% of men spend time with them every day or several times a week. Sixty four percent of those women and 45% of those men who have grandchildren said they frequently took care of them. Finally, 42% of those women and 33% of those men who have adult relatives in need said they often looked after them. Women over 45 perform these activities more often than their younger counterparts. Among men, no such connection was established.

Table 6.9
"How often do you pursue the following extra-work activities?" (%)

	Women				Men			
	Every day	Several times a week	Rarely	Never	Every day	Several times a week	Rarely	Never
Household chores	77	18	5	1	31	44	20	5
Looking after children*	58	16	17	10	33	30	27	10
Looking after adult family members*	17	25	35	23	8	25	35	32
Looking after grandchildren*	14	33	31	23	7	38	31	24
Interests and hobbies	17	42	34	7	24	44	29	3
Self-education	11	25	36	28	12	25	33	30
Sports, active leisure	6	24	40	30	14	29	35	22
Voluntary or pro bono activities	0	6	28	66	1	6	32	60
Political activities	0	1	8	91	0	2	9	89

Note: The answers "I don't know" were disregarded.
* – features only the answers of respondents to whom the particular activities apply.
Source: Institute for Public Affairs, August 2006.

As for other extra-work activities, women and men most frequently devote their time to their interests and hobbies; 59% of women and 66% of men do so every day or several times a week. Sports and active leisure activities are significantly less common, particularly among women (30% of women compared to 43% of men). A detailed analysis showed that men under 45 pursue these activities much more frequently than older men, as well as women, especially the older ones.

Self-education is a specific extra-work activity. It is important to women and men regardless of age, because education is one of the basic prerequisites for succeeding on the labor market (Bodnárová – Džambazovič – Filadelfiová – Gerbery – Kvapilová – Porubänová, 2005; Gyárfášová, 2006). According to Table 6.9, these activities are frequently pursued by 36% of women and 37% of men. However, there are substantial differences in terms of age (see Table 6.10). While 84% of women and 82% of men younger than 45 educate themselves at least sporadically, this share among older people is only 60% and 56%, respectively. While 16% of women and 17% of men under 45 pursue this activity every day, only 6% of women and men over 45 do the same. Needless to say, this age difference has to be eliminated in order to strengthen the participation of older people on the labor market. This requires not only a change in the attitudes of employers and better availability of education to all age groups, but also a more open and motivated approach on the part of older women and men themselves.

At the bottom of the list of extra-work activities are two activities that promote civic participation. A marginal 6% of women and men regularly participate in voluntary or *pro bono* activities pursued by civic associations, clubs or churches; 28% of women and 32% of men participate occasionally, while 66% of women and 60% of men never devote time to these activities. Even less popular among women and men is political activity (for instance within local self-government or a political party), which is regularly pursued by 1% of women and 2% of men; occasionally by 8% of women and 9% of men; and never by 91% of women and 89% of men.

Let us now look at the impact of educational attainment on extra-work activities of women and men. As Table 6.10 shows, the frequency of four activities increases hand in hand with

Table 6.10
Frequency of select extra-work activities – by education and age (% of answers "every day" : "several times a week" : "rarely" : ""never")

		Sports, active leisure	Self-education	Voluntary or pro bono activities	Political activities
Women by education	Elementary	8 : 15 : 22 : 56	6 : 14 : 26 : 53	2 : 5 : 24 : 69	0 : 1 : 4 : 96
	Secondary without A levels	3 : 22 : 48 : 27	5 : 18 : 45 : 32	0 : 5 : 26 : 69	0 : 0 : 7 : 93
	Complete secondary	8 : 26 : 46 : 19	14 : 30 : 41 : 15	0 : 6 : 28 : 66	0 : 2 : 11 : 88
	University	5 : 36 : 44 : 13	24 : 57 : 23 : 6	0 : 5 : 43 : 52	0 : 0 : 14 : 86
Men by education	Elementary	13 : 26 : 26 : 35	14 : 19 : 23 : 44	2 : 6 : 26 : 64	1 : 1 : 5 : 93
	Secondary without A levels	11 : 30 : 37 : 23	6 : 19 : 39 : 36	0 : 6 : 34 : 60	0 : 2 : 9 : 89
	Complete secondary	18 : 30 : 41 : 11	15 : 30 : 41 : 14	1 : 6 : 35 : 58	0 : 2 : 12 : 87
	University	19 : 35 : 34 : 12	27 : 53 : 15 : 5	7 : 9 : 27 : 57	3 : 3 : 11 : 83
Women by age	Under 45	8 : 33 : 46 : 13	16 : 31 : 37 : 16	0 : 5 : 29 : 66	0 : 1 : 9 : 90
	Over 45	4 : 14 : 34 : 48	6 : 19 : 34 : 40	1 : 6 : 27 : 66	0 : 0 : 8 : 92
Men by age	Under 45	19 : 42 : 32 : 7	17 : 31 : 34 : 18	1 : 7 : 32 : 60	1 : 1 : 8 : 90
	Over 45	8 : 12 : 39 : 41	6 : 17 : 33 : 44	2 : 5 : 33 : 60	0 : 3 : 10 : 88

Note: The answers "I don't know" were disregarded.
Source: Institute for Public Affairs, August 2006.

education: sports and active leisure, self-education, voluntary and *pro bono* activities and political activities. This documents that the progressive lifestyle, consisting in spending more time on education, physical fitness and civic or political involvement, is more typical of women and men with greater cultural capital.

However, is should be added that the structure of extra-work activities depends to a great extent on the financial situation of people as well as on the presence of children in the family. As time use surveys carried out in 14 EU member states between 1998 and 2004 indicated, in countries with higher per capita income, women spend less time on unpaid domestic work and men spend less time at their paid jobs, while both women and men are more involved in social activities. On the other hand, countries with lower per capita income (e.g. Estonia, Lithuania, Latvia, Poland or Hungary) tend to have a higher volume of unpaid and paid work and a lower degree of public involvement (*The Life...*, 2008, pp. 111 – 131).

All in all, women and men in Slovakia devote their extra-working time primarily to performing household chores and looking after family members. They spend much less time on sports, active leisure and self-education, let alone voluntary, *pro bono* and political activities. Their intensive involvement in paid and unpaid work significantly limits their opportunities for self-fulfillment through leisure activities. From the gender viewpoint, it is important that women's double burden of paid work on the labor market and unpaid work at home is substantially greater than that of men, and is also more influenced by their family situation. Consequently, women in Slovakia have less time for pursuing their hobbies and interests, as well as for civic and political activities than men.

6.4. CONFLICT BETWEEN FAMILY AND PROFESSIONAL OBLIGATIONS

Women in Slovakia carry on their shoulders a considerable load of domestic obligations. That is why it is important to know how they solve the conflict between the work and family demands. To what extent is their professional career affected by their family obligations? And to what extent are their decisions regarding family influenced by the work demands?

6.4.1. IMPACT OF FAMILY OBLIGATIONS ON PROFESSIONAL CAREER

Family obligations influence the professional careers of women and men both indirectly and directly. In the former case, they may give employers a reason to discriminate against women and men in the hiring process and in the process of their promotion. In the latter case, family obligations may directly affect people's performance at work and have less serious consequences (e.g. being late for work, bringing children to the workplace, etc.) or more serious ones (e.g. being reassigned to a job with fewer responsibilities, being forced to find a different job, to interrupt or abandon the professional career or even to withdraw from the labor market).

In the following analysis, we focus on the more serious implications of family obligations for professional careers. According to Table 6.11, the most common way of adjusting one's professional career to one's family obligations is to find a different job, followed by inter-rupting a professional career, and by being reassigned to a job with fewer responsibilities. Women reported all three consequences more frequently than men: 26% of them had to find another job (compared to 5% of men), 17% were forced to interrupt their professional career (compared to 3% of men) and 10% were reassigned to a job with fewer responsibilities (com-pared to 3% of men). The figures in brackets illustrate an important, though not surprising finding: while the mothers of dependent children experienced these negative impacts slightly more frequently than the average for all women, it was not the case of fathers of dependent children.

Table 6.11
"In the course of your professional career, did you ever have to adjust your work to family obligations in any of the following ways?" (% of affirmative answers)

	Women's experience			Men's experience		
	Under 45	Over 45	Total	Under 45	Over 45	Total
Find a job that allowed you to take care of children or other family members	25 (28)	28 (29)	26 (28)	3 (2)	6 (6)	5 (4)
Interrupt your career for a certain period of time	19 (21)	16 (14)	17 (17)	2 (1)	3 (3)	3 (2)
Ask to be assigned to a job with fewer responsibilities	9 (11)	10 (11)	10 (11)	1 (1)	4 (4)	3 (3)

Note: This table features the answers of respondents that are or were active on the labor market. The data in brackets are for respondents with at least one child. The answers "I don't know" were disregarded.
Source: Institute for Public Affairs, August 2006.

A comparison of women and men under and over 45 indicates that the negative implications of family obligations for professional career are slightly more common among older women and men. The only exception is the experience of interrupting a professional career, which was more frequently reported by younger women than older women (19% vs. 16%). The difference was even greater among the younger and older mothers (21% of mothers under 45 vs. 14% of mothers over 45). This can be attributed to the following three factors: first, the weaker protection of employed mothers after 1989 (the increased reluctance of employ-ers to rehire women after they return from maternity leave); second, more frequent volun-tary decision by young mothers to stay home and take care of the children; finally, fewer options for balancing work and family demands.[8]

As Table 6.12 shows, tensions between family and professional obligations tend to increase especially under the influence of parenthood. Other important factors include marital and education status. Divorced and widowed women; mothers with many children, as well as women with the lowest education reported such negative experiences more frequently.

The overall picture is clear: women are more frequently forced to find a different job, inter-rupt their professional career, or accept a less responsible and worse paid job due to their family obligations. The share of women whose professional careers suffer due to their family obli-gations is three to six times higher than that of men. Let us now look at the perception of this reality by women and men.

---

[8] The importance of these factors has been corroborated by a number of surveys. For instance, a survey examining the needs of young families (Bodnárová – Džambazovič – Filadelfiová – Gerbery – Pafková – Porubänová, 2004) documented the strat-egies used by employers to obstruct women's return from maternity leave or to push for their earlier return, as well as the existence of a group of young women who prefer to take care of their pre-school children rather than to have a paid job. The lack of measures by employers to accommodate the needs of parents of dependent children was also noted by other surveys (e.g. Marošiová – Šumšalová, 2006; *Práca versus...*, 2007).

Table 6.12
Impact of family obligations on the professional career – by number of children, marital status and education (% of affirmative answers of women : % of affirmative answers of men)

		Being forced to find a more suitable job	Interrupting the professional career	Being assigned to a job with fewer responsibilities
Number of children	No children	5 : 8	8 : 2	0 : 0
	One child	22 : 0	14 : 1	9 : 1
	Two children	27 : 6	16 : 3	11 : 3
	Three or more children	34 : 4	22 : 1	11 : 4
Marital status	Single	13 : 7	11 : 3	3 : 0
	Divorced, widowed	30 : 4	18 : 6	16 : 2
	Married, cohabiting	26 : 5	17 : 2	8 : 3
Education	Elementary	30 : 5	19 : 5	9 : 1
	Secondary without A levels	27 : 5	19 : 3	12 : 2
	Complete secondary	26 : 5	16 : 1	10 : 3
	University	17 : 2	7 : 1	6 : 4

Note: This table features the answers of respondents that are or were active on the labor market. The answers "I don't know" were disregarded.
Source: Institute for Public Affairs, August 2006.

According to Table 6.13, there are far more women than men who feel that they had to sacrifice something in their professional careers for the family (71% and 57%, respectively). One in three women perceived this sacrifice as substantial (6% sacrificed "very much" and 27% "quite a lot"), compared to one in five men (2% sacrificed "very much" and 18% "quite a lot").

When we compare the actual impact of family obligations on the professional careers of women and men and their feeling of sacrifice, we get an interesting picture (compare Tables 6.11 and 6.13). Among women, the feeling of sacrifice more or less corresponds to their actual professional losses, as 33% of them described their sacrifice as substantial while 10 – 26% have actually had a negative professional experience. Men, for their part, tend to overestimate their professional sacrifice; 20% described their sacrifice as substantial, but only 3 – 5% of them were actually forced to sacrifice something.

While there are only minor differences between the perception of younger and older women, in case of men the age matters more. Younger men described their sacrifices as less substantial than their older counterparts.

Table 6.13
"If you look back at your professional career, how much had you sacrificed for the sake of your family?" (%)

	Views of women			Views of men		
	Under 45	Over 45	Total	Under 45	Over 45	Total
Very much	6	7	6	2	2	2
Quite a lot	26	27	27	14	22	18
Little	37	38	38	39	36	37
Nothing	31	28	29	46	40	43

Note: This table features the answers of respondents that are or were active on the labor market. The answers "I don't know" were disregarded.
Source: Institute for Public Affairs, August 2006.

As one would expect, the number of children is an important factor: childless women and men show the weakest feeling of professional sacrifice (see Table 6.14). People's marital status is relevant, too. Single women and men fell that they have made the fewest professional sacrifices due to family obligations. Divorced and widowed men feel they had to sacrifice more than men who live in a partnership, while such a difference was not found among women. This could be another illustration of the fact that family obligations represent a different burden for women and men: while living with a partner usually liberates men of many domestic obligations, women living in a partnership are burdened by these obligations equally or even more than divorced or widowed women (for details, see Section 6.3.2. of this chapter).

The more educated women and men are, the stronger is their conviction that family obligations have hurt their professional careers. While 39% of women and 59% of men with elementary education did not view family obligations as a hindrance to their professional careers, this opinion was shared only by 28% of women and 30% of men with university degrees.

Table 6.14
"If you look back at your professional career, how much had you sacrificed for the sake of your family?" (by number of children, marital status and education – in %)

		Views of women			Views of men		
		Very much and quite a lot	Little	Nothing	Very much and quite a lot	Little	Nothing
Number of children	No children	19	26	55	4	28	68
	One child	34	38	28	24	38	38
	Two children	36	43	21	26	44	30
	Three or more children	35	35	30	22	33	45
Marital status	Single	22	22	56	6	23	71
	Divorced, widowed	35	38	27	31	32	37
	Married, cohabiting	34	40	26	22	41	37
Education	Elementary	31	30	39	17	24	59
	Secondary without A levels	33	38	29	19	38	42
	Complete secondary	34	42	24	20	43	37
	University	34	38	28	30	40	30

Note: This table features the answers of respondents that are or were active on the labor market. The answers "I don't know" were disregarded.
Source: Institute for Public Affairs, August 2006.

6.4.2. IMPACT OF THE PROFESSIONAL CAREER ON FAMILY DECISIONS

Let us now examine the conflict between professional and family demands from the opposite angle. To what extent do professional obligations of women and men affect their decisions on family issues? Table 6.15 takes into account two such situations: the decision to return to work from maternity or parental leave sooner than originally planned and the decision to postpone having children.

Decisions by women to return to work from maternity leave earlier than planned are relatively common. Almost one in four female respondents (24%) said they had made this decision. Women over 45 reported it more frequently than their younger counterparts (28% and 18%, respectively). This difference may be due to the different length of maternity leave in the past. Currently, the maximum length of paid maternity leave is three years, while it was significantly shorter at the time when most women over 45 were mothers.

The share of men who decided to cut short their parental leave in order to resume their professional careers is marginal; such experience was reported by 1% of younger and 3% of older

Table 6.15
"In the course of your professional career, were your decisions on family issues ever subordinated to your professional obligations in the following ways?" (% of affirmative answers)

	Experience of women			Experience of men		
	Under 45	Over 45	Total	Under 45	Over 45	Total
Return to work from maternity/ parental leave earlier than planned	18	28	24	1	3	2
Postpone children due to work	8	4	6	6	3	4

Note: This table features the answers of respondents that are or were active on the labor market. The answers "I don't know" were disregarded.
Source: Institute for Public Affairs, August 2006.

respondents. This is largely related to the fact that very few men choose to go on parental leave; in most cases it is a way out of non-standard family or professional situations (e.g. in case of the death, serious illness, runaway of the mother, unemployment of the father, etc.). There have been very few examples of "new fatherhood" in Slovakia, based on taking joint care of infants and splitting parental leave, although it has been allowed by law since 2002.

Let us now look at decisions to postpone parenthood. In this case the gender difference was not so pronounced, as 6% of women and 4% of men said they had made such a decision. Younger respondents reported making this decision twice as frequently as respondents over 45. But the overall share of women and men who postponed children due to their work is generally very low, indicating that a substantial majority of them do not let their work interfere with their parenthood strategies.

Let us look at the impact of the marital and education status on women's decision to cut short their maternity leave. Table 6.16 shows that divorced and widowed women most frequently choose to return from maternity leave prematurely, followed by women who live in a partnership and single mothers. The share of women who opt for this solution falls as the number of children increases. Women with university degrees cut their maternity leave short more frequently than women with lower education. This may reflect not only their fear of losing

Table 6.16
Subordinating family ideals to professional careers by women and men – by number of children, marital status and education (% of affirmative answers of women : % of affirmative answers of men)

		Earlier return to work from maternity/ parental leave	Postponing children
Number of children	No children	–	11 : 14
	One child	24 : 1	8 : 5
	Two children	25 : 4	5 : 3
	Three or more children	19 : 0	2 : 1
Marital status	Single	15 : 0	14 : 7
	Divorced, widowed	30 : 0	3 : 2
	Married, cohabiting	21 : 3	6 : 4
Education	Elementary	14 : 3	1 : 1
	Secondary without A levels	20 : 2	6 : 6
	Complete secondary	29 : 2	7 : 0
	University	33 : 0	9 : 7

Note: This table features the answers of respondents that are or were active on the labor market. The answers "I don't know" were disregarded.
Source: Institute for Public Affairs, August 2006.

a good job or the acquired qualifications and skills, but also the pressure from employers urging qualified women to return to work earlier.

As for the postponement of parenthood, single women and men have made such a decision approximately twice as frequently as persons who live in a partnership and approximately four times as frequently as divorced and widowed persons. Needless to say, this experience is the most frequent among childless women and men, in fact reflecting their unrealized parenthood. Last but not least, more educated women and men tend to postpone parenthood due to career reasons more frequently than persons with lower education.

6.5. MATERIAL WELL-BEING AND LIFE SATISFACTION
6.5.1. INCOME SITUATION AND POVERTY RISK

In 2005, the EU-SILC established the highest poverty risk rate among economically active population in Poland (20%), followed by Latvia, Lithuania, Portugal, Greece, Spain, Estonia and Romania (between 17% and 18%). The lowest values (under 10%) were recorded in Sweden, the Czech Republic, the Netherlands, Finland and Slovenia. Slovakia with 11% ranked in the bottom quarter of the list, i.e. among countries with a low poverty risk rate.

Generally speaking, women in EU member states are slightly more at risk of poverty than men, as 15% of economically active women and 14% of economically active men lived below the poverty line in 2005. In sixteen EU member states, women were more endangered by poverty than their male counterparts; in five member states, men were more at risk of poverty than women and in six member states – including Slovakia – no relevant gender differences were found.

In the category of people over 65, women are significantly more at risk, as 21% of these women and only 16% of men lived below the poverty line in 2005. In 25 EU member states, women over 65 were more endangered by poverty than men; in Luxembourg, the situation of elderly men was worse and in Portugal, no relevant gender differences were confirmed.

What is the income situation of women and men of different ages and what is their perception of it? Let us first examine statistics on people with low incomes, and focus particularly on gender and age differences. We will rely on the findings of the European Union Statistics on Income and Living Conditions (EU-SILC), which has measured living conditions in individual EU member states including Slovakia since 2004.

In Slovakia, 11.6% of people lived below the poverty line in 2005, a decline compared to 13.3% in 2004.[9] Available data from 2006 indicate a continuation of this trend, as the poverty rate declined further to 10.7% (11.5% for women and 9.8% for men). In 2005, children younger than 15 were the most endangered by poverty; 16.6% of them inhabited households below the poverty line. As for population of productive age, the highest poverty rate was among people between 16 and 24 (14.1%). The share of people endangered by poverty tends to decline with increasing age. The lowest

---

[9] The poverty line is defined from the median income of the population. The poor are considered households with incomes below 60% of the median income in a given country. People whose income is below this limit are viewed as at risk of poverty; their share of the total population forms the poverty risk rate http://portal.statistics.sk/showdoc.do?docid=12683).

poverty rate was established among people between 50 and 64 (7.7%) and people over 65 (8.5%).

According to this source, there were no gender differences in terms of the poverty rate within Slovakia's economically active population in 2005, as the overall shares of women and men living below the poverty line were approximately 11%. However, a more detailed analysis revealed slight differences between women and men within individual age groups. In the 16 – 24 age group the gender difference was 2% to the detriment of men; men were also slightly worse off in the 25 – 49 age group (0.6%) and the 50 – 64 age group (0.9%).[10] These gender differences were heavily made up for in the oldest age group, as women over 65 are threatened by poverty more than twice as frequently (10.8%) as their male counterparts (4.5%).

Table 6.17
Share of women and men in Slovakia below the poverty line – by age (2004 and 2005 – in %)

		2004	2005
0 – 15	Total	18.4	16.6
16 – 24	Women	16.6	13.1
	Men	17.1	15.1
	Total	16.8	14.1
25 – 49	Women	17.7	11.9
	Men	13.4	11.3
	Total	14.1	11.6
50 – 64	Women	8.3	7.3
	Men	8.3	8.2
	Total	8.3	7.7
Over 65	Women	9.8	10.8
	Men	2.7	4.5
	Total	7.1	8.5
Slovak population		13.3	11.6

Source: *EU-SILC*, 2005 and 2006.

Let us now look at poverty through the prism of material deprivation, which the EU-SILC defines as the involuntary insufficient satisfaction of regular needs emerging from the lack of the economical resources.[11] According to the 2004 data, the highest share of materially deprived people was found within the over 65 age group (12% – see Table 6.18) – although this age group is not particularly severely threatened by income poverty (see Table 6.17). People in the 50 – 64 age group, for their part, have not only a low risk-of-poverty rate, but also a weak feeling of material deprivation.

Table 6.18
Share of materially deprived people in Slovakia – by age (2004 – in %)

0 – 15	16 – 24	25 – 49	50 – 64	Over 65	Slovak population
8.4	7.9	8.0	6.9	12.0	8.3

Source: *EU-SILC*, 2005.

A number of surveys corroborated that the poverty rate and material deprivation rate depend primarily on the status of household members on the labor market (i.e. whether they are employed or not) as well as on the family profile (i.e. number of children, number of employed adult members, etc.), age and the region of residence (Gerbery – Džambazovič, 2006; Džambazovič, 2007; Schmidt, 2001).

A survey by the Institute for Public Affairs brought data on the material situation of Slovak women and men of different ages in 2006. As Table 6.19 shows, the most common house-

---

[10] This finding was surprising for three reasons: first, Slovak women earn significantly less than men on average; second, women more frequently run single-parent households, which are the most endangered by poverty; finally, a large proportion of women between 50 and 64 are retirees and their old-age pension, which is substantially lower on average than that of men, is their only source of income. (See also Filadelfiová, 1993.)

[11] The EU-SILC monitors three criteria of material deprivation: economic strain; enforced lack of durable goods; and poor housing conditions. Each of them comprises 4 to 5 items. Individuals are considered materially deprived if they feel a shortage of at least two items from the former two categories and of at least one item from the latter category (*EU-SILC*, 2005).

hold incomes were between Sk15,000 and Sk20,000 (20% of women and men), followed by the Sk10,000 – Sk15,000 category (15% of women and 18% of men) and the Sk20,000 – Sk25,000 category (18% of women and 17% of men). These three income categories comprised households inhabited by 53% of all women and 55% of all men. Households in the lowest income category (i.e. less than Sk10,000 per month) were more frequently inhabited by women (15%) than men (12%). On the other hand, households whose monthly income exceeded Sk30,000 were more frequently inhabited by men (22%) than women (19%). This general perspective does not reveal dramatic gender imbalances, as the overall difference did not exceed 3% in any income category.

Table 6.19
"What is the combined monthly income of all members of your household including all pensions, benefits, allowances, stipends and other types of income?" (%)

	Women			Men		
	Under 45	Over 45	Total	Under 45	Over 45	Total
Under 10,000 Sk	8	21	15	6	19	12
10,001 – 15,000 Sk	10	21	15	9	29	18
15,001 – 20,000 Sk	22	19	20	22	17	20
20,001 – 25,000 Sk	22	14	18	22	12	17
25,001 – 30,000 Sk	15	12	14	13	8	11
30,001 – 35,000 Sk	9	5	7	12	6	9
35,001 – 40,000 Sk	7	2	5	8	3	6
40,001 – 45,000 Sk	3	2	3	4	2	3
Over 45,000 Sk	4	3	4	5	3	4

Note: The answers "I don't know" were disregarded.
Source: Institute for Public Affairs, August 2006.

However, when we add the age dimension to the gender one, we get quite a different picture. This perspective reveals that the average monthly income of households inhabited by people under 45 is substantially higher than that of households inhabited by people over 45. This difference applies to women as well as men. In 2006, only 8% of women under 45 but 21% of women over 45 lived in households whose combined monthly income was less than Sk10,000. Among men, the difference between the two age categories was the same (13%), but the shares of younger and older men living in the poorest households were lower than those of women (6% of younger men and 19% of older men).

Significant differences are typical also of the women and men from households whose average combined monthly income exceeds Sk30,000. In 2006, twenty three percent of women under 45, but only 12% of women over 45 lived in such households. On the other hand, those shares were higher among men of both age categories (29% and 14%, respectively).

If we rank the four principal gender/age categories according to the average combined monthly income of the households they inhabit, men under 45 are at the top of the list, followed by women under 45, men over 45 and women over 45.

Obviously, the combined monthly income of each household depends on its make-up and particularly on the number of employed household members. The higher the number of employed household members, the higher the household's combined income.

Women make up a substantial majority of all low-income households, which comprise mostly the households of lone individuals and single-parent families. According to the most recent population census carried out in Slovakia in 2001, two in three households of lone individuals were inhabited by women, particularly widowed pensioners. In the category of single-parent families, the difference was even greater, as 87% of these families were led by women (*Sčítanie...*, 2001; Pilinská, 2005). Needless to say, women from this category are at the greatest risk of poverty.[12]

Generally speaking, women who run their households single-handedly (either as single mothers or as widowed pensioners) are worse off than women who live in other types of households. The main reason is that they cannot compete with men in terms of income, whether in the form of wages or old-age pensions.

Let us now look at the perception of income situation by women and men of different ages. Respondents were asked to evaluate their households' financial condition by placing it on a standard six-degree scale (see Table 6.20). People who placed their households into one of the bottom two categories (i.e. their household was able to buy only the cheapest groceries or not even that) were defined as those experiencing subjective poverty.

Most respondents (73% of men and 70% of women) placed their households in one of the top three categories. Eight percent of women and 10% of men described their household's financial condition as completely problem-free. About one third of respondents (34% of women and men alike) said they could afford everything but had to be thrifty at the same time; 28% of women and 29% of men said they had to be very thrifty in order to afford more expensive goods.

Table 6.20
"How does your household manage on your current income? Choose the most fitting of the options presented." (%)

	Views of women			Views of men		
	Under 45	Over 45	Total	Under 45	Over 45	Total
1. Our income comfortably covers everything.	10	6	8	14	4	10
2. Our income covers everything but we must be thrifty.	34	33	34	33	35	34
3. We must be very thrifty in order to afford more expensive goods.	32	23	28	32	24	29
4. We have just enough to afford the cheapest goods.	15	23	19	13	17	14
5. Our income covers only the cheapest groceries.	6	13	9	5	16	10
6. Our income does not cover even the cheapest groceries.	3	2	2	3	4	3

Note: The answers "I don't know" were disregarded.
Source: Institute for Public Affairs, August 2006.

Some 30% of women and 27% of men placed their households into one of the bottom three categories, which represent various degrees of hardship in satisfying material needs. While women more frequently admitted that they had just enough to afford the cheapest goods (19% of women and 14% of men), men slightly more frequently placed their households into one of the bottom two categories (11% and 13%, respectively). This largely corresponds to data in Table 6.17, according to which the poverty rate in Slovakia based on EU-SILC methodology neared 12% in 2005.

Table 6.20 also indicates that the income situation of the younger generation is somewhat different from that of older people. Women and men under 45 placed their households into

---

[12] According to EU-SILC, the poverty risk rate of single-parent families reached 29% in 2005. A higher rate of poverty risk was only in the category of unemployed persons' households, 44% of which were considered below the poverty line.

the top category two or three times more frequently than their older counterparts. Respondents over 45, for their part, more frequently located their households into the fourth and especially the fifth category.

As we see, older women and men are generally more critical about their material situation than their younger counterparts. Among people who perceive themselves as poor are often pensioners; unemployed or those who share households with them; the heads of single-parent families with several children; people with lower education; and the residents of smaller settlements. In some households, two or more of these factors combine to produce a negative synergetic effect.

A similar conclusion can be drawn from the status self-identification of women and men of different ages. A comparison of women and men as such does not expose significant differences (see Table 6.21). Approximately three in five respondents (61% of women and 56% of men) saw themselves as members of the middle class, while 28% of women and 29% of men felt they belonged to the lower middle class. Only 7% of female as well as male respondents placed themselves in the upper middle class, while just 1% of men and no women described themselves as upper class. At the opposite pole, 5% of women and 7% of men positioned themselves into the lowest class.

However, under this general surface, there are significant differences. Divorced and widowed people, pensioners, the unemployed, people without university degrees and the residents of rural areas tend to identify with one of the bottom two social classes. Also, women and men over 45 more frequently feel to adhere to the lower middle class or the lowest class than their younger counterparts.

Table 6.21
"Which social class would you place yourself and your family in?" (%)

	Women's views			Men's views		
	Under 45	Over 45	Total	Under 45	Over 45	Total
Upper class	0	0	0	1	0	1
Upper middle class	9	4	7	9	4	7
Middle class	64	57	61	62	49	56
Lower middle class	24	32	28	25	35	29
Lowest class	2	7	5	4	11	7

Note: The answers "I don't know" were disregarded.
Source: Institute for Public Affairs, August 2006.

6.5.2. LIFE SATISFACTION

An important component of the life situation of women and men is their overall happiness and life satisfaction. As Table 6.22 illustrates, most people in Slovakia are happy with their family life (91% of women and 89% of men said they were very or somewhat satisfied) and partner relationship (84% and 89%, respectively).[13] It is worth of mentioning that according to the *European Values Survey*, people in Slovakia attach most importance to these two aspects of life (*European Values...*, 1999).

---

[13] As one would expect, marital status is an important factor affecting people's satisfaction with their family and emotional life as well as their overall satisfaction with life. Divorced or widowed women and men typically expressed less satisfaction than people who live in partnerships, and even less than single people.

Table 6.22
"To what degree are you satisfied with the following aspects of your life?" (% of answers "very satisfied" : "somewhat satisfied" : "very and somewhat unsatisfied")

	Views of women			Views of men		
	Under 45	Over 45	Total	Under 45	Over 45	Total
Family life	37 : 54 : 9	28 : 62 : 10	33 : 58 : 9	37 : 51 : 13	31 : 60 : 9	34 : 55 : 11
Partner relationship	35 : 49 : 16	25 : 57 : 18	31 : 53 : 16	42 : 44 : 14	36 : 55 : 9	39 : 50 : 11
Social life	18 : 66 : 16	13 : 70 : 17	16 : 68 : 16	27 : 61 : 12	15 : 69 : 16	22 : 64 : 14
Leisure time	16 : 62 : 22	16 : 70 : 14	16 : 65 : 19	27 : 59 : 14	16 : 66 : 18	22 : 62 : 16
Working life	12 : 54 : 34	13 : 57 : 30	12 : 55 : 33	16 : 51 : 33	17 : 57 : 26	17 : 54 : 30
Participation in public life	7 : 65 : 28	6 : 66 : 28	6 : 66 : 28	11 : 63 : 26	9 : 63 : 28	10 : 63 : 27
Overall life satisfaction	18 : 66 : 16	12 : 69 : 19	15 : 67 : 17	18 : 64 : 18	12 : 67 : 21	16 : 65 : 18

Note: The answers "I don't know" and "Does not concern me" were disregarded.
Source: Institute for Public Affairs, August 2006.

On the other hand, women and men are most critical of their working life and participation in public life. Thirty three percent of women and 30% of men expressed dissatisfaction with their work life, 28% of women and 27% of men felt unhappy about their participation in public life.

Last but not least, respondents placed their social life and leisure time in the middle, between the most favorable evaluation of the two exclusively private aspects of life (i.e. family and partner relationship) and between the most critical assessment of the two predominantly public aspects of life (i.e. work and public participation).

To obtain a clearer picture of the level of satisfaction that women and men feel with various aspects of their life, we created a satisfaction index ranging from 0 to 100. Graphs 6.6 through 6.8 illustrate the differences between women and men as well as the differences between women of different education levels and ages.

Although the differences between women and men in terms of subjective happiness are not pronounced, they are symptomatic. In all six areas, women expressed dissatisfaction slightly

Graf 6.6
Satisfaction of women and men with particular aspects of their lives (satisfaction index ranging from 0 to 100)

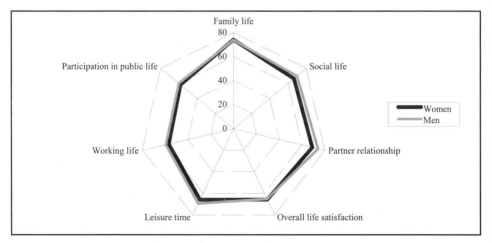

Source: Institute for Public Affairs, August 2006.

Graf 6.7
Satisfaction of women with particular aspects of their lives –by education (satisfaction index ranging from 0 to 100)

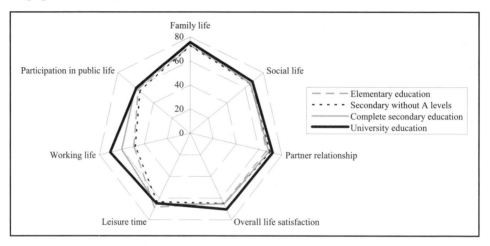

Source: Institute for Public Affairs, August 2006.

Graf 6.8
Satisfaction of women with particular aspects of their lives –by age (satisfaction index ranging from 0 to 100)

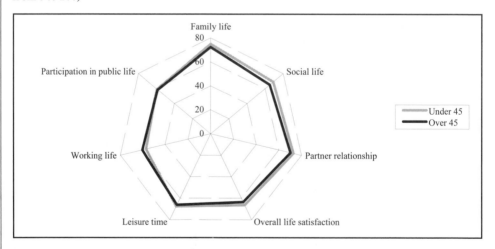

Source: Institute for Public Affairs, August 2006.

more frequently than men. They also less frequently described themselves as completely happy – with the sole exception of satisfaction with family life. It is interesting that these gender differences disappear in the women's and men's evaluation of overall life satisfaction.

As one would expect, the subjective happiness of women and men with particular aspects of their life is closely related to their educational attainment. Generally speaking, women and men with higher education feel happier than those with lower education. This factor most strongly affects people's satisfaction with their working life and their overall subjective happiness. The role of education is much less obvious in the case of family, partner relationship and social life as well as participation in public life.

A comparison of people under and over 45 indicates that younger women and men feel happier than their older counterparts in three areas – family, partner relationship and social life. On the other hand, older women and men expressed more satisfaction with their working life.

Worth of attention are also differences in the satisfaction of women and men with their leisure time. While younger men are happier than older ones, this is not the case of younger women. Apparently, their greater dissatisfaction with leisure time mirrors the fact that they are under stronger time pressure and more burdened by work and family obligations than men of the same age.

Interestingly, the overall subjective happiness of women and men declines with increasing age. This tendency was proved also by other surveys, which revealed that older people in Slovakia, similarly to other Central and Eastern European countries, feel less content with their lives than younger people (Varnum, 2008, p. 219). Repeated surveys carried out in the United States document the opposite trend.

We may assume that the decline of overall life satisfaction among older women and men in Slovakia and in other countries in transition is largely influenced by the complex and demanding economic, political and societal changes that took place after the collapse of Communism. This new and challenging situation has brought about feelings of social uncertainty, material deprivation and frustration in large strata of the population. The feelings of life dissatisfaction are particularly strong among those older people who do not dispose of sufficient educational and cultural capital and of good health, which would boost their adaptation to the new circumstances. Another negative phenomena are widespread ageism and insufficient promotion of the concept of active ageing within society (for details, see Section 3.2.1. in this publication).

7. WOMEN AND MEN IN PUBLIC LIFE AND POLITICS[1]

Oľga Gyárfášová – Zora Bútorová – Jarmila Filadelfiová

Oľga Gyárfášová and Zora Bútorová co-authored Sections 7.1., 7.2., 7.3.1. and 7.3.3. Jarmila Filadelfiová wrote Section 7.3.2.

---

[1] This chapter was written as part of a project implemented by the Center of Excellence for Research on Citizenship and Participation: Facing the Challenges of 21st Century (COPART) at the Department of Social and Biological Communication at the Slovak Academy of Sciences.

7. WOMEN AND MEN IN PUBLIC LIFE AND POLITICS

7.1. PERCEPTION OF SOCIETY AND POLITICS

7.1.1. OLD AND NEW REGIME AS SEEN BY WOMEN AND MEN

The views of women and men about the development of Slovak society after the collapse of communism saw some interesting changes. After the euphoria sparked by the Velvet Revolution of November 1989 had subsided, people had to cope with tough challenges related primarily to economic transformation and the uncertainty caused by the end of the Czechoslovak federation. For more than a decade, supporters of the new democratic regime were outnumbered by its opponents who saw more advantages in the old regime, and by those who did not see any great difference between the two regimes. In recent years however, especially since Slovakia's accession to the European Union, the citizens have grown more optimistic. Since 2006, supporters of the new regime have prevailed over its opponents.

As Table 7.1 shows, the opinion shift was more significant among women than among men. While Slovak women in the past were more critical of the new regime, their views nowadays are more favorable than those of men. By the end of 2007, eighteen years after the Velvet Revolution, 51% of women and 46% of men saw more positives in the current system, while 27% of both women and men saw more advantages in the previous one and the rest could not choose.

Table 7.1

Perception of the current regime compared to the system before November 1989 (% of answers "it has more positives" : "there is not much difference" : "it has more negatives" : "I don't know")

	Views of women	Views of men
1994	32 : 18 : 48 : 2	42 : 14 : 42 : 2
2002	34 : 17 : 42 : 7	39 : 17 : 37 : 7
2007	51 : 17 : 27 : 5	46 : 19 : 27 : 9

Source: FOCUS, November 1994; Institute for Public Affairs, March 2002 and November 2007.

7.1.2. HIERARCHY OF SOCIAL PROBLEMS

Sociological surveys carried out since 1990 have repeatedly confirmed that the views of Slovak women and men regarding economic transformation, political developments and foreign policy are very similar, but not identical.

In a poll done in spring 2006, respondents were presented a list of 26 social problems and asked to identify three that they saw as the most urgent. As Table 7.2 illustrates, women and men placed identical problems at the top of their respective lists. They agreed that the most serious social problem was unemployment, followed by the poor state of health care, poverty, and the living standard of ordinary people. Next on the list were such issues as opportunities for young people, crime and organized crime, corruption and bribery, regional economic and social disparities, abuse of power, problems in the pension system and opportunities for elderly people.

The status and opportunities of women came further down the list, in a group that included the social security system; solidarity with poor people; effectiveness of the judiciary and law enforcement; performance of economy; respect for the constitution and laws; environmental issues; xenophobia, racism, intolerance and extremism. Finally, the list of urgent social problems included protection of employees' rights; standard of education; quality of democracy, living standard and opportunities for residents of Romany settlements; living standard and opportunities for members of the Hungarian minority and the country's performance within various international institutions.[2]

Table 7.2
"Slovakia faces a great number of serious problems that need to be tackled. Choose three issues from the list that you consider the most pressing" (2006 – in %)

	Views of women	Views of men
Unemployment	52	47
Quality of health care	33	29
Poverty	29	28
Living standard of people like you	27	27
Status and opportunities of young people	16	18
Crime and organized crime	16	14
Corruption and bribery	14	17
Economic and social disparities between Slovakia's regions	13	16
Abuse of power	11	16
Pension system	10	12
Status and opportunities of elderly people	10	7
Social security system	8	8
Solidarity with poor people	8	7
Effectiveness of the judiciary and law enforcement	7	11
Status and opportunities of women	7	1
Performance of economy	6	8
Respect for the constitution and laws	5	6
Environmental issues	5	4
Xenophobia, racism, intolerance and extremism	5	4
Protection of employees' rights	4	6
Standard of education at elementary and secondary schools	4	2
Standard of education at universities	3	2
Quality of democracy	2	6
Living standard and opportunities for residents of Romany settlements	2	3
Living standard and opportunities for members of the Hungarian minority	2	0
Slovakia's performance in international institutions such as the EU	1	1

Note: Respondents were free to choose three answers, which is why the total sum exceeds 100%.
Source: Institute for Public Affairs, April 2006.

Table 7.2 also shows some gender differences. Women put greater emphasis on unemployment, health care, the status and opportunities of elderly people and women, the quality of education at elementary and secondary schools, and the living standard and opportunities of the Hungarian minority.[3] On the other hand, men assign greater importance to corruption and bribery, economic and social disparities between regions, abuse of power, the effectiveness

---

[2] The rather marginal importance of foreign policy on the list of pressing social problems has been documented by most surveys carried out after 1989. According to them, foreign policy orientations of women and men are not essentially different and their support of Slovakia's membership in the EU and NATO is virtually identical. The main difference is that women are less interested and oriented in foreign policy (Bútorová, 1996; *Empirical Data...*, 2006c).

[3] A greater emphasis of women in Slovakia on the status and rights of ethnic Hungarians was detected also in earlier surveys (Bútorová – Filadelfiová – Guráň – Gyárfášová – Farkašová, 1999).

of the judiciary and law enforcement, performance of economy, protection of employees' rights, and the quality of democracy (see also Bútorová, 1996; Bútorová – Filadelfiová – Guráň – Gyárfášová – Farkašová, 1999; *Empirical Data...*, 2006c and 2007c).

Women's greater sensitivity to such issues as unemployment, health care and education was established also in other studies (Bútorová, 1996; *Empirical Data...*, 2007c). This is likely related to women's traditional role of homemakers, which entails greater responsibility for the everyday life of the family, including the education of the children and the health of family members. In this context, it is worth noting that women assign greater weight to the government's responsibility for the living standard of individuals and expect the government to help people in need (*Empirical Data...*, 2005c).

The existence of gender differences in professed values was also confirmed by a survey carried out by the International Republican Institute in 2007 (Gyárfášová – Slosiarik, 2008). The study revealed women's stronger inclination towards such values as responsibility, tolerance, environment, government care, compassion, solidarity and charity.[4] Men, for their part, tend to emphasize values related to the free market, especially competition and material well-being.

At the same time, the survey identified significant differentiation of professed values within both groups, i.e. among women and among men. It also showed that women's values tend to change with age. The middle generation, which is the most active on the labor market, is more interested in public affairs and politics and assigns greater importance to the value of work and politics than young or elderly women. Young women, for their part, attach greater weight to their private life and entertainment. Older women emphasize values such as religion, tradition and the neighborhood or local community.

Education is an important factor, too. Women with lower education tend to emphasize religion and to attribute far less importance to work and democracy than better educated women.[5]

The third dividing line influencing women's professed values is type of environment in which they live. While women from the rural settlements are more anchored to traditional values and religion, women from large towns tend to prefer values such as responsibility and work. This reflects the structure of the urban population that is more educated and has greater social capital. In general, people with higher education endorse values such as modernity, meritocracy, aspiration and instrumentality, while those with lower education prefer traditional values.

All in all, values professed by women are rather heterogeneous and the same is truth about men's values as well. Empirical data show that age is an important factor, as both women and men at different stages of the life cycle have different priorities. Values professed by women and men in their younger and older years are more similar than those of middle-aged women and men. Another factor behind the value diversity is education. Value priorities of women with higher education are closer to those of well-educated men, and more distant from those of elderly and less educated women living in rural areas.

---

[4] Other values that are more important to women than to men include matrimony, God, neighborhood community, religion and tradition (Gyárfášová – Slosiarik, 2008).

[5] Needless to say, education is a significant factor that affects also views on the economy, the role of government, etc. Better educated people tend to regard the economic changes after 1989 more positively, and perceive themselves as the winners of the transformation process, while less educated people generally view themselves as the losers.

7.1.3. POLITICAL ORIENTATIONS

How do women and men feel about the four principal ideologies or opinion mainstreams, namely social democrats, nationalists, conservatives and liberals? As Table 7.3 shows, women – and to an even greater degree men – identify especially with social democrats and nationalists. On the other hand, they feel more distant from liberals and particularly conservatives. This negative self-identification is stronger among men than among women.

Table 7.3
"How close or distant do you feel to the following political orientations?" (% of answers "very and rather close" : "very and rather distant" : "I don't know")

	Views of women	Views of men
Social democrats	44 : 25 : 30	50 : 24 : 26
Nationalists	36 : 38 : 26	45 : 32 : 23
Liberals	27 : 36 : 37	27 : 42 : 31
Conservatives	18 : 45 : 37	19 : 50 : 31

Source: Institute for Public Affairs, August 2006.

Where do women and men see themselves on the traditional right-left[6] political spectrum? As Table 7.4 shows, their orientations over the past decade have tended mainly towards the political center. At the same time, more of them preferred the left to the right. Throughout the whole period, there was a relatively strong portion of ambiguous and uninformed views. Developments over the past decade have shown that citizens' greater experience with a pluralist democracy has not led to a corresponding crystallization of political self-identification.

Table 7.4
Political self-identification of women and men (% of answers "strong and moderate left" : "political center": "strong and moderate right": "I don't know")

	Views of women	Views of men
October 1997	19 : 35 : 17 : 29	21 : 41 : 22 : 16
January 1999	23 : 39 : 11 : 28	26 : 40 : 17 : 17
June 2002	18 : 37 : 14 : 32	24 : 36 : 20 : 20
November 2004	20 : 45 : 16 : 19	29 : 43 : 17 : 11
August 2006	20 : 40 : 14 : 26	26 : 40 : 14 : 20

Source: Institute for Public Affairs, October 1997, January 1999, June 2002, November 2004, August 2006.

As for the gender differences, especially in the first half of the examined period, women's views were more ambiguous. On the other hand, the share of declared leftists among women was lower than among men throughout the whole examined period. Another gender difference before 2002 was

Table 7.5
Political self-identification of women and men – by age and education (% of answers "strong and moderate left" : "political center": "strong and moderate right": "I don't know")

		Orientations of women	Orientations of men
Age	15 – 17	9 : 36 : 2 : 53	7 : 19 : 9 : 65
	18 – 45	17 : 42 : 14 : 28	22 : 41 : 15 : 22
	45 – 64	24 : 38 : 14 : 24	31 : 40 : 13 : 16
	Over 65	19 : 29 : 14 : 38	41 : 34 : 8 : 17
Education	Elementary	18 : 33 : 10 : 39	25 : 35 : 11 : 29
	Secondary without A levels	27 : 32 : 10 : 31	26 : 42 : 12 : 20
	Complete secondary	19 : 47 : 15 : 19	27 : 42 : 18 : 13
	University	15 : 47 : 25 : 13	28 : 45 : 16 : 11

Source: Institute for Public Affairs, August 2006.

---

6   In Slovakia, the right-left spectrum is defined primarily by socio-economic criteria. With a certain simplification, one could say that the more people emphasize the role of government the closer they are to the leftist pole; the more weight they attribute to free market the closer they are to the rightist pole.

women's weaker inclination towards the right pole of the political spectrum, which is not the case any more.

Political orientations of women and men are significantly influenced by their age (see Table 7.5). While teenage girls are politically more articulate than teenage boys, at later stages their political views become more ambiguous compared to men. This difference is the largest in the oldest category.

With the increasing education, the political orientations of women and men become less ambiguous and slightly more centrist. Among women, the share of rightists becomes more numerous, too. Men with elementary, complete secondary and university education incline to the left significantly more often than their female counterparts.

7.1.4. CREDIBILITY OF POLITICAL AND SOCIAL INSTITUTIONS

What is the degree of trust in key political and social institutions among women and men in Slovakia? As Table 7.6 illustrates, the most credible among the top political institutions in 2007 was the presidency, followed by the Constitutional Court. As for the credibility of the parliament and the cabinet, the distrust toward them prevailed over the trust among women, but especially among men.

As for other institutions, the most credible were local self-governments, followed by non-governmental organizations (NGOs). On the other hand, trade unions and particularly political parties ranked among the least trustworthy institutions.

In general, men's views differed from those of women by a somewhat higher degree of distrust toward most of the examined institutions.

Table 7.6
Credibility of select institutions (% of answers "I completely and rather trust" : "I definitely and rather distrust")

		Views of women	Views of men
Top political institutions	President	69 : 27	68 : 29
	Constitutional Court	49 : 43	48 : 47
	Parliament	44 : 51	40 : 57
	Cabinet	41 : 54	38 : 59
Other institutions	Local self-governments	54 : 38	55 : 41
	Non-governmental organizations	43 : 48	39 : 51
	Trade unions	31 : 50	27 : 55
	Political parties	18 : 76	18 : 77

Note: The remainder of the 100% figure comprises the answer "I don't know".
Source: Institute for Public Affairs, August 2007.

7.1.5. ATTITUDES TOWARD NON-GOVERNMENTAL ORGANIZATIONS

Let us now take a closer look at the attitudes of women and men toward non-governmental organizations. As Table 7.7 shows, these views have seen ups and downs since 2002. Throughout the examined period, women's attitudes were more favorable than those of men. There was also a remarkable decline in the share of ambiguous views among both women and men, which indicates that they became more familiar with the activities of the NGOs.

Table 7.7
Credibility of non-governmental organizations among women and men (% of answers "I completely and rather trust" : "I definitely and rather distrust" : "I don't know")

	Views of women	Views of men
2002	33 : 38 :29	30 : 46 : 24
2003	41: 39 : 20	42 : 42 : 16
2004	43 : 42 : 15	40 : 48 : 16
2005	50 : 38 : 12	46 : 42 : 12
2006	49 : 34 : 17	44 : 42 : 14
2007	43 : 48 : 9	39 : 51 : 10

Source: Institute for Public Affairs, June 2002, September 2003, November 2004, November 2005, November 2006, August 2007.

The credibility of NGOs is based on people's views about their usefulness, which in turn largely depend on what issues are the NGOs dealing with (Bútora – Bútorová, 1996; Bútorová, 2004; Strečanský – Bútora – Vajdová – Szatmáry – Bútorová – Kubánová – Woleková, 2006). Also according to a survey carried out by the Institute for Public Affairs in 2005, women attribute the greatest importance to NGOs that provide social services to people in need as well as to NGOs that operate in the field of health care. Women's NGOs ranked third,[7] followed by NGOs striving for environmental protection; by NGOs promoting community development, by NGOs exposing and combating corruption in public life, and by NGOs defending citizens' rights against the government and private owners (see Table 7.8).

In terms of usefulness, the second category comprises NGOs that combat racial, ethnic and other forms of intolerance, NGOs supervising and demanding improvement of the performance of state administration, local self-governments and courts of law, NGOs monitoring political party financing and publicly criticizing exposed problems, NGOs whose expertise and civic initiatives intervene into the process of political decision-making and advance citizens' interests; and NGOs that provide humanitarian aid and pro-

Table 7.8
Views of women and men about the usefulness of non-governmental organizations (% of grades "1" and "2")

	Views of women	Views of men
NGOs providing social services to people in need	94	93
NGOs operating in the field of health care	93	93
NGOs dealing with the problems of women and furthering their rights	86	69
Environmental NGOs	83	83
NGOs promoting community development	79	81
NGOs exposing and combating corruption in public life	78	81
NGOs defending citizens' rights against the government and private owners	78	79
NGOs combating racial, ethnic and other intolerance	70	70
NGOs supervising and demanding improvement of the performance of state administration, local self-governments and courts of law	67	68
NGOs providing expertise and civic initiatives that intervene into the process of political decision-making and advance citizens' interests	65	65
NGOs monitoring political party financing and publicly criticizing exposed problems	64	68
NGOs providing humanitarian aid and promoting democracy in other countries	64	65
Public policy think tanks	49	51
NGOs striving for the social and moral advancement of the Romany community	49	50

Note: Respondents evaluated the usefulness of NGOs on a scale from 1 to 5, in which 1 = usefulness and 5 = uselessness.
Source: Institute for Public Affairs, November 2005.

---

[7] On the "male" list of usefulness, women's NGOs ranked eighth. However, more important than this actual ranking is that as many as 69% of male respondents considered these NGOs useful.

mote democracy in other countries. Finally, the least useful according to Slovak women are public policy think tanks and NGOs striving for the social and moral advancement of the Romany community.

7.2. ELECTORAL BEHAVIOR OF WOMEN AND MEN
7.2.1. ARE SLOVAK VOTERS DIVIDED BY A "GENDER GAP"?

As we demonstrated in the opening section, women's views of current social problems, their professed values, political orientations and attitudes to political and social institutions are only slightly dissimilar from those of men. It is therefore little surprise that these subtle differences in opinions and values have not resulted in substantial gender differences in electoral behavior. Since the early 1990s, the lack of a deep gender gap has been typical not only of the voter turnout, but to some extent also of women's' and men's preferences for individual political parties (Bútorová – Filadelfiová – Guráň – Gyárfášová – Farkašová, 1999; Filadelfiová – Bútorová – Gyárfášová, 2002).

In the following analysis, we will take a closer look at the electoral behavior of Slovak women and men in the 2006 parliamentary elections and their voting preferences in 2007. We will base our conclusions on an exit poll carried out by the MVK agency in June 2006, as well as on aggregate data on citizens' voting preferences collected throughout 2007 by the FOCUS agency.

The exit poll from June 2006 revealed several similarities but also some remarkable differences in the electoral behavior of women and men. Two parties – namely the Christian Democratic Movement (KDH) and the Freedom Forum (SF) – received significantly more votes from women than from men. This was the case of the KDH, which has traditionally relied on female rather than male supporters.[8] The greater support of the KDH among women, particularly elderly residents of smaller villages, originates in their strong religious background and their inclination towards traditional values (Gyárfášová – Slosiarik, 2008).

On the other hand, the far-right Slovak National Party (SNS) and the Communist Party of Slovakia (KSS) were more successful among men (see Table 7.9). The KSS received greater support from men in the 2002 parliamentary elections as well. The electorates of the two strongest parties, namely Smer-Social Democracy (Smer-SD) the Slovak Democratic and Christian Union (SDKÚ-DS), are quite balanced in terms of gender make-up (*Exit poll MVK*, 2006).

Table 7.9
Support for political parties in the 2006 elections (% of voters)

	Smer-SD	SDKÚ-DS	SNS	SMK	KDH	ĽS-HZDS	KSS	SF
Women	27.6	19.1	8.5	12.2	9.6	7.7	3.2	5.2
Men	27.8	18.8	12.0	11.1	6.5	8.5	5.3	3.1

Note: The remainder of the 100% figure comprises voters of other political parties.
Source: MVK exit poll, June 2006.

---

[8]   This was also corroborated by election surveys in 1992, 1994 and 2002 (Filadelfiová – Bútorová – Gyárfášová, 2002).

Had the parliament been created solely based on women's votes after the 2006 elections, it would also have comprised SF deputies, while the position of the KDH would have been stronger. On the other hand, the SNS, which ranked third in the actual elections, would have dropped by two places, and would have controlled fewer seats than Smer-SD, the SDKÚ-DS, the SMK and the KDH (Bútorová – Gyárfášová – Krivý, 2007).

Let us now compare the voting patterns of women and men in the 2006 parliamentary elections to their voting preferences in the course of 2007. The voter support of the major parties has been relatively stable since the 2006 elections, with Smer-SD enjoying great popularity and all other parliamentary parties stagnating.

In the post-election period, three parties preserved a specific gender profile, namely the KDH, which has continued to rely on a predominantly female electorate; the SNS, which has remained a "male party"; and the ĽS-HZDS, which has also preserved its prevailingly male character, though not as distinct as in case of the SNS.

As for the education, voter support for Smer-SD was spread relatively evenly throughout all education categories of women and men. The SDKÚ-DS, for its part, tended to be preferred by women and men with a higher education, particularly those with university degrees. On the other hand, the ĽS-HZDS continued to appeal to less educated women and men. In all education categories, women were less supportive of the SNS and more supportive of the KDH compared to men.

Another factor that strongly affected voting preferences of women and men in 2007 was the age, especially in the case of KDH and ĽS-HZDS supporters, as both parties attracted particularly women and men over 45. The SMK is another party that appeals mostly to older voters, though to a smaller extent. On the opposite pole is the SNS, whose supporters are predominantly young men.

The share of non-voters and undecided voters is significantly higher among women and men under 45.

Table 7.10
"Imagine that parliamentary elections were held this weekend and the following political parties ran. Which party would you vote for?" (% of all eligible voters)

		Smer-SD	SDKÚ-DS	SNS	SMK	ĽS-HZDS	KDH	I would not vote	I don't know
Women	Elementary	19.3	4.8	5.4	7.2	8.2	9.6	21.4	14.4
	Secondary without A levels	23.5	6.9	6.6	6.4	4.4	5.9	22.3	11.9
	Secondary	20.2	12.1	6.3	5.7	3.1	5.4	19.4	13.6
	University	18.0	22.6	3.9	3.7	2.9	7.5	14.1	15.3
Men	Elementary	19.3	4.4	8.4	6.1	7.6	4.3	22.9	14.2
	Secondary without A levels	23.5	6.7	10.1	7.1	6.5	2.9	20.0	9.6
	Secondary	20.2	14.2	10.3	4.7	4.0	3.2	20.2	10.8
	University	18.5	20.9	8.0	3.4	3.2	3.6	15.2	9.6
Women	Under 45	21.2	10.8	6.3	5.4	2.3	3.9	21.2	17.1
	Over 45	21.4	9.2	5.5	6.8	7.2	9.9	18.9	9.5
Men	Under 45	21.8	10.6	10.4	4.3	2.9	2.1	22.2	13.9
	Over 45	20.0	8.6	8.4	7.8	9.5	5.1	17.6	7.2
Women		21.3	10.0	5.9	6.1	4.6	6.8	20.1	13.5
Men		21.0	9.7	9.5	5.8	5.7	3.4	20.3	11.1

Note: Average voting preferences for 11 months of 2007 (February – December).
Source: FOCUS, February – December 2007.

7.2.2. PERCEPTION OF PARTIES' ABILITY TO DEAL WITH GENDER AGENDA

When examining women's electoral behavior, the question arises whether their support of a specific political party is determined by their conviction that this party is able to solve pressing women's issues. Theoretically, the relevance of this question should be high, as the sensitiveness of the population to women's issues has grown (see Chapter 5 of this publication).

However, women have very unclear or skeptical ideas about political parties' attitude toward the gender agenda. When asked in a survey by the Institute for Public Affairs before the 2002 elections "Which political party is the most capable of addressing women's problems?" 64% of women answered "I don't know" or "none". The remaining 36% of women who believed that their favorite party addressed women's issues the best, based this conviction rather on their general belief in that party than on positive evaluation of its gender politics (Gyárfášová – Pafková, 2002; Filadelfiová – Bútorová – Gyárfášová, 2002).

During the following four years, this situation has not changed for better. Before the 2006 parliamentary elections, the election programs of major political parties dedicated to explicitly formulated gender agenda only very little attention or no attention at all (Kobová – Maďarová, 2007; Kollár – Mesežnikov, 2006).

Thus we can speak about the perpetuation of a vicious circle. By neglecting the gender agenda in their election programs, political parties support the indifference of voters on the matter; in turn, the voters do not expect political parties to tackle this agenda.

7.3. CIVIC AND POLITICAL PARTICIPATION
7.3.1. FORMS OF CIVIC AND POLITICAL PARTICIPATION

The political and civic participation of women and men is an important dimension of the quality of democracy. A survey in summer 2007 by the Institute for Public Affairs focused on 12 select forms of this participation.[9] Graph 7.1 ranks them according to the ratio of women and men who used them over the past 10 years. The most common form of participation among women and men is voting in elections (80% and 76%, respectively). Other activities are much less common. Less than half of women (46%) and men (44%) tried to influence public affairs by signing a petition. Twenty five percent of women and 35% of men joined the others in solving a community problem and about the same percentage attended a political meeting (24% and 32%, respectively) or contacted an official in order to solve a problem (25% and 30%, respectively). Seventeen percent of women and 20% of men participated in the activities of a non-governmental organization; 14% of women and 18% of men tried to persuade their friends to vote for a concrete political party. The remaining forms of participation in the past decade included attending a protest demonstration (8% of women and 10% of men), working for a political party (7% and 9%, respectively), working in trade unions (6% each), commenting political matters in the media (5% and 6%, respectively) and running for a public office (2% and 5%, respectively).

---

[9] These data were collected by the project *Launching e-Governance in Slovakia: Empowering Citizens to Participate, Influence and Control,* carried out by the Institute for Public Affairs and supported by The Trust for Civil Society in Central & Eastern Europe – CEE Trust (Velšic, 2008).

These findings suggest that men are more active than women in exercising certain forms of political and civic participation, in particular in helping to solve community problems, attending political meetings and contacting officials in order to solve a problem. Men have also slightly more frequently worked in non-governmental organizations and run for public office. Some activities have been exercised with approximately the same intensity among women and men. However, none of them has been significantly more common among women than among men.

A comparison of these findings to those of earlier surveys shows that gender differences in the forms of participation are relatively stable and have not changed significantly over the past 13 years (*Current Problems...*, 1996; Bútorová – Filadelfiová – Guráň – Gyárfášová – Farkašová, 1999; *Empirical Data...*, 2004).

Graph 7.1
"There are various forms of citizens' participation in public affairs. Have you used any of the following over the past ten years?" (% of affirmative answers)

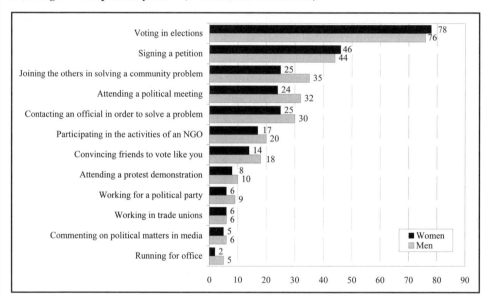

Source: Institute for Public Affairs, August 2007.

Most forms of political and civic participation are more frequent among people of a mature age, people with university education, white-collar workers and entrepreneurs. At the same time, certain forms of participation, especially those related to municipal politics, are far more common among residents of smaller towns. These differences were confirmed also by previous surveys (*Empirical Data...*, 2004; *Current Problems...*, 1996).

Let us look whether these general conclusions about the role of age and education apply also to the political and civic participation of women. Graph 7.2 gives a clear answer. Women over 45 are more active than younger women in 10 out of 12 forms of participation.[10] In the past

---

[10] The minimum age was set at 28 because the question examined the activities over the past decade. Younger women between 18 and 28 would have been put in disadvantage by this formulation of question.

decade, women over 45 have more frequently attended political meetings, tackled community problems, contacted political officials; participated in the activities of NGOs and trade unions, and convinced their friends to vote like them. Differences in other forms of participation were not statistically significant.

Graph 7.2
Rate of political and civic participation among women by age (% of affirmative answers)

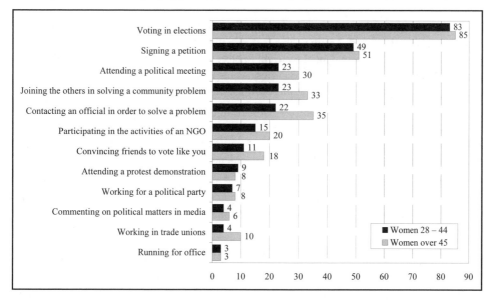

Source: Institute for Public Affairs, August 2007.

And what role does educational attainment play in women's civic and political participation? As one would expect, the higher is the education, the greater is the participation. Somewhat surprisingly, the mobilization effect of education is weaker among women than among men. As a result, in 10 out of 12 forms of participation, women with university degrees lag behind

Table 7.11
Rate of political and civic participation among women and men by education (% of those with elementary education : % of those with university education)

	Women	Men
Voting in elections	63 : 85	59 : 91
Signing a petition	33 : 54	37 : 72
Attending a political meeting	20 : 27	33 : 53
Joining the others in solving a community problem	21 : 24	29 : 59
Contacting an official in order to solve a problem	27 : 22	27 : 48
Participating in the activities of an NGO	14 : 37	20 : 35
Convincing friends to vote like you	18 : 14	19 : 29
Attending a protest demonstration	4 : 12	8 : 28
Working for a political party	7 : 10	11 : 16
Commenting on political matters in media	2 : 19	4 : 12
Working in trade unions	4 : 10	3 : 14
Running for office	4 : 6	4 : 10

Source: Institute for Public Affairs, August 2007.

men with the same level of education to a greater extent than women with elementary education behind their male counterparts. The fact that the participatory potential of women with the highest education is not sufficiently mobilized indicates that there are other barriers standing in their way.

7.3.2. REPRESENTATION OF WOMEN IN POLITICS

The codification of political rights for women has been slower than for men. Although the 19th century is generally regarded as the period when political rights were formed, this did not apply to women. Women were denied the right to elect political representatives and help decide the fate of their countries. In some countries, women were allowed to participate in political life after World War I as a result of strong suffrage movements at the turn of the century.[11]

Compared to other European countries, women in Slovakia were granted the right to vote relatively early, in 1919, immediately after the formation of the Czechoslovak Republic. Despite this, the right of women to be elected and participate in the process of shaping and executing policies is still not sufficiently implemented.[12]

Since 1989, the participation of women in political decision-making has been unsatisfactory, mostly because of the absence of the basic prerequisite for participation, i.e. the equal representation of women in political bodies at the national, regional and local levels.

Women's Representation in Parliament

Before the fall of communism in Czechoslovakia, several formal quotas were in place regarding the appointment of deputies to parliamentary seats. One was a quota requiring a 30% proportion of women in the parliament. As a result, women regularly obtained over 20% of parliamentary seats. However, their participation in shaping policies was merely formal, as it took place in an undemocratic framework under the power monopoly of the communist party.

When the quota system was abolished as a relic of past, the share of women elected to the Slovak parliament in the first free elections in 1990 dropped to 12%. Since then, women have controlled between 18 and 24 out of 150 seats, i.e. between 12% and 16% of mandates.

Table 7.12
Women running on the candidate lists of political parties for parliamentary elections between 1998 and 2006 (in total numbers and %)

Election year	Number of parties running	Number of candidates			% of female candidates
		Women	Men	Total	
1998	17	274	1,344	1,618	16.9
2002	25	604	2,014	2,618	23.1
2006	21	532	1,808	2,340	22.7

Source: *Zoznamy kandidátov...*, 2008; *Volebná...*, 2008.

---

[11] The first country to enact women's suffrage was New Zealand in 1893, followed by Australia in 1902. The first European country to do so was Finland in 1906, still a province of the Russian Empire at the time.

[12] In Western Europe, some of those obstacles were overcome in the 1970s and 1980s when a number of countries introduced special measures to encourage political participation of women (*Women...*, 1999; *Women 2000...*, 2000; Filadelfiová, 2001, 2002; *Women and Men...*, 2008).

The gender structure of the Slovak parliament is largely predetermined by the share of women appearing on the candidate lists of political parties. The overall share of women running for parliament was 15% in the 1994 parliamentary elections, 16.9% in 1998, 23.1% in 2002 and 22.7% in 2006. It has remained below one third of all candidates and is far from proportional (see Table 7.12).

Of the six political parties that won parliamentary seats in the 2006 elections, only three (the ĽS-HZDS, SNS and SDKÚ-DS) nominated at least one woman to the top three spots on their respective tickets. Compared to 2002, the overall share of women increased only on the SDKÚ-DS candidate list. The share of women on other political parties' tickets slightly declined. Only 3 out of 21 parties running in the 2006 elections featured a woman at the top of their candidate lists, namely the ANO, the Freedom Forum and Nádej (Hope); however, none of these parties won parliamentary seats.

Unlike before the 2002 parliamentary elections or elections to the European Parliament in 2004, when several women's non-governmental organizations advocated the greater representation of women in politics (Filadelfiová, 2003), the election campaign in 2006 was almost completely free of similar activities. Although some NGOs tried to spark public debate on the issue,[13] their activities did not draw the desired public response and had no effect on the election results and on the formation of the new administration.

Parliamentary elections in Slovakia use a proportional electoral system with closed candidate lists, which is generally regarded as less favorable for the final representation of women (Jalušić, 2000). Political parties have exclusive authority to decide whether candidates are placed in electable or non-electable spots on their lists – and they are predominantly male organizations. According to Slovak electoral law, however, voters may cast "preferential" ballots (singling out favored candidates) and thus change the order of the candidates as set by

Graph 7.3
Representation of women in the Slovak parliament between 1985 and 2006 (%)

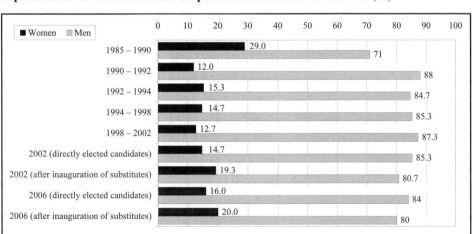

Source: Filadelfiová 2002; *Zoznam poslancov...*, 2008; www.nrsr.sk.

---

[13] Worth of mentioning are the information materials disseminated through the websites of feminist organizations such as Možnosť voľby or Aspekt (www.aspekt.sk; www.gender.sk) as well as discussion forums organized by the Profesionálne ženy [Professional Women] civic association.

political parties. This process sometimes helps even low-seeded candidates win parliamentary seats. In the 2006 elections, preferential votes helped nine female candidates from four parties move up on their respective candidate lists, giving three of them a seat in parliament. Given the general reluctance of political parties to amend the existing legislation (e.g. to introduce formal quotas or a "zipper system" alternating male and female candidates), the preferential vote system remains the only tool that voters have to influence political leaders' decisions regarding the seeding of women on candidate lists.

Based on the election results, the overall share of seats clinched by women in 2006 was slightly higher than in previous elections, i.e. 16% compared to 14.7% in 2002 and 11.3% in 1998. In order to increase their overall representation to one third, which is generally considered the critical mass needed for influencing decision-making processes, women must almost double their current number. After some MPs relinquished their mandates to take up top executive posts, opening room for replacement MPs to be nominated, women eventually clinched 20% of all seats, compared to 19.3% in 2002 and 12.7% in 1998. As for individual political parties, the ĽS-HZDS and Smer-SD have the highest share of women in their parliamentary caucuses, at 25% and 24%, respectively; the KDH is at the opposite pole with 14.3% (see Table 7.13).

Table 7.13
Representation of women in parliamentary caucuses (as of January 1, 2007 – in total numbers and %)

	Total number of seats	Women	Men	% of women	Caucus chairperson
Smer-SD	50	12	38	24.0	Man
SDKÚ-DS	31	6	25	19.4	Man
SNS	19	3	16	15.8	Man
SMK	20	3	17	15.0	Man
ĽS-HZDS	16	4	12	25.0	Man
KDH	14	2	12	14.3	Woman
Total	150	30	120	20.0	5 men and 1 woman

Note: Since the beginning of 2007, the make-up of the parliament has seen some changes, which also led to changes in the assembly's overall gender ratio. As of April 28, 2008, the total number of female deputies was 28, i.e. 18.7% of total seats. The representation of women in individual caucuses changed as well; the share of women was 22.0% in the Smer-SD caucus, 20.0% in the SDKÚ-DS caucus, 15.8% in the SNS caucus, 15.0% in the SMK caucus; 20.0% in the ĽS-HZDS caucus and 22.2% in the KDH caucus. There is no woman among independent MPs.
Source: *Zoznam poslancov...*, 2008.

Approximately one third of the 30 female MPs were elected to executive parliamentary posts. Anna Belousovová (SNS) took one of the four deputy speaker chairs, Mária Sabolová became the chairperson of the KDH caucus (the only woman among six caucus chairs), and 11 women were elected chairperson or vice-chairperson of the various parliamentary committees (out of a total of 57 such posts).

Women's Representation in Regional Parliaments

In its modern history, Slovakia has held two elections to regional self-government, in 2001 and 2005. Voters elected eight regional governors and members to eight regional parliaments.

In 2001, a total of 133 candidates ran for the post of regional governor, including 13 women (9.8%). Eight of them had been nominated by political parties with little political weight and two ran as independent candidates; only three were backed by political parties represented in parliament. In the end, not a single female candidate won a post as regional governor.

The situation was pretty much the same four years later, as no woman was elected as regional governor. The share of women running for the post in 2005 remained virtually unchanged, with only 7 women running alongside 57 men (10.9% of the total). Another constant was the "political weight" of the female candidates, as they ran either on minor parties' tickets or as independents, and thus stood no chance of being elected against candidates running for major parties in various election coalitions.

In 2001, the overall share of women running for seats in eight regional parliaments was 17.3% of all candidates and four years later, it was 18.6% (see Table 7.14). Women's share of the total number of elected members was even smaller than their percentage on candidate lists: 12.7% in 2001 and 14.3% in 2005.

Generally speaking, the political participation of women at the regional level of government is far from satisfactory. So far, not a single woman has been elected governor, and the representation of women in regional parliaments is below 15%. For women, the first two regional elections in 2001 and 2005 brought worse results than the two most recent parliamentary elections in 2002 and 2006.

Table 7.14
Representation of women among candidates for governor of regional parliament and elected as governors and representation of women among candidates for member and elected members of regional parliaments in regional elections (2001 and 2005 – in total numbers and %)

	Candidates for governor		Elected governors		Candidates for member		Elected members	
	Total / women	Women (%)	Total / women	Women (%)	Total / women	Women (%)	Total / women	Women (%)
2001	133/13	9.8	8/0	0	3,976/ 690	17.3	401/51	12.7
2005	64/7	10.9	8/0	0	2,833 / 526	18.6	412/59	14.3

Source: Ministry of Interior, 2001 (www.civil.gov.sk); *Ženy a muži na Slovensku II…*, 2002; *Volebná…*, 2008.

Women's Representation in Local Parliaments

Slovakia has held four municipal elections since it emerged as an independent country in 1993. In the last municipal elections in 2006, women won 601 posts out of the total of 2,905 mayors elected. Their overall share increased to 20.7% from 18.6% four years before. In the first two municipal elections, this share was even smaller, at 17.5% in 1998 and only 15.2% in 1994. The share of women holding the post of mayor has been slowly, but surely increasing, at 5 percentage points in 15 years.

While the representation of women at the local level of politics is somewhat better than at the regional or national levels, the situation is still far from satisfactory.

Table 7.15
Representation of women among mayors elected between 1994 and 2006 (in total numbers and %)

	Total elected	Women elected	% of women
1994	2,750	418	15.2
1998	2,766	484	17.5
2002	2,913	541	18.6
2006	2,905	601	20.7

Note: On its official website, the Statistical Office of the Slovak Republic provides information only on the two most recent municipal elections. The format of the data does not allow calculating the share of women out of the total number of all candidates running or of those elected to local councils.
Source: *Ženy a muži na Slovensku II …*, 2002; *Volebná…*, 2008.

Women and the Presidency

In its short history, Slovakia has not yet had a female president. After direct presidential elections were introduced in 1999, the president of the Slovak Foreign Policy Association and Czechoslovakia's former Ambassador to Austria, Magda Vášáryová, was among the 10 candidates who ran for the country's highest constitutional post in 1999. In the next elections of 2004, there were no women among the 12 candidates. However, this is about to change, as sociologist Iveta Radičová, an MP for the SDKÚ-DS and former minister of labor, social affairs and family, will challenge incumbent president Ivan Gašparovič for the post in 2009. Radičová was endorsed by all three parliamentary opposition parties in parliament – the SDKÚ-DS, KDH and SMK.

Women's Representation among Members of the European Parliament for Slovakia

From the viewpoint of women's representation, the most successful elections so far were the first elections to the European Parliament (EP) that Slovakia held in 2004. Female candidates clinched 5 of 14 EP seats earmarked for Slovak deputies, or 35.7%.[14] This share is even 4 percentage points higher than the average representation of women in the EP, which is currently 30.4%.

Women's Representation in Government

The representation of Slovak women in top executive posts is even lower than their representation in the legislative assembly. While the ratio of female cabinet members has fluctuated since 1989, it has never exceeded 15% (see Graph 7.4). The poor gender sensitivity of Slovak political leaders was particularly evident in the formation of the two most recent administrations. The second Mikuláš Dzurinda administration, formed after the 2002 elections, did not include a single female minister, something that had not happened since the Vladimír Mečiar administration, formed after the first free elections in 1990. It was not until the end of the Dzurinda government's term that two women were put in charge of the Ministry of Labor, Social Affairs and Family and the Ministry of Justice. In the following Robert Fico administration, formed after the 2006 elections, the only female cabinet member was initially Minister of Labor, Social Affairs and Family Viera Tomanová. By the end of 2007, she was joined by Zdenka Kramplová, who took the post of agriculture minister until she was ousted in August 2008. Although the principal election winner and the dominant coalition party is Smer-SD, which claims to be a social-democratic party, its leaders disregarded the principle of gender equality when forming the Smer-SD – SNS – ĽS-HZDS coalition government.

The situation in Slovakia contrasts sharply with that of most original EU member states, where the share of female cabinet members usually exceeds one-fifth and in some countries is close to equal representation or even goes beyond it.[15] These countries' political leaders obviously take gender criteria into consideration when forming governments, as they are bound to do by international conventions as well as EU political strategies and objectives.[16]

---

[14] Anna Záborská of the KDH was elected chairwoman of the Parliamentary Committee for Women's Rights and Gender Equality.
[15] The only exceptions from this rule are Greece and Portugal.
[16] The European Commission cited promoting equal representation of women and men in decision-making processes among six priorities of its gender agenda for the period of 2006 – 2010 (*A Roadmap…*, 2006).

Graph 7.4
Representation of women in Slovak cabinets between 1989 and 2008 (%)

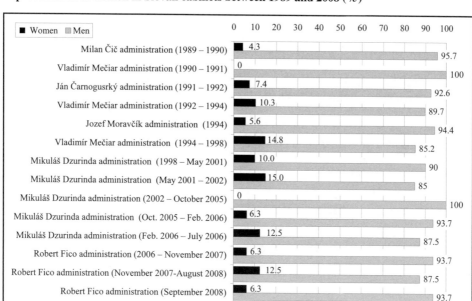

Source: *Vláda SR...,* 2008.

On the other hand, six of Central and Eastern European countries (Slovenia, Romania, Moldavia, Hungary, Slovakia and the Czech Republic) were ruled in 2005 by exclusively male cabinets, while in other countries women made up only about 10% of cabinet members. Although this region continues to lag behind the original EU member states, the representation of women in some of these countries' national governments has increased slightly, and by November 2007 it reached or exceeded 20%. Unfortunately, Slovakia continues to be an unflattering exception, and in terms of women's representation in government it is at the bottom of the list of EU member states along with Romania, Greece, Portugal and Slovenia (*Women and Men...,* 2008).

These data illustrate the low participation of women in the legislative and executive branches and testify to the political marginalization of women in Slovakia, which is an important – and not particularly favorable – indicator of the country's overall degree of cultural development.

In recent years, Slovakia has not adopted any law to strengthen women's political rights. Although three such bills were drafted, parliament turned them down even though people in Slovakia were ready to endorse measures to increase women's participation in politics. According to a survey in 2002 by the Institute for Public Affairs, a majority of citizens (64% of women and 52% of men) agreed that political parties should set quotas for women or introduce a "zipper system" alternating men and women on candidate lists (Filadelfiová – Bútorová – Gyárfášová, 2002).

In March 2001, the cabinet adopted the *Conception of Equal Opportunities for Women and Men* (*Koncepcia...,* 2001). In the document, it pledged to "support amending the Law on Political Parties and the Election Law in order to guarantee the representation of women in politics and political parties, for instance via introducing quotas and other short-term temporary measures". Eight years later, the government has yet to adopt such changes.

7.3.3. OPINIONS ON WOMEN'S REPRESENTATION IN POLITICS

Over the long term, people in Slovakia have been critical of the insufficient representation of women in top politics (Bútorová, 1996; Bútorová – Filadelfiová – Guráň – Gyárfášová – Farkašová, 1999; Filadelfiová – Bútorová – Gyárfášová, 2002; Filadelfiová – Bútorová, 2007a). This criticism was reiterated in August 2006, when 73% of women and 59% of men evaluated the representation of women in the cabinet as inadequate; 67% of women and 53% of men felt the same way about parliament. Public perception of women's representation in local politics was a little less critical (52% and 38%, respectively). In all three cases, women were substantially more dissatisfied. The need to increase women's participation in political decision-making was more frequently acknowledged by women and men with higher education.

Table 7.16
Views of women's representation in political institutions (% of answers "sufficient" : "insufficient" : "I don't know")

	Views of women	Views of men
Parliament	21 : 73 : 6	33 : 59 : 8
Cabinet	27 : 67 : 6	38 : 53 : 9
Local self-government	37 : 52 : 11	48 : 38 : 14

Source: Institute for Public Affairs, August 2006.

A comparison with earlier surveys shows that people's criticism of the insufficient representation of women in political decision-making grew stronger between 2000 and 2006. This is true not only of women but even more so of men, whose views underwent greater changes. Despite the positive shift, however, the criticism of men continues to lag behind that of women.

Table 7.17
Development of views on women's political representation in 2000 – 2006 (% of answers "insufficient")

	Views of women			Views of men		
	2000	2002	2006	2000	2002	2006
Representation of women in parliament	57	68	67	35	48	53
Representation of women in cabinet	61	68	73	39	49	59
Representation of women in local self-government	38	42	52	22	26	38

Source: Institute for Public Affairs, March 2000, June 2002 and August 2006.

The criticism of women's low political representation stems from the fact that a majority of the Slovak population believes that "women should have an equal say in politics as men". In August 2006, this view was shared by 81% of women ad 65% of men. Only 16% of women and 29% of men expressed the opposite opinion that "women should not meddle in politics". Again, the differences in the opinions of women and men are significant (see Graph 7.5). The higher is the education of women and men, the stronger is their support of equal political representation of women.

Generally speaking, a more active role of women in politics is hindered by socio-cultural expectations within society. As we could see in Chapter 1 of this publication, the "ideal woman" is rarely expected to be an active citizen. Only 48% of people imagine that an ideal woman would be interested in public affairs, and only 10% find this attribute very important. The image of the "ideal man" has a more pronounced dimension of active political participation: 60% of people expect him to be well-versed in politics and 14% consider this attribute very important. Women's views do not differ greatly from those of men. Interestingly, these normative expectations have changed little since 1995 (Bútorová, 1996, p. 151). For most people in Slovakia, the ideal woman is selfless, taking care of others, particularly of her family and household. Few people see the ideal woman also as *homo politicus.*

We have thus exposed an interesting paradox. On the one hand, the public increasingly acknowledges the importance of women's equal participation in political decision-making. On the other hand, most of people continue to believe that it is not important for women to be active in public life. This indicates that public support for the active political and civic participation of women is rather superficial.

Graph 7.5
"Which of the following statements do you support:
A. Women should not meddle in politics.
B. Women's say in politics should be equal to that of men"
(support of statement A : undecided : support of statement B – in %)

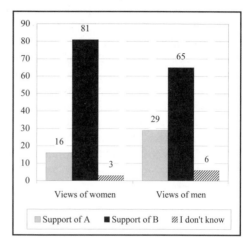

Source: Institute for Public Affairs, August 2006.

What do people in Slovakia see as the principal reasons for the insufficient representation of women in politics? According to the findings of a survey carried out in 2002 by the Institute for Public Affairs, 79% of women and 70% of men believed that the entry of women into politics is hindered primarily by their family obligations (see Table 7.18).

This key limiting factor was also corroborated by an in-depth survey examining the role of women in politics (Filadelfiová – Radičová – Puliš, 2000). According to the survey findings, family obligations represent a universal barrier to women's entry into politics. It usually requires the consent and support of their spouses and often of other family members as well. Most women who desire to enter politics are "excused" from family chores under the condi-

Table 7.18
Reasons for the low representation of women in top political posts as perceived by women and men (%)

	Views of women	Views of men
Women's entry into politics is hindered by family obligations.	79	70
It is the result of systematic efforts by men to keep decision-making in their own hands.	47	29
Women are not interested in politics.	43	54
Politics is dirty and unscrupulous, which is why women prefer to avoid it.	42	37
Women are insufficiently prepared for public and political posts.	27	25
Women have low self-esteem.	21	22
Women do not have the necessary skills and make-up for politics.	7	15

Note: Respondents were free to choose three reasons, which is why their sum exceeds 100%.
Source: Institute for Public Affairs, June 2002.

tion that "the family must not bear the brunt". Public office amounts to yet another activity, and even if other family members are willing to help run the household, most household chores remain on the woman's shoulders during the weekends, increasing her workload considerably. The family vs. public office conflict is easier to handle at the local level. Complications arise when a woman decides to accept public office at the national level, which usually entails repeated one-week separations from her family.

In the eyes of women, the second most important reason is systematic efforts by men to keep decision-making in their own hands (47%); among men, this reason ranked fourth (29%). Forty three percent of women, but 54% of men cited a lack of interest in politics among women. The dirty and unscrupulous nature of politics was mentioned by 42% of women and 37% of men. Women's insufficient preparation of women for public and political posts was cited by approximately one fourth of female and male respondents, and their low self-esteem by one fifth. Finally, 7% of women, but twice as many men (15%) said that women do not have the necessary skills for politics. Needless to say, this form of argumentation is not sustainable given the educational attainment of women in Slovakia, which is slightly higher than that of men. Furthermore, there are new and new examples from other European countries, which prove that it is possible to find sufficient number of qualified female candidates for top political posts.

8. IMAGE OF WOMEN IN SLOVAK MEDIA

Monika Bosá – Milan Minarovič – Martina Sekulová

Monika Bosá authored Sections 8.1.3. and 8.1.4. and co-authored Sections 8.1.1. and 8.1.2.
Milan Minarovič is the co-author of Sections 8.1.1. and 8.1.2.
Martina Sekulová authored Section 8.2.

8. IMAGE OF WOMEN IN SLOVAK MEDIA

8.1. SEARCHING FOR STEREOTYPES OF FEMININITY AND OLD AGE[1]

8.1.1. MEDIA, SOCIETY AND GENDER ISSUES

The mass media play a very important role in defining the social reality. They participate in shaping public discourses on various issues, reproduce these discourses and involve in them also people who have not been directly confronted with the particular issues yet.

In the words of Jean Baudrillard, the mass media not only "represent" the world around us; they increasingly define what this world is really like (quoted in Giddens, 1999, p. 373). The media produce and reproduce the language that is used in the discourse and that incorporates designations, distinctions, stereotypes, myths, statuses and roles. That is why it is fair to conclude that the media possess not only political but especially social power.

Paraphrasing Pierre Bourdieu, the media's role in presenting and reproducing the individual discourses may be explained with the metaphor of eyeglasses. Journalists have special "glasses", Bourdieu argues, through which they see certain things and not others, and through which they see the things they see in the special way they see them (Bourdieu 2002, pp. 15 – 16).

Naturally, the media are an important factor that affects the overall situation of women on the labor market and in society as such. What is the image of women that the media offer us? At first glance, it seems rather agreeable. Women are often portrayed as devoted, caring, loving and selfless at every age and – on top of everything else – attractive. Many are successful in the public sphere as artists, managers, scientists or other professionals. But if we take a close look at this positive image, is it truly as flattering as it seems?

In order to answer this question, we analyzed select print media to examine the media discourse on femininity issues on the one hand and issues of ageing and old age on the other. We assumed that by deconstructing the media image of women in general and mature women in particular, we would understand how the media influence the everyday life of women and their status on the labor market and in society.

To do so, we carried out content analysis of select dailies and magazines. Our identification of media images of femininity, ageing and old age in select daily papers was followed up by examination of the images of successful women and men in select magazines.

Before we present the results of our analysis, let us note that we base our study on the theoretical distinction between gender and sex that was catalyzed by the second wave of feminism. The term "gender" came to refer to socially (i.e. culturally, historically and geographi-

[1] Articles for the content analysis were collected by Andrea Brndiarová, Dávid Bosý, Jana Fedorková, Daniela Greššová, Eva Kručayová and Veronika Strýčková.

The authors would like to express their gratitude to Marianna Szapuová and Zuzana Kiczková with the Center of Gender Studies, Katarína Minarovičová and Dávid Bosý with the EsFem civic association and Jarmila Filadelfiová with the Institute for Public Affairs for their valuable advice in the field of gender theory and gender-sensitive research. Also, they would like to thank Zora Bútorová for her help at all stages of the research as well as her careful editing of the final text.

cally) set characteristics that are attributed to people based on their biological sex. This bred new methodological approaches that use gender as a central category.

In traditional approaches to studying the social relations between women and men, biological differences were the principal platform to explain and interpret all observable differences, and, even more importantly, to derive generalized and stereotypical approaches to masculinity and femininity. Due to this philosophy, almost all known phenomena – particularly social inequalities and the division of labor – could be considered "natural", taken for granted and unchangeable. This perception and justification of social inequalities remains widespread even today. An argument against purely biological interpretations of "natural" differences between women and men was poignantly formulated by Ann Oakley: "It is true that every society proceeds from biological sex as the basic criterion; beyond this point, however, no two cultures completely agree on what sets one gender apart from another… Every society believes it is its own definition of gender that best captures the biological duality of sexes" (Oakley, 2000, p. 121).

A particularly productive definition of gender was introduced by Sandra Harding, who described three mutually connected aspects of gender:

Gender symbolism, i.e. assigning a gender to phenomena that have no relation to sex differences. Gender symbolism is inherently present in our language and the ways we use it. Most importantly, assigning a "masculine" or "feminine" connotation implies an evaluating, hierarchical standpoint and creates an impression of society's generally dichotomous structure.

Gender structure of human activities. i.e. assigning gender characteristics to entire fields of human activity and institutions, regardless of whether they are actually performed by women or men. The division of labor thus gains a "natural" character. Again, an element of hierarchy is present with respect to masculine or feminine characteristics: "whatever is thought of as manly is more highly valued than what is thought of as womanly".

Individual gender, i.e. the socially constructed individual identity that individual members of society create, accept and deal with (Harding, 1986, p. 18).

There are many surveys examining the gender aspects of the media discourse on women and men. They focus mostly on the content of media statements, especially on how they define femininity and construct social gender inequalities by using direct negative connotations related to femininity or endorsing and proliferating gender stereotypes (Curran – Renzetti, 2003, p. 183). A favored research focus is the media's influence on society.

The media confirm and cement society's gender structure and strengthen inequalities between women and men. Gender connotations become even more distinct in combination with age. From the viewpoint of the multiplication of disadvantages based on gender and age, interesting findings were produced by a survey carried out in 1994 for the American Association of Pensioners, which showed that television shows broadcast in prime time featured only 15 percent of women over 45. Only 3 in 100 main characters were older than 65, and only one in 100 was a woman (Curran – Renzetti, 2003, p. 194).

8.1.2. IMAGES OF FEMININITY AND OLD AGE IN SELECT DAILY PAPERS
Selection of the Sample

The content analysis set out to identify images of femininity and ageing as presented by the four nationwide daily papers *Nový Čas*, *Sme*, *Pravda* and *Hospodárske noviny*. The dailies were selected based on two criteria: readership or circulation, and type of coverage.

Nový Čas is a tabloid that was the country's largest nationwide daily in terms of circulation and readership at the time of the survey. *Sme* and *Pravda* are serious dailies that shared the second and third place on the list of Slovakia's largest daily papers. *Hospodárske noviny* is a daily specializing in business news that ranked sixth in terms of sold copies.

The time frame of the analysis was 12 months between July 1, 2004, and June 31, 2005.

The analysis examined selected newspaper articles and pictures. The basic selection criterion was that they feature key words listed in the "vocabulary of relevant expressions" related to women, femininity, ageing and old age. The vocabulary featured roots and derivatives of the following words: a) woman, mother, wife, female forms of professions such as artist, actor, architect, etc.; b) pensioner, old age, grandmother, grandfather, elderly, old man, old woman, senior citizen, pension, pension reform.

The selection of articles and photographs for the sample or rejecting them was a six-step process:

- Steps 1 to 3: selection of articles based on a direct reference to women or femininity and to ageing or old age, respectively, in an article's headline, subhead or lead paragraph;

- Step 4: selection of articles based on featured photographs in cases where they did not make a direct reference to the examined issues in their headlines, subheads or leads. The photographs had to depict a woman or a person showing physical characteristics usually associated with old age (e.g. wrinkles, grey hair, bald head, bent back, etc.);

- Step 5: elimination of articles that discussed or reported only the legislative and financial aspects of the pension reform, and not elderly people or the phenomenon of ageing;

- Step 6: a control cycle to verify the completeness of the sample. For this purpose we used the database of the Slovak National Bibliography and carried out an electronic newspaper search using the same key words and relevant expressions (http://www.cd-rom.uniba.sk/).

The place of Mature Women in the Daily Press

Based on the selection process described above, we identified 723 articles discussing women, elderly people, and the pension reform (see Table 8.1). Of those, 313 were published by the *Sme* daily, 143 by the *Pravda* daily, 145 by the *Nový Čas* daily, and 122 by the *Hospodárske noviny* daily. In line with step 5, 131 articles discussing exclusively the legislative and financial aspects of the pension reform were eliminated from the sample. The resulting sample comprised 592 articles.

Table 8.1
Occurrence of select topics in nationwide (total numbers)

	Sme	Pravda	Nový Čas	Hospodárske noviny	Total
Women in general	90	71	32	32	225
Mothers	77	16	46	26	165
Elderly people and population ageing	86	33	56	27	202
Pension reform	60	23	11	37	131
All topics together	313	143	145	122	723
All topics except pension reform	253	120	134	85	592

Source: *Sme, Pravda, Nový Čas* and *Hospodárske noviny* dailies, July 1, 2004 – June 31, 2005.

The place of mature women in the daily press is clear almost at first glance. The front pages of daily papers do not often carry explicit references to women; on the other hand, the back pages feature ample references to them. Women are referred to especially as the recipients of assistance, as those that are cared for or neglected by the law, or as the source of problems.[2] The low visibility of women on the front pages reflects their low representation in decision-making positions in politics and business.[3]

Let us now look at the placement of articles on women in each of the daily papers examined. Most articles concerning women and elderly people that the *Sme* daily ran on its front pages (i.e. in the *News* and *Business* sections) discussed the pension reform. The situation of mature women and men on the labor market was addressed mostly by articles in the paper's regular *Career* supplement published on Tuesdays (from page 34 onward). These articles focused on the difficulties that elderly people encounter when seeking jobs, as well as on discrimination and gender inequality in the field of remuneration; they often provided information on ways to help this disadvantaged category of citizens, and other assistance projects.

Sometimes, gender equality issues were touched upon by articles in the *Foreign News* section (from page 9 onward), which occasionally discussed violations of women's universal rights around the world and featured positive examples from some countries.

Images of women presented by women themselves – often in the form of an interview with women from the culture or art community – were found especially in the *Culture* supplement. These images were often accompanied by various research findings on women in their mature years (e.g. on their increased dependence on drugs, addiction to computer games, on lonely women suffering from isolation, etc.). Articles on women in the pages of the *Weekend* supplement carried a similar tone. Women, particularly their health, also formed an important part of the *Health* supplement.

The *Pravda* daily also tended to carry articles on women in the back pages of the paper. The *Saturday* supplement was devoted mostly to the "lighter" side of the news, but also featured interviews with successful women from the health care sector, culture, politics or other walks of public life. The *Couple* supplement, which focused on famous couples, offered a specific type of space for women. The daily's supplements on career and culture were comparable to those of the *Sme* daily. *Pravda*'s specialty was the *Intimacy* supplement, which may have been designed to educate readers on sexuality and partnership relations, but in fact supported gender stereotypes and focused on piquant and *risqué* information. This supplement carried brief interviews with three women and men from three age categories focused exclusively on partnership (i.e. heterosexual) relations that were presented in the vein of gender stereotypes. Besides in these supplements, articles on women also appeared in the *World* and *Home* sections, which apart from information on legislative changes featured mostly curiosities and other space-fillers.

The *Nový Čas* daily occasionally focused on women and their problems in its *Slovakia* and *Regions* sections. Elsewhere, however, these issues were covered only sporadically and usually formed part of a story with a different central topic such as health, services, the labor market or the topic of the day. The daily's specialty was various so-called series of stories that represented yellow journalism at its best. During the period examined, *Nový Čas* pub-

---

[2]   Compare to Curran – Renzetti, 2003, p. 184. Various minorities and risk population groups have a similar place in the coverage of daily papers.

[3]   One should note that at the time this content analysis was carried out, the Slovak government had no female cabinet members, while in the Slovak parliament, women controlled 19% of seats and virtually no important parliamentary posts (see Section 7.3. of this publication).

lished series entitled *Crane Operator, Alcoholic's Confession, This Is How We Live, Expectant Mother in a Coma* or *Prostitute's Confession*. True to its tabloid format, *Nový Čas* teemed with articles on female celebrities, their makeup, love affairs, etc.

In line with its business focus, the *Hospodárske noviny* daily published far fewer articles on women than the other three papers. Stories on successful women were a rarity and – as in the *Sme* and *Pravda* dailies – were usually run in supplements, such as *Career, Enterprise* or *Europe*. For every five interviews with men, the daily ran one interview with a woman. During the period examined, *Hospodárske noviny* published several articles that discussed the harmonization of professional and family life. But like the other dailies, the paper viewed the problem primarily as a women's issue, as opposed to a broader social problem.

Images of femininity

Image One: Family as the Primary Sphere of a Woman's Activity

The most distinct image revealed by our analysis of articles on women is that of a strong bond between women and family. Regardless of the topic of these articles – legislative changes concerning the family, social security, education, success stories or commemorative pieces on the lives of anniversary-celebrating pensioners – all of them document that the main issues determining the media discourse on women in Slovakia include family relations, taking care of relatives, and love as the central pillar of life.

Taking care of relatives – be it children or adults – is considered a natural role for women. Not a single article described a case in which these activities were performed by a man – of course, apart from the atypical cases of lonely fathers forced to play the role of their wives. The anchoring of women in the family was presented as "natural" and ensuing from a biological foundation.[4] Being devoted to family and taking care of children is considered a woman's key obligation throughout her life.

In this context, women's professional career, their personal ambitions and interests are regarded as something secondary. The private sphere, represented by family as the principal "platform" for women's self-definition and self-fulfillment, pushes their professional interests to the background. As Zuzana Kiczková pointed out, "there are various reasons why a woman is not considered a full member of the labor force – either she must fulfill her maternal obligations, or it is assumed that even a single and childless woman will eventually get married and have children" (Kiczková, 1997, pp.10 – 12).

One of the main qualities of women is selflessness, something that is expected of them throughout their adult lives. Articles on harmonizing professional and family life are almost exclusively about women-mothers. Slovak daily papers take two basic approaches to the subject: first, they discuss models for providing support and assistance to employed mothers; second, they glorify the self-sacrificing nature of women via the memories of older women.

In one article, the wife of a leading Slovak politician talks about her life. When she speaks of an ambition she was unable to satisfy due to family obligations, she does not say whether her husband helped take care of the household:

---

[4] As Hana Haveľková writes, the argument that the placement of women in the private sphere (particularly as mothers-educators) is "natural" is historically determined. She refers to the historian Ute Gerhard, who argues that this role was viewed as a *social necessity* for women at the end of the 18th century, but by the mid-19th century it had come to be perceived as *natural* (Haveľková, 1995, pp. 30 – 31).

> *"I didn't begin to study until this late because I didn't go to university right after high school; a year later I got married and had children."*

("Figeľová zostáva na Slovensku – študuje teológiu"
['Figeľová Stays in Slovakia, Studies Theology']
Sme, October 11, 2004)

Another story concerns a 90-year old high school graduate who is happy finally to have fulfilled an old ambition:

> *"I have achieved something I promised myself I would achieve a long time ago… But back in 1931, I preferred marriage to a farmer over my studies."*

("Deväťdesiatročná maturantka"
['Ninety-Year-Old Graduate']
Sme, June 5, 2004).

All articles that speak of the bonds between women and their families have a strong normative tone. They speak positively of, and even exalt, selflessness by women and their willingness to accept "the woman's lot" and "the rhythm of life" as mothers and grandmothers.

In this context, maternity or motherliness is not understood as a concrete situation in a concrete woman's life but rather as a quality that is tied to motherhood, i.e. a willingness to perform unpaid and invisible work, self-sacrifice, and empathy for the problems of others, emotionality and a permanent readiness to help others. Maternity thus becomes a quality that is expected of women regardless of their actual marital status, age, personal ambitions or attitudes. Consequently, society comes to appreciate such abilities, talents and "natural gifts" in women that are of little use on the labor market; they are more useful on the level of interpersonal relations, emotionality and empathy than with respect to performance and growth strategies, for either the woman herself or the company she works for. This concept expects that women will always treat their job as something secondary. It is assumed that they will be absent from work for longer periods, that they will not perform at 100%, and therefore they will earn less, again regardless of each concrete woman's marital status.

Motherhood thus becomes a trap: women are treated as if every single one of them were a mother. Social control of women's maternal behavior is extremely strong. Since childhood, women are raised to be selfless and to put aside their ambitions for the benefit of others, all of which is interpreted as part of their preparation for motherhood. It is assumed that these qualities are "natural" and that women must respect them. Their reward, in their role as mothers, is to be put on a pedestal. In other words, maternity is interchangeable with femininity.

And what is society's attitude towards women who do not have children? Many people think of them as "unfeminine women" or as "bad mothers". Consequently, not only mothers but also childless women risk being accused of failure and selfishness.

Image Two: Compulsory Beauty

Clichés such as "the fair sex", "the prettier half" and others suggest that beauty is considered a "natural" characteristic of women and one of the "typical" attributes of femininity. At the same time, articles that discuss female beauty often question its "natural quality". They provide readers with detailed information on what some women have to do to retain their good appearance, or what others are able or willing to endure if they lack this "natural" quality. By pointing out the effort women must make to attain beauty, the press questions the very natural character of this beauty. Therefore, female beauty becomes a social imperative rather than the natural and inherent characteristic of a woman.

In this context, Naomi Wolf (2000) argues that women in Western culture are damaged by the pressure to conform to an idealized concept of female beauty. She says that the beauty myth is political, a way of maintaining the patriarchal system and the unequal status of women within society.

The strength of this imperative may be seen in the fact that most stories on older women feature photographs of them when they were young. For instance, a story on a woman celebrating her 106th birthday was accompanied by two photographs – one from her most recent birthday celebration, and one from her youth. The accompanying comment stated that *"sprightly Alžbeta Budínska is as beautiful today as she was when she was young"* ("Alžbeta Budinská už žije v treťom storočí" ['Alžbeta Budinská's Life Spans Three Centuries'] *Sme*, January 13, 2005).

Articles on older men rarely feature such archival photographs. The only exception is stories on successful men that document their entire professional careers; however, the purpose of running such photographs is to illustrate their activity, profession or long-term experience, as opposed to their physical appearance.

Beauty is particularly important to women in certain professions. In this context, Naomi Wolf speaks of "professional beauty qualification", referring to occupations that view good looks as an indispensable prerequisite. The author notes that in the past, these professions included dancers, models, courtesans, etc. Their social status was very low, as most of their practitioners were morally condemned and poorly paid. In recent years, however, all occupations in which women achieve success are quickly reclassified as showcase professions – of course, this only applies to the women working in them (Wolf, 2000, p. 32).

One of chief attributes of beauty is a slim body that supports a youthful image. There is no femininity without beauty; and there is no beauty without a slim body. This is the clear message of the next article:

> *"She lives in a small apartment for seniors... Although she is over 60, she still longs for a slim figure. Age: 64."*

> ("Naďa Urbánková: Stále chcem byť štíhla"
> ['Naďa Urbánková: I Still Want to Be Slim']
> *Nový Čas*, November 8, 2004)

The recent arrival of plastic surgery has further strengthened the beauty imperative. On the other hand, the "obligation" of women to look beautiful also carries a requirement that she do so in a "natural" way. One often comes across articles portraying women who chose to "improve" their face or figure as being "caught in the act".

In the daily press, the issue of plastic surgery is associated exclusively with "beautifying" and "rejuvenating" operations. The medical aspects are pushed into the background, and plastic surgery becomes a domain reserved primarily for women and femininity:

> *"The event is supposed to show that all women want to be beautiful. We also want society to stop mocking those who want to change their looks."*

> ("Cenu za najkrajšiu ženu získava plastický chirurg"
> ['Prize for the Most Beautiful Woman Goes to a Plastic Surgeon']
> *Pravda*, December 14, 2004)

To summarize: The beauty imperative restricts the potential of women by forcing them to pay excessive attention to improving their appearance at the expense of developing their skills and creativity. Still, most women "voluntarily" submit to it.

Image Three: Women for Men – Women as (Sexual) Objects

Even in the modern age, when all women's rights are formally guaranteed, women must overcome barriers that ensue from the way femininity is defined. In the words of Viera Bačová, "femininity is defined as adaptation to the power of men. The main quality of femininity and the women has to be – and also is –their attractiveness for men. Attractiveness includes physical appearance, encouraging a man's ego, exclusive heterosexuality, sexual availability without sexual assertiveness, taking care of children, suppressing 'strong' emotions such as anger, and sociability – men like women that are 'nice'" (Bačová, 2005, p. 180).

The perception of women as sexual objects who are attractive for men affects the employment sphere and cements the unequal status of women and men. Ľuba Kobová speaks about the disqualification of women within the public sphere: "It takes place in the form of pinning up degrading, almost pornographic depictions of women, not only in men's locker rooms, but also on billboards, on buses, and in other forms of advertising; it takes place through sexual harassment. The practice disqualifies women and constantly reminds them that although they have entered the public sphere, 'sex matters'" (Kobová 2005, p. 275).

While the sexual harassment of women is usually seen as involving only sexual behavior, it actually represents a demonstration of power to someone who is assumed to be submissive.[5] During the period examined, the four daily papers did not publish many articles on the subject. Let us mention some examples.

One article on sexual harassment in the workplace, which was aimed primarily at men, used an informative tone. As the article poignantly began:

> "Harassment is not a ridiculous American invention but a serious problem that causes stress and depression in its victims and affects their performance at work."

> "Pozor na pohľady do výstrihu"
> ['Beware of Staring Down a Woman's Top']
> Pravda's Intimacy supplement, November 12, 2004)

The article also presents statements by women with experience of harassment. One passage describes various forms of harassment:

> "Harassment may be not only verbal but also visual – pictures of naked women in lascivious poses on computer monitors, vulgar e-mails or gestures; those certainly do not boost work morale."

> (ibid)

Despite its commendable intention of pointing out the seriousness of sexual harassment, the article featured an illustration that made light of the issue and allowed sexual harassment to be interpreted as a source of amusement.

---

5   In most cases it is a woman, but sometimes a man who is in subordinated position. Regardless of whether sexual harassment is perpetrated on a woman by a man or the other way round, it is equally a demonstration of power in the workplace. In a heteronormative environment, where men are expected to be active and women to be passive, a male victim of sexual harassment is stigmatized in other attributes of manhood as well (e.g. prestige, authority, strength, activity, career, etc.).

Humor is an extremely dangerous form of disqualification of women in the public sphere: if remarks, comments and statements on the supposed unreliability, incompetence, weakness or other shortcomings of women are presented as a joke, it is very difficult to object. In the best case, refusing to accept such humor may make others think that the person has a poor sense of humor; in the worst case, it provokes further mockery, accusations of hysteria, etc. Ridicule can be extremely hurtful. Moreover, statements presented in a joking way are emotional and usually easy to remember, which amplifies their normative function.[6]

When analyzing the print media's attitude to sexual harassment, it is important to note where the topic is placed. For instance, if a paper runs an article informing readers of this form of violent treatment of women in a supplement called *Intimacy – special section dedicated to issues of love and sex*, it predetermines the context in which the topic will be perceived. The human rights and labor law aspects of the problem are pushed into the background, and the paper gives the impression that this is a personal or even an intimate subject and that the main motive behind sexual harassment is sexuality. Responsibility for sexual harassment is thus indirectly shifted onto women themselves. Associating sexual harassment with sex and sexuality is a frequent and serious mistake that further victimizes the victims of sexual harassment. A public and political problem is transformed into a private issue, and women who actively participate on the labor market become sexual objects. It even invites the question of whether the frivolous placement and treatment of this topic might not sometimes itself be seen as a form of sexual harassment.

But the reduction of women to sexual objects can take other forms as well. All the daily papers we analyzed are designed for a mixed male and female readership. Despite that, it was sometimes difficult to escape the impression hat these papers assume a male reader, perhaps due to an unintentional identification of mankind with manhood. A telling example of this could be an article that apparently set out to eliminate prejudices regarding the sexual activity of older people. Although it described an active sex life as a good way for mature women and men to maintain their physical and mental fitness, it could not avoid falling into stereotypical lines of thought:

> "*A substantially younger partner may truly revive sexual activity – this was known not only by 80-year-old Russian generals who maintained their physical fitness by having sex with young girls, but also by sexologists.*"

> ("Najúčinnejší liek na starobu? Sex"
> ['Best Medicine for Old Age? Sex']
> *Pravda*, October 1, 2004)

While the article was originally addressed to mature women as well, and set out to endorse and "defend" their sexual activity, it somehow forgot all about mature women. The author neglected the mature woman with her autonomous female sexuality, and replaced her with a younger woman as a tool to enhance male sexuality, as a pill for rejuvenation. Needless to say, this approach endorses the image of women as non-autonomous beings that are here "for others".

Even more explicit are these stereotypes in articles on men who – in keeping with the stereotype of men's uncontrollable sexuality and childishness – seek to build up their confidence

---

[6] Who doesn't remember at least one joke about blondes, mothers-in-law, female teachers or wives? Of course, there are also jokes about men, for instance policemen. However, they are not ridiculed as men but as representatives of a certain profession.

through extramarital affairs with much younger partners. While these articles are primarily aimed at criticizing the behavior of these men, one does not have to look far to see also the other dimension of presenting the problem. On the one hand, they feature either passive or manipulative mistresses that are interested in mature men because of their social status or wealth; on the other hand, they present wives that "save" or "help" their husbands:

> *"... paradoxically, they may be saved by the first wife that fails to fly off the handle at her husband's infidelity."*
>
> ("Mladá milenka vracia druhý dych"
> ['Young Mistress Brings Second Wind']
> *Pravda*, February 11, 2005)

Image Four: Successful Women

When writing about working women in their mature years, the four daily papers examined presented them mostly as successful women. Articles on them were placed mostly in specialized weekly supplements and focused on their activities in professional fields such as culture, art, show business, etc. The exception was interviews with women that were run in sections on employment and careers; here, mature women were represented mostly by managers and executives.

When introducing women in management positions, most articles did not omit to point out that their success was "not exactly an everyday occurrence". This invites the question of whether portraying successful women as something exceptional helps to motivate other women or whether it supports the stereotype that successful women are an "unnatural" phenomenon.

One article on women in managerial posts that explicitly rejected gender stereotypes and interpreted them as one reason for the low representation of women in higher posts, also came to conclusions along the same lines.

> *"This process* [i.e. the entrance of women onto the labor market and into upper management posts at work] *is hindered by obstacles consisting of prejudices, fears and clichés."*
>
> ("Mojou šéfkou je žena"
> ['My Boss Is a Woman']
> *Hospodárske noviny*, November 4, 2004)

First, the article lists some "typically female qualities" to establish the pluses or advantages of women:

> *"But women are – not always but in many respects – better bosses than their male colleagues. They are more communicative, they are able to juggle several things at once, they have a team spirit, and they are creative."*
>
> (ibid)

Next, the article tries to "advise" women by listing other female qualities that women in management posts should avoid showing or using:

> *"Do not advertise your feminine side too much ... it doesn't support your authority."*
>
> (ibid)

Although the article verbally condemns gender stereotypes, they still "show up" through the author's way of thinking, as a subconscious mechanism that works on a symbolic level or as a control mechanism that shows up in the language used. Gender stereotypes thus become an undisputed and even indisputable fact of the "world order". This example illustrates how complicated it is to expose and reflect critically on stereotypes within ourselves, so to speak. At the same time, it shows that without deeper understanding of gender as the principle on which society is organized, it is impossible to avoid the pitfalls created by stereotypical concepts of masculinity and femininity.

Interestingly, the media seem to view preserving femininity, i.e. the ability to *be a woman*, as more important than women's actual performance at work. Men do not have to expend energy on justifying their presence in the world of labor to the media. Although the stereotypical image of masculinity also plays a role in building a career, masculinity never becomes an obstacle to getting a job or a promotion, which is why the media do not view it as noteworthy. Unlike interviews with women that discuss the issue of femininity at great length, interviews with men completely avoid the masculinity issue. On the labor market, masculinity is considered natural, a standard. Women, for their part, are more frequently confronted with the need to prove their professional and managerial qualities and to explain the professional success they have achieved "despite" being women.

A number of articles, particularly those published in the *Career* supplement, featured advice for women on how to achieve success. One offered a "manual on how to survive within a male work team":

> *"Overall professional appearance: A woman should make a fresh and pleasant impression. She should have nice manners, moves and gestures – everything in moderation. An appropriate outfit puts a nice finishing touch on the professional look.*

> *"Behavior: A woman must have a good command of etiquette. She should not be audacious, arrogant or too self-assured, nor too apprehensive or easily intimidated. While men appreciate a sense of humor, it is important to avoid too close friendships, let alone flirting. It is important to concentrate on your work performance, which does not require close friendships. On the other hand, if the remarks or statements of a colleague offend you, you should admonish him in an acceptable form.*

> *"Communication: Speak calmly, serenely, to the point, and look your partner in the eye. Excessive gesturing takes attention away from the subject and may undermine the woman's position. Also, remember to avoid being impertinent.*

> *"Professional performance: A professional attitude to your job is the only way to win authority among men. Remember to avoid excessive openness and do not share your personal problems with a colleague.*

> *"Take men's advice: The authority of a woman will not suffer if she asks a colleague to help her when she is at her wit's end. They will not take it as incompetence and will be only too glad to show off their knowledge and skills."*

> ("Ženy v mužskom kolektíve"
> ['Women in a Male Team']
> *Pravda*'s *Career* supplement, February 5, 2005)

The quoted advice documents the stereotypical and dichotomous perception of the female and male worlds as completely different from each other. The article creates the impression that men are "natural" players on the labor market but women must learn "special" communication skills. While most of the advice given would be equally useful to men as to women, the article repeatedly emphasized "femininity", as opposed to "masculinity", to guarantee results.

In the words of Naomi Wolf, if a woman wants to be successful on the labor market and in her professional career, she must be *feminine, but not too feminine* (Wolf, 2000). Of course, this kind of recommendation is too vague as it does not clearly demarcate the limits of "acceptable" femininity. Besides, the definition of "adequate femininity" always depends on the circumstances – i.e. who sets the limits, and what the motives are. So, women face the constant risk that their behavior will be viewed either as too much or too little feminine.

The challenge of using the "survival kit" correctly was illustrated by a photograph of an exhausted woman with her head on a desk. The caption said: *Successful woman.*

One of the world's greatest accolades for achieving success in the domain of science, art and community involvement is the Nobel Prize. During the period examined, the prize was awarded to two women – Austrian author Elfriede Jelinek and Kenyan environmental activist Wangari Maathai. Slovakia's leading daily papers presented these successful women in a rather controversial manner.

The jury's decision to bestow the Nobel Prize for Literature on Jelinek made the *Pravda* daily dispute the point of awarding a Nobel Prize in this area in a story called "Akú cenu má Nobelova cena za literatúru?" ['What Is the Value of the Nobel Prize for Literature?'], published on December 11, 2004. Apart from running her picture, the daily mentioned the laureate only in the lead paragraph of the article, noting that she had not accepted the prize in person and calling her the *enfant terrible* of Austrian literature. The article focused on controversies surrounding the laureates of the Nobel Prize for Literature. The *Sme* daily, for its part, published an article on October 8, 2004, headlined "Nobelova cena Rakúšanke Elfriede Jelinek" ['Nobel Prize to Austrian Elfriede Jelinek'] using matter-of-fact, informative language and featuring a brief biography of the author.

On the other hand, *Sme* showed considerable reserve in commenting on Wangari Maathai, the most recent laureate of the Nobel Peace Prize:

> "The decision from Oslo surprised many. The favorites included the boss of the International Atomic Energy Agency, the Pope or... Václav Havel... Kenyan Maathai is almost unknown around the world."
>
> ("Afričanka, ktorá sadila stromy"
> ['An African Woman Who Planted Trees']
> *Sme*, October 9, 2004)

The article was accompanied by a photograph that showed a man holding up a portrait of Wangari Maathai and a woman planting trees in the background. The picture further underlined the insignificant and even "unreal" nature of the Nobel Peace Prize laureate.

In this case *Pravda* did better. On December 11, 2004 it published an interview with Maahtai headlined "Príroda tiež potrebuje slobodu" ['Nature Needs Freedom Too']. The questions in the interview were aimed directly at the work of the fresh Nobel Prize laureate. The text was illustrated with a photograph of Maathai posing with her award.

The way in which these papers covered the stories of women who had received one of the world's most coveted awards for professional achievement indicates a certain division, even schizophrenia, in the daily press in Slovakia. On the one hand, the papers declared support for the equality of women and presented successful women in their pages; on the other hand, they questioned the very nature of women's ambitions and even made skeptical comments on the performance and qualities of the most successful women. We believe that the main reason women and their professional achievements are portrayed in this way is that journalists succumb to gender stereotypes in juxtaposing the male and female worlds, identifying the former with "the public sphere" and the latter with "the private sphere". Although most articles were undoubtedly written with good intentions, the media images of women and men that they presented were not truly equal.

Attempts at Alternative Perceptions

The content analysis of these dailies also identified some articles, particularly run by *Hospodárske noviny*, which strove to expose and undermine gender stereotypes. For instance, an article titled "Práca alebo rodina? Stála dilema" ['Career or Family? The Eternal Dilemma'] published on February 17, 2005 stressed that the division of labor within families had to be changed if women and men were to enjoy equal opportunities on the labor market. The article concluded that Slovak women have fewer options than women in other European countries. Besides measures to optimize the work regime of women and enable the employment of mothers, the daily stressed the need to "break mental barriers", to "eliminate inequalities between men and women on the labor market" and to "share family roles and duties".

On April 18, 2004, *Hospodárske noviny* ran a story titled "Rovnaké zaobchádzanie v pozornosti EÚ" ['Equal Treatment Under EU Scrutiny'] that discussed the phenomenon of gender segregation in certain economic sectors and professions, which according to the authors was one of the main causes of the lingering inequalities in the remuneration of women and men. A week later, the paper ran a story headlined "Nové programy na podporu žien" ['New Programs to Support Women'] which discussed positive measures to eliminate gender segregation. Another article titled "Slovenky patria k najpracovitejším v Európe" ['Slovak Women Among Hardest Working in Europe'] from April 26, 2005 was devoted to gender segregation and unpaid labor.

The articles examined rarely criticized lingering gender stereotypes as one of the main reasons for the inequalities between women and men. One exception was a story headlined "Mojou šéfkou je žena" ['My Boss Is a Woman'] that was run by *Hospodárske noviny* on November 4, 2004. The story analyzed statistical data on the representation of women and men in top executive positions and explicitly criticized the harmfulness of gender stereotypes.

Another encouraging example of an approach free of gender stereotypes was an article published by *Hospodárske noviny* in April 2005. The story observed that stereotypes of femininity and the role of women formed one of the main obstacles to female entrepreneurship and the success of women on the labor market in general:

> *"A man should not be dominant and a woman should not be limited to taking care of the family; a woman has the right to do business and to work, which is why support is extended to female entrepreneurs."*

("Záujem žien muži neberú často vážne"
['Women's Interests Often Not Taken Seriously by Men']
Hospodárske noviny, April 1, 2005)

The article emphasized that employment is the key to the economic independence and self-reliance of women. It pointed out the greater willingness of women to perform "auxiliary" and "support" (mostly unpaid) labor, as well as the general tendency to underrate women wanting to launch their own businesses.

"Wives who help their husbands run a business can be underestimated. The status of men [on the labor market] *is simpler; they have no respect for a businesswoman or a woman who wants to launch her business."*

(ibid)

During the period examined from 2004 – 2005, all four daily papers were dominated by stereotypical images of women and femininity. The only difference was in how they were presented. While gender stereotypes were hardly apparent in *Sme*, *Pravda* (except for its *Intimacy* supplement) and *Hospodárske noviny*, *Nový Čas* presented them explicitly.

Although all dailies examined, except *Nový Čas*, strove to present positive portraits of women based on a conscious rejection of gender discrimination, they still reflected subconscious gender stereotypes as their overall image of women featured the following:

• Women are predestined to find fulfillment within the family, especially through maternity;

• Maternity (i.e. care and self-sacrifice) along with the duty to be attractive and beautiful is identified with femininity.

• Women always focus their efforts on others rather than on themselves;

• The perception of women as sexual objects that are attractive to men also affects the employment sphere; society sexualizes male dominance and female subordination;

• Successful women achieve their success "despite" their femininity; this success must be "justified" as not threatening their femininity;

• The success of women is often exposed to doubts.

Images of Ageing and Old Age

Image One: An Inexorable Process Leading to the Physical Decline of "Beauty"

Beauty, good physical or mental health, and money – those are the three things we can wave goodbye to as we grow older. Or at least this is the message that the four Slovak daily papers we examined send to their readers with respect to ageing and old age.

Let us begin with the first media image, which presents ageing as a decline of beauty and old age as a state incompatible with beauty. The media repeatedly point out that elderly people are no longer beautiful and therefore should avoid performing certain roles that do not correspond to their status as old people.

This is a favorite topic in countless stories on Slovak celebrities, particularly mature female ones. Most of the articles examined minutely described and graphically documented the physical changes caused by increasing age. A good example was an article titled "Slovenské celebrity. Ako budú vyzerať na dôchodku?" ['Slovak Celebrities: What Will They Look Like after Retirement?'] published by *Nový Čas* on August 21, 2004. The story discussed the physical appearance of three women and one man 20 years from now, commenting on various attributes of old age such as wrinkles, baldness, grey hair or a bent back.

On the other hand, our content analysis also came across articles that made ironic comments about mature women who tried to improve their looks. This approach was present in a series of articles on a famous Slovak actress and her experimentation with plastic surgery:

"More than two years ago, this charming artist underwent plastic surgery on her eyelids ... she yearned to be younger, now she is paying for it."

("Chcela byť krajšia, teraz pyká!"
['She Wanted Good Looks, Now She Suffers!']
Nový Čas, June 30, 2004)

"It's only understandable that she does everything she can to avoid being marked by time."

("Priznanie: mám plastiku!"
['Confession: I Have Had Plastic Surgery!']
Nový Čas, October 30, 2004)

The articles described the actress's ageing and discussed the tricks and procedures that were supposedly going to help her "cheat old age". The series of accompanying photographs was supposed to demonstrate the shortcomings of the plastic surgery she had undergone, and to present her wrinkles as a symbol of old age. The actress is portrayed as someone trying to resist the inevitable and unable to accept her new status. On the other hand, these articles admitted such behavior was "natural" because old age meant fewer opportunities in show business, particularly acting.

Daily papers reproduce the beauty imperative. They suggest what is or is not beautiful, and decide what professions should be sensitive to signs of old age such as wrinkles and grey hair for women and baldness for men.

In other words, old age is incompatible with beauty according to the media discourse. All famous people are criticized if they fail to meet the beauty standard. If some strive to meet it via plastic surgery, they are ridiculed because that is not done at their age! In other words, plastic surgery ceases to be the answer if the public finds out. The media compete in exposing attempts by celebrities to eliminate the "stigma" of old age, and delight in presenting such attempts as swindles.

In Slovakia, the media associate beauty with youth, and fail to define beauty standards for older generations. Since beauty is a socially appreciated value, the media show some understanding for the efforts of ageing people to bring their appearance up to the beauty standard, but at the same time condemn these efforts as pointless because they see them as part of a losing battle against the inevitable and irreversible physical deterioration of ageing.

Image Two: Old Age as Poverty

The daily press in Slovakia describes the financial situation of elderly people as a factor that can have a decisive impact on the quality of their lives upon retirement.

"The third age may be the most beautiful period in life as long as people are not burdened by financial problems."

(*Nový Čas*, April 7, 2005)

At the same time, the dailies we examined occasionally tried to legitimize or justify the existing state of affairs by relativizing the position of elderly people and attributing values to their status that are not financially demanding. They argued that a lack of money should not be seen as tragic as the hierarchy of values changes upon retirement, implying that elderly people should shift their focus from material values to spiritual ones.

> "*Seventy-year-old people don't need to ride a motorcycle or go diving in the Caribbean in order to enjoy their retirement.*"

> ("Penzie: Nič nie je isté"
> ['Pensions: Nothing Is Certain']
> *Nový Čas*, November 10, 2004)

The accompanying photograph showed an old woman with grey hair, wearing a worried expression on her face and a traditional village outfit: an apron, a sweater and a scarf.

Interestingly, articles discussing the future, i.e. the old age of the contemporary young and middle generations, were quite different. Spirituality was pushed to the background and all arguments were subordinated to the inexorable demands of financial security. This was further documented by photographs (mostly from foreign databases) showing happy and affluent elderly people; they were used to illustrate articles on pension reform. The financial situation of most contemporary pensioners was presented as a warning: "You don't want to end up like this!"

One example was an article headlined "Zabezpečte si starobu bez finančných ťažkostí" ['Secure Yourself an Old Age Free of Financial Problems'] published by *Nový Čas* on September 23, 2004. The article featured two photographs: one symbolized poverty (a contemporary pensioner from the countryside) and the other prosperity (a future pensioner, i.e. you!).

The first photograph showed an old man in old-fashioned clothes counting coins. Its caption said: *Start saving now if you don't want to watch every penny after you retire* (*Nový Čas*, September 23, 2004). The photograph is a perfect example of media manipulation, as it illustrates how the media image of old age is constructed. The picture of the man counting his change was one of several the daily used repeatedly to illustrate the link between old age and poverty. But when we searched for the photograph in the daily's archive, we found that the uncut color photograph actually showed a man at a currency exchange office counting his cash after exchanging from one currency to another. Apparently, a picture of an old man counting his change in a normal transaction did not sufficiently illustrate the link between old age and poverty; hence, the photograph had to be cropped.

According to this approach, old age is practically incompatible with affluence. Old age and poverty are synonymous, with no way out for contemporary pensioners:

> "*For most people, retiring means one thing: relaxing at last, in whatever manner people associate with that word, be it fishing, knitting or weeding the garden ... Eventually, however, everyone will have to ask himself: what will I live on?*"

> ("Dôchodcovia dnes a zajtra"
> ['Pensioners Today and Tomorrow']
> *Hospodárske noviny*, June 24, 2005)

On the other hand, the media discourse on the poor socio-economic situation of elderly people goes sometimes beyond just presenting negative images of old age; it also tries to analyze and reflect on this phenomenon. One good example of this approach was an article published in the *Hospodárske noviny* daily.

> "*Pensioners are unable to compensate for the increased costs of housing, food and health care through tax write-offs or bonuses; and in some areas, their needs are greater (e.g. drugs, etc.).*"

> ("Strach zo staroby: Rub kultu mladosti"
> ['Fear of Old Age: The Seamy Side of the Youth Cult']
> *Hospodárske noviny*, January 23, 2005)

Image Three: Old Age as Illness

While the process of ageing cannot be equated to illness, let alone physical handicaps, it cannot be denied that health problems tend to increase as people get older. The dailies we examined do not question this chronobiological causality:

"Around the age of 50, unexpected blows may come: a weaker heart, osteoporosis, problems in the field of sexuality ... Still, every woman seems to be caught unawares when she finds out that something is happening to her. She feels as if her own body has just betrayed her ... What can we do about the beginning of old age?"

(Hospodárske noviny, November 3, 2004)

The images used by all the daily papers we examined to illustrate the public discourse on health and old age had a lot in common. Images of elderly people served as a traditional background to discussions of health and illness; in many cases, old age was directly identified with illness. The special supplements that all dailies carried on health and health care ran pictures of elderly people, showing that old age precludes good health. Although most articles offered solutions on how to remain in good health, they often created the impression that doing so amounted to resisting the inevitable. For younger people, good health was generally considered normal while illness was viewed as an exception. This logic was reversed with respect to elderly people, as illness was considered normal while good health was seen as a deviation from the norm.

From this viewpoint, old age is actually presented as a cluster of illnesses. Most articles create an atmosphere of anxiety and fear regarding old age. In fact, fear is a constant in the media discourse on old age. The focus is on risk categories, death, disability, limited health and stigma.

The public discourse on old age in the print media is filled with images of health and illness. At an older age, "the 'I' gradually becomes a problem for others" (Alan, 1989). In other words, elderly people require increased attention and care because they suffer from various health problems. All the daily papers examined presented references supporting this stereotype. Most articles interwove or blended old age with disability or illness, which was often amplified by graphic descriptions.[7]

This blurring of issues also appears in photographs published with articles on health and the health service in general. Although some of these articles did not make a single direct or indirect reference to old people, most were illustrated with photographs of old people.

We should note that the link between old age and health is not nearly as strong indisputable as presented in the articles. Research shows that "a deterioration in health and advanced age do not necessarily have to accompany one another ... It is difficult to separate the effect of physical decay from the social and economic factors an elderly person is exposed to" (Giddens, 1999, p. 153). Upon retirement, most elderly people lose contact with their former colleagues and lose their social networks; at the same time, their material wealth as well as their standard of living declines. These socio-economic factors may have an equal or even greater impact on the health of elderly people than their biological age.

---

[7] What is worse, the graphic material featured often did not correspond to the contents of the concrete articles. One example was a business article on disability that did not feature a single reference to senior citizens, and yet the featured photograph suggested a link between old age and disability.

Image Four: Less Adaptability and Return to Infancy

The daily papers we examined reproduced the stereotype of old age as a synonym for impaired flexibility, ability to learn and overall adaptability. "When people grow older, their orientation in the world and the related process of social adaptation become in many respects much more demanding." (Alan, 1989, p. 385).

A number of articles portrayed elderly people as unable to learn new things. At the same time, they offered a solution in the form of new technologies or education techniques that were "custom-made" for elderly people.

> *"Do you want to be able to reach your grandmother, but she refuses to use a cell phone because she doesn't understand it? There is a solution."*

> *(Nový Čas,* February 15, 2005)

The picture accompanying the story showed an elderly woman whose ignorance of information technologies is the reason why her family members have lost touch with her. Using a strong advertising tone, the article offers a solution in the form of an appliance specifically designed for elderly people.

A similarly pro-active tone was used in an article published by the *Sme* daily. It reported on a project aimed at teaching computer skills to elderly people, and observed that it had aroused significant interest.

> *"Similar projects are frequently sought by elderly people who never worked with a computer ... Almost every class is attended by some 80-year-old man who would, for instance, like to communicate via e-mail with his son who lives in Canada."*

> "Nebojte sa myší"
> ['Do Not Be Afraid of Mice']
> *Sme,* June 21, 2005.

The illustrating photograph showed an old man with a grey beard sitting behind a computer. The caption said: *Do not be afraid of a computer. It is never too late to start.*

On the other hand, some articles presented old age as a return to childhood. Most reported on institutions and facilities that provide care to elderly people. On March 29, 2005, an article run by *Nový Čas* tried to capture readers' attention with the following headline: "Máte doma dôchodcu a bojíte sa ho nechať doma samého? Pošlite ho do škôlky" ['Are You Afraid to Leave Pensioners Home Alone? Send Them to Kindergarten'].

A different example of the same approach was found in another article published by *Nový Čas.* The story was about people over 60, whom the author compared to infants:

> *"Conditions are exactly the same as in a kindergarten... The only difference is that the inmates are not under 6 years of age but older than 60!"*

> "Obedy mi prinesú na bicykloch"
> ['They Bring My Lunches by Bike']
> *Nový Čas,* August 19, 2005.

The authors of these articles rarely showed adequate respect for elderly people. They regularly addressed their sources as if speaking to small children. It seemed that the older the source, the more likely the author was to refer to them by their first name.[8]

---

[8] On the other hand, this approach also meets with criticism. A director of a retirement home quoted by the *Nový Čas* daily claimed that pensioners demanded that people respect their dignity and refer to them by their proper names, as opposed to diminutives of their first names.

Image Five: Elderly People as Victims

Impaired social adaptability and the gradual deterioration of one's mental and physical capacities are negative aspects of old age that lead elderly people to be presented as defenseless children or victims. The media pay close attention to the fact that elderly people easily fall victim to crime, often citing their age as the main reason. Such was the case of an article titled "Zlodeji berú sliepky, ovce, psov aj býky" ['Thieves Steal Hens, Sheep, Dogs and Bulls'] published by *Nový Čas* on December 5, 2005, which presented the stories of two 71- and 81-year old women who became the victims of thievery.

The old age is victimized. The main reason is the reduced cognitive abilities of people in their old years, which is implicitly assumed:

> *"The theft of the paintings was due to the pensioner's negligence."*

("Dôchodca strážca múzea zabudol zapnúť alarm"
['Pensioner Guard in Museum Forgot to Turn on Alarm']
Nový Čas, December 3, 2004).

While a modern Western society comprises four generations of people, they live side by side rather than together (Giddens, 1999). The Western model of the nuclear family also prevails in Slovakia. Elderly people who live alone often fall victim to various assaults because their loneliness invites perpetrators of all kinds. A story headlined "Falošný vnuk" ['False Grandson'] run by *Nový Čas* on December 3, 2004, told of a con on several elderly women; the swindle was facilitated by the victims' loneliness and lack of social networks.

Old age and naivety are the motifs of many articles on victims of frauds, swindles and similar cons. An article headlined "Spomedzi uterákov jej zmizlo 300-tisíc!" ['300,000 Snatched from Between Woman's Towels'] highlighted this image of "incompetence" with an unjustified generalization: "Gullible pensioners were again tricked by swindlers," wrote *Nový Čas* on December 14, 2004. A similar tone is regularly used especially by *Nový Čas*, for instance in the following article:

> *"A 33-year-old woman persuaded a 55-year-old to give her the money to take to a temple in Ukraine where she would pray in order to break the spell."*

("Modlitby za 668-tisíc Sk"
['Prayers Cost 668,000 Sk']
Nový Čas, January 14, 2005).

These articles usually feature a stereotypical observation that elderly people are easy to deceive. They use a whole range of euphemisms for elderly people such as pensioner, elder, senior, granny, grandpa, old man, etc. Virtually every story on swindles uses these euphemisms to indicate the age of the victims or divulges it directly, sometimes even in headlines: "Starenku (85) obrali o vyše štvrť milióna korún" ['Old Woman (85) Conned of over a Quarter Million'] read a *Nový Čas* headline on December 18, 2004. With the media reiterating that old age is the main reason for criminal offences against elderly people, the vicious circle is complete.

Attempts at Alternative Perceptions

Very few of the articles we examined tried to promote an active image of old age. This image was particularly to be found in stories on the activities and hobbies of retired people. Most activities corresponded to the traditional gender-specific division of labor. While men kept busy chopping wood or farming, women did craftwork, cooking, baking or making traditional pastries. Any "untraditional" activities in the portfolio of retirement homes or clubs were presented as curiosities, for instance dancing ("Babičky tancovali kankán" ['The Grannies Danced the Cancan'], *Nový Čas*, October 18, 2004) or playing darts and working out on a step-machine ("Má 92 rokov, hrá šípky a vyšíva" ['92-Year-Old Woman Plays Darts and Embroiders'], *Nový Čas*, July 28, 2005).

A different image of active old age was to be found in an article headlined "Dôchodcovia sa ešte nelúčia" ['Pensioners Aren't Yet Saying Farewell'] published by *Nový Čas* on June 15, 2005. The story covered a race for senior citizens, and quoted one of the participants: "Farewell should be said from the top, not from a wheelchair."

During the examined period, spanning summer 2004 and summer 2005, the four daily papers analyzed mostly reproduced negative age stereotypes; however, we also ran across hints of critical reflection that explicitly rejected the image of old age as inferior, and identified age stereotypes as well as their negative implications. One example was found in a series of articles published by *Hospodárske noviny* that also emphasized the strengths of old people:

> *"Old age is portrayed as something negative. It is rarely noted that elderly people are often able to remain independent in their thinking and in coping with life's many problems. They often have a detached point of view and the necessary distance; they can assess things in the context of the past as well as anticipate the future..."*

("Strach zo staroby: Rub kultu mladosti"
['Fear of Old Age: The Seamy Side of the Youth Cult'],
Hospodárske noviny, January 23, 2005)

8.1.3. IMAGES OF SUCCESSFUL WOMEN AND MEN IN SELECT MAGAZINES

Selection of the Sample and Basic Parameters of Interviews

Our analysis of weekly magazines examined interviews with professionally successful women and men, which provided ample material for a comprehensive analysis of several aspects of gender and age.

The analysis focused on interviews published by four nationwide weekly magazines. The sample comprised *Plus 7 dní*, the country's largest weekly magazine in terms of circulation, *Život*, a leading lifestyle weekly with a long tradition, *Slovenka*, the country's oldest weekly focusing on women, and the *Trend* weekly, which specializes in economic and business issues.

The time frame of the analysis was three months from March 1 to May 31, 2007, and was chosen in order to gain a fresher perspective and a distance in time from the media material examined during the content analysis of the daily papers.[9] During the examined period, these four weekly magazines published 66 interviews with successful women and men of different ages. All but one interview featured economically active professionals.

Our content analysis of the magazine interviews was a continuation of our content analysis of the daily articles, and used identical methods.

While the content analysis of the interviews with successful women and men applied a qualitative approach, it is useful to outline their basic quantitative characteristics as well. As Ta-

---

[9]   We assumed that magazines would pay increased attention to women during this period, as it included International Women's Day as well as the Mother's Day; however, this assumption was wrong.

ble 8.2 shows, all four magazines during the examined period provided substantially more space to successful men than to successful women. The ratio was approximately two to one, as 43 out of 66 interviews examined featured men while only 23 featured women.

Of course, there were differences between the various magazines. The ratio was most balanced in the *Slovenka* weekly, which published 18 interviews with women and 13 interviews with men during the period examined. At the opposite pole was the *Trend* weekly, which over the same period did not publish a single interview with a woman but ran 12 interviews with men.

Table 8.2
Number of interviews published by select weekly magazines

		Slovenka	Život	Plus 7 dní	Trend	Total
Women	Under 45	10	1	0	0	**11**
	Over 45	8	3	1	0	**12**
	Total	18	4	1	0	**23**
Men	Under 45	3	9	1	5	**18**
	Over 45	10	4	4	7	**25**
	Total	13	13	5	12	**43**

Source: The weekly magazines *Slovenka, Život, Plus 7 dní* and *Trend* , March 1 – May 31, 2007.

Let us now take a closer look at the amount of attention that the weeklies paid to issues from the public and private spheres. When interviewing successful men, all of the weekly magazines placed the main emphasis on professional issues; in the *Trend* weekly it was 100%, and in the *Plus 7 dní* weekly it was almost 100% (see Table 8.3). Professional issues also prevailed over family and partnership issues in interviews featuring women published by the *Plus 7 dní* ; however, the dominance was not as striking as in the interviews featuring men.

The *Život* and *Slovenka* weekly magazines focus on leisure and social issues. Compared to the other two weeklies, they placed a far greater emphasis on partnership relations and love, as well as on health, lifestyle and personal interests. Even their interviews featuring men focused largely on family and partnership issues.

Table 8.3
Representation of work and family issues in select weekly (%)

		Slovenka		Život		Plus 7 dní		Trend		Total	
		Work	Family	Work	Family	Work	Family	Work	Family	Work	Family
Women	Under 45	43	32	47	27	–	–	–	–	44	31
	Over 45	47	23	27	39	79	7	–	–	45	25
Men	Under 45	53	8	48	22	100	0	100	0	66	12
	Over 45	43	21	43	22	94	0	100	0	67	12

Note: Figures for the representation of issues were calculated based on the number of questions inquiring about work and family relative to the total number of questions in interviews. The remainder of the 100% figure comprises other issues.
– The magazine did not publish any interviews with successful women.
Source: The weekly magazines *Slovenka, Život, Plus 7 dní* and *Trend*, March 1 – May 31, 2007.

The difference in the professions of the women and men interviewed was also symptomatic. Interviews with successful men were not only more frequent but also more diverse in terms of their professions (see Table 8.4). Most of the interviews were with men who wielded economic or political power (e.g. as managers or politicians); they were followed by entrepreneurs and professionals from the fields of culture, entertainment and media (e.g. actors, singers or news readers) as well as from the fields of sport, business, church, services and science. On the other hand, the successful women featured in the interviews examined came mostly from the "visible" professions, such as singers, actresses, news readers and models, while there were far fewer interviews featuring female judges, managers or politicians.

Table 8.4
Professions of successful women and men interviewed by select weekly magazines

Number of interviews	Women	Men
8	–	Manager
7	–	Politician
5	Singer	–
4	Actress	Actor; singer; entrepreneur
3	News reader	–
2	Model; judge*	Sportsman; banker; news reader
1	Manager; politician	Economist; director; priest; hairstylist; oceanographer

* Two interviews with the same person.
Source: The weekly magazines *Slovenka*, *Život*, *Plus 7 dní* and *Trend*, March 1 – May 31, 2007.

Finally, let us take a look at the gender make-up of the reporters who conducted the interviews. In three out of four magazines examined, female interviewers prevailed over their male counterparts. Women contributed 90% of the interviews published by the *Slovenka* weekly, 88% of interviews run by the *Život* weekly, and 67% of interviews published by the *Plus 7 dní* weekly. The *Trend* weekly again stood at the opposite pole, as 75% of all published interviews were conducted by male reporters.

Images of Successful Women and Men Up Close

Residents of Two Worlds – Private and Public

Like the newspaper articles, the magazine interviews with successful women teemed with stereotypes as they portrayed the dichotomy of women's public and private spheres and emphasized the family as every woman's principal domain. This approach was apparent from the tone of the interviews, despite the fact that the magazine's decision to publish these interviews was motivated primarily by the professional success of the interviewees.

While all women interviewed were successful professionals, the reporters' questions repeatedly suggested that their professional accomplishments were less important than their family success in the role of wife and mother:

> *"You are a very attractive woman and very successful, too. And yet you are single. That's quite unusual – one would more expect you to be married, to have two children and a husband, along with the career."*
>
> ("V súkromí nie som lovkyňa" ['I Am No Huntress in Private'])
> (an interview with a woman over 45)
> *Život* No.10, March 5, 2007.)

If the women interviewed show no interest in the concept of matrimony, the reporters find it baffling. In another interview, the interviewee resists the way the interview is going, but the reporter continues to ask questions that shed doubts on her way of life:

"I know you keep hearing the question 'why' from journalists..." Answer: *"Oh, yes. Nobody wants to believe that I am really not unhappy, that I am really not depressed..."*

The reporter continues in the same vein:

"The only thing missing is the ring – that must keep everybody wondering ... Doesn't even your mommy pressure you?" Answer: *"No."*

Although the interviewee repeatedly rejects the notion that being unmarried is an "unhappy fate", the reporter clearly does not believe her assertions, which apparently seem "unwomanly" to her. Finally, she completely gives in to her prejudices and "finds a way out":

"So you're not a feminist after all?"

At least here the interviewee reacts in line with the reporter's expectations:

"No, God forbid!"

("Mala som byť chalan" ['I Should Have Been a Boy']
(an interview with a woman over 45)
Slovenka No. 17, April 30, 2007)

In this interview, we can see several elements of the stereotypical image of femininity, above all the reporter's fixation on the concept of a woman as a being that yearns for matrimony. Although the interviewee emphasized that she did not feel lonely and that she found her emotional life completely fulfilling, the reporter insisted that the only life model that could bring satisfaction was matrimony. The idea that *every woman yearns for marriage* is strongly present. The negative concept of feminism that is inherent in the ironic question *"So you're not a feminist after all?"* may be interpreted as a threat of "punishment" for the interviewee's failure to comply with the conventions.

The reporter eventually wraps up the subject in a positive and even admiring fashion:

"Perhaps you just know how to live, because although you live alone, you seem neither lonely nor tearful nor upset."

("V súkromí nie som lovkyňa" ['I Am No Huntress in Private']
(an interview with a woman over 45)
Život No.10, March 5, 2007.)

Still, it is interesting that the reporter phrased her conclusion as admiration for the "strength to live despite the fate you have been handed", although the interviewee reiterated that she was happy with her lifestyle and that it was the result of a conscious choice:

"My female colleagues can be divided into two categories: those who are independent like me and live without a partner – they are very happy and successful – and those who are married and are either getting divorced or continue to live in unhappy marriages."

(ibid)

Another interview in a different magazine took a similar course.[10] Its central topic was matrimony, which the reporter viewed as the basic prerequisite of a satisfying emotional life; therefore, she searched for reasons why the interviewee had chosen not to get married:

---

[10] It was the same respondent, a well-known female judge.

> *"I know you had a lot of suitors during your university studies; men were hovering around you..."*

("Mala som byť chalan" ['I Should Have Been a Boy']
(an interview with a woman over 45)
Slovenka No. 17, April 30, 2007)

As we see, the interview starts out with a question that is supposed to help readers understand that the interviewee was an attractive woman. Consequently, the life situation of a woman who was "left alone" despite all those possibilities seems all the more baffling. Following the initial assurance, the reporter sets out to find the motives for such an "unusual choice":

> *"Have you met your ideal guy? ... If he was ideal, why didn't you marry him?"*

In light of other circumstances, the interviewee's decision to lead an independent life seems even less comprehensible. Although the reporter declares her "admiration for your courage", she issues a "threat" like in the other aforementioned interview:

> *"Aren't you afraid of being lonely after you retire?"*

(ibid)

In this interview, the reporter showed understanding and even admiration for the interviewee's choice; yet she found it difficult to conceal her disapproval, which was clear in her enumeration of the possible "threats" that such a choice invited. Despite everything, this interview stands out as an exception, as most of the interviews with women clearly portrayed matrimony as the only way to secure happiness in a partnership.

In the interviews we identified four basic methods designed to reinforce the dichotomy between women's public and private spheres as well as the primary anchoring of women in the family. These methods emphasize the following issues:

- The threat of loneliness or unhappiness as the price of professional success;
- Family and partner as the criterion for and limitation on a successful career;
- The imperative of motherhood;
- The harmonization of family and professional life.

Successful Women and the Threat of Loneliness

The first method of cementing the dominance of the private sphere over the public one is to suggest that unhappiness of women will ensue from "wrong choices" such as "preferring a career to a family". Sometimes, the very choice of a professional career, associated with time constraints or intellectual demands, is presented as the "wrong choice":

> *"Oh, that professional success! Is it so important to you? Would you sacrifice anything for it?"* The interviewee's answer is negative, although people around her doubt it: *"...I want to be able to devote myself to a new and promising relationship. My friends warn me that I will miss this creative if hectic work. But I believe I would be able to give it up, because success is a relative thing."*

("Neťahám v zákulisí nitky" ['I Don't Pull Strings from Behind the Scenes']
(an interview with a woman under 45)
Slovenka No. 21, May 28, 2007)

The opening formulation – *"Oh, that professional success!"* – sounds like a sigh of resignation over some bad habit, rather than an unprejudiced opening to a conversation about the interviewee's views. By urging the interviewee to think about her willingness to "sacrifice" professional success, the reporter insinuates that professional success should be viewed as something "extra" or secondary, as opposed to something central. In interviews with successful men, not a single reporter presented this way of thinking. Men's achievements were depicted as something admirable but "normal". They did not carry any risks, and there was no reason to believe that men should give them up. Perhaps the closest to this line of thought would be urging a man to "slow down at work", especially if his health was at stake.

The reasons why the reporter questioned the interviewee's preparedness to sacrifice her professional success became clear later in the interview:

> *"You are a very successful woman, but people usually don't get everything they want. Some time ago, you were divorced after several years of marriage ... Was the failure of your relationship due to your excessive preoccupation with work? Or did you seek comfort and satisfaction at work because your relationship was not fulfilling you?"*

(ibid)

This quotation illustrates the reporter's view that women's devotion to their work is something suspicious. The reporter assumes that it either undermines functional relationships (*"Was the failure of your relationship due to your excessive preoccupation with work?"*) or makes up for failed ones (*"Or did you seek comfort and satisfaction at work because your relationship was not fulfilling you?"*).

Some successful women seem to have it all figured out: professional success is easier to achieve than success in a relationship.

> *"I was rather successful professionally in the past, I had fans but I did not have a complete family. The entire time I was looking for contentment and a family background. It's not easy to find an ideal partner or at least a partner that fits with your ideas."*

("Mojou výhrou je rodina" ['My Family Is My Victory']
(an interview with a woman under 45)
Slovenka No. 12, March 26, 2007)

In another interview, the reporter's question sounds like a generalization that can be applied to other successful women as well:

> *"Is it difficult for a successful and pretty woman to find an adequate partner? Are men afraid of such women?"*

("Neťahám v zákulisí nitky" ['I Don't Pull Strings from Behind the Scenes']
(an interview with a woman under 45)
Slovenka No. 21, May 28, 2007)

If the question was phrased as *"Is it difficult to find an adequate partner"*, it would be possible to view it as a "warm-up question". But the reporter insinuated that it was even more difficult for *successful* women than for "regular" ones. Besides, the suggestive formulation of the follow-up question (*"Are men afraid of such women?"*) creates the feeling that this perspective has to be endorsed, albeit reluctantly. In this particular case, the question may also be interpreted as a warning to women who yearn for professional success.

Emphases on the threat of loneliness associated with women's success at work were found in other interviews as well, for instance:

> *"I know you are divorced. How does it feel being alone? ... Do you want to spend the rest of your life alone like this, with only a son?"*
>
> ("Vie o nich najviac" ['She Knows Them Best']
> (an interview with a woman under 45)
> *Život* No. 14, April 2, 2007)

This question creates the impression that the interviewee keeps failing in her partnerships because she is so busy at work that she does not even try (*"Do you want to spend the rest of your life alone like this?"*). Later on, the reporter questions the interviewee's qualities as a mother, as she admits to doubts as to whether she is a good mother to her son, and misgivings that she has neglected something in his education, and says she is determined to "pay him back" for it.

This interview is no exception, as many women publicly try to "justify" their professional success as secondary, and say they are willing to sacrifice their careers (because of a husband or a family) in order to "preserve the relationship".

The issue of divorce or separation also came up in interviews with successful men. Although reporters also tried to seek links between the interviewees' professional occupation and their divorce, the image of men who succeed at work as well as in their partnerships still prevailed. At the same time, the end of the previous relationship usually meant the beginning of a new one. A new partner is the embodiment of a man's "success"; success at work brings a new relationship with a more "lucrative" partner. In this case, women are portrayed as rewards or status symbols.

> *"Was the failure of your first marriage related to your business accomplishments? I mean, often a successful man suddenly sets his heart on a new partner."*
>
> ("Dom na Tenerife" ['House on Tenerife']
> (an interview with a man over 45)
> *Život* No. 17, April 23, 2007)

Similar attempts to find the reasons behind the failure of an interviewee's marriage were also present in interviews with other successful men.

What Does the Partner Have to Say?

Emphases on the importance of family along with the assumption that a woman should be prepared to "sacrifice" her career were also seen in questions about the opinions of family members, particularly husbands or partners, which were subsequently presented as approving or disapproving of women's professional activities.

> *"Even at this stage of pregnancy, you still work and take part in social events. Your husband is not exactly happy about it..."*
>
> ("Tehotenstvo? Vyriešil ho osud" ['Pregnancy? Fate Solved It']
> (an interview with a woman under 45)
> *Slovenka* No. 19, May 14, 2007)

> *"Rumor has it that you declined an offer to appear in the Celebrity Camp show because of your husband. Did he forbid it?"*
>
> ("Sviatkujem najradšej doma" ['I Prefer to Spend My Holidays at Home']
> (an interview with a woman under 45)
> *Slovenka* No. 14, April 9, 2007)

The views of husbands or partners are presented as a limit on women's successful careers or, more generally, on their participation in the labor market at all. This cements the notion of the man as the head of the family, who has the right to decide on what course the life of its members will take. While interviewees in both cited interviews said their partners had not "forbidden" their professional activities, they were not taken aback at the notion that their partners had a right to do so in the first place.

In interviews with successful men, reporters did not enquire about their partners' opinions; on the contrary, sometimes they asked whether and how they influenced the decisions of their wives or partners, as well as their daughters, sisters and other relatives.

> *"Didn't you try to talk her out of the job? True, it is brave of her but it's still dangerous work, particularly for a woman ... Where did she find the courage?"*
>
> ("Keď šoumen nestarne" ['When a Showman Defies Age'] (an interview with a man over 45) *Slovenka* No. 20, May 21, 2007)

The interviews were conducted as if men were the ones who do or should decide, and as if women were the ones who do or should subordinate themselves to men's decisions.

The older the female interviewee, the less the "family pressure". Questions such as "did he not forbid it" or "did he not try to talk you out of it" are replaced by more neutral formulations, for instance "the family's opinion" or "the impact on the family".

> *"How did your family take the fact that you would have to commute to work across the country?"*
>
> ("Prvá žena" ['First Woman'] (an interview with a woman over 45) *Plus 7 dní* No. 11, March 16, 2007)

Similar formulations also appear in interviews with younger men:

> *"Constant travel is an inseparable part of a sportsman's life ... You have certainly become more sensitive about spending time away from your family since your daughter was born."*
>
> ("Maká na zlato" ['Toiling for Gold'] (an interview with a man under 45) *Život* No. 18, April 30, 2007)

Let us describe the differences in the reactions to the same question. A mature woman usually deems it necessary to explain the circumstances and relations within her family, for instance that her children are already grown up and that her husband has the kind of job that allows him to be with her. Younger men, for their part, limit themselves to admitting that they do not spend enough time with their families or simply agreeing that it is difficult and that they have to sacrifice a lot in the name of success (in this case, spending time with their children). Unlike mature women, younger men do not mention any remedies to alleviate the negative effects that their absence has on their families.

Our content analysis revealed only one such reaction by a female interviewee:

> *"But I view it in a way that if I want to do my job properly, the family must also sacrifice something. I take it as a mission..."*
>
> ("Občas som zúrivá blondína" ['Sometimes I Am a Furious Blonde'] (an interview with a woman under 45) *Slovenka* No. 20, May 21, 2007)

In this one case, the female interviewee presented her career like men do, i.e. as a "mission", as an urge, as part of the way she defines herself and a source of personal happiness. For this woman, work is an inseparable part of her life, which includes her family life as well.

Am I a Good Mother?

Interviews with successful women often present motherhood as an imperative or a "compulsory ideal", as opposed to an individual choice for each woman or a personal and unique relationship to their children. Most interviewees' statements about this "paramount mission" are clichés that emphasize the importance of the woman's role as a mother:

> *"A woman's role in society cannot be replaced. She is the bearer of life."*

("Čo ma rakovina naučila" ['What Cancer Taught Me']
(an interview with a woman over 45)
Slovenka No.10, March 12, 2007)

> *"A woman is the one that takes care of education. I believe in God and I believe that he created two different beings – a man and a woman. I think that the role of a woman is more important than the role of a man ... After all, what is more important than raising a human being?"*

("Obchod je životný štýl" ['Business Is a Way of Life']
(an interview with a woman under 45)
Slovenka No. 16, April 23, 2007)

This glorification of maternity is closely related to treating women's professional activities as secondary. Reporters' questions assume that all women should subordinate their lives to their femininity, which is identified with maternity:

> *"Pregnancy and family life have certainly changed you."*

("Tehotenstvo? Vyriešil ho osud" ['Pregnancy? Fate Solved It']
(an interview with a woman under 45)
Slovenka No. 19, May 14, 2007)

As they grow older, successful women are increasingly often confronted with questions regarding motherhood:

> *"Women around 40 often set their hearts on having one last baby; they peek in other women's prams and so on. Is that happening to you as well?"*

("V súkromí nie som lovkyňa" ['I Am No Huntress in Private']
(an interview with a woman over 45)
Život No.10, March 5, 2007.)

The answer – "I guess I'm not the typical maternal type" – indicates that the interviewee also identifies femininity with maternity, which she views as an "obligation". Even women who do not have children and do not want to become mothers are nevertheless expected to show care and love for children. In this case, the interviewee emphasizes that she "fulfills her role as a mother" by taking care of her sister's children.

In the case of men, questions about fatherhood were asked exclusively of young interviewees.

> *"I have the feeling that the only thing missing from your perfect happiness is a child. Are you ready to become a father?"*

("Do roka sa oženi" ['He Will Get Married Within a Year']
(an interview with a man under 45)
Život No. 18, April 30, 2007)

"To wrap things up, let me put the classic question: when will there be more of you at home?"

("Hľadá si vlastnú cestu" ['Searching for His Own Way']
(an interview with a man under 45)
Slovenka No 15, April 16 2007)

These questions addressed to young men presented fatherhood as yet another "success" that must be accomplished. Besides parenthood, some reporters also reminded their interviewees of the need to enter into marriage:

"You live together under one roof; you have three children – your two sons and your partner's daughter. I can't escape the feeling that the only thing missing is a marriage certificate and mutual offspring."

("Už to prebolelo" ['Pain Has Subsided']
(an interview with a man under 45)
Život No.19, May 7, 2007)

"Will marriage bells chime soon for you?"

("Do roka sa ožení" ['He Will Get Married Within a Year']
(an interview with a man under 45)
Život No. 18, April 30, 2007)

But in order to fulfill the ideal of maternity, it is not enough to love, raise and even sacrifice for children, as was clearly shown in an interview with a man who proudly spoke of his daughter who is raising four adopted children but has remained single:

"How did she, a single woman, ever get the idea of adopting a child?"

("Dom na Tenerife" ['House on Tenerife']
(an interview with a man over 45)
Život No. 17, April 23, 2007)

What *"Harmonization"*?

As a direct result of the dichotomy of public and private spheres and of the anchoring of women in the latter, the harmonization of public and private life is seen primarily as a woman's problem and is in fact interpreted as harmonizing *family* and professional life. This fact was also clearly reflected in interviews with successful women:

"I try not to be constantly burdened by professional duties, although I always carry them out to 100%... In order to keep everything content, peaceful and pleasant at home, everything must be managed and must fit together."

("Ochranka jej prekáža" ['Security Constrains Her']
(an interview with a woman over 45)
Život No. 16, April 16, 2007)

In this statement, we can detect the interviewee's awareness of the stereotype of women as homemakers. For most men, family and household is a place of regeneration, but for women it is a work environment, often one of *primary* importance. Consequently, the term "harmonization" loses its positive connotation and becomes an extra burden that will not disappear as long as the traditional division of family roles between women and men remains. The concept of a successful woman that is able to cope with everything becomes problematic:

"How are you dealing with the challenge of being an actress and a mother at the same time?" Answer: *"Who told you I was dealing? I can't manage it ... And*

> *without the help of my older children and my mother, it would not be possible at all."*

("Materstvom som nič nezmeškala" ['I Didn't Miss a Thing Due to Motherhood']
(an interview with a woman over 45)
Slovenka No. 19, May 14, 2007)

The perception of this stress as the cost of entertaining professional ambitions further underlines the concept that the right to work and to derive satisfaction from it is an "extra bonus" for women, for which they have to "pay" accordingly.

> *"In any case, you are managing to harmonize your career and your family."* Answer: *"I'm managing like most on-the-go, out-of-breath mothers in this country … As soon as the biggest work stress is gone, the first thing I do is start cooking. I want to compensate my family for everything I missed."*

("Mojou výhrou je rodina" ['My Family Is My Victory']
(an interview with a woman under 45)
Slovenka No. 12, March 26, 2007)

The sentence "I want to compensate my family for everything I missed" reveals the interviewee's conviction that a woman's principal sphere is the family, as well as her feeling of guilt for the success she has achieved.

These examples reflect the most common notion of "harmonization". Although the original concept means harmonizing private and professional life and should therefore concern all people on the labor market, it seems that the private life of women is merely a misname for family life consisting of household chores and care for family members.

The relationship between the public and private spheres does not amount to the same thing for women and men. While most men place family at the top of their list of values, they still perceive their family roles differently. For women, taking care of the family and its members is their primary personal responsibility and principal "workplace". Most men are not forced to choose between the public and the private, but for women this choice is fundamental; most struggle with it throughout their lives. A number of female interviewees showed uncertainty and even guilt when the interview turned to family and partnership issues. This is largely the consequence of the stereotypical image of successful women as careerists who only think of themselves, for which they may be punished by a lonely and loveless life.

Professionally successful men, for their part, are not so much threatened by the "loss of a partner". Work is an integral part of their identity. A successful man is primarily a successful professional; to his family, he represents security that is often viewed through his traditional role as a breadwinner. Slovakia's dominant double-income household model does not fully correspond with such model. However, the stereotypical division of male and female duties affects women's opportunities and their motivation to participate on the labor market, as well as the expectations men face within their families and households. According to this gender stereotype, employment is always viewed as "secondary" for women but natural for men.

This largely affects people's perception of the possibilities and ways of harmonizing private and professional life. For men, it is a question of "finding time for the family" while it is presumed that this time may well be limited due to their desire to succeed professionally. Women, for their part, are free to devote themselves to their professions only "as far as the family permits". For most Slovak women, private life does not truly mean time for themselves but primarily time for a different kind of work. Men's work is often identified with their private life and interests, while a woman's household chores and care for family members are perceived as her principal "personal" interest.

According to this logic, people without "family obligations" are not targeted by company measures to harmonize private and professional life. Unmarried and childless men as well as unmarried women are thus excluded in this respect. It is also interesting that unmarried women are often considered "lonely", even if they live in an informal partnership.

Ageing and Its Gender Dimensions

The issues of ageing and old age showed up relatively frequently in the interviews with successful women and men. While successful mature men faced questions regarding their age mostly when asked to sum up their accomplishments, successful mature women were asked about their age in the context of their desire to turn back the clock:

> *"Wouldn't you like – and not just in your imagination – to return to the past and postpone getting old?"*

("Materstvom som nič nezmeškala" ['I Didn't Miss a Thing Due to Motherhood']
(an interview with a woman over 45)
Slovenka No. 19, May 14, 2007)

Most reporters tend to assume that mature women – unlike their male counterparts – resort to working as hard as they can as a way of "postponing" old age:

> *"You embarked on a challenging business even though you weren't exactly 20 years old. Did you want to extend your youth?"*

("Nezávislosť je na nezaplatenie" ['Independence Is Invaluable']
(an interview with a woman over 45)
Slovenka No. 9, March 5, 2007)

This formulation indicates that the reporter views a woman's professional life as a "substitution" or a compensation – just as in the case of a dysfunctional or unfulfilling partnership. In line with this logic, work is not viewed as a key part of a woman's life but merely as a substitution – for a partnership, for motherhood, for youth. This view is based on the idea that the public sphere is not a "natural" environment for women.

Interviews with successful men much more frequently approached these issues from a lighter side, for instance by discussing "effective" methods to avoid ageing.

> *"In my opinion, age is just a number that can't be fooled, you can only slow it down … And I have one special trick – I soak up energy from younger people … I'm one of those people who listen to the young. Their views are clearer. They bring me fresh air."*

("Zberateľ zážitkov" ['Experience Collector']
(an interview with a man over 45)
Slovenka No. 13, April 2, 2007)

This statement is based on the notion of youth as an ideal that gradually deteriorates, or as a quality that requires care and deserves maintenance. Consequently, ageing and old age are defined as losing this quality.

A similarly humorous but nevertheless negative connotation of ageing can be found in another interview with a mature man:

"There's always plenty of time for getting old! I believe that old age is largely a temptation – and that it can be successfully resisted. Ageing is also relatively contagious, so beware!"

("S rodinou ma baví svet" ['Family Life Is Fun']
(an interview with a man over 45)
Slovenka No. 9, March 5, 2007)

Ageing and old age is portrayed as something unpleasant that must be "coped with".

"From playing handsome characters, you have gradually worked your way into playing the role of Grandpa Pepa, for instance … Have you come to terms with it?"

(ibid)

Also, old age is often presented as a degradation, a loss of courage, abilities, energy or beauty.

"At the age of 68, don't you feel exhausted? I mean, you would be entitled to."

("Keď šoumen nestarne" ['When a Showman Defies Age']
(an interview with a man over 45)
Slovenka No. 20, May 21, 2007)

The interviewed man's reaction is adverse, even taunting:

"Do I strike you as that?"

Of course, this kind of answer did not satisfy the reporter, who apparently felt the interviewee was trying to "avoid the truth". Still convinced, she raised a warning finger:

"Still, wouldn't you like to slow down in some areas?"

(ibid)

In interviews with successful mature women, reporters repeatedly tried to "discover the truth". For instance, the following question sounds like an attempt to "expose the true intentions" of the interviewee behind the change in her lifestyle or her professed values:

"Perhaps you are no longer as willing to take risks as you were years ago."

("Neťahám v zákulisí nitky" ['I Don't Pull Strings from Behind the Scenes']
(an interview with a woman under 45)
Slovenka No. 21, May 28, 2007)

Unless strictly limited to the content of the interviewees' work, almost all questions asked of mature women and men betrayed the reporters' expectations that they would soon end their professional careers. Particularly for women, working in their mature years is considered admirable but simultaneously as something "out of the ordinary":

"Recently, she became a grandmother … Despite that, she does numerous activities and even runs a business."

("Nezávislosť je na nezaplatenie" ['Independence Is Invaluable']
(an interview with a woman over 45)
Slovenka No. 9, March 5, 2007)

Reporters rarely contemplate the future professional plans of mature women and men. It is interesting that in this case, the phrasing of questions asked of women and men is almost identical.

"Do you still have any dreams?"

("Keď gitary žiarlia" ['When Guitars Are Jealous']
(an interview with a woman over 45)
Slovenka No. 17, April 30, 2007)

"Have any of your dreams not come true yet?"

("Keď šoumen nestarne" ['When a Showman Defies Age']
(an interview with a man over 45)
Slovenka No. 20, May 21, 2007)

Worth of attention are also the gender differences in most reporters' understanding of the concept of ageing. While men face questions about ageing usually around the age of 60, but rarely before they turn 50, women are confronted with this type of question much earlier:

"You strike people as remarkably youthful, but still ... Recently, you celebrated your 40th birthday. In Slovakia, television journalism is largely interchangeable with modeling. Are you mentally prepared for the day they say 'thank you'? Or do you believe the day is coming when a young and pretty face will no longer be enough?"

("Mojou výhrou je rodina" ['My Family Is My Victory']
(an interview with a woman under 45)
Slovenka No. 12, March 26, 2007)

This was not the only interview in which the age of 40 was presented as a crucial age limit for women. One of the first challenges that most women face is the threat of losing their youthful appearance. The pressure of the beauty imperative accompanies women throughout their lives and intensifies as they get older, particularly in professions where good appearance is viewed an important qualification. Most successful women in the interviews belonged to this category of professionals. The interviewees' answers to the questions confirm the reporters' assumptions and further elaborate on them:

"Sometimes I almost feel like an old woman when I start moralizing that journalists should not be superficial ... I agree that young people should be given a chance; after all, many of them have a great command of foreign languages and are ambitious. But their young age should not be the only criterion."

(ibid)

Most interviews contained no positive images of ageing or old age. Only two of them featured references to old age as something positive. In both cases, the question was directed at mature men and inquired about their life models:

"You have become a pedagogue yourself ... Are you trying to continue what your teacher taught you?"

("Kaskadér z reklamy" ['Advertising Stuntman']
(an interview with a man over 45)
Slovenka No. 18, May 7, 2007)

In both cases, the interviewees spoke of other mature men as their models and praised the wide life and professional experience they had passed down to them. Here, a mature age was associated with specific knowledge and inspiring wisdom. None of the interviews with successful women featured even a remotely positive reference to mature years.

Beauty and Its Gender Dimensions

Media interviews with successful women pay excessive attention to their appearance, and to keeping and even "improving" their looks. Most reporters seem to believe that a woman's appearance is important, that it is threatened by age, and therefore deserves special care. They find it particularly difficult to conceal their admiration when the interviewee is a mature woman:

"You give the impression that you are ready to step in front of the camera at any moment – always neat and elegant. Has this become a habit or even a need for you during your years of working in television?"

("Žijem a užívam si!" ['I Live and Savor Life!']
(an interview with a woman over 45)
Slovenka No. 13, April 2, 2007)

The phrasing of the question emphasizes the importance of beauty for the interviewed woman's professional career; in her answer, though, the interviewee suggests that she considers good looks an important quality of every woman, regardless of her profession:

"But that didn't start with television! I was always neat and tidy in public."

(ibid)

The interviews paid specific attention to the interviewed women's appearance, particularly when it was unusual in some way. One such situation arose in the aforementioned question, which highlighted the interviewee's "beauty despite her age". At the opposite pole was a situation when the interviewed woman did not "care" about her good appearance as much as the reporter expected her to:

"You came to our meeting wearing no make-up. Don't you feel that you should look perfect at all times, given that people recognize you on the street?"

("Mám rada adrenalín" ['I Love Adrenalin']
(an interview with a woman under 45)
Slovenka No. 16, April 23, 2007)

Successful women are often asked how they "maintain" their good looks. They are often forced to discuss the issue of plastic or aesthetic surgery:

"Would you also undergo plastic surgery?" Answer: *"No problem."*

("Mala som byť chalan" ['I Should Have Been a Boy']
(an interview with a woman over 45)
Slovenka No. 17, April 30, 2007)

"But they say you have undergone a cellulite treatment … Already at your age?"

("Modelka aj šťastná mama" ['A Model and a Happy Mother']
(an interview with a woman under 45)
Slovenka No. 11, March 19, 2007)

All interviewees who were asked this kind of question said they did not have a problem with plastic surgery and that they were willing to undergo it. They only disagreed over the extent to which it was socially acceptable to discuss these issues in public. Some agreed that beauty was important, but emphasized that it must be "natural".

"Do you also approve of external interventions, say surgical?" Answer: *"I approve of everything a woman does for herself, but I don't think it's right to discuss it in public. There are things I wouldn't mind doing, but it's wrong for somebody to ask me about them."*

("Žijem a užívam si!" ['I Live and Savor Life!']
(an interview with a woman over 45)
Slovenka No. 13, April 2, 2007)

Beauty is not only an important stereotypical attribute of femininity; it is often identified with femininity itself. From the viewpoint of gender stereotypes, we are seeing an interesting situation: if a woman is not attractive, her "femininity" is undermined. On the other hand, beauty is viewed as something natural or "given". Consequently, if feminine charms are achieved by "artificial interventions", it is impossible to call them natural. When discussing aesthetic "improvements", reporters repeatedly used expressions such as "confession" or "disclosure", even if the interviewed woman spoke openly of her personal experience with plastic surgery:

> *"What else do you have to confess? What else have you improved on your body?"*
>
> ("Modelka aj šťastná mama" ['A Model and a Happy Mother']
> (an interview with a woman under 45)
> *Slovenka* No. 11, March 19, 2007)

Female beauty may also be the "standard" of the success or status of others, for instance men or institutions. The following statement was published as part of the public debate on changes in the health and pension insurance systems:

> *"... this does not mean that you will receive more expensive drugs, a better room, or a prettier nurse at the hospital."*
>
> ("Na starobu žobrákmi" ['Old Age Reduces People to Beggary']
> (an interview with a man under 45)
> *Plus 7 dní* No. 15, April 13, 2007)

In this context, a "pretty nurse" represents a kind of benefit that is placed at men's disposal under certain conditions. The nurse's beauty is presented as something that is not meant for her but for someone else.

Let us now take a closer look at the perception and presentation of men's beauty. In interviews with successful men, prevailingly female reporters often discussed their appearance, but in a completely different context. The attractiveness of the men interviewed was not associated with their profession; it was not portrayed as a quality that a successful man ought to strive for, but rather as something admirable. The reporters often called the interviewees' appearance the source of their sex appeal and the reason that they attracted women's attention. This issue appeared exclusively in interviews with mature men.

> *"You were an attractive southern type. Did women throw themselves at you? Did you have to chase them away?"*
>
> ("Keď šoumen nestarne" ['When a Showman Defies Age']
> (an interview with a man over 45)
> *Slovenka* No. 20, May 21, 2007)

Female reporters tended to associate the interviewed men's sex appeal with their professional success and fame rather than their looks:

> *"There were crowds of beautiful women going wild at your concerts. They surrounded you away from your concerts as well. But you have been married to the same woman for years. How did you manage to cope with fame?"*
>
> ("Večne mladý muzikant" ['Ageless Musician']
> (an interview with a man over 45)
> *Slovenka* No. 16, April 23, 2007)

Given the interviewed man's sex appeal, the female reporter found it difficult to conceal her surprise over the fact that he lived in a stable and long-term partnership:

"You travel around the world and act with beautiful women, but you have been married to the same woman for an unbelievable 30 years. What about temptations? How did you resist them?"

("Moja najťažšia rola je Juraj Kukura" ['My Hardest Role Is That of Juraj Kukura']
(an interview with a man over 45)
Slovenka No. 10, March 12, 2007)

The stereotypical portrayal of men's success as increasing their attractiveness was found in a number of interviews. They did not describe men's attractiveness as something expected or as a part of masculinity, but rather as the source of temptation and potential problems in the emotional lives of the interviewees. In one interview, the reporter apparently had a fixed notion of men's "natural promiscuity". Although the interviewee rebuffed her attempts to portray him as a lady-killer, the reporter did not believe him; on the contrary, she repeatedly tried to "uncover the truth" and make him "confess", as illustrated by the following questions:

"How did you chase away your suitors?"
"And what did you do when women threw themselves at you?"
"But she must have been jealous quite often, no?"
"Juraj Kukura as an ageless idol..." Answer: (laughter, refusal)
"Okay, let's say an eternal idol then!"

(ibid)

Although the interviewee repeatedly rejected the image of the seducer that the reporter tried to foist on him, he did not manage to convince her. Finally, she offered a "compromise":

"Then you camouflage yourself very well."

(ibid)

Division of Labor in Household

The concrete nature of the division of household labor is of fundamental importance to the performance of women in the public sphere, and particularly to their performance at work. Without a more just division of household labor, it is impossible to improve women's participation on the labor market. While the interviews primarily discussed the professional life of successful women and men, they touched upon their household obligations as well. It turned out that most celebrities saw these duties as women's duties.

Most interviewed women spoke of trying to cope with all their "obligations" at work and at home. Men, for their part, did not spontaneously address this issue, and only spoke of it when confronted with a direct question. Unfortunately, most of these questions focused only on the typically "masculine" work (e.g. small repairs, etc.) or portrayed household chores as the principal domain of women and even praised the men for "helping" their women.

"Tidiness is not something I was born with. But my partner tidies up with love, I guess. Sometimes I try to play responsible, and I'm happy to do it."

("Do roka sa ožení" ['He Will Get Married Within a Year'])
(an interview with a man under 45)
Život No. 18, April 30, 2007)

The formulation "sometimes I try to play responsible" indicates that the interviewee does appreciate his partner's taking care of their common household, but treats her duties with certain disrespect because he views them as intellectually shallow and physically unchallenging, as something anyone could do. Most men perform a small proportion of the domestic chores, and are free to choose what part they will perform, depending on their time constraints or willingness; women, for their part, are "obliged" to carry them out without much choice in the matter. The admiration some men earn for "helping" their women may seem inspiring, while in fact it only underlines the exceptional nature of such help.

Most women's statements indicated that they had accepted the responsibility for running their household; few disputed the fact that taking care of their family was their highest priority. Family represented a precious value to the men as well; however, they did not associate it with the work that must be performed in order to keep it running. Quite the contrary, the interviews with successful men gave a rather clear picture of the division of labor in their household, in which the burden of domestic chores was shouldered primarily by women.

> *"My sweetheart now helps take care of my diet ... My diet has changed considerably because I am perfectly taken care of."*

(ibid)

> *"I don't waste time going to restaurants because my wife is an excellent cook and we have eaten sparingly our entire lives."*

("Nič by som nemenil" ['I Wouldn't Change a Thing']
(an interview with a man over 45),
Život No. 16, April 16, 2007)

In both cited examples, the interviewed men praised their partners for improving their health. Taking care of the diets and health of family members is also on the list of chores performed by women. These activities form an integral part of the stereotypical image of femininity, and neglecting them would undermine their image as a "good woman". The same goes for the notion of women's "natural" sense of fashion and style.

> *"Do you listen to your wife when it comes to your wardrobe?"*

("Moja najťažšia rola je Juraj Kukura" ['My Hardest Role Is That of Juraj Kukura']
(an interview with a man over 45)
Slovenka No. 10, March 12, 2007)

It is interesting that many women spontaneously spoke of their domestic chores and the burden they represent. Some showed regret or even guilt for failing to perform their duties as expected or as they wished to perform them. They viewed the imbalance in the division of labor in their households as natural; they did not question it, although it was the main thing holding them back from devoting themselves more intensively to their work.

8.1.4. INCREASING THE SENSIBILITY OF JOURNALISTS AS A WAY OF ELIMINATING STEREOTYPES

The media images of women in general and mature women in particular as identified by the content analysis of select daily papers from summer 2004 to summer 2005 were confirmed by the content analysis of magazine interviews with successful women and men in spring 2007. In other words, no signs that gender and age stereotypes were being eliminated from the Slovak media were detected in more than two years. Despite their formal condemnation of any kind of discrimination, the weekly magazines often reproduced the same images of femininity seen in the daily papers.

Profile interviews in all magazines featured successful men rather than successful women, who received the most space in lifestyle magazines (*Život* and *Slovenka*). On the other hand, weekly magazines specializing in economic and political issues published exclusively (*Trend*) or almost exclusively (*Plus 7 dní*) interviews with successful men.

All interviews with successful women reflected the dichotomy of the public and private spheres and emphasized the precedence of family over work and profession. Most presented women as persons whose principal mission in life is or should be helping others, as supportive mothers, wives, partners, etc.

The appearance of women was portrayed as an important factor that was directly related to the performance of their jobs and their professional success. An important characteristic of interviews with successful women was that they mostly featured representatives of professions that view good looks as extremely important (i.e. actresses, models, etc.). Interviews with successful men were not only more frequent but were also more diverse in terms of professional focus.

Some interviews with successful men presented women as sexual objects – either as "temptresses" that successful men must resist, or as potential replacements for their original partners. In this context it was particularly important that these stereotypes were presented by female reporters as opposed to the interviewed men themselves.

On the other hand, the magazine interviews offered different findings about successful women, for instance that they feel guilty because they have problems balancing their professional duties and their household chores; that their professional success undermines their relationships; that they fear their partner might "replace" them and leave them alone; that they are expected to invest more into their appearances as time goes by. Successful men, for their part, may expect that their increasing success will enhance their attractiveness for potential partners, and that their increasing age will make them role models for younger men. In other words, men are expected to be successful, while successful women are less obvious and run more risks.

The magazine interviews portrayed ageing and old age quite differently than the newspapers did, primarily because they featured active and successful women and men. Although many interviewed celebrities were already past the retirement age, most continued to be professionally active. This is why the magazine interviews were almost completely free of the three images of old age that appeared in the daily press: old age as poverty; old age as a return to infancy; and elderly people as victims. Despite that, old age still inspired mostly negative associations and anxiety.

Portrayals of ageing as a degradation of physical beauty appeared mostly in interviews with successful women. On the other hand, interviews with successful men presented ageing as a deterioration of one's health and an accumulation of illnesses, and spoke mostly of how hard work and the related stress causes problems for mature people in particular. The interviews also discussed other types of "decline", such as a reduced willingness to take risks, poorer adaptability and work performance, impaired capacity and motivation to learn new things, and changed life ambitions.

Our content analysis exposed several differences in the attitudes of particular magazines towards presenting successful people. For instance, the *Trend* weekly, which specializes in "traditionally male" issues (i.e. economy, trade, business, etc.) completely avoided interviewing successful women. Also, the focus of interviews with successful men was strictly professional, which is seen as yet another attribute of masculinity. None of the interviews deviated even once from the "paramount" and overriding subject, i.e. business.

Interviews with successful people published by the *Plus 7 dní* weekly focused primarily on political issues and rarely wandered off into "female" issues such as family or emotional life. Successful men strongly outnumbered successful women in the weekly's interviews.

It was interesting to compare *Život* and *Slovenka* magazines. While only *Slovenka* is explicitly designed for a female readership, *Život* is very similar in terms of its structure and focus on relaxation, discussing mostly leisure and social issues. Both magazines represent almost bottomless sources of gender and age stereotypes – especially dichotomous concepts of masculinity and femininity, as well as of young and mature years.

Still, a comparison of the way that the questions were put indicated that *Život* was more balanced than *Slovenka* with respect to women and men, as it gave a relatively equal chance to its female and male interviewees to describe their family relations, their professional backgrounds, and the way they combined their public and private lives.

In the *Slovenka* weekly, interviews with successful men used a different style than those with successful women. While the former often featured questions that tried to present men's professional success in a rather erotic context, the latter frequently put women's professional careers in the light of the potential risks for their relationships. They also used explicitly stereotypical formulations and reproduced the dichotomous image of masculinity and femininity. Also, female interviewees were more frequently asked about their appearance and its maintenance.

This finding was particularly surprising because in other articles, *Slovenka* relatively often covered issues such as equal opportunities and gender equality. It even ran a special series of stories featuring disadvantaged people. This is why it is even more surprising that reporters' questions repeatedly reproduced gender and age stereotypes. During the period examined, *Slovenka* did not publish a single interview that challenged gender stereotypes.

Despite the *Slovenka* weekly's conscious efforts to endorse and promote gender equality, its interviews in fact reproduced gender and age stereotypes. This seemingly paradoxical finding proves that measures aimed at supporting women (or other disadvantaged groups) cannot be successful unless based on a perfect understanding of the reasons behind their social disadvantages as well as the mechanisms by which these disadvantages are reproduced.

Particularly serious in this context is the fact that these stereotypes were reproduced also as a part of the image of the successful women. This indicates that the stereotypical images of femininity are reproduced on several levels of the public discourse. This is why the attempts to eliminate stereotypes can only be successful if aimed at all levels of the gender universe as defined at the beginning of this chapter (Harding, 1986). As our analysis has shown, the symbolic dimension of gender order endures despite some positive changes within society. This inertia is clearly seen in journalists' attempts at gender-sensitive reporting and also in their attempts at the critical reflection on social prejudices and on the reasons for which some social groups are disadvantaged.

Gender stereotypes, as part of the symbolic dimension of gender, endure in language and affect people's perceptions, views and ways of thinking, often without their realizing it. The analysis of the interviews with successful women and men has proved that it is impossible to overcome them by formally subscribing to the principle of equality or even by practicing such a type of individual behavior that is based on their rejection.

Our analysis of the magazine interviews has showed how important it is for the media to understand gender aspects of media praxis. Education, and especially sensibilization of journalists are indispensable to producing discrimination-free and gender- and age-sensitive media coverage.

8.2. HERALDING A NEW APPROACH

8.2.1. PROFILES OF SUCCESSFUL WOMEN IN THE *SME ŽENY* SUPPLEMENT OF THE *SME* DAILY

In November 2006, the liberally-oriented *Sme* daily launched the publication of a special supplement to its Saturday edition called *Sme Ženy*.[11] It was the first supplement designed primarily for a female readership to be published by a serious daily paper.[12] Each edition features a profile interview in a section called *Female Personality* that introduces a different woman who has performed exceptionally in the public sphere.

In the following pages, we present the basic findings of a content analysis of all the interviews published by *Sme Ženy* in issues No. 1, 2006 to No. 11, 2008, i.e. during the first 18 months of the weekly's existence.[13]

Our content analysis focused on three aspects: first, the profile of the women viewed as interesting by the editorial staff, which says a great deal about women's media image; second, the way questions were asked, and the issues that were selected by the reporters who conducted the interviews; finally, the thematic focus of the interviews and women's opinions and positions. Topics were identified based on particular phrases or on the concrete situations described or discussed.

We paid particularly close attention to the interviews of women over 40, as well as to the similarities and differences in the focuses of interviews with younger and mature women.

The analysis used a deductive method for creating units of analysis according to Mayring (Mayring, 2007). All interviews were analyzed in three phases; the first two phases fulfilled analytical purposes, while the third phase had verification purposes. In the final phase, we paid attention to interviews that we considered of paramount importance.

Between November 2006 and March 2008, *Sme Ženy* published seventy one interviews with outstanding women between the ages of 17 and 86. Younger women prevailed: forty six of the interviewees (or two in three) were younger than 40, while ten were between 40 and 49, eight were between 50 and 59 and seven were over 60.

Women with university degrees formed the substantial majority of interviewees (59 out of 71). Several of the remaining 12 women had foregone their university studies after professional career prospects opened up while they were at secondary school, whether in music, theatre, sports or modeling. Almost all women over 40 had university degrees, and two had achieved higher scientific titles or academic degrees.

As Table 8.5 shows, the respondents had all kinds of professional backgrounds. Most were actresses (16), followed by top sportswomen (9) singers (7), doctors, musicians and models

---

[11] The supplement has been available as a separate weekly magazine since April 2007.

[12] Six months later, beginning in April 2007, the *Pravda* daily followed suit and began to publish a supplement for women under the name *Ženy*.

[13] While the content analysis was limited to these interviews, the supplement's entire profile would also deserve a detailed evaluation.

(4 each) and scientists, news readers, artists and managers (3 each). The list also included politicians, leaders of non-governmental organizations, authors, businesswomen, dance instructors and fashion designers (2 each) as well as three women who won recognition in occupations that are traditionally considered "male" professions: a police chief, a banker and a protestant vicar.

The professional make-up of the women interviewed indicates a relatively high representation of professions that are in the media limelight; 30 out of the 71 interviews featured celebrities such as actresses, singers, models, moderators or newscasters.[14]

Table 8.5
Professions of women interviewed for the *Female Personality* section of the *Sme* daily

Actress	16
Sportswoman	9
Singer	7
Musician, model, doctor	4
Scientist, news reader, artist, manager	3
Member of parliament, businesswoman, author, leader of a non-governmental organization, dance teacher, fashion designer	2
Vicar, banker, police chief	1

Source: *Sme Ženy* supplement of the *Sme* daily, November 2006 – March 2008.

Most interviews that we examined presented the women through their "life stories" as they summed up their academic and professional careers, highlighted their greatest accomplishments, and described their paths toward achieving them. They tried to interweave the respondent's story with her expert views on particular problems, giving a more complex picture of her personality to readers. Such was the case of an interview on cancer with Doctor Eva Sirácka, an interview about the social status of women with ethnographer Soňa Kovačevičová, an interview on visual arts with sculptress Zora Palová, and an interview about the role of classical music in contemporary society with Andrea Serečinová, editor-in-chief of the *Hudobný život* magazine.

A substantially smaller category of interviews offered the general views of the interviewed women, particularly the younger ones, who had become celebrities thanks mostly to the media, such as actresses or models. These interviews tended to slide into moderately yellow journalism at times.

8.2.2. CRUCIAL TOPICS OF EVERYDAY LIFE

Work and Career

The main topic in all the interviews was the women's work and professional careers. As all interviewees were successful women who had won recognition in their respective field, the common feature of them was that they were ambitious professionals who knew what they wanted and tried to pursue their values. In all interviews, the main emphasis was on the respondent's domain, her achievements and her plans for the future. In short, the interviews presented the image of a professional woman.

---

[14] Still, the occurrence of these interviews in *Sme Ženy* supplement between March and May 2007 was substantially lower compared to weekly magazines *Slovenka*, *Život* and *Plus 7 dní* (see Table 8.4 in Section 8.1.3.).

Especially when the interviews featured mature women, the reporters went into greater depth and offered a more comprehensive portrait that covered ground beyond the interviewees' work and career. In interviews with younger women, reporters focused almost exclusively on their work and career, based on the assumption that the life experience of these women – models, actresses, singers or sportswomen – was rather thin.

Some reporters put the respondent's professional career in the context of her self-fulfillment, which she viewed as crucial. The readers were thus offered a portrait of a woman who seeks and pursues forms of self-expression that were specific to her. The most outstanding examples of such interviews featured the director of a charity non-governmental organization, Denisa Augustínová (No. 9, 2008), the artist and photographer Dorota Sadovská (No. 20, 2007), and dance teacher Magdaléna Thierová (No. 43, 2007).

It is particularly noteworthy that work was the main topic of discussion with all interviewees, even those who had already reached retirement age. Not only that: even elderly women were portrayed as professionals full of vitality and energy who continued to develop their expertise.

Some of the respondents had succeeded in fields that are normally considered the domain of men, or had climbed to top executive posts. These interviews allowed reporters to discuss the gender barriers that hinder women in their careers. One of the interviewees, the parasitologist Markéta Derdáková, argued that women's achievement of high executive or management posts in the field of science was hampered by family obligations and a lack of ambition:

> "*Many women are not interested in higher executive posts because they demand a lot of time that they usually don't have – because of the family. Besides, I don't think women have this sort of ambition.*"

> (*Sme Ženy*, No. 2, 2008)

The interviewees presented different opinions on the preparedness of women to assume a more equal position on the labor market and in public life in general. Some did not conceal their nostalgia for "the good old days", when traditionally perceived dissimilarities between the female and male mentality were considered "natural". For instance, actress Lucia Gažiová observed that modern women were more independent – not because they wanted to be, but because they were "forced" to be so by life. This opinion reproduces traditional gender stereotypes, i.e. the perception of women as emotional, weaker, and therefore belonging to the private sphere, and of men as more rational, independent and therefore belonging to the public arena.

> "*I believe that girls today are generally more self-confident. Women could once afford to be 'flowers', but nowadays we have to be more independent, rational and strong. We have to be a bit like men, so to speak. But I am rather the pretty flower.*"

> (*Sme Ženy*, No.7, 2008)

Ways of Balancing Work and Family

While the emphasis was on the respondent's work, the interviews usually did not avoid family and partnership issues. Family was discussed in several contexts: balancing professional and family obligations; limitations on spending time with the family; the absence of family contact while working abroad; or support from the family as a prerequisite for women to perform well at work. The interviewees approached the issue of balancing professional and family obligations from different angles.

The image that constantly resurfaced in these interviews was that of women who are overwhelmed by family and professional obligations. According to ethnographer Soňa Kovačevičová, the burden that most Slovak women bear has always been heavier than that of Slovak men.

> *"My mother had an aunt whose husband was an ambassador in Moscow after the war. When she returned from there, she said: 'You have no idea what Czechoslovak women go through. In Moscow as well as in Warsaw, it is common for a family to have domestic help. Only here do women haul everything by themselves.' This remains true until the present day. But it is in women themselves and their education. Why on earth should they have to iron or preserve vegetables like their mothers once used to? Of course, it's good if a woman can manage everything by herself at home; on the other hand, it becomes a drag when the children arrive."*

> *(Sme Ženy, No. 37, 2007)*

In the same interview, the reporter seconds that opinion by saying that a woman's burden has not become lighter over time:

> *"The household continues to be primarily a woman's domain."*

> *(Sme Ženy, No. 37, 2007)*

Some reporters presented stereotypical views and emphasized that family was the right place for women to find true self-fulfillment. For instance, in an interview with a protestant vicar, Anna Polcková, the reporter asked:

> *"The natural fulfillment of every woman is having a family and children. Is this your case as well?"*

> *(Sme Ženy, No. 11, 2008)*

Similar notes were sounded in an interview with Karin Cíleková-Habšudová, who once ranked among the world's top 10 tennis players, but who perceives family as the best source of self-fulfillment:

> *"The sports life was an interesting stage, during which I managed to bring some of my ambitions to fruition thanks to hard work. But being a mother gives me a greater feeling of self-fulfillment."*

> *(Sme Ženy, No. 5, 2007)*

Some interviews criticized overburdening women with household and family chores, and painted an image of women as needing self-fulfillment besides the family. Such was the case of the interview with Gabriela Mlsnová, the former world fitness champion, who argued that after women get married they are overwhelmed with family obligations and feel that in pursuing their own goals and dreams they are stealing time from their families. She appreciated that this state of affairs was improving as more and more women were not afraid to pursue their ideas of self-fulfillment.

> *"Many women who started a family simply abandoned their sports careers because they felt it cost them too much time, and that it was somewhat inappropriate. Today it is different, thank goodness. Most women realize that having children does not automatically mean quitting their own activities."*

> *(Sme Ženy, No. 27, 2007)*

While some reporters' questions and some interviewees' answers were rooted in the traditional and stereotypical view that women's primary role is as homemakers, others documented a recent shift in how the role of women is seen in modern society. Some interviews offered the image of a professional woman who is not afraid to delegate caring for her household to another person. For instance, the director of the Slovak National Theatre (SND), Silvia Hroncová, advocated balancing professional and family obligations with the use of domestic help.

> *"I openly admit that at the moment I don't [manage my household duties too well].*
> *But I have a very tolerant family and domestic help as well."*
>
> (*Sme Ženy*, No. 12, 2007)

These interviews also presented another alternative harmonization model that remains exceptional in Slovakia. According to this model, tested by parasitologist Markéta Derdáková, a young mother entrusts a dependant child to the care of her husband or partner in order to pursue her career. To the reporter's question of whether "it is true that your husband became a househusband and accepted the principal responsibility for taking care of your son", the scientist reacted quite frankly and even outlined the problems of this solution:

> *"Thanks to him, I was really able to stay at the laboratory as long as I needed,*
> *although after some time he took an evening job at a veterinary emergency clinic.*
> *But he still claims that sometimes I carried it too far and that when our son saw*
> *me, he tried to hide behind him."*
>
> (*Sme Ženy*, No. 2, 2008)

Cooperation with Men

The interviews often discussed whether men adequately respect female colleagues who have won recognition in their professions or achieved high management posts within their organization.

SND Director Silvia Hroncová and police chief Zuzana Zajacová were asked whether men around them had problems respecting them as superiors. This question implicitly assumes that women in management positions may not be judged based on their expertise and practical managerial abilities, but rather based on their gender. Neither interviewee "swallowed the bait". Hroncová refused to speak for her subordinates:

> *"That's more a question for them. As for myself, I can only say that I do not have*
> *any problems with them."*
>
> (*Sme Ženy*, No. 12, 2007)

Zajacová, for her part, admitted that her beginnings in her new management post were not free of embarrassment:

> *"I think they accepted me rather professionally, although at the beginning, I sensed*
> *rather their stares. One could say that initially they were quite confused, surprised*
> *and perhaps curious about who had just joined them."*
>
> (*Sme Ženy*, No. 34, 2007)

Some women who worked in professions dominated by men expressed opinions on co-operation between women and men. All evaluated it positively and viewed the presence of women in these fields as beneficial. They argued that both men and women contributed specific qualities. These interviewees did not feel negatively about the fact that they were surrounded by men in their workplaces. On the contrary, they positively evaluated women's abilities as well as the opportunity to win recognition in these environments.

In the words of banker Ingrid Brocková:

> "*The World Bank is an institution where ... everybody ... is given an equal chance and there are many women in management posts. Men and women contribute their individual assets to the organization and its management; moreover, it cultivates communication ... I am not disturbed by the fact that banking is considered a male domain. I believe that we live in a century of women. Women are tremendously on the rise. Most are long-distance runners; but often they are too hard on each other and show little solidarity.*"

> (*Sme Ženy*, No. 39, 2007)

Police chief Zuzana Zajacová offered a similar opinion:

> "*If I should compare the time when I began my career with the police to the present, I would say that the profession is no longer a taboo for women. This job is ceasing to be the domain of men. Of course, the job is physically and mentally challenging and requires fitness, expertise and certain skills, such as shooting, which is why it may seem that men are better cut out for it. On the other hand, a woman can be more decisive and precise in a number of activities...*

> "*Women can be more uncompromising than men and do not need to discuss a problem endlessly ... Another very important asset of women on the force is their assertiveness in contact with people, accompanied by a very desirable professional smile. That is an effective and time-tested 'female weapon'.*"

> (*Sme Ženy*, No. 34, 2007)

Differences in Remuneration

When discussing gender inequalities on the labor market, the issue of lower wages for women than men surfaced most frequently, and was usually brought up spontaneously by the interviewees.

Ethnographer Soňa Kovačevičová put the unequal remuneration of women and men into the broader historical context of women's status in society.

> "*... I can hardly answer from my personal experience, because I come from a family where women were very free two generations before I was born – not exactly in terms of modern feminism, but they were certainly free to decide for themselves, men respected their opinions, and they were not reduced just to taking care of the family. Likewise, I was raised to obey, but also to be independent ... I did not encounter actual inferiority until later, particularly at work, when men simply approved higher wages for one another while us women had to haggle over every penny.*"

> (*Sme Ženy*, No. 37, 2007)

An indirect experience of unequal pay was also mentioned by actress Zuzana Krónerová, who said that discrimination against women had been quite prevalent during Communism, and lingers until the present day.

"I am no dissident, but I do recall one sad experience from those earlier days. I was on an advisory committee in a theatre and I spoke up for an outstanding professional, our stage manager. I said: 'She is here sixteen hours a day and works more than any of us, so why is her wage so low?' And the director, at that point comrade director, told me: 'She's just a woman.' At that, I hit the roof ... I'm not sure whether he increased her wages. I think not. This kind of discrimination remains today, and must change."

(*Sme Ženy*, No. 16, 2007)

Standard of Female Beauty

The issue of women's appearance surfaced in about one in three of the interviews. The most frequently discussed question was female beauty as a social standard, and the obligation of modern women to maintain it. Several women observed that society set strict standards regarding a woman's appearance, and defines beauty attributes that many women are unable to meet. All women seemed aware of this pressure and presented various opinions on it.

The imperative of female beauty was often brought up by the reporters themselves. In an interview with actress and comedian Petra Polnišová, the reporter asked: *"Do you notice the pressure society puts on the modern woman's appearance?"* (No. 13, 2007). The reporter who interviewed corrective dermatologist Jana Šrámeková sought an expert opinion on the subject: *"To what degree does society force women to improve their appearance, and to what degree does it reflect their own initiative?"* (No. 49, 2007) A similar question was asked of actress Zuzana Krónerová: *"In your opinion, is beauty important in life? Society pressures women more than men when it comes to good looks..."* (No. 16, 2007)

The women's answers differed significantly. Some automatically linked professionalism and beauty, and even viewed beauty as a prerequisite for professionalism. In their views, beauty implied an obligation to care for one's body and appearance. Their answers reflected the normative concept that a woman should look good regardless of her age. For instance, actress Michaela Čobejová said:

"A woman should be particular about her appearance at every age."

(*Sme Ženy*, No. 14, 2007)

It is worth noting that even women who were critical of the beauty imperative confirmed the strength of this stereotype and the pressure from society. They offered the image of a woman who succumbs to society's beauty standards even if she does not accept them. In the words of Petra Polnišová:

"I laugh at the notion that a woman should be perfect, but sometimes I succumb to it myself. I bother my husband and people around me that it would perhaps be better if I dropped a few pounds. On the other hand, I can live with it and turn my social handicap into an asset. Why should I have to submit to some fashion dictate of the period? I like people who are able to ignore this."

(*Sme Ženy*, No. 13, 2007)

Besides interviewees who presented stereotypical views of female beauty, there were also those who argued that decisions about a woman's appearance were up to the woman herself. In other words, it was up to women to decide what beauty meant, how to dress and how to care for their appearance. Zuzana Krónerová had this to say on the subject:

"The pressure to look good is worth resisting. Islands of individual freedom should be preserved. Let everyone dress however they like and as authentically as they feel, without insulting the taste of passers-by. I believe that internal beauty radiates on its own, and even the best make-up cannot replace it. Regardless of whether you are a woman or a man, your internal beauty will come to the surface."

(*Sme Ženy*, No. 16, 2007)

The media often find it difficult to resist the temptation to comment on the appearance of professional women. According to MP Magda Vášáryová, this media behavior disparages women and undermines their position:

"Even in serious interviews, female politicians are often asked: 'How can you harmonize your work and your household?' or 'What on earth are you wearing?' Reporters would never ask a man such a question ... In doing so, they disparage women and make readers believe that they actually belong in the kitchen."

(*Sme Ženy*, No. 4, 2006)

Embarrassments Related to Feminism

The issue of feminism was explicitly mentioned in only two interviews. In an interview with actress Ingrid Timková, the reporter wanted to know whether a woman who perceived that women and men had different opportunities in society should feel like a feminist: *"Are you a feminist? When a woman applies for a job, they ask her whether she has children. Men are not asked these questions..."* But the interviewee refused the association and emphatically distanced herself from feminism:

"Do you have to be a feminist to be able to speak about these issues? Or does speaking of these issues make you a feminist? This is about justice."

(*Sme Ženy*, No. 28, 2007)

In another interview, the reporter asked Zuzana Krónerová to present her own understanding of feminism in the context of defending women's rights in the private sphere: *"If a woman intends to defend her rights with respect to her husband and her micro-environment, does that make her a feminist?"* Unlike Timková, Krónerová did not dissociate herself from this definition of feminism; on the contrary, she openly subscribed to it. According to her, women should stand up for their rights.

"A woman must honestly believe her feelings. I like feminists very much."

(*Sme Ženy*, No. 16, 2007)

8.2.3. PERSONALITY OF A MATURE WOMAN

What the Age of 40 Entails

Out of the 71 women interviewed, 25 were older than 40, and almost all were women with university degrees who had achieved professional success or held high management posts. The scope of their professions was diverse, ranging from medicine to science and research, from culture and art to politics, sports and business. Some had achieved success in fields that are traditionally perceived as the domain of men (e.g. the police). Others had received international accolades for their work. In profiling women that had won recognition in their respective fields through hard work, the interviews presented an image of women as successful professionals who had been able to get past "the glass ceiling".

Interviews with mature women presented their life stories, including the twists and turns, but remained focused on their work and profession. All 25 women interviewed were portrayed as renowned professionals. Such was the case of interviews with television announcer Jarmila Košťová (No. 6, 2007) or oncologist Eva Sirácka (No. 22, 2007). The retrospective story of the interviewee's life was usually interwoven with her expert views on the issues she specialized in: dance teacher Magdaléna Thierová spoke of dance (No. 7, 2006), sculptress Zita Palová discussed art (No. 4, 2008) and MP Magda Vášáryová presented her views on political issues (No. 4, 2006).

Interviews with mature women differed from interviews with younger women. Because they had enjoyed longer professional careers, mature women had much richer life experience and professional expertise; some were even experienced in management, business or politics.

Reporters usually did not ask their respondents direct questions on ageing and old age. These issues mostly surfaced naturally in the course of the interview that discussed various aspects of the women's views of ageing. Some of them exposed negative age stereotypes.

For instance, the issue of old age was addressed by 40-year-old actress Szidi Tobias, who recalled her previous fears of losing her playfulness and spontaneity; however, she did not say whether her fears had come true:

> *"I have the feeling that life passes by very quickly. Sometimes it makes me sad. It is probably a woman's perception, too. I always remember this: when I was a child or a teenager, a 40-year-old woman looked old to me. I felt as if they did not know how to be spontaneous anymore. Perhaps I now see myself from a different angle. What if I am not so joyful either anymore?"*
>
> (*Sme Ženy,* No. 23, 2007)

Actress Ingrid Timková was asked a direct question about old age. The formulation used by the reporter revealed a negative age stereotype. At first she said that the age of 40 was truly a mature age, and then she amplified her observation with a follow-up question:

> *"This year you celebrated your 40th birthday. It's not an advanced age, but still … Are you not depressed because of your age?"*
>
> (*Sme Ženy,* No. 28, 2007)

Some interviews discussed ageing in the context of the degradation of female beauty. Based on her ample professional experience, corrective dermatologist Jana Šrámeková observed that mature women were more sober and therefore better able to estimate the need for corrective dermatological surgery:

> *"Some women look fantastic considering their age, but there are also ladies who have problems … Younger women tend to give in to fashion. We need to direct them and explain to them how fragile the line between beauty, elegance and vulgarity is. I don't think that ladies around 40 would come in with such demands."*
>
> (*Sme Ženy,* No. 49, 2007)

One interview stretched the issue of old age to terminal consequences as it discussed the prospects of nearing death, which is a taboo for most Slovak media. Actress Božidara Turzonovová entertained the thought that people should consciously prepare for old age and death the same way expectant mothers prepare for motherhood:

"Several weeks after a woman gets pregnant, she gets a pregnancy book ... for nine months, the woman learns to build a relationship to pregnancy and to prepare for maternity ... Wise people ask why we don't prepare to leave this world as well."

(*Sme Ženy*, No. 30, 2007)

Active Ageing as a Life Credo

The interviews profiled several female personalities who had already reached retirement age but continued to be active in their fields. They emphasized especially the professional side of these women, presenting readers with an image of active ageing through the examples of women who lead a full professional life.

Active ageing as a life credo was presented in an interview with sculptress Zita Palová, who at the age of 60 feels she is at the top of her creative skills, and has many plans and projects:

"We could publish yet another book ... It's great that we accomplished this goal now, when we feel at the top of our strength. We want to move forward, which is why from now on we will only discuss future projects."

(*Sme Ženy*, No. 4, 2008)

The *Sme Ženy* supplement presented mature women as successful professionals, as experienced and independent personalities who live for their work and yearn for professional recognition. This message resonated not only in interviews with mature women but was also present in some of the younger interviewees' statements. For instance, 23-year-old sport shooter Danka Barteková presented exactly this kind of level-headed mature woman as a role model from her own professional field:

"... I like the beautiful example of a Finnish woman who shortly after turning 50 wrapped up her shooting career and began to run marathons. Since sport shooting has no age limits, it's all about how one feels ... In my opinion, older shooters are more level-headed and especially more experienced."

(*Sme Ženy*, No. 3, 2008)

Doctor Jana Šrámeková emphasized that women in their mature years nowadays yearn for self-fulfillment and have better opportunities to achieve it because they are no longer so burdened by taking care of their households and families.

"Modern 50-year-old women are at the top of their strength. They are active, they have a solid professional background, they have raised children that have already become independent, and so they feel the need to devote time to themselves."

(*Sme Ženy*, No. 49, 2007)

8.2.4. ON THE PATH TOWARDS REAL CHANGE

The images of women profiled in the *Female Personality* section of the *Sme Ženy* supplement focused especially on their work and professionalism, proceeding from the crucial assumption that women have a legitimate right to professional self-fulfillment. The interviewees were presented as experts who are firmly established in their respective fields, who strive for perfection, who try to live in harmony with their values, and who apply various strategies to harmonize their professional careers with their private lives. The interviews emphasized the importance of women's self-fulfillment outside the family and the household.

The interviews offered readers a media image of women that questioned the traditional stereotype of women. The *Female Personality* section strove not to reduce the women's personalities to their private lives, as shown by the fact that several interviews discussed family background or emotional life only briefly. The difference between this media image and the common standard (for details, see section 8.1.3 of this chapter) may also be corroborated by the selection of professionals from various occupations, including those that are traditionally viewed as typically male (i.e. banker, police chief, protestant vicar, etc.).

Unfortunately, not all interviews managed to avoid reproducing traditional images of femininity. The most commonly reiterated stereotypes included describing caring for the household and family members as the principal area in which women find true self-fulfillment, or portraying this care as the exclusive responsibility of women.

The tendency to highlight the imperative of female beauty and emphasize the importance of a woman's appearance was particularly problematic. This traditional stereotype was further underlined by the editorial decision to feature pictures of the interviewed women dressed up in fashionable outfits and groomed by professional stylists. So, the principal way in which these female personalities were visually presented was through artificial photographs that, due to the layout, dominated the complementary amateur pictures taken from the interviewed women's private archives. Several women's attempts to preserve their authentic appearance met with an adamant editorial rejection.

From this viewpoint, our analysis of the interviews published by *Sme Ženy* must arrive at the same conclusion as the analysis of the select daily newspapers and weekly magazines in Section 8.1 of this chapter: it is truly necessary to critically reflect and overcome the often subconscious gender and age stereotypes in journalists' heads.

The degree to which the interviews managed to capture the interviewees' personality and their professional expertise varied depending on the reporter's professional quality. During the 18 month period examined, the interviews were conducted by eleven female journalists, which was inevitably reflected in variations in quality. While some went quite deep, others indicated that the author had not done her homework, which is crucial for such interviews. In such cases, the interview remained superficial and had a rather light, even "yellow" character. Thus the editorial staff of *Sme Ženy* supplement has not managed to fully extricate itself from the mainstream tendency to "celebritize" the media domain (Jesenková, 2008).

However, despite all the deficiencies mentioned, the *Female Personality* section of the *Sme Ženy* supplement should be praised for its systematic endeavor to present readers with examples of successful women who might inspire other women and simultaneously encourage male readers to respect women with outstanding professional resumes. This kind of editorial policy, combined with increasing gender and age sensitivity among journalists, might in the long term strengthen the position of women on the labor market and in society in general.

CONCLUSION

This publication features the research findings of a three-year project called *Plus for Women 45+* by the EU Community Initiative EQUAL, which was implemented between 2005 and 2008 and financed by the European Social Fund. The eight chapters of this book cover a relatively broad spectrum of issues and problems that are interrelated, but each has its own "life" as well. One could almost say that readers can begin to read the book at any chapter they please.

When examining a number of topics, we capitalized on our previous survey research that has been conducted since the early 1990s, which enabled us to analyze long-term trends in Slovakia. In the case of other topics, this publication is a pioneering effort and we believe it will blaze the trail for future followers. Whereas the former category comprises mostly gender analyses, the latter is represented by those chapters that combine gender and age perspectives while paying particular attention to the category of women in their mature years, i.e. women between the ages of 45 and 64.

This publication places great emphasis on describing the life situations of Slovak women and men, as well as on analyzing their views of these situations in light of their ideals and expectations. We are aware that the tremendous amount of facts and statistical data provided in this book will be interpreted differently by individual readers, who will approach them from various positions and will view them through the prism of their own life experiences and convictions. The plurality of opinions within the readership community reflects the fact that a particular situation, which may be considered "natural" or "normal" in one social environment, can be seen as unsatisfactory or even completely unacceptable in another. Precisely this tension between the *status quo* and what is desirable, between reality and the ideal can catalyze social change. That is why we have strived to capture that conflict in our research as well as in this publication.

This also explains why the book avoids suggesting public policy measures to be taken in this area: we believe that they can be effective only provided they are based on an intimate knowledge of the social environment for which they are designed.

With all these circumstances in mind, it seems appropriate to describe the pillars that buttressed our scientific approach to this project in general and this publication in particular.

The first pillar is *furthering the idea of equality and non-discrimination*, which in case of this publication focuses primarily on women and men of different ages. Of course, we are not referring to some mechanical form of equal treatment that ignores the diversity in people's qualities, make-ups and living conditions. We are not saying that individuals should be forced to conform to a uniform mould. On the other hand, since we respect the right of every human being to dignity and the right to develop their own potential, we believe it is necessary to reduce the sometimes enormous gaps among the chances of individuals or entire social groups.

The second pillar is our *conviction that Slovak society needs to mobilize all of its potential* to cope with the formidable challenges that it will face in future, such as alleviating the effects of population ageing and eliminating the lingering discrimination against women and elderly people on the labor market as well as within society in general.

In broader terms, mobilizing this potential requires a fundamental change in people's attitudes and behavior. First and foremost, it is necessary to overcome the widespread skepticism and resignation regarding the very possibility of remedying the *status quo*. This goes for men but even more so for women, who are more critical than men of their status and opportunities within the public and private spheres, yet they do not create enough pressure to effect a change.

Examples are not difficult to find. As we have shown in this book, Slovak women are less satisfied with the lingering traditional unbalanced division of labor within the family, and they are also more critical of their status and opportunities on the labor market and in politics. Compared to men, however, they have less clear ideas on how to fight discrimination on the labor market, and tend to prefer a strategy of passive adaptation. In doing so, they actually help to cement their weaker position within the public sphere. Numerous research findings show that the syndrome of learned helplessness is particularly prevalent among mature women, who grow increasingly passive and gradually withdraw from the public sphere especially after they reach the age of 55. That is why Slovakia needs the activist redefinition of the prevailing concept of ageing.

Our analysis also revealed that younger and more educated women are particularly critical of gender inequalities, while younger men tend to see fewer reasons to change the *status quo*, indicating that differences between the views of women and men are deeper within the younger generation. This tension could spark a positive reversal, provided that women are sufficiently assertive in advocating their demands within the public as well as the private spheres. When emphasizing the need to overcome the syndrome of learned helplessness, we do not mean to provoke an irreconcilable gender conflict, but rather to outline a viable path towards a more equal partnership between women and men. Naturally, women cannot walk this path alone, as it requires active participation on the part of men in terms of seeing gender differences, acknowledging the need for change, and implementing this change in everyday life.

The third pillar of our research is *promoting a realistic attitude* to the current situation of women in the public and private spheres. This includes also the conviction that society's increasing diversity and the growing plurality of individual life courses and personal strategies should not be a priori seen as a negative departure from "sound traditions", but rather as trends that offer possibilities for extending the boundaries of individual freedom and responsibility.

That is why we do not approve of such public policy solutions that would prefer and privilege only one type of family, namely the matrimonial family. In the period of diversification of partnership and family forms and of increasing number of children born outside matrimony, such policies would disadvantage children who grow up in one-parent families who also deserve to be treated equally.

In a similar way, we regard it as unrealistic to require women to withdraw on a wider scale from the public sphere and to return to the private one. Even though some women prefer this model, most of them view paid employment not only as a necessary source of family income but also as an opportunity for self-fulfillment and for the satisfaction of their other social needs.

At the same time, however, it should be emphasized that most labor related to household chores and to looking after family members remains on the shoulders of women in Slovakia. Numerous research findings indicate that the unbalanced division of labor between women and men that is typical of the traditional family model not only survived the communist regime but persists even two decades after its collapse. Women still carry a double burden, and while their normative ideas about the division of labor within the family continue to drift towards the balanced partnership model, the views of men have remained almost unchanged.

As the present publication shows, the range of life courses and the spectrum of timing of life stages is increasing, which in turn strengthens the diversity of relationships between work and family, as well as the diversity of the needs of working women and men. Obviously, such varied professional and family lives also require a differentiated approach on the part of employers and broader society.

This book presents significant facts about various aspects of women's current status on the labor market. It illustrates the lingering concentration of women in those sectors, industries and professions that are inadequately rewarded by society; the substantial pay gap between women and men, which is among the greatest within the European Union; and the insufficient representation of women in managerial and decision-making posts. Sociological surveys have repeatedly proved that the general public – both women and men – is growing increasingly critical of the disadvantages that women face on the labor market.

The representation of women in political decision-making processes and the level of their civic participation are equally unsatisfactory in the long term. On the one hand, there are two grounds for cautious optimism on this score: first, the visibility of this problem has increased in recent years; second, public opinion strongly endorses measures aimed at increasing the representation of women in politics. On the other hand, neither women nor men regard the low participation of women in political decision-making as a key problem of Slovak women. This completes a vicious circle in which the marginal position of the gender agenda among other political agendas persists.

A particularly serious problem in Slovakia is the media image of women in general and of women in their mature years or old age in particular. The results of a content analysis of select print media justify the conclusion that the image of women that is reproduced and disseminated by the media is largely based on gender stereotypes or a combination of gender and age stereotypes. Some isolated attempts to change this general approach have been seen in recent years, but they have not become the part of the mainstream. In this respect, increasing the sensitivity of the creators of media messages – i.e. reporters, journalists, editors, newscasters, moderators, etc. – is essential to developing non-discriminatory and gender- and age-sensitive media in Slovakia.

Finally, let us say a few words on the category of women over 45. Their position on the labor market does not differ much from that of women in general. Their employment profile tends to include gender segregation; low representation in managerial posts; relatively poor prospects for promotion; the predominance of full-time labor contracts; the relatively high occurrence of overtime, night and weekend work; relatively low incomes and equally low satisfaction with their pay. What sets women over 45 apart from their younger counterparts is the higher occurrence of long-term unemployment; their tendency to solve the problem of unemployment by early retirement; their lower educational attainment and lower interest in improving their qualifications; their greater exposure to discrimination in the workplace; their more fragile sense of employment security; and their greater preparedness to make concessions to keep their jobs. All in all, our analysis produced ample evidence of the disadvantaged position of women in their mature years on the labor market.

Needless to say, women over 45 have remarkable employment potential. However, if we are to capitalize on it, we must overcome a whole range of social barriers, both structural and individual. Paradoxes abound: Slovakia's economy needs to increase the participation of older workers in labor market, but society is teeming with negative age stereotypes, and the corporate sector is a hotbed of ageist prejudices; the population is ageing, but employers do not seem prepared for this demographic scenario; demand for older employees is increasing, but employers do not take their specific needs into account sufficiently.

Remedying this situation will be neither quick nor easy. As we indicated in the foreword to this book, it will require a profound cultural change. Enacting that change calls for the partnership and involvement of many stakeholders, including the government; corporations; workers and worker organizations; research, academic and educational institutions; the media; and last, but not least, older women and men themselves.

The development of Slovakia towards the society for all ages must include the promotion of the concept of active ageing and the all-round participation of older women and men in the economic, social, cultural and political life of the society. There is no doubt that they have a lot to offer our society, and that society needs their contribution.

We would like to conclude by expressing the hope that embracing the concepts of gender equality and active ageing will become yet another in a long line of tough challenges that people in Slovakia have mastered successfully following the fall of communism in 1989.

REFERENCES

A Roadmap for Equality between Women and Men 2006 – 2010. COM(2006) 92 final. Brussels, Commission of the European Communities 2006. Available at: http://ec.europa.eu/employment_social/news/2006/mar/com06092_roadmap_en.pdf

Aburdene, P. – Naisbitt, J.: *Megatrends for Women.* New York, Vilard Books 1992.

Alan, J.: *Etapy života očima sociologie* [Life Stages through the Eyes of Sociology]. Prague, Panorama 1989.

Analýza rozdielov v priemerných zárobkoch žien a mužov v SR [An Analysis of the Differences between the Average Wages of Women and Men in the Slovak Republic]. Bratislava, Ministry of Labor, Social Affairs and Family 2005.

Anketa medzi manažérmi ľudských zdrojov o firemných politikách voči starším pracovníkom a pracovníčkam [Poll of Human Resources Managers on Corporate Policies towards Elderly Employees]. Bratislava, Institute for Public Affairs July – August 2007.

Bačová, V.: "Ako sa vytvára ženskosť: Spojenie moci a sebadefinovania" ['Shaping Femininity: Linking Power and Self-Definition'] in Cviková, J. – Juráňová, J. – Kobová, Ľ. (eds.): *Žena nie je tovar: komodifikácia žien v našej kultúre* [Women Are Not Products: The Commodification of Women in Our Culture]. Bratislava, Aspekt 2005, pp. 173 – 191.

Bahna, M.: "Gender Equality and the Labor Market in Slovakia (Report on a Representative Survey)" in Piscová, M. (ed.): *Slovakia on the Path toward Gender Equality.* Bratislava, Institute of Sociology of the Slovak Academy of Sciences – European Roma Working Agency 2006.

Barošová, M.: *Monitoring rodovej segregácie na trhu práce – analýza dopadov transformačných zmien* [Monitoring of Gender Segregation on the Labor Market: An Analysis of the Consequences of Transformation Changes], the final report on VÚ No. 2120. Bratislava, Research Institute of Labor and Family 2006.

Bauman, Z.: *Individualizovaná společnost* [The Individualized Society]. Prague, Mladá fronta 2004.

Beck, U.: *Riziková společnost* [The Risk Society]. Prague, SLON 2004.

Bednárik, R.: *Sociálno-ekonomická situácia starších ľudí na Slovensku* [The Socio-Economic Situation of Elderly People in Slovakia], a report from a sociological survey. Bratislava, Research Institute of Labor and Family 2004.

Benassi, M. P.: "Women's Earnings in the EU: 28 % Less Than Men's" in *Statistics in Focus – Population and Social Conditions*, theme 3 – 6/1999. Brussels, Eurostat 1999.

Bertola, G. – Blau, F. D. – Kahn, L. M.: *Labor Market Institutions and Demographic Employment Patterns*, a CEPR Working Paper No. 3448, 2002.

Bitušíková, A.: "Ženy a veda v krajinách strednej a východnej Európy" ['Women and Science in Central and Eastern European Countries'] in *Spravodajca Universitas Matthiae Belii* [Newsletter of Universitas Matthiae Belii]. Banská Bystrica, UMB March – April 2004.

Bleha, B. – Vaňo, B.: "Niektoré teoretické a metodologické aspekty populačnej politiky a náčrt jej koncepcie pre Slovenskú republiku" ['Certain Theoretical and Methodological Aspects of Population Policy and an Outline of a Concept for the Slovak Republic'] in *Sociológia* No. 39, 2007, pp. 62 – 80.

Bodnárová, B. – Džambazovič, R. – Filadelfiová, J. – Gerbery, D. – Kvapilová, E. – Porubänová, S.: T*ransformácia sociálneho systému na Slovensku: stav, výsledky, riziká narušenia sociálnej súdržnosti a modely riešenia* [Transformation of the Welfare System in Slovakia: Status Quo, Results, Risks of Disrupting Social Cohesion, and Possible Solutions], a report from the 1st stage of a survey. Bratislava, Research Institute of Labor and Family 2004.

Bodnárová, B. – Džambazovič, R. – Filadelfiová, J. – Gerbery, D. – Pafková, K. – Porubänová, S.: *Rodinná politika a potreby mladých rodín* [Family Policy and the Needs of Young Families], the final report on a survey. Bratislava, Research Institute of Labor and Family 2004.

Bodnárová, B. – Džambazovič, R. – Filadelfiová, J. – Gerbery, D. – Kvapilová, E. – Porubänová, S.: *Transformácia sociálneho systému na Slovensku: stav, výsledky, riziká narušenia sociálnej súdržnosti a modely riešenia* [Transformation of the Welfare System in Slovakia: Status Quo, Results, Risks of Disrupting Social Cohesion and Solution Models], the final report on a survey. Bratislava, Research Institute of Labor and Family 2005.

Bodnárová, B. – Filadelfiová, J. – Gerbery, D.: *Výskum potrieb a poskytovania služieb pre rodiny zabezpečujúce starostlivosť o závislých členov* [Survey of Needs and Services Extended to Families Providing for Dependent Members], the final report on a survey. Bratislava, Research Institute of Labor and Family 2005.

Bodnárová, B. – Filadelfiová, J. – Gerbery, D. – Džambazovič, R. – Kvapilová, E.: *Premeny sociálnej politiky* [Alterations of Social Policy]. Bratislava, Research Institute of Labor and Family 2006.

Bodnárová, B. – Filadelfiová, J. – Guráň, P.: *Reflexia súčasnej demografickej situácie v rodinných a sociálnych politikách krajín strednej a východnej Európy* [Reflections on the Current Demographic Situation in Families and the Social Policies of Central and Eastern European Countries], the final report on a survey. Bratislava, International Center for Family Studies 2001.

Bosá, M.: "Výchova a problém násilia páchaného na ženách" ['Education and the Issue of Violence against Women'] in Bútorová, Z. – Filadelfiová, J. (eds.): *Násilie páchané na ženách ako problém verejnej politiky* [Violence against Women as a Public Policy Issue], Bratislava, Institute for Public Affairs 2005.

Bosá, M. – Minarovičová, K.: *Rodovo citlivá výchova* [Gender Sensitive Education]. Bratislava, EsFem 2005.

Bourdieu, P.: *O televizi* [On Television]. Brno, Doplněk 2002.

Braun Levine, S.: *The Woman's Guide to Second Adulthood: Inventing the Rest of Our Lives.* London, Bloomsbury Publishing 2005.

Brinkerhoff, D. B. – White, L. K.: *Sociology.* St. Paul, West Publishing Company 1988.

Bútora, M. – Bútorová, Z.: *Mimovládne organizácie a dobrovoľníctvo na Slovensku očami verejnej mienky* [Non-Governmental Organizations and Volunteerism in Slovakia through the Eyes of Public Opinion]. Bratislava, S.P.A.C.E. 1996.

Bútorová, Z. et al: *She and He in Slovakia: Gender Issues in Public Opinion.* Bratislava, FOCUS 1996.

Bútorová, Z. (ed.): *Krehká sila. Dvadsať rozhovorov o životných cestách žien* [Fragile Strength: Twenty Interviews about the Life Stories of Women]. Bratislava, Institute for Public Affairs and Kalligram 2001.

Bútorová, Z.: "Mimovládne organizácie a dobročinnosť vo svetle verejnej mienky" ['Non-Governmental Organizations and Charity in Public Perception'] in Majchrák, J. – Strečanský, B. – Bútora, M. (eds.): *Keď ľahostajnosť nie je odpoveď. Príbeh občianskeho združovania na Slovensku po páde komunizmu* [When Indifference Is Not the Answer: The Story of Civic Associating in Slovakia after the Fall of Communism]. Bratislava, Institute for Public Affairs 2004.

Bútorová, Z.: "Growing Diversity in the Lives of Slovak People (The Sociological Background to Domestic Cultural Disputes)" in Gyárfášová, O. – Mesežnikov, G. (eds.): *Slovakia "in the Draft": Cultural and Ethical Challenges and the New Nature of Disputes after Accession to the European Union*. Bratislava, Institute for Public Affairs 2005.

Bútorová, Z. (ed.): *Tu a teraz. Sondy do života žien 45+* [*Here and Now: Probes into the Lives of Women 45+*]. Bratislava, Institute for Public Affairs 2007.

Bútorová, Z . et al.: Ona a on na Slovensku. Zaostrené na rod a vek [She and He in Slovakia: Focused on Gender and Age]. Bratislava, Institute for Public Affairs 2008.

Bútorová, Z . – Filadelfiová, J. (ed.): *Násilie páchané na ženách ako problém verejnej politiky* [Violence against Women as a Public Policy Issue]. Bratislava, Institute for Public Affairs 2005.

Bútorová, Z. – Filadelfiová, J.: "Frauen und FrauenOrganizationen in der Slowakei" ['Women and Women's Organizations in Slovakia'] in *Stillstand oder Roll-back? Zur Situation der Frauen in den „neuen" mittel-europäischen EU-Ländern und der Ukraine* [Stillness or Roll-Back? The Situation of Women in the "New" Central European EU Member States and Ukraine]. Warsaw, Heinrich Böll Stiftung, 2006.

Bútorová, Z. – Filadelfiová, J. – Guráň, O. – Gyárfášová, O. – Farkašová, K.: "Gender Issues in Slovakia" in Mesežnikov, G. – Ivantyšin, M. – Nicholson, T. (eds.): *Slovakia 1998 – 1999: A Global Report on the State of Society*. Bratislava, Institute for Public Affairs 1999.

Bútorová, Z. – Filadelfiová, J. – Cviková, J. – Gyarfášová, O. – Farkašová, K.: "Women, Men, and Equality of Opportunities" in Mesežnikov, G. – Kollár, M. – Nicholson, T. (eds.): *Slovakia 2002: A Global Report on the State of Society*. Bratislava, Institute for Public Affairs 2002.

Bútorová, Z. – Filadelfiová, J. – Marošiová, L.: "Ženské mimovládne organizácie: trendy, problémy, výzvy" ['Women's Non-Governmental Organizations: Trends, Problems and Challenges'] in Majchrák, J. – Strečanský, B. – Bútora, M. (eds.): *Keď ľahostajnosť nie je odpoveď. Príbeh občianskeho združovania na Slovensku po páde komunizmu* [When Indifference Is Not the Answer. The Story of Civic Associating in Slovakia after the Fall of Communism]. Bratislava, Institute for Public Affairs 2004.

Bútorová, Z. – Gyárfášová, O: "Public Opinion" in Bútora, M. – Kollár, M. – Mesežnikov, G. (eds.): *Slovakia 2006: A Global Report on the State of Society*. Bratislava, Institute for Public Affairs 2007.

Bútorová, Z. – Gyárfášová, O.: "Verejná mienka" ['Public Opinion'] in Kollár, M. – Mesežnikov, G. – Bútora, M. (eds.): *Slovensko 2007. Súhrnná správa o stave spoločnosti* [Slovakia 2007: A Global Report on the State of Society]. Bratislava, Institute for Public Affairs 2008.

Bútorová, Z. – Gyárfášová, O – Krivý, V.: "Slovakia Votes: Public Opinion and Electoral Behavior" in Bútora, M. – Gyárfášová, O. – Mesežnikov, G. – Skladony, W. T. (eds.): *Democracy and Populism in Central Europe: The Visegrad Elections and Their Aftermath*. Bratislava, Institute for Public Affairs 2007.

Bútorová, Z. – Gyárfášová, O. – Velšic, M.: "Public Opinion" in Kollár, M. – Mesežnikov, G. – Kollár, M. (eds.): *Slovakia 2003: A Global Report on the State of Society*. *Bratislava*, Institute for Public Affairs 2004.

Bútorová, Z. – Gyárfášová, O. – Velšic, M.: "Public Opinion" in Kollár, M. – Mesežnikov, G. – Kollár, M. (eds.): *Slovakia 2004: A Global Report on the State of Society*. *Bratislava*, Institute for Public Affairs 2005.

Commission Acts to Bridge Gender Pay Gap, a press release by the European Commission. Brussels, European Commission, July 18, 2007.

Confronting Demographic Change: A New Solidarity between the Generations, the Green Book. Brussels, European Commission 2005.

Crompton, R. (ed.): *Restructuring Gender Relations and Employment: The Decline of the Male Breadwinner*. Oxford, Oxford University Press 1999.

Curran, D. J. – Renzetti, C. M.: *Ženy, muži a společnost* [Women, Men, and Society]. Prague, Karolinum 2003.

Current Problems of Slovakia after the Split of the ČSFR – March 1993. Bratislava, Center for Social Analysis 1993.

Current Problems of Slovakia – December 1995. Bratislava, FOCUS 1996.

Cviková, J.: "Nerodíme sa ako ženy a muži. Pohlavie a rod" ['We Are Not Born as Women and Men: Sex and Gender'] in Cviková, J. – Juráňová, J. (eds.): *Ružový a modrý svet. Rodové stereotypy a ich dôsledky* [Pink and Blue World: Gender Stereotypes and Their Implications]. Bratislava, Občan a demokracia – Aspekt 2003.

Cviková, J. (ed.): *Aká práca, taká pláca? Aspekty rodovej nerovnosti v odmeňovaní* [Same Work, Same Pay? Aspects of Gender Inequality in Remuneration]. Bratislava, Aspekt 2008.

Cviková, J. – Juráňová, J.: *Ružový a modrý svet. Rodové stereotypy a ich dôsledky* [Pink and Blue World: Gender Stereotypes and Their Implications]. Bratislava, Občan a demokracia – Aspekt 2003.

Čermáková, M. – Maříková, H. – Tuček, M.: "Role mužů a žen v rodině a ve společnosti I. a II." ['The Role of Men and Women in Family and Society'] in *Data & fakta* [Data & Facts], information from surveys 5 and 6. Prague, Institute of Sociology of the Czech Academy of Sciences 1995.

Čornaničová, R.: "Idea vzniku a založenie UTV na Slovensku" ['The Idea of the Founding and the Emergence of UTV in Slovakia'] in *Hist17ia a súčasnosť UTV na Slovensku* [The Past and Present of UTV in Slovakia], a collection on the occasion of the 15th anniversary of the establishment of universities of the third age in the Slovak Republic. Bratislava, Comenius University 2007. Available at: http://www.cdv.uniba.sk/index.php?id=2466

Daučíková, A. – Bútorová, Z. – Wallace-Lorencová, V.: "The Status of Sexual Minorities" in Mesežnikov, G. – Kollár, M. – Nicholson, T. (eds.): *Slovakia 2002: A Global Report on the State of Society*. Bratislava, Institute for Public Affairs 2002.

Debrecéniová, J. – Očenášová, Z.: *Equal Opportunities for Women and Men. Monitoring Law and Practice in Slovakia.* Bratislava, OSI/Network Women's Program 2005.

Demographic Challenges – Family Needs Partnership, documentation of a specialist conference held on February 2 – 4, 2006, within the framework of Austria's EU Presidency. Vienna, Federal Ministry of Social Security, Generations and Consumer Protection 2006.

Demographic Outlook: National Reports on the Demographic Developments in 2007. Brussels, European Communities 2007. Available at: http://epp.eurostat.ec.europa.eu/cache/ITY_OFFPUB/KS-RA-07-026/EN/KS-RA-07-026-EN.PDF

Discrimination in the European Union: Special Eurobarometer 263. Brussels, European Commission 2007.

Džambazovič, R.: "Premeny rómskej rodiny" ['Metamorphoses of the Romany Family'] in *Rodina v spoločenských premenách Slovenska* [The Family amidst Slovakia's Societal Changes], proceedings from a conference. Prešov, Faculty of Arts at Prešov University 2001.

Džambazovič, R.: *Chudoba na Slovensku: Diskurz, rozsah a profil chudoby* [Poverty in Slovakia: Discourse on the Extent and Profile of Poverty]. Bratislava, Comenius University 2007.

Empirical Data from a FOCUS Sociological Survey. Bratislava, FOCUS, December 1994.

Empirical Data from a FOCUS Sociological Survey. Bratislava, FOCUS, June 1995.

Empirical Data from an IVO Sociological Survey. Bratislava, Institute for Public Affairs, January 1999.

Empirical Data from an IVO Sociological Survey. Bratislava, Institute for Public Affairs, March 2000.

Empirical Data from an IVO Sociological Survey. Bratislava, Institute for Public Affairs, June 2002.

Empirical Data from an IVO Sociological Survey. Bratislava, Institute for Public Affairs, September 2003.

Empirical Data from an IVO Sociological Survey. Bratislava, Institute for Public Affairs, November 2004.

Empirical Data from an IVO Sociological Survey. Bratislava, Institute for Public Affairs, July 2005a.

Empirical Data from an IVO Sociological Survey. Bratislava, Institute for Public Affairs, September 2005b.

Empirical Data from an IVO Sociological Survey. Bratislava, Institute for Public Affairs, November 2005c.

Empirical Data from a Sociological Survey. Bratislava, Slovak National Centre for Human Rights, November 2005d.

Empirical Data from an IVO Sociological Survey. Bratislava, Institute for Public Affairs, April, 2006a.

Empirical Data from an IVO Sociological Survey. Bratislava, Institute for Public Affairs, August 2006b.

Empirical Data from an IVO Sociological Survey. Bratislava, Institute for Public Affairs, November 2006c.

Empirical Data from an IVO Sociological Survey. Bratislava, Institute for Public Affairs, April 2007a.

Empirical Data from an IVO Sociological Survey. Bratislava, Institute for Public Affairs, August 2007b.

Empirical Data from an IVO Sociological Survey. Bratislava, Institute for Public Affairs, November 2007c.

Empirical Data from an IVO Sociological Survey. Bratislava, Institute for Public Affairs, May 2008.

Employment in Europe 2007. Brussels, European Commission's DG for Employment, Social Affairs and Equal Opportunities, October 2007. Available at: http://www.igfse.pt/upload/docs/gabdoc/2008/01-Jan/keah07001_en.pdf

Employment Initiatives for an Ageing Workforce in the EU 15. Dublin, European Foundation for the Improvement of Living and Working Conditions 2006.

Esping-Andersen, G.: *A Welfare State for the 21st Century*, a report to the Portuguese presidency. Brussels, European Commission 2000. Available at: http://www.nnn.se/seminar/pdf/report.pdf

Esping-Andersen, G. et al: *Why We Need a New Welfare State?* Oxford, Oxford University Press 2002.

Europe's Demographic Future: Facts and Figures on Challenges and Opportunities. Brussels, European Commission's DG for Employment, Social Affairs and Equal Opportunities 2007. Available at: http://ec.europa.eu/employment_social/spsi/docs/social_situation/demo_report_2007_en.pdf

European Values Studies. Názory obyvateľov Slovenska v medzinárodnom porovnaní, 1. časť [European Values Studies: Views of Slovakia's Inhabitants in an International Comparison, Part 1. Tilburg University – Institute of Sociology of the Slovak Academy of Sciences 1999/2000.

European Working Conditions Survey 2005. Dublin, European Foundation for the Improvement of Living and Working Conditions 2005. Available at: http://www.eurofound.eu.int/ewco/surveys/index.htm

EU-SILC 2005: Zisťovanie o príjmoch a životných podmienkach domácností v SR [EU-SILC 2005: Examining the Income and Living Conditions of Households in the Slovak Republic]. Bratislava, Statistical Office of the Slovak Republic 2006.

EU-SILC 2006: Zisťovanie o príjmoch a životných podmienkach domácností v SR [EU-SILC 2006: Examining the Income and Living Conditions of Households in the Slovak Republic]. Bratislava, Statistical Office of the Slovak Republic 2007.

Exit poll MVK pre TV Markíza [MVK Exit Poll for TV Markíza]. Bratislava, MVK agency, June 2006.

Falťan, Ľ. et al.: *Regionálna diferenciácia, regionálny rozvoj v Slovenskej republike v kontexte integračných dosahov* [Regional Differentiation and Regional Development in the Slovak Republic in the Context of Integration Implications]. Bratislava, Institute of Sociology of the Slovak Academy of Sciences 2004.

Farrell, W.: *Why Men Earn More (The Startling Truth Behind the Pay Gap – and What Women Can Do about It.* New York, AMACOM 2005.

Fialová, Z.: *Ženy v mimovládnych organizáciách* [Women in Non-Governmental Organizations]. Bratislava, Alliance of Slovak Women 1997.

Filadelfiová, J.: "Bytová a ekonomická situácia starších ľudí" ['The Housing and Economic Situation of Elderly People'] in *Životná situácia starších ľudí v regióne Malacky* [The Living Situation of Elderly People in the Malacky Region], the final report on a survey. Bratislava, Institute of Sociology of the Slovak Academy of Sciences – Research Institute of Gerontology 1993.

Filadelfiová, J.: "Stratégie a postupy zvyšovania účasti žien v politickom a verejnom živote" ['Strategies and Methods of Increasing Women's Participation in Political and Public Life'] in *Mozaika rodiny 2001* [Family Mosaic 2001]. Bratislava, International Center for Family Studies 2001.

Filadelfiová, J.: "O ženách, moci a politike: úvahy, fakty, súvislosti" ['On Women, Power and Politics: Reflections, Facts, Context'] in Cviková, J. – Juráňová, J. (eds.): *Hlasy žien: Aspekty ženskej politiky* [Women's Voices: Aspects of Female Policy]. Bratislava, Aspekt 2002.

Filadelfiová, J.: "Rovnosť príležitostí" ['Equal Opportunities'] in Mesežnikov, G. – Gyárfášová, O. – Kollár, M.: *Slovenské voľby '02. Výsledky, dôsledky, súvislosti* [Slovak Elections '02: Results, Consequences, Context]. Bratislava, Institute for Public Affairs 2003.

Filadelfiová, J.: "Demografický vývoj a rodina" ['Demographic Development and the Family'] in Szomolányiová, S. (ed.): *Spoločnosť a politika na Slovensku: cesty k stabilite 1989 – 2004* [Society and Politics in Slovakia: Paths toward Stability between 1989 and 2004]. Bratislava, Comenius University 2005a.

Filadelfiová, J.: "Demografická situácia a správanie rodín vz. verejná politika v SR" ['The Demographic Situation and Family Behavior vs. Public Policy in the Slovak Republic'] in *Sociológia* No. 5, 2005b.

Filadelfiová, J.: "Populačný vývoj a štruktúra rodín" ['Demographic Development and Family Structure'] in Kollár, M. – Mesežnikov, G. (eds.): *Slovensko 2004. Súhrnná správa o stave spoločnosti* [Slovakia 2004: A Global Report on the State of Society]. Bratislava, Institute for Public Affairs 2005c.

Filadelfiová, J.: "Demografický vývoj a posuny v štruktúre populácie a domácností ako predpoklad a dôsledok zmien v sociálnej sfére" ['Demographic Development and Shifts in the Structure of the Population and Households as the Prerequisite for and Consequence of Changes in the Welfare System'] in Bodnárová, B. – Filadelfiová, J. – Gerbery, D. – Džambazovič, R. – Kvapilová, E.: *Premeny sociálnej politiky* [Changes in Social Policy]. Bratislava, Research Institute of Labor and Family 2006a.

Filadelfiová, J.: "Zmeny v rodinnej politike" ['Changes in Family Policy'] in Bodnárová, B. – Filadelfiová, J. – Gerbery. D. – Džambazovič, R. – Kvapilová, E.: *Premeny sociálnej politiky* [Changes in Social Policy]. Bratislava, Research Institute of Labor and Family 2006b.

Filadelfiová, J.: "Vek, životný cyklus a medzigeneračný prenos chudoby." ['Age, Life Cycle and Intergenerational Transmission of Poverty'] in Gerbery, D. – Lesay, I. – Škobla, D. (eds.): *Kniha o chudobe: Spoločenské súvislosti a verejné politiky* [The Book on Poverty: Social Context and Public Policies]. Bratislava, Friends of Earth-CEPA – Friedrich Ebert Stiftung – Slovak Anti-Poverty Network 2007.

Filadelfiová, J.: "Rodová priepasť: Čo (ne)hovoria štatistiky a výskumné dáta o odmeňovaní žien a mužov" ['Gender Gap: What Statistics and Research Data (Do Not) Say about the

Remuneration of Women and Men'] in Cviková, J. (ed.): *Aká práca, taká pláca? Aspekty rodovej nerovnosti v odmeňovaní* [Same Work, Same Pay? Aspects of Gender Inequality in Remuneration]. Bratislava, Aspekt 2008a.

Filadelfiová, J.: *Učiteľské povolanie. Aspekty rodovej rovnosti v škole* [Teaching Profession: Aspects of Gender Equality in School]. Bratislava, Aspekt 2008b.

Filadelfiová, J. – Bútorová, Z.: "Equality of Women and Men" in Bútora, M. – Kollár, M. – Mesežnikov, G. (eds.): *Slovakia 2006: A Global Report on the State of Society.* Bratislava, Institute for Public Affairs 2007a.

Filadelfiová, J. – Bútorová, Z. (ed.): *Ženy, muži a vek v štatistikách trhu práce* [Women, Men and Age in Labor Market Statistics]. Bratislava, Institute for Public Affairs 2007b.

Filadelfiová, J. – Bútorová, Z. – Gyarfášová, O.: "Women and Men in Politics" in Mesežnikov, G. – Kollár, M. – Nicholson, T. (eds.): *Slovakia 2002: A Global Report on the State of Society.* Bratislava, Institute for Public Affairs 2002.

Filadelfiová, J. – Cuperová, K.: *Rôznorodosť demografického vývoja v Európe* [The Diversity of Demographic Development in Europe]. Bratislava, International Center for Family Studies 2000.

Filadelfiová, J. – Guráň, P.: *Demografické trendy a rodina v postkomunistických krajinách Európy* [Demographic Trends and the Family in European Post-Communist Countries]. Bratislava, International Center for Family Studies 1997.

Filadelfiová, J. – Guráň, P.: "Demographic Development" in Bútora, M. – Skladony, T. W. (eds.): Slovakia 1996 – 1997: A Global Report on the State of Society. Bratislava, Institute for Public Affairs 1998.

Filadelfiová, J. – Guráň, P. – Šútorová, D.: *Rodové štatistiky na Slovensku* [Gender Statistics in Slovakia], the second updated edition. Bratislava, Ministry of Labor, Social Affairs and Family – International Center for Family Studies 2002.

Filadelfiová, J. – Radičová, I. – Puliš, P.: *Ženy v politike* [Women in Politics]. Bratislava, International Center for Family Studies – Ministry of Labor, Social Affairs and Family – S.P.A.C.E. 2000.

Fourth European Working Conditions Survey. Dublin, European Foundation for the Improvement of Living and Working Conditions 2007. Available at: www.eurofond.eu.int/ewco/surveys/index.htm.

Franco, A.: "The Entrepreneurial Gap between Men and Women" in *Statistics in Focus* No. 30, 2007. Brussels, Eurostat, European Commission 2007a.

Franco, A.: "The Concentration of Men and Women in Sectors of Activity" in *Statistics in Focus* No. 53, 2007. Brussels, Eurostat, European Commission 2007b.

Friedan, B.: *The Fountain of Age.* New York, Simon & Schuster 1993.

Garcia, A. B. – Gruat, J. V.: *A Life Cycle Continuum Investment for Social Justice, Poverty Reduction and Sustainable Development.* Geneva, International Labor Organization 2003.

Gauthier, A.: *The State and the Family.* Oxford, Oxford University Press 1996.

Gender Pay Gaps in European Labor Markets – Measurement, Analysis and Policy Implication, a Commission Staff working paper, SEC (2003)937. Brussels, Commission of the European Communities September 4, 2003.

Gerbery, D. – Džambazovič, R.: "Vývoj systému sociálnej pomoci a boj proti chudobe" ['Developing the System of Social Assistance and Combating Poverty'] in Bodnárová, B. – Filadelfiová, J. – Gerbery, D. – Džambazovič, R. – Kvapilová, E.: *Premeny sociálnej politiky* [Alterations of Social Policy]. Bratislava, Research Institute of Labor and Family 2006.

Gerbery, D. – Lesay, I. – Škobla, D. (eds.): *Kniha o chudobe: Spoločenské súvislosti a verejné politiky* [The Book on Poverty: Social Context and Public Policies]. Bratislava, Friends of Earth-CEPA – Friedrich Ebert Stiftung – Slovak Anti-Poverty Network 2007.

Ghosheh, N.: "Conditions of Work & Employment for Older Workers: Understanding the Issues" in *Competence 50+: Age as an Opportunity*, Programme and Abstract Book of the European Conference on Age Management. Göteborg, Life Competence 50+ 2007.

Giddens, A.: *Sociologie* [Sociology]. Prague, Argo 1999.

Gilster, A. P.: *Digital Literacy*. New York, John Wiley & Sons 1997.

Grimshaw, D. – Rubery, J.: *Undervaluing Women's Work*. Manchester, European Work and Employment Research Centre – University of Manchester 2007. Available at: http://83.137.212.42/sitearchive/eoc/PDF/WP53_undervaluing_womens_work.pdf?page=20331

Guillemard, A.: "The Ageing Workforce in Europe and 'Age Cultures'" in *Competence 50+: Age as an Opportunity*, Programme and Abstract Book of the European Conference on Age Management. Göteborg, Life Competence 50+ 2007.

Guráň, P. – Filadelfiová, J.: *Hlavné demografické trendy a rodina: Svet – Európa – Slovensko* [The Main Demographic Trends and the Family: World – Europe – Slovakia]. Bratislava, International Center for Family Studies 1995.

Gyárfášová, O.: *Hlasy žien. Správa z kvalitatívneho výskumu* [Women's Voices: A Report from a Qualitative Survey]. Bratislava, Institute for Public Affairs 2002.

Gyárfášová, O. et al: *Evaluácia sociálnej politiky zameranej na zníženie dlhodobej nezamestnanosti.* [Evaluation of the Social Inclusion Policy Aimed at Reducing Long-Term Unemployment]. Bratislava, Institute for Public Affairs 2006. Available at: http://www.ivo.sk/buxus/docs/socialna_inkluzia/Evaluacia_soc_politiky_SK.pdf

Gyárfášová, O. – Krivý, V. – Velšic, M. et al: *Krajina v pohybe. Správa o politických názoroch a hodnotách ľudí na Slovensku* [Country on the Move: A Report on the Political Views and Values of People in Slovakia]. Bratislava, Institute for Public Affairs 2001.

Gyárfášová, O. – Pafková, K.: *Potenciál aktívnej účasti žien na verejnom živote. Výsledky sociologického výskumu* [The Potential for the Active Participation of Women in Public Life: Results of a Sociological Survey]. Bratislava, Institute for Public Affairs 2002.

Gyárfášová, O. – Slosiarik, M.: "Rodové súradnice hodnotového priestoru. Analýza hodnotových orientácií žien a mužov na Slovensku" ['Gender Coordinates of the Value Dimension: An analysis of the Value Orientations of Women and Men in Slovakia'] in Cviková, J. (ed.): *Aká práca, taká pláca? Aspekty rodovej nerovnosti v odmeňovaní* [Same Work, Same Pay? Aspects of Gender Inequality in Remuneration]. Bratislava, Aspekt 2008.

Harding, S.: *The Science Question in Feminism*. New York, Cornell University Press 1986.

Harmonized European Time Use Survey. Available at: https://www.testh2.scb.se/tus/tus/StatMeanMact1.html

324

Hašková, H.: "Práce a plodnost: Bezdětní třicátníci a třicátnice na trhu práce" ['Labor and Fertility: Childless Women and Men in their Thirties on the Labor Market'] in Dudová, R. (ed.): *Nová rizika pracovního trhu: flexibilita, marginalizace a soukromý život* [New Risks of the Labor Market: Flexibility, Marginalization and Private Life]. Prague, Institute of Sociology of the Czech Academy of Sciences 2008 (in print).

Havelková, H.: "Dimenze 'gender' ve vztahu soukromé a veřejné sféry" ['The 'Gender' Dimension in the Relationship between the Private and Public Spheres'] in *Sociologický časopis* No. 1, 1995, pp. 25 – 37.

Havelková, H.: *Political Representation of Women in Czech Republic: Political Institutions, Public Polls and Intellectual Discourse* , a paper presented at the international workshop "Perspectives for Gender Equality Policies in Central and Eastern Europe". Ljubljana, the Peace Institute 2000.

Havlíková, J.: "Věk v sociologické teorii: perspektiva životního běhu" ['Age in Sociological Theory: The Perspective of the Life Course'] in *Sociální studia*. Brno, Faculty of Social Studies at Masaryk University, 2007/1.

Heinz, W. R. – Krüger, H.: "Life Course: Innovations and Challenges for Social Research" in *Current Sociology* No. 49, 2001, pp. 29 – 45.

Hrapková, N.: "Genéza a súčasný stav UTV v SR" ['The Genesis and Current Situation of UTV in the Slovak Republic'] in *História a súčasnosť UTV na Slovensku* [Past and Present of UTV in Slovakia], a collection on the occasion of the 15th anniversary of the establishment of universities of the third age in the Slovak Republic. Bratislava, Comenius University 2007. Available at: http://www.cdv.uniba.sk/index.php?id=2466

Changes in Parenting: Children Today, Parents Tomorrow, the Conference of European Ministers Responsible for Family Affairs, 28th Session in Lisbon, May 16 – 17, 2006. Strasbourg, Council of Europe 2006.

Ilmarinen, J.: *Ageing Workers in the European Union – Status and Promotion of Work Ability, Employability and Employment*. Helsinki, Finnish Institute of Occupational Health – Ministry of Social Affairs and Health – Ministry of Labor 1999.

Ilmarinen, J.: *Toward a Longer Work Life! Ageing and the Quality of Work Life in the European Union.* Helsinki, Finnish Institute of Occupational Health – Ministry of Social Affairs and Health 2006.

Ilmarinen, J.: *Ako si predĺžiť aktívny život. Starnutie a kvalita pracovného života v Európskej únii* [Toward a Longer Work Life! Ageing and the Quality of Work Life in the European Union]. Bratislava, Klub strieborných hláv – Príroda 2008.

Ilmarinen, J. – Louhevaara, V. (eds.): *FinnAge – Respect for the Aging: Action Programme to Promote Health, Work Ability and Well-Being of Aging Workers in 1990 – 1996.* Helsinki, Finnish Institute of Occupational Health 1999.

Indicators of Quality in Work, a report by the Employment Committee to the European Council, 14263/01. Strasbourg, Council of Europe, November 23, 2001.

Informácia o demografickom vývoji v roku 2006 [Information on Demographic Developments in 2006]. Bratislava, Statistical Office of the Slovak Republic 2007. Available at: portal.statistics.sk/showdoc.do?docid=8435

Informačný systém o priemerných zárobkoch [Information System on Average Wages]. Bratislava, Trexima 2006.

Informačný systém o priemerných zárobkoch [Information System on Average Wages]. Bratislava, Trexima 2007.

Inglehart, R. – Baker, W. E.: "Modernization, Culture Change, and the Persistence of Traditional Values" in *American Sociological Review* No. 65, 2000, pp. 19 – 51.

Integrated Guidelines for Growth and Jobs. COM (2005) 141, final. Brussels, European Commission 2005. Available at: http://ec.europa.eu/growthandjobs/pdf/integrated_guidelines_en.pdf

Jakuš, D.: "Uchádzači po štyridsiatke a trh práce – mýty a fakty" ['Job Seekers over Forty and the Labor Market: Myths and Facts'], a paper presented at the expert seminar *Personality Zoom: Tretia kariéra – zaostrené na zamestnávanie starších* [Personality Zoom: Third Career – Focused on Employment of Elderly]. Bratislava, Trenkwalder 2007.

Jalušić, V.: "Public Agenda, Women's Groups and Equal Opportunity Politics in Slovenia", a paper presented at the international workshop *Perspectives for Gender Equality Policies in Central and Eastern Europe*. Ljubljana, the Peace Institute 2000.

Jesenková, A.: "Obraz matiek maloletých detí v časopise *Slovenka* a *Život*" ['The Image of Mothers of Dependent Children in the Magazines *Slovenka* and *Život*'] in Marošiová, L. (ed.): *Matky samy sebou* [Mothers Themselves]. Bratislava, Institute for Public Affairs 2008.

Juráňová, J.: "Stav feministickej reflexie slovenskej spoločnosti päť rokov po…" ['State of Feminist Reflection in Slovak Society Five Years After…'] in *Päť rokov po* [Five Years After], proceedings from an international conference held in Budmerice in December 1994. Bratislava, Association of Writers' Organizations of Slovakia – Institute of Slovak Literature of the Slovak Academy of Sciences 1995.

Jurčová, D. et al: *Populačný vývoj v okresoch SR 2005* [Population Developments in Slovakia's Districts in 2005]. Bratislava, Infostat – Demography Research Centre 2006.

Kauppinen, K.: "Gender, Age and Myths of Reality" in *Women 45+ on Labor Market: Gender, Age and Equality of Opportunities*, proceedings from an international conference. Bratislava, Institute for Public Affairs 2007.

Keller, J.: *Teorie modernizace* [Theory of Modernization]. Prague, SLON 2007.

Key Data on Higher Education in Europe. Brussels, European Commission's DG for Education and Culture 2007.

Kiczková, Z.: "Vzájomný vzťah medzi verejnou a súkromnou sférou z pohľadu žien" ['The Mutual Relationship between the Public and Private Spheres from the Perspective of Women'] in *Aspekt* No. 1, 1997, pp. 189 – 196.

Kiczková, Z. – Szapuová, M. – Zezulová, J.: *Ženy a muži na univerzitách podľa kvantitatívneho empirického výskumu* [Women and Men at Universities According to a Quantitative Empirical Survey], the second survey report from a project. Bratislava, Club of Feminist Philosophers 2006.

Kobová, Ľ.: "Keď na pohlaví záleží: Návod na čítanie" ['When Sex Matters: A Reading Manual'] in Cviková, J. – Juráňová, J. – Kobová, Ľ. (eds.): *Žena nie je tovar: komodifikácia žien v našej culture* [Women Are Not Products: The Commodification of Women in Our Culture]. Bratislava, Aspekt 2005, pp. 271 – 275.

Kobová, Ľ. – Maďarová, Z.: *Kradmá ruka feministky rozvažuje za plentou* [Feminists Surreptitiously Ponder behind a Partition]. Bratislava, Aspekt 2007.

Kohout, A. – Stokes, B.: *Amerika proti svetu. V čom je iná a prečo ju nemajú radi* [America against the World: How Is It Different and Why Is It Disliked]. Bratislava, Slovart 2006.

Kollár, M. – Mesežnikov, G. (eds.): *Voľby 2006. Analýza volebných programov politických strán a hnutí* [Elections 2006: An analysis of the Election Programs of Political Parties and Movements]. Bratislava, Institute for Public Affairs 2006.

Koncepcia rovnosti príležitostí žien a mužov Slovenskej republiky [Conception of Equal Opportunities for Women and Men of the Slovak Republic]. Bratislava, Ministry of Labor, Social Affairs and Family 2001.

Korpi, W.: "Gender, Class and Patterns of Inequalities in Different Types of Welfare States" in Kohli, M. – Novak, M. (eds.): *Will Europe Work?* London, Routledge 2001.

"Kult tela nás vháňa do pasce" ['The Cult of the Body Drives Us into a Trap'], in *Pravda*, November 14, 2005.

Lanzieri, G.: "First Demographic Estimates for 2006" in *Statistics in Focus* No. 41, 2007. Brussels, Eurostat 2007.

Lewis, J.: "Gender and the Development of Welfare Regimes" in *Journal of European Social Policy* No. 2, 1992, pp. 159 – 173.

Light, D. – Keller, S. – Calhoun, C.: *Sociology*. New York, Alfred A. Knopf 1989.

Marody, M – Giza-Poleszczuk, A.: "Changing Images of Identity in Poland: From the Self-Sacrificing to the Self-Investing Woman?" in Gal, S. – Klingman, G. (eds.): *Reproducing Gender: Politics, Public and Everyday Life after Socialism.* Princeton, Princeton University Press 2000.

Marošiová, L.: "The Young Generation and Its Views on Family, Women's Reproductive Rights and Discrimination" in Gyárfášová, O. – Mesežnikov, G. (eds.): *Slovakia "in the Draft": Cultural and Ethical Challenges and the New Nature of Disputes after Accession to the European Union.* Bratislava, Institute for Public Affairs 2005.

Marošiová, L. (ed.): *Matky samy sebou.* [Mothers Themselves]. Bratislava, Institute for Public Affairs 2008.

Marošiová, L. – Šumšalová, S. (eds.): *Matky na trhu (práce a života)* [Mothers on the Market (of Labor and Family Life)]. Bratislava, Institute for Public Affairs 2006.

Matoušek, O.: *Rodina jako instituce a vztahová síť* [The Family as an Institution and a Network of Relations], Prague, SLON 1993.

Mayring, Ph.: "Qualitative Content Analysis" in *Forum Qualitative Sozialforschung/Forum Qualitative Social Research* No. 2, June 2000 as quoted by *Časopis online* on April 20, 2008. Available at: http://www.qualitative-research.net/fqs-texte/2-00/2-00mayring-e.htm

Määttä, P.: *Equal Pay Policies: International Review of Select Developing and Developed countries*. Geneva, ILO 2007. Available at: http://www.ilo.org

McNay, K.: *Women's Changing Roles in the Context of the Demographic Transition*, a background paper prepared for the Education for All Global Monitoring Report 2003/4. Florence, UNESCO 2003.

Mesežnikov, G.: "The Political Context of the Dispute between Conservatives and Liberals" in Gyárfášová, O. – Mesežnikov, G. (eds.): *Slovakia "in the Draft": Cultural and Ethical Challenges and the New Nature of Disputes after Accession to the European Union.* Bratislava, Institute for Public Affairs 2005.

Mesochoritisová, A.: "Médiá a násilie páchané na ženách" ['The Media and Violence Against Women'] in Bútorová, Z. – Filadelfiová, J. (eds.): *Násilie páchané na ženách ako problém verejnej politiky* [Violence against Women as a Public Policy Issue], Bratislava, Institute for Public Affairs 2005.

Mesochoritisová, A.: "Gender Sensitive Education: Experience and Inspiration from the Project *Plus for Women 45+*" in *Women 45+ on Labor Market: Gender, Age and Equality of Opportunities*, proceedings from an international conference. Bratislava, Institute for Public Affairs 2007.

Minarovičová, K.: "Čo sa v škole o nerovnosti naučíš… Rodové stereotypy v správaní a postojoch učiteliek a učiteľov" ['What You Learn in School about Inequality… Gender Stereotypes in the Behavior and Attitudes of Teachers'] in Cviková, J. – Juráňová, J. (eds.): *Ružový a modrý svet. Rodové stereotypy a ich dôsledky* [Pink and Blue World: Gender Stereotypes and Their Implications]. Bratislava, Občan a demokracia – Aspekt 2003.

Možný, I.: *Rodina vysokoškolsky vzdělaných manželů* [Families of Spouses with University Education]. Brno, UJEP 1983.

Možný, I.: *Moderní rodina (Mýty a skutečnosti)* [The Modern Family (Myths and Truths)]. Brno, Blok 1990.

Možný, I.: *Sociologie rodiny* [The Sociology of the Family]. Prague, SLON 1999.

Možný, I.: *Rodina a společnost* [Family and Society]. Prague, SLON 2006.

National Human Development Report: Slovak Republic 2000. Bratislava, UNDP 2000.

Názory obyvateľov SR na firemné politiky [Views of Slovakia's Inhabitants on Corporate Policies], a selection from research data. Bratislava, Association of Businesswomen 2006.

Oakley, A.: *Pohlaví, gender a společnost* [*Sex, Gender and Society*]. Prague, Portál 2000.

Obyvateľstvo Slovenska podľa SODB [Slovakia's Population According to Population Census]. Bratislava, Infostat – Demography Research Centre 2005.

Olsen, W. – Walby, S.: *Modelling Gender Pay Gaps.* London, UK Equal Opportunities Commission 2004. Available at: http://www.lancs.ac.uk/fass/sociology/papers/walby-modellinggenderpaygapswp17.pdf

Ondrisová, S.: "Homofóbia a heterosexizmus. Postoje ku gejom, lesbickým ženám a bisexuálom" ['Homophobia and Heterosexism: Attitudes to Gays, Lesbians and Bisexuals'] in Ondrisová, S. – Šípošová, M. – Červenková, I. – Jójárt, P. – Bianchi, G.: *Neviditeľná menšina. Čo (ne)vieme o sexuálnej orientácii* [The Invisible Minority: What Do We (Not) Know about Sexual Orientation]. Bratislava, Občan a demokracia foundation 2002.

Opinion on Gender Pay Gap. Brussels, European Commission, Advisory Committee on Equal Opportunities for Women and Men 2007. Available at: http://ec.europa.eu/employment_social/gender_equality/docs/2007/opinion_pay_gap_en.pdf

Orloff, A. S.: "Gender and the Social Rights of Citizenship: State Policies and Gender Relations in Comparative Research" in *American Sociological Review* No. 58, 1993, pp. 303 – 328.

Pendakur, K.: "Consumption Poverty in Canada" in *Canadian Public Policy* No. 2, June 2001.

Petrusek, M.: *Společnosti pozdní doby* [Societies of the Late Age], Prague, SLON 2006.

328

Pietruchová, O.: *Dôchodková reforma znevýhodňuje ženy* ['Pension Reform Discriminates against Women'], November 9, 2006. Available at: http://www.changenet.sk/?section=forum&x=238902

Pietruchová, O.: *Čo DSS-ky ženám určite nepovedia* ['What DSSs Will Surely Not Tell Women'], April 6, 2008. Available at: http://www.jetotak.sk/ekonomika/co-dssky-zenam-urcite-nepovedia

Pilinská, V. et al: *Demografická charakteristika rodiny na Slovensku* [Demographic Characteristics of the Family in Slovakia]. Bratislava, Infostat 2005.

Pirošík, V. – Janišová, M. – Šuterová, V.: "Marginalized Groups" in Mesežnikov, G. – Kollár, M. – Nicholson, T. (eds.): *Slovakia 2000: A Global Report on the State of Society*. Bratislava, Institute for Public Affairs 2001.

Poslanci/Poslanecké kluby [Deputies/Caucuses]. Bratislava, NR SR 2008. Available at: http://www.nrsr.sk/default.aspx?sid=poslanci/kluby/zoznam

Potančoková, M.: "Reprodukčné stratégie a sociálne vplyvy na rozhodovanie o materstve v transformujúcej sa spoločnosti: teoretický rámec k začínajúcemu výskumu" ['Reproduction Strategies and Social Factors Affecting Decisions on Maternity in a Society in Transition: A Theoretical Framework Based on Initial Research'] in *Gender Studies* No. 4, 2004, pp. 15 – 16.

Práca verzus rodina? Zosúlaďovanie pracovného a rodinného života očami zamestnankýň a zamestnávateľov [Work versus the Family: Harmonizing Professional and Family Life in the Eyes of Employees and Employers]. Bratislava, ZZŽ MYMAMY maternity centre 2007.

Program of Action of the International Conference on Population and Development (ICPD – Cairo 1994). New York, United Nations 1995.

Provazník, D. (ed.): *Aktuálne problémy sociológie rodiny* [Topical Problems in Family Sociology]. Bratislava, Veda 1989.

Přidalová, M.: "Mezi solidaritou a konfliktem. Zkušenosti pečujících dcer a synů" ['Between Solidarity and Conflict: The Experience of Caregiving Daughters and Sons'] in *Sociální studia*. Brno, Faculty of Social Studies at Masaryk University, 2007/1.

Recent Demographic Developments in Europe 2000. Strasbourg, Council of Europe Publishing 2000.

Recent Demographic Developments in Europe 2003. Strasbourg, Council of Europe Publishing 2003.

Reconciling Working and Family Life, the Conference of European Ministers Responsible for Family Affairs, 27th session in Portorož, June 20 – 22, 2001. Strasbourg, Council of Europe 2001.

Report from the Commission to the Council, the European Parliament, the European Economic and Social Committee and the Committee of the Regions on Equality between Women and Men. COM(2006)71. Brussels, Commission of the European Communities 2006. Available at: http://www.uil.it/pari_opportunit%C3%A0/Equality-report-2006%20En.pdf

Report of the Second World Assembly on Ageing. Madrid, United Nations, April 8 – 12, 2002. Available at: http://www.un-ngls.org/pdf/MIPAA.pdf

Reprezentatívny výskum vnímania ľudských práv a zásady rovnakého zaobchádzania u dospelej populácie v SR [Representative Survey on Perceptions of Human Rights and the Equal

Treatment Principle among Slovakia's Adult Population]. Bratislava, Slovak National Center for Human Rights 2007.

Rowe, J. W. – Kahn, E. L.: *Successful Aging*. New York, Random House 1999.

Rubery, J. – Fagan, C. – Grimshaw, D. – Figueiredo, H. – Smith, M.: *Indicators on Gender Equality in the European Employment Strategy*. Manchester, European Work and Employment Research Centre, Manchester School of Management, UMIST 2002.

Sčítanie obyvateľov, domov a bytov SR 1991 a 2001 [Population Census of the Slovak Republic for 1991 and 2001]. Bratislava, Statistical Office of the Slovak Republic 1992, 2002.

Schaefer, R. T.: *Sociology*. New York, McGraw-Hill Inc. 1989.

Schmidt, V.: *The Evolution of Gender Inequalities in the European Union: Labor Market Participation, Wage Inequalities and Unemployment in Cross-National Comparison*, CEuS Working Paper 2001/2. Bremen, Jean Monnet Centre for European Studies – University of Bremen 2001.

Silva, E. – Smart, C. (eds.): *The New Family?* London, Sage 1999.

Sirovátka, T.: "Rodinné chování a rodinná politika v České republice" ['Family Behavior and Family Policy in the Czech Republic'] in Možný, I. (ed.): *Modernizace a česká rodina* [Modernization and the Czech Family]. Brno, Barrister and Principal 2003.

Slovensko na ceste k rodovej rovnosti. Pramenná publikácia z reprezentatívneho kvantitatívneho výskumu [Slovakia on the Path toward Gender Equality: Empirical Data from a Representative Quantitative Survey]. Bratislava, Institute of Sociology of the Slovak Academy of Sciences – European Roma Working Agency 2006.

Slovstat. Bratislava, Statistical Office of the Slovak Republic 2008. Available at: http://www.statistics.sk/pls/elsiw/vbd

Statistics in Focus – Population and Social Conditions No. 41, 2007. Brussels, Eurostat 2007.

Stav a pohyb obyvateľstva v SR [Population of the Slovak Republic and Its Development], data for 1921 – 2003. Bratislava, Statistical Office of the Slovak Republic, 1921 – 2004.

Steinhorn, L.: *The Greater Generation: in Defence of the Baby Boom Legacy*. New York, Thomas Dunne Books and St. Martin's Griffin 2007.

Strečanský, B. – Bútora, M. – Vajdová, K. – Szatmáry, Z. – Bútorová, Z. – Kubánová, M. – Woleková, H.: "Non-Governmental Organizations and Volunteerism" in Bútora, M. – Kollár, M. – Mesežnikov, G. (eds.): *Slovakia 2005: A Global Report on the State of Society*. Bratislava, Institute for Public Affairs 2006.

Súhrnná správa o realizácii Národného programu ochrany starších ľudí [A Global Report on Implementing the *National Program for the Protection of Elderly People'*]. Bratislava, Ministry of Labor, Social Affairs and Family, July 2006.

Sýkorová, D.: "Senioři v České republice. Mýty a jejich dekonstrukce" ['Seniors in the Czech Republic: Deconstructing Myths'] in *Sociológia* No. 38, 2006.

Sýkorová, D.: *Autonomie ve stáří. Kapitoly z gerontosociologie* [Autonomy in Old Age: Chapters from Gerontosociology]. Prague, SLON 2007.

Šípošová, M. – Jójárt, P. – Daučíková, A.: *Správa o diskriminácii lesbických žien, gejov, bisexuálov a bisexuálok na Slovensku* [Report on Discrimination of Lesbians, Gays and Bisexuals in Slovakia]. Bratislava, Ganymedes – Q Archív 2002. Available at: http://diskriminacia.altera.sk/vyskum

Štatistické ročenky SR 1985 – 2007 [Statistical Yearbooks of the Slovak Republic 1985 – 2007]. Bratislava, Statistical Office of the Slovak Republic 1985 – 2007.

Šumšalová, S.: "Keď sa z koníčka stane podnikanie: skúsenosti žien z Lučenca a okolia" ['When Hobby Becomes Business: The Experience of Women from the Lučenec Area'] in Bútorová, Z. (ed.): *Tu a teraz. Sondy do života žien 45+* [Here and Now: Probes into the Lives of Women 45+]. Bratislava, Institute for Public Affairs 2007.

Tackling the Pay Gap between Women and Men. Brussels, Commission of the European Communities 2007. Available at: http://ec.europa.eu/employment_social/news/2007/jul/genderpaygap_en.pdf.

Terénny výskum dodržiavania zásady rovnakého zaobchádzania pri vzniku a skončení pracovnoprávneho vzťahu vybraných kategórií obyvateľov [Field Research Examining Adherence to the Principle of Equal Treatment during the Process of Hiring and Discharging of Select Population Categories], the final report on a project. Bratislava, Slovak National Center for Human Rights 2006.

The Future of the European Employment Strategy (EES): A Strategy of Full Employment and Better Jobs for All. Brussels, European Commission 2003. Available at: http://ec.europa.eu/employment_social/news/2003/jan/ees_03_com_en.pdf

The Life of Women and Men in Europe: A Statistical Portrait. Brussels, European Communities 2008. Available at: http://epp.eurostat.ec.europa.eu/cache/ITY_OFFPUB/KS-80-07-135/EN/KS-80-07-135-EN.PDF

The Lisbon Strategy. European Council, signed at Lisbon, March 23 – 24, 2000. Available at *europa.eu/lisbon_treaty/index_en.htm*

The Social Situation in the European Union 2003. Brussels, European Commission 2004.

The Story behind the Numbers: Women and Employment in Central and Eastern Europe and the Western Commonwealth of Independent States. New York, UNIFEM 2006.

The Treaty of Rome of 1957. Available at: http://www.hri.org/docs/Rome57/

Úloha mužov pri podpore rodovej rovnosti: Participácia otcov na domácej starostlivosti (názory a skúsenosti populácie SR) [The Role of Men in Furthering Gender Equality: The Participation of Fathers in Taking Care of Households (Views and Experience of Slovakia's Population)]. Bratislava, Slovak National Center for Human Rights 2006. Available at: http://www.snslp.sk/rs/snslp_rs.nsf/0/1BF2229F7C4E9001C125722700633CF5?OpenDocument

Van der Meer, M. – Leijnse, F.: *Life-Course Schemes and Social Policy Reform in Netherlands.* Amsterdam, Amsterdam Institute for Advanced Labor Studies at University of Amsterdam 2005.

Vaňo, B.: *Demografická charakteristika rómskej populácie v SR* [Demographic Characterization of the Romany Population in the Slovak Republic]. Bratislava, Infostat 2001.

Vaňo, B. (ed.): *Populačný vývoj v Slovenskej republike 2002* [Population Development in the Slovak Republic in 2002]. Bratislava, Infostat – Demography Research Centre 2003.

Vaňo, B. (ed.): *Populačný vývoj v Slovenskej republike 2004* [Population Development in the Slovak Republic in 2004]. Bratislava, Infostat – Demography Research Centre 2005.

Vaňo, B. (ed.): *Populačný vývoj v Slovenskej republike 2006* [Population Development in the Slovak Republic in 2006]. Bratislava, Infostat – Demography Research Centre 2007.

Varnum, M. E. W.: "Rapid Adaptation to Social Change in Central Europe: Changes in Locus of Control, Attribution, Subjective Well-Being, Self-Direction and Trust" in *Slovak Sociological Review* No. 3, spring 2008.

Velšic, M.: *Digital Literacy in Slovakia*. Bratislava, Institute for Public Affairs 2005.

Velšic, M.: *Digitálna gramotnosť na Slovensku* [Digital Literacy in Slovakia]. Bratislava, Institute for Public Affairs 2007.

Velšic, M.: *E-demokracia na Slovensku* [E-democracy in Slovakia]. Bratislava, Institute for Public Affairs 2008.

Vláda SR/História vlád Slovenskej republiky [Government of the Slovak Republic/History of Governments of the Slovak Republic], 2008. Available at: http://www-8.vlada.gov.sk/index.php?ID=1073

Volebná štatistika [Electoral Statistics]. Bratislava, Statistical Office of the Slovak Republic 2008. Available at: http://portal.statistics.sk/showdoc.do?docid=30

Výberové zisťovanie o štruktúre miezd [Selective Survey on the Structure of Wages]. Bratislava, Statistical Office of the Slovak Republic 2007.

Výsledky výberového zisťovania pracovných síl za tretí štvrťrok 2005 [Results of the Selective Workforce Survey for the Third Quarter of 2005]. Bratislava, Statistical Office of the Slovak Republic 2005.

Vývoj obyvateľstva v SR 2003 [Population Development in the Slovak Republic in 2003]. Bratislava, Statistical Office of the Slovak Republic 2004.

Waste of Talents: Turning Private Struggles into a Public Issue: Women and Science in the ENWISE Countries. Brussels, European Commission's DG for Research 2004.

Wolf, N.: *Mýtus krásy. Ako sú obrazy krásy zneužívané proti ženám. [The Beauty Myth: How Images of Beauty Are Abused against Women]*. Bratislava, Aspekt 2000.

Women 2000: An Investigation into the Status of Women's Rights in Central and South-Eastern Europe and the Newly Independents States. Vienna, International Helsinki Federation for Human Rights – IHF Research Foundation 2000.

Women and Men in Decision-Making 2007: Analysis of the Situation and Trends. Brussels, European Commission 2008.

Women Have a Long Way to Go – Average EU Women Earns A Quarter Less than Men. Even Allowing for Structural Gap, It's still around 15 %, News Release No. 48/99. Brussels, Eurostat, June 8, 1999.

Women in Politics in the Council of Europe Member States, an information document. Strasbourg, Council of Europe, December 1999.

Women 45+ on the Labor Market: Gender, Age and Equality of Opportunities, proceedings from an international conference. Bratislava, Institute for Public Affairs 2007.

Working Conditions and Gender in an Enlarged Europe. Dublin, European Foundation for the Improvement of Living and Working Conditions 2005.

Working Conditions in the European Union: The Gender Perspective. Dublin, European Foundation for the Improvement of Living and Working Conditions 2007. Available at: http://www.eurofound.europa.eu/pubdocs/2007/108/en/1/ef07108en.pdf

Working Together for Growth and Jobs. A New Start for the Lisbon Strategy. COM(2005)24. Brussels, European Commission 2005a. Available at: http://ec.europa.eu/growthandjobs/pdf/COM2005_024_en.pdf

Zoznam poslancov NR SR [List of Members of the National Council of the Slovak Republic]. Bratislava, National Council of the Slovak Republic 2008. Available at: http://www.nrsr.sk/default.aspx?sid=poslanci/kluby/zoznam

Zoznamy kandidátov zaregistrovaných Ministerstvom vnútra SR pred voľbami [Lists of Candidates Registered with the Interior Ministry before Elections], 2008. Available at: http://www.civil.gov.sk

Ženy a muži na Slovensku II [Women and Men in Slovakia II]. Bratislava, Coordination Committee for Women's Problems 2002.

Ženy a muži na univerzitách podľa kvantitatívneho empirického výskumu [Women and Men at Universities According to a Quantitative Empirical Survey]. Bratislava, Club of Feminist Philosophers 2006.

Ženy a muži SR v EÚ 2007 [Slovak Women and Men in the EU in 2007]. Bratislava, Statistical Office of the Slovak Republic 2007.

Sme, *Pravda*, *Nový Čas* and *Hospodárske noviny* daily papers, July 1, 2004 – June 31, 2005.

Slovenka, Život, Plus 7 dní and *Trend* weekly magazines, March 1 – May 31, 2007.

The *Sme Ženy* supplement of the *Sme* daily paper, issues 1/2006 through 11/2008.

http://epp.eurostat.ec.europa.eu/portal/page?_pageid=1913,47567825,1913_58814988&_dad=portal&_schema=PORTAL; http://portal.statistics.sk/showdoc.do?docid=12683

http://portal.statistics.sk/showdoc.do?docid=12683

http://portal.statistics.sk/showdoc.do?docid=69

http://www.altera.sk

http://www.aspekt.sk

http://www.cd-rom.uniba.sk

http://www.civil.gov.sk

http://www.diskriminacia.sk

http://www.eijtur.org/

http://www.esfem.sk

http://www.europarl.europa.eu

http://www.family.sk

http://www.ganymedes.info

http://www.gender.sk

http://www.genderstudies.cz

http://www.inakost.sk

http://www.ivo.sk

http://www.lesba.sk

http://www.medzipriestor.sk

http://www.moznostvolby.sk

http://www.nrsr.sk

http://www.oad.sk

http://www.piatazena.sk

http://www.pravonazivot.sk

http://www.regiony.sk/

http://www.ruzovyamodrysvet.sk

http://www.senior.sk

http://www.testh2.scb.se/tus/tus/

http://www.timeuse.org/

http://www.uips.sk/statis/index.html

http://www.zastavmenasilie.sk

http://www.zenyamedia.cz

ABOUT THE AUTHORS

Zora Bútorová – project director and head of the team of authors of *Plus for Women 45+*

She earned a master's degree and a doctorate in sociology at the Faculty of Arts of Comenius University in Bratislava. Before 1989 her major field of study was the sociology of science. After 1990 she got involved in public opinion research in Slovakia. From 1993 – 1997 she was researcher at the FOCUS agency. Since 1997 she has been a senior research fellow at the Institute for Public Affairs, focusing on political culture, public opinion, and gender relations. She has edited and co-authored a number of books, including *She and He in Slovakia: Gender Issues in Public Opinion* (1996); *Democracy and Discontent in Slovakia: A Public Opinion Profile of a Country in Transition* (1998), *The 1998 Parliamentary Elections and Democratic Rebirth in Slovakia* (1999); *Krehká sila. Dvadsať rozhovorov o životných cestách žien* [Fragile Strength: Twenty Interviews about the Life Stories of Women] (2001); *Slovakia: Ten Years of Independence and a Year of Reforms* (2004); *Násilie páchané na ženách ako problém verejnej politiky* [Violence against Women as an Issue of Public Policy] (2005); *Democracy and Populism in Central Europe: The Visegrad Elections and Their Aftermath* (2007). Besides writing studies and articles for academic journals and print media, she regularly contributes analyses of public opinion and gender issues to annual comprehensive country reports *Slovakia: A Global Report on the State of Society* (1996 – 2009). Her most recent contributions are *Equality of Women and Men* (2007) and *Public Opinion* (2008 and 2009). In 2005 – 2008 she was the leader of the project *Plus for Women 45+*. Within this project, she edited the publication *Ženy, muži a vek v štatistikách trhu práce* [Women, Men and Age in Labor Market Statistics] and co-authored and edited the book *Tu a teraz: sondy do života žien 45+* [Here and Now: Probes into the Lives of Women 45+]. In 2008 she was the chief author and editor of the book *Ona a on na Slovensku – zaostrené na rod a vek* [She and He in Slovakia: Focused on Gender and Age].

Monika Bosá

She graduated in history and philosophy from the Faculty of Arts of Comenius University in Bratislava, Slovakia (1998). She worked as a teacher at primary and secondary schools in Bratislava (1997 – 2001). She is the president of the civic association EsFem, and the author of the *Model of Gender-Sensitive Education* project. She acts as a coordinator, expert and consultant for educational and research projects focused on establishing gender equality, the human rights of women and the elimination of gender stereotypes. She is a founding member of the civic associations EsFem, Pro-Choice Slovakia, The Fifth Woman Initiative and The Women's Lobby of Slovakia. She is also a member of the Club of Feminist Philosophers and of the Slovak Family Planning Association. Currently she lectures in epistemology, social philosophy and gender theory at the Faculty of Arts of Prešov University. She is an external PhD student at the Faculty of Education of Comenius University in Bratislava.

Jarmila Filadelfiová

She is a sociologist and a graduate of Comenius University's Department of Sociology in 1979. Until 1994 she worked at the Sociology Institute of the Slovak Academy of Sciences and from 1994 – 2006 at the Bratislava International Center for Family Studies, which in 2003 was transformed into the Research Institute for Labor and Family. Since March 2006 she has worked at the Institute for Public Affairs in Bratislava. She has done research on demographic developments, family and gender issues and social policy. She is the author of numerous scholarly articles and has contributed to several books, including *Ženy v politike* [Women in Politics]; *Domáce násilie a násilie páchané na ženách v SR [Domestic* Violence and Violence against Women in Slovakia] (2003); *Die Partizipation von Frauen am politischen Leben in der Slowakei* [Participation of Women in Political Life in Slovakia] (2004), *Populačný vývoj a štruktúra rodín [*Demographic Developments and Family Structure] (2004), *Násilie páchané na ženách ako problém verejnej politiky [*Violence against Women as an Issue of Public Policy] (2005), *Demografický vývoj a rodina* [Demographic Developments and Family] (2005), *Equality of Women and Men* (2007); *Ženy, muži a vek v štatistikách trhu práce* [Women, Men and Age in Labor Market Statistics] (2007); and *Učiteľské povolanie: Aspekty rodovej rovnosti v škole* [Teaching Profession: Aspects of Gender Equality in School] (2008).

Oľga Gyárfášová

She earned a master's degree in sociology and a doctorate in political science at the Faculty of Arts of Comenius University in Bratislava. She has been a program director at the Institute for Public Affairs since 1999. She specializes in exploring public opinion, political culture, electoral behavior, and gender issues. She has co-authored a number of books and studies, for instance *She and He in Slovakia: Gender Issues in Public Opinion* (1996); *Democracy and Discontent in Slovakia: A Public Opinion Profile of a Country in Transition* (1998), *The 1998 Parliamentary Elections and Democratic Rebirth in Slovakia* (1999); *Krajina v pohybe. Správa o politických názoroch a hodnotách ľudí na Slovensku* [Country on the Move: A Report on the Political Views and Values of People in Slovakia] (2001); *Potenciál aktívnej účasti žien na verejnom živote.* [The Potential for Active Participation by Women in Public Life] (2002); *Slovak Elections '02: Results, Implications, Context* (2003); *Slovakia: Ten Years of Independence and a Year of Reforms* (2004); *Democracy and Populism in Central Europe: The Visegrad Elections and Their Aftermat*h (2007). She also contributes regularly to the series of annual comprehensive country reports called *Slovakia: A Global Report on the State of Society* (1997 – 2009). She is a founding member of the Institute for Public Affairs and a member of its Board of Trustees. She lectures at the Faculty of Social and Economic Sciences of Comenius University in Bratislava.

Milan Minarovič

He majored in political science at the Faculty of Arts of Comenius University in Bratislava. In 2006 he received a bachelor's degree upon completing his combined studies in sociology and political science at the Faculty of Social Studies of Masaryk University in Brno. Since 2005 he has been pursuing a doctorate at the Department of Political Science at Comenius University. In the field of sociology he specializes in the analysis of social discourse; his specialty in the domain of political science is the statistical analysis of the stability of the governments in Central and Eastern European countries.

Martina Sekulová

She studied ethnology and cultural anthropology at the Faculty of Arts of Comenius University in Bratislava, Slovakia. From 2005 – 2006 she worked at the International Visegrad Fund. Since 2006 she has been working as a researcher for the Institute for Public Affairs, where she concentrates on social policy, social inclusion, unemployment, and anti-discrimination. As part of her external doctoral studies at the Faculty of Arts of Comenius University, she specializes in tourism issues. In 2007, she co-authored the book *Tu a teraz: sondy do života žien 45+* [Here and Now: Probes into the Lives of Women 45+].

Sylvia Šumšalová

She graduated in sociology from the Faculty of Arts of Comenius University in Bratislava, Slovakia. From 1993 – 1995 she worked at the Institute of Sociology of the Slovak Academy of Sciences, and from 1995 at the FOCUS agency. As an analyst and project manager, she has participated in the preparation, realization and evaluation of numerous social and marketing research projects. She co-edited and co-authored the publication *Matky na trhu (práce a života)* [Mothers on the Market (of Labor and Family Life)] (2006) and co-authored the books *Tu a teraz: sondy do života žien 45+* [Here and Now: Probes into the Lives of Women 45+] and *Matky samy sebou* [Mothers Themselves] (2008).

Marián Velšic

He earned a master's degree in sociology and a doctorate in political science at the Faculty of Arts of Comenius University in Bratislava. From 1993 – 1994 he worked as an analyst for various political parties. Between 1995 and 1998 he was a researcher at the Political Science Institute of the Slovak Academy of Sciences. During the same period, he co-founded and was one of the editors of the political review *Quo vadis, Slovensko?* Since 1998 he has been with the Institute for Public Affairs. He has authored and co-authored a number of publications, including *Dva roky politickej slobody* [Two Years of Political Freedom] (1992); *Dva roky politickej slobody – ex post* [Two Years of Political Freedom Ex Post] (1993); *Democracy and Discontent in Slovakia: A Public Opinion Profile of a Country in Transition* (1998); *Slovensko a jeho volebné pravidlá* [Slovakia and Its Election Rules] (1998); *The 1998 Parliamentary Elections and Democratic Rebirth in Slovakia* (1999); *Krajina v pohybe. Správa o politických názoroch a hodnotách ľudí na Slovensku* [Country on the Move: A Report on the Political Views and Values of People in Slovakia] (2001); *Slovak Elections '02: Results, Implications, Context* (2003); *Slovakia: A Global Report on the State of Society* (1998 – 2009); *Digital Literacy in Slovakia* (2005, 2007); *Citizens Online* (2007); *e-Government na Slovensku* [E-Government in Slovakia] (2007); *e-Demokracia na Slovensku* [E-Democracy in Slovakia] (2008). Currently he specializes in issues related to the information society.

Ilona Németh

She was born on 28 January 1963 in Dunajská Streda. She studied typography and book art at the Academy of Applied Arts in Budapest (1981 – 1986), and in 2005 received PhD degree at the Academy of Fine Arts in Budapest (2000 – 2003). She has participated in group exhibitions since 1988 (1988 Čuňovo; 1989 Budapest; 1990 Komárno; 1991 Budapest; 1992 Bratislava, Žilina, Nové Zámky, Dunajská Streda; 1993 Nové Zámky, Piešťany, Klatovy, Klenová; 1994 Tatranská Lomnica, Žilina, Munich; 1995 Bratislava, Prague, Žilina; 1996 Lake Taechong, Bratislava, Prague, Trnava, Žilina, Dolný Kubín; 1997 Žilina, Klatovy, Osová Bitýška, Štúrovo, Budapest; 1998 Bratislava, Budapest; 1999 Vienna, Stockholm, Venice, Bratislava; 2000 Budapest, Nové Zámky, Bratislava, Hamburg, Berlin, Prague, Trnava, Žilina, Vienna, Paris; 2001 New York, Maribor, Pisa, Pforzheim, Bratislava, Prague, Luxemburg, Chur, Trnava, Banská Bystrica, Leipzig, Budapest, Washington; 2002 Vienna, Valencia, Zagreb, Saint Etienne, Luzern, Berlin, Graz; 2003 Bratislava, Budapest, Valencia; 2004 Berlin, Saint Etienne, Bratislava; 2005 Hiroshima, Osaka, Tokyo, Prague, Washington, Budapest; 2006 New York, Hannover, Žilina, Bratislava, Györ, Frankfurt am Main, Krakow, Bucharest, Tokyo, Budapest, Prague, Helsinki; 2007 Poznan, Budapest, Prague, Saint Etienne, Providence, Nitra, Bratislava, Györ, Ljubljana, Bucharest).

She has held solo exhibitions since 1990 (1990 Bratislava; 1993 Prague; 1995 Budapest; 1996 Trnava, Budapest, Šamorín; 1997 Šamorín, Košice, Budapest; 1999 Bratislava, Sausalito, Budapest, Prague, Vienna; 2000 Hannover; 2001 49th Venice Biennial; 2002 Budapest, Bratislava; 2003 Bratislava, Šahy; 2004 Brno, Banská Bystrica; 2005 Pécs; 2006 Oxford, Bratislava, Dunajská Streda, Šamorín; 2007 Budapest, Dunajská Streda; 2008 Rome, Stockholm).

In 1978, she evinced her attitude to art events in Slovakia when she became involved in establishing an alternative association Erté Studio in Nové Zámky which concentrated on the presentation of action art on Slovak, Central European and international scenes.

While searching for her own artistic identity, she focused on various art disciplines, from drawings with political contents, through brisk paintings with daring erotic themes, to ephemeral installations. She found the artistic maturity when she admitted the forcefulness of her talent and started creating large-scale objects, installations and environments with unambiguous messages. For a long time, Ilona Németh has focused on social issues ranging from postfeministic and socio-critical to political ones. She conveys her unconventional attitudes through visual language using the latest technologies. Her perception of female artist's role is very sensitive; she often deals with marginal issues and thus makes them worthy of our attention.

She received many awards in Slovakia and abroad, for instance the Young Visual Artist of the Year (1998), Open Europe (Sándor Márai Foundation, 1998), or Mihály Munkácsy Prize (2001). Since 1994 she has worked as a lecturer at the Academy of Fine Arts in Bratislava where she heads the "IN" studio. She lives and works in Dunajská Streda.

ABOUT THE ARTISTS OF THE EDITION

Zuzana Bartošová

Recognition characteristic of the series of publications issued within the project *Plus for Women 45+* is an unobtrusive, informal cover with selected illustrations of work of four contemporary Slovak female artists working with video. Jana Želibská (1941), Anna Daučíková (1950), Ilona Németh (1963) and Pavlína Fichta Čierna (1967) represent four different ways how to comment on the social reality of present days using the current media.

Free-thinking Jana Želibská[1] had a meteoric career in the second half of the 1960s already. By exposing masculine concepts of erotic, morality and view of a woman as a sexual object, her exhibition projects provoked the audience not only in Slovakia and Czechoslovakia, but through her exhibition in Paris also in Europe. In addition to subjects related to her personal mythology, she has been always interested in a hidden side of socially relevant subjects, approaching it with an ironical distance. After removing taboo from the then patterns of sexual behavior, valid despite a certain degree of liberalization in the early period in her work, the artist focused on the issues related to the devastation of the environment. Since the 1990s she has paid attention mainly to the realm of everydayness. Her artistic expression of banal subjects is suggestive, even disturbing. She finds their white spaces, and exactly like in the past, i.e. without moralizing, reveals the treacherousness of conventional solutions.

A video by Anna Daučíková: *How Are You?* (2004).

Anna Daučíková[2] studied at the Academy of Fine Arts in the studio Glass in architecture, headed by a Czech artist, Václav Cígler. The meaning of this creative environment has to be understood in the context of that period: most other lecturers at the academy subordinated their artistic opinion, and their teaching as well, to ideological requirements. It was at the academy where she found courage to search for sophisticated dimensions of art creation and concentrate on the subjects from undiscovered territories. Initially she was engaged in abstract painting in which she worked with numerical signs, their variations and combinations. Since the early 1990s she has focused especially on performances made up through video. In terms of the content, her individual artistic poetics is related to the feministic activities and the activities pointing out the specifics of gender differences (she is a co-founder of the feminist magazine *Aspekt*). By her video work, the

---

[1] Literature on work of Jana Želibská is relatively abundant. A detailed description of her work can be found in introductory studies to solo and group exhibitions, as well as in historical and critical studies and publications written by Radislav Matuštík and Katarína Rusnáková.

[2] Video work of the artist is described by Katarína Rusnáková in the publication *História a teória mediálneho umenia na Slovensku* [History and Theory of Media Art in Slovakia] (Rusnáková, 2006).

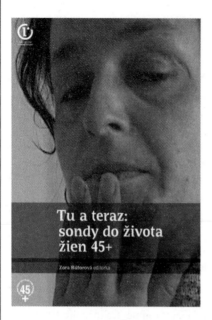

A video by Pavlína Fichta Čierna:
Reconstruction (2005).

A video installation by Jana Želibská:
Meditation in the Year ? (1996).

artist has tried to intermediate the emotional and erotic levels of "different" experience of the world. Currently she uses video to comment on social issues which, from a different perspective, reveal the same theme. Her artistic statement has become even more critical.

While searching for her own artistic identity, Ilona Németh[3] focused on various art disciplines, from drawings with political contents and brisk paintings depicting daring erotic themes, to ephemeral installations. She found the artistic maturity when she admitted the forcefulness of her talent and started creating large-scale objects and installations with unambiguous messages. One of her most persuasive installations is the installation "The Way" (1996) created for the synagogue in Šamorín: a vigorous, ascetic and suggestive interpretation of the trauma of holocaust. She also deals with other social themes, ranging from feministic and socio-critical to political ones. She expresses her unconventional attitudes through actual visual language using the latest technologies. She deliberately crosses the conventional borders of the fine art closed within its own world: many of her projects with intimate subjects are realized in public premises.

Pavlína Fichta Čierna[4] initially used video and video-installations to deal with the subjects referring to her life story. She conveyed the story of caressed, vulnerable and treated body, and did not hesitate to capture the banal side of it. However, she told the story with a certain distance to underline its general validity. At the same time she gave a true picture of paradoxical feelings of impersonality that deluges the consciousness of the protagonists of a life and death game. In her current works, Pavlína Fichta Čierna focuses on individual people from her surroundings. The artist reconstructs their stories in clearly, even statically set up segments, while she often uses radical editing. Visual level of her videos is artistically sophisticated by its unobtrusiveness. She reckons on a realistic, however sophisticated use of dispersed light that is able to modify color undertones

---

[3] Work of Ilona Németh was interpreted by Gábor Húshegyi in introductions to exhibition catalogues, in texts for experts as well as broader public (Katarína Kišová, too, pays attention to Németh's work). Gábor Húshegyi is also an author of the monograph about the artist.
[4] Video work of the artist is described by Katarína Rusnáková in her publication *História a teória mediálneho umenia na Slovensku* [History and Theory of Media Art in Slovakia] (Rusnáková, 2006).

of individual pictures. The counterpoint to this moderation is realistic commentary of the protagonists which sometimes goes into drastic details, and usually points out their social exclusion without direct criticism.

The fact that the covers of four successive publications within the project *Plus for Women 45+* show works of female artists is not a coincidence. Their art has several common denominators. The first one, already mentioned within the interpretation of individual artists, is the concentration on social issues. Another one is the fact that all of these artists opted for video when they wanted to express the current social issues in a topical and timely manner. The selection of video makes clear at the first sight that they comment on the issues "here and now".

Entry of video to the fine art is related to the crucial role of media in modern society on the one hand, and to the transient, ephemeral character that the fine art acquired in the 1960s on the other hand.

An interactive multimedia installation by Ilona Németh: *Exhibition Room* (1998).

In the Slovak environment, the first video works did not appear, except for several previous exceptions, until the early 1990s.[5] This fact was related rather to the generally low accessibility of video than to the low preparedness of Slovak artists to express themselves through actual artistic means. Today, it is not the case any more.

The video (art) has completed a radical change in the themes and language of the contemporary fine art. At the same time, it brought back to the fine art a human being, his and her figure and face – body – as well as a story. In the 20th century, the narration was overlaid with analytical art of avant-gardes and neo-avant-gardes and with sophisticated tendencies which had both the philosophical and the linguistic ambitions. For a long time it was believed that the narration belongs to the art of historical periods or to the mainstream art which is not worth noticing (obviously, with certain exceptions). However, its return has been indicated by happening and performance in the 1960s and confirmed by a wild, spontaneous and eclectic painting. Finally it has been legitimized by contemporary video and photography, i.e. disciplines which replace the classical painting. Today it is automatically used by both the young and the youngest generations.

In Slovakia, the video itself underwent a radical transformation of its language, themes and objectives and became an obvious way of artistic expression. Initially it was necessary to master new techniques, while applying the specifics of work of an individual artist who created as a sculptor or a painter, and exceptionally also as a performer. A video made possible to capture the very process of creation. In terms of themes it initially focused on the inner world of artist's personality, which it depicted in a way similar to the classical media. It concentrated on the issue of human body and body art. Through video art, the intimate became the public without the necessity to decode the complicated clues.

---

5   Radislav Matuštík dates this fact to 1993 (Matuštík, 1994).

Today, the video art can comment on the subjects of everydayness in its various forms better than any other art discipline. Diversity of human fates that are shaped by the inability of the society to cross the closed circles of excluded or marginalized individuals and groups, finds in the video art its patient observer. Thus the artist may become an intermediary in the process of considering the solutions to the issues of the quality of life which arise in the civil society.[6]

Literature

Rusnáková, K.: *História a teória mediálneho umenia na Slovensku* [History and Theory of Media Art in Slovakia]. Bratislava, Academy of Fine Arts and Design 2006.

Matuštík, R.: "Videoumenie na Slovensku" ['Video Art in Slovakia'] in Jungo, E. – Rusnáková, K. – Smolenická, M. (eds.): *Video, vidím, ich sehe* [Video, I see, ich sehe]. Žilina – Bern, Museum of Art Žilina 1994.

Manovich, L.: "Ilúzia naratív a interaktivita" ['Illusion of Narratives and Interactivity'] in Rusnáková, K. (ed.): *V toku pohyblivých obrazov* [In the Flow of Moving Pictures]. Bratislava, Academy of Fine Arts and Design 2005.

---

[6] A few years ago, even the experts did not believe in such communication function of new media including video when they asserted that "social sphere... is beyond new media" (Manovich, 2005, p. 89).